International Trade and the World Economy

International Trade and the World Economy

Charles van Marrewijk

Erasmus University, Rotterdam

OXFORD
UNIVERSITY PRESS

Great Clarendon Street, Oxford OX2 6DP

Oxford University Press is a department of the University of Oxford.
It furthers the University's objective of excellence in research, scholarship,
and education by publishing worldwide in

Oxford New York

Athens Auckland Bangkok Bogotá Buenos Aires Cape Town
Chennai Dar es Salaam Delhi Florence Hong Kong Istanbul Karachi
Kolkata Kuala Lumpur Madrid Melbourne Mexico City Mumbai Nairobi
Paris São Paulo Singapore Taipei Tokyo Toronto Warsaw

with associated companies in Berlin Ibadan

Oxford is a registered trade mark of Oxford University Press
in the UK and in certain other countries

Published in the United States
by Oxford University Press Inc., New York

© Charles van Marrewijk 2002

A catalogue record for this book is available from the British Library

Library of Congress Cataloging in Publication Data
ISBN 0 19 925004 9

Typeset by Newgen Imaging Systems (P) Ltd., Chennai, India
Printed in Great Britain
on acid-free paper by
Bath Press Ltd., Bath, Avon

Preface

The objective of this book is to give a succinct, yet fairly complete, up-to-date, and thorough introduction to the forces underlying all 'real' international economics, such as trade and investment flows, imperfect competition, trade policy, multinationals, economic integration, etc. The book's target audience includes first and second year university and college students in economics, management, and business with a working knowledge of microeconomics and macroeconomics. Elementary comprehension of mathematics for economists (simple functions and differentiation) is recommended. The approach is based on the student's active participation using the companion study guide and the website. These provide, for example, empirical questions to test theories and simulation questions to get a better feel for the structure of economic models by performing small, user-friendly computer simulations and interpreting the results. In part based on Fig. A, of the book's structure, I briefly discuss its main features.

Four-part organization

The book's primary organizational structure is in four parts. Part I (introduction and classical trade) gives an overview of the main economic forces in the world economy today, and of the classical explanation for international trade flows based on

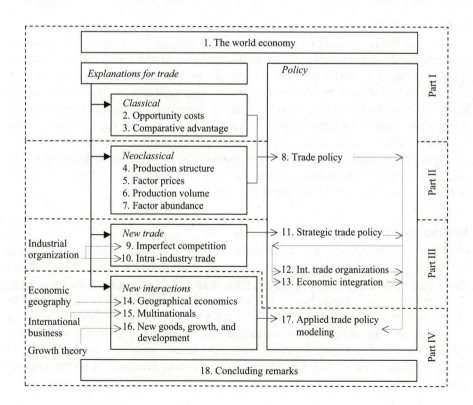

opportunity costs and comparative advantage, as a result of technological differences. Part II (neoclassical trade) analyses comparative advantage in perfectly competitive economies with identical technologies as a result of differences in factor abundance. It also discusses the (distributional) welfare implications of trade policy, such as tariffs, quotas, and voluntary export restraints, for the classical and neoclassical models of Parts I and II. Part III (new trade) investigates the impact of imperfect competition, economies of scale, and product differentiation on the structure of the international economy and the size and type of its trade flows. This 'new trade' approach is the fruitful result of incorporating elements of the industrial organization literature into international economics. Part III also analyses the impact of new trade theory on (strategic) trade policy, discusses the main international organizations, and applies the economic insights on the structure of the world economy learned in Parts I–III to an investigation of the process of (European) economic integration. Finally, Part IV (new interactions) brings the reader up to date with recent developments in international economics which have occurred in the last decade or so. These are based on new interactions between international economics and other fields of economics; with economic geography leading to a better explanation of location, with international business leading to a better explanation of multinational firms, and with economic growth theory leading to a better understanding of international differences in growth and development. Part IV also discusses the implications of these developments for applied trade policy modelling.

Two-tier analysis

The body of the text represents the first tier of analysis, by providing extensive verbal, graphical, and intuitive explanations of the structure of the international economic system. The reader's understanding of the first tier is supported by limited structural analysis, empirical data, special interest boxes, and applications. The second tier of analysis is provided by the Technical Notes at the end of most chapters, which explicitly derive most results used and discussed in the body of the text. As such, the second tier represents background information for a better understanding of the body of the text. A proper understanding of the first tier, however, does not require knowledge and comprehension of the Technical Notes, as long as the reader is willing to take the results derived in those notes for granted.

Empirics: applications, boxes, and examples

The ultimate objective of economic model building is to provide a better understanding of the (forces of the) world economy. The empirical information provided throughout the book therefore serves a dual purpose. First, to give a better insight in the structure of the world economy, e.g. on the size of trade and capital flows or the rising importance of multinational firms, such that the reader has a better idea what we should be trying to explain. Second, to test the main conclusions of the economic models by applying them to real world problems. By directly using the models we also make the exposition livelier, through case studies and by pointing out vivid examples in special interest boxes.

Thorough, but simple

As mentioned above, we want to provide a thorough analysis, indicating that all the results we discuss will be based on explicit economic models. Nonetheless, we want to keep the analysis as simple and tractable as possible. Without reservation, therefore, all the discussions in the text and derivations in the Technical Notes at the end of each chapter will be based on the most simple functional forms.

Study guide and simulations

There is a clear and consistent interaction between the book, the study guide, and the website supporting the book. For example, since the exposition in the text and many illustrations are based on actual calculations using specific functional forms (see the feature above), we can use this to our advantage in the 'simulation' questions of the study guide. These questions are based on colour versions of the figures in the book and available on the website. The student not only immediately recognizes the material in the questions of the study guide, but also becomes acquainted with practical computer tools, thus learning first hand what happens with production and consumption if the capital stock increases or the preference structure changes.

C.v.M.

Website: www.oup.com/uk/marrewijk

Acknowledgements

In the course of writing this book I have accumulated a substantial intellectual debt to the co-authors of work forming the basis for some chapters or sections, in particular Steven Brakman, Harry Garretsen, and Jeroen Hinloopen, and to persons providing comments and suggestions for improvements on earlier versions of (parts of) this book, in particular Koen Berden, Steven Brakman, Joe Francois, Ger Lanjouw, Doug Nelson, Teun Schmidt, and Jean-Marie Viaene. Of these persons Koen Berden and Teun Schmidt are my excellent and inspirational colleagues for the course *International Economics* at Erasmus University, where Koen reaches levels of student praise in the evaluations which I unfortunately will never achieve, and Teun has been my valuable mentor in the history of (international) economic thought for two decades. My special thanks go out to Stephan Schueller and Daniel Ottens, the authors of the accompanying study guide, who not only worked very hard, provided and processed a substantial part of the data material, gave detailed comments, did a wonderful job on writing the study guide, refining the simulations, and organizing the website, but through their presence also made it a pleasure to go to work over the past two years. Finally, I would like to thank Tim Barton, Matthew Cotton, and John Grandidge of Oxford University Press and Edwin Pritchard, the copy-editor, for their encouragements, support, and excellent organisational skills in producing and publishing this book.

Rotterdam
31 August 2001

Contents

Part One **Introduction and Classical Trade**

Part Two **Neoclassical Trade**

Part Three **New Trade**

Part Four **New Interactions**

Detailed Contents

Part One Introduction and Classical Trade

Part Two **Neoclassical Trade**

Part Three **New Trade**

Part Four **New Interactions**

List of Figures

List of Tables

List of Boxes

List of Technical Notes

Part One

Introduction and Classical Trade

Part I (Introduction and Classical Trade) gives an overview of the main economic forces in the world economy today, and of the classical explanation for international trade flows based on opportunity costs and comparative advantage, as a result of technological differences.

Chapter 1
The World Economy

Objectives/key terms

International real/monetary analysis	General equilibrium approach
Land area	Population
Gross domestic product (GDP)	Gross national product (GNP)
Purchasing power	Tradeable/non-tradeable
International comparison project (ICP)	Income per capita
Exports/imports	Balance of payments
Current account/capital account	Trade balance
Capital inflow/outflow	Globalization

We present basic information on (the development of) the structure of the world economy in terms of land area, population, income, and (the connection between) trade flows and capital flows. This serves as background information for observations to be explained by international economics models discussed in the remainder of this book.

1.1 Introduction

What is international economics? To paraphrase a well-known definition of economics, it is 'what international economists do'. Although this does not seem very helpful at first sight, the underlying message is clear: you will only know what international economics is about once you have studied it yourself. In fact, this probably holds for many fields of study, also outside economics. This does not mean that you have to devote four years of your life to studying international economics before you get an idea why we like this field so much, although I can highly recommend it. After you have studied this book in one course you will roughly know what *half* of international economics entails. 'Half?', you say. Well, yes, because the field is divided into two parts, namely international *monetary* analysis and international *real* analysis. As the name suggests, international monetary analysis investigates the demand for and supply of money and other financial assets, and the interactions between nations in this respect, through the exchange rate and otherwise. This book does *not* cover international monetary analysis. Instead, we focus attention on international real analysis, investigating trade and investment flows, imperfect competition, trade policy, multinationals, economic integration, etc.

The remainder of this chapter gives a brief empirical overview of the world economy, based on data from the World Bank Development Indicators CD-ROM 2001, covering the forty years from 1960 to 1999.[1] This serves as background information for observations to be explained by international economics models discussed in the rest of this book. More detailed empirical information on specific topics, raising new questions to be answered, will be presented as we go along. A final remark before we get started. I was asked by students what sets international economics apart from other fields of study. After contemplating the question for a while, I think an important distinguishing characteristic is the *general equilibrium* nature of the approach. It is true that many discussions in the chapters to follow are of a *partial equilibrium* nature, for example determining the optimal production level for a producer *given* the demand for its good, or determining the optimal consumption level for a labourer *given* the wage rate she earns and the prices charged for the goods on the market. However, international economists are not truly satisfied with an explanation of empirical observations until the partial equilibrium explanations are put together like a jigsaw puzzle in a consistent general equilibrium framework, providing a miniature world in which the producer's demand for its goods is explained by the consumer's optimization problem and in which the wage rate and the prices are also determined within the model. The main advantage of insisting on a general equilibrium framework is, of course, that it forces us to be precise and complete in our explanations. Essentially, it prevents us from cheating. It is important to keep this in mind as we continue.

1.2 Land area and population

There are many countries in the world. On its CD-ROM the World Bank distinguishes 207 different countries, a fair number of which are so small in terms of land area, population, and economic clout that you may have never heard of them. As a result of political pressure from China, which considers it one of its provinces, Taiwan is the only significant country missing on the World Bank CD-ROM. In the discussions in this chapter, we focus attention on the most important countries. But important in what sense? Clearly, if you are one of the few inhabitants of Vanuatu, this is an important country to you and your family. However, for the world as a whole we will assume that 'large' countries are important. Again, the question is raised: large in what sense? There are, of course, several options available, their suitability depending on the object of study. In general terms, we can look at land area or population. Since this is a book on economics, we can look at various income measures. More specifically, since this is a book on *international* economics, we can look at exports or international capital flows. In the rest

---

[1] Unless stated otherwise, the source of all data in this chapter is the World Bank Development Indicators CD-ROM 2001. If data for 1999 are reported, the most recent observation in the period 1996–1999 was used, which in most cases is indeed the 1999 observation.

of this chapter we will have a brief look at all these aspects, indicating some of the relationships between them if appropriate.

Land area

As the central piece left over after the break-up of the Soviet Union, the Russian Federation, henceforth Russia for short, is still by far the largest country in the world in terms of land area. With almost 17 million km^2, as indicated in Table 1.1 some 13 per cent of the world total, Russia is more than 80 per cent larger than China, the world's second-largest country. Other non-surprising large countries are Canada, the USA, and Brazil. Perhaps more remarkable countries in the top fifteen list are the ninth place for Kazakhstan, formerly a part of the Soviet Union, and the African countries: Algeria (tenth), Sudan (eleventh), Congo (Zaire[2], twelfth), and Libya (fifteenth). As a result of the most frequently used methods for projecting the world globe on a flat piece of paper, see for example Fig. 1.3 in section 1.4, most people tend to underestimate the size of the African land area. Finally note that, taking into consideration that by far the biggest part of Russia is on the Asian continent, there are no European countries in the top fifteen of Table 1.1, which taken together account for about 63 per cent of the total land area in the world.

Table 1.1 Top fifteen land area (1,000 km^2), 1999

Country	Size	% of world	Sum %
1 Russia	16,889	13.0	13
2 China	9,327	7.2	20
3 Canada	9,221	7.1	27
4 USA	9,159	7.0	34
5 Brazil	8,457	6.5	41
6 Australia	7,682	5.9	47
7 India	2,973	2.3	49
8 Argentina	2,737	2.1	51
9 Kazakhstan	2,671	2.1	53
10 Algeria	2,382	1.8	55
11 Sudan	2,376	1.8	57
12 Zaire	2,267	1.7	59
13 Mexico	1,909	1.5	60
14 Indonesia	1,812	1.4	61
15 Libya	1,760	1.4	63
World	130,079		

[2] There are two 'Congo' countries in Africa, the largest of which in terms of both population and size, a former Belgian colony, is better known under the old name Zaire.

Population

As an indicator of economic importance, a country's land area is of limited use. Many of the countries listed in Table 1.1 incorporate vast stretches of desert, rocks, swamps, or areas frozen solid year round. Such uninhabitable land cannot be used to sustain and feed a population engaged in commerce, production, and trade. In this respect, the total population of a country is a better indicator of its fertility and potential economic viability. Table 1.2 lists the top fifteen countries in terms of population, only seven of which also make it to the top fifteen in terms of land area.

Two Asian countries, China and India, clearly stand out in terms of total population. Together they have 2.25 billion inhabitants, or almost 38 per cent of the world total of 6 billion people. The USA, ranked third with 278 million inhabitants, has less than 28 per cent of the Indian population, which is ranked second. Asian countries dominate the population list. Apart from China and India this includes Indonesia (fourth), Pakistan (seventh), Bangladesh (eighth), Japan (ninth), Vietnam (thirteenth), the Philippines (fourteenth), and Turkey (fifteenth). Note that we do not include Russia in this list of Asian countries, despite the fact that its largest land mass is in the Asian continent, because the largest share of its population is on the European continent. Thus, together with Germany (twelfth), there are two European countries in the top fifteen. With 124 million people Nigeria is the only African country. The top fifteen countries together account for about 66 per cent of the world population.

Table 1.2 Top fifteen population (millions), 1999

Country	Size	% of world	Sum %
1 China	1,254	21.0	21
2 India	998	16.7	38
3 USA	278	4.7	42
4 Indonesia	207	3.5	46
5 Brazil	168	2.8	49
6 Russia	146	2.4	51
7 Pakistan	135	2.3	53
8 Bangladesh	128	2.1	55
9 Japan	127	2.1	58
10 Nigeria	124	2.1	60
11 Mexico	97	1.6	61
12 Germany	82	1.4	63
13 Vietnam	78	1.3	64
14 Philippines	74	1.2	65
15 Turkey	64	1.1	66
World	5,978		

Box 1.1 **Are nations rational?**

Sometimes it is hard for outsiders to understand the disagreements between nations. In July 2001 the government of South Korea became so upset about the 'missing' parts in a Japanese history book for 13–15-year-old students that it decided to break off the (limited) military cooperation with Japan and not to open up its market for Japanese cultural goods, such as computer games. The South Korean government objected to the portrayal of history in the Japanese book on about thirty-five points. Partially, this reflects irritation at the fact that the book does not acknowledge that many cultural innovations, such as Chinese writing, Buddhism, and baking porcelain, reached the Japanese islands through the Korean peninsula. Most irritation, however, is related to the occupation of Korea by Japan in the twentieth century, in particular the fact that the book does not mention the 'comfort girls', a gentle term for (Korean) women forced into prostitution by the Japanese military in the Second World War. The description of the Korean–Japanese history in the book is biased. Whether this is important enough to warrant the Korean excitement and (trade) restrictions is another matter. The costs of trade restrictions are discussed in the sequel.

Information source: NRC (2001*d*).

1.3 Income

The best indicator of the economic power of a nation is, of course, obtained by estimating the total value of the goods and services produced in a certain time period. Actually doing this and comparing the results across nations is a formidable task, which conceptually requires taking three steps. First, a well-functioning statistics office in each nation must gather accurate information on the value of millions of goods and services produced and provided by the firms in the economy. This will be done, of course, in the country's local currency, that is dollars in the USA, pounds in the UK, yen in Japan, etc. Second, we have to decide what to compare between nations: gross domestic product or gross national product. Third, we have to decide *how* to compare the outcome for the different nations. We will elaborate on the second and third steps below.

Domestic or national product?

As mentioned above, we can compare either gross domestic product (GDP) or gross national product (GNP) between nations. GDP is defined as the market value of the goods and services produced by labour and property *located* in a country. GNP is defined as the market value of the goods and services produced by labour and property of *residents* of a country. If, for example, a Mexican worker is providing labour services in the USA, these services are part of American GDP and Mexican GNP. The term 'located in' sometimes has

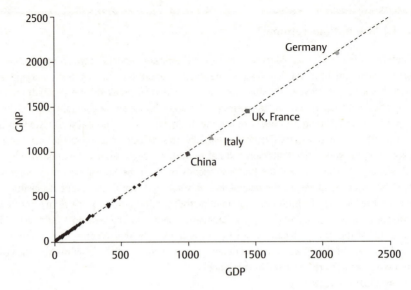

Fig. 1.1 Gross domestic and gross national product. The dotted line is a 45° line. Observations for Japan and the USA are outside the shown range

to be interpreted broadly, for example if a Filipino sailor is providing labour services for a Norwegian shipping company, this is part of Norwegian GDP despite the fact that the ship is not actually located in Norway most of the time. The difference between GNP and GDP does not only hold for labour services, but also for other factors of production, such as capital, that is:

(1.1) $$\text{GDP} + \text{net receipts of factor income} = \text{GNP}$$

So does it really matter whether we compare countries on the basis of GDP or GNP? No. This is illustrated in Figure 1.1 for the GDP and GNP values measured in current US $. Since almost all observations are very close to a straight 45-degree line through the origin, the values of GDP and GNP are usually very close to one another. For example, French GDP was $1,432 bn, about 0.5 per cent below its GNP of $1,440 bn. Note that both values are so close to the UK values that it is not possible to distinguish between the two observations in Figure 1.1. The difference between GDP and GNP is not always small, at least not in relative terms. For example, capital income from abroad for some of the small oil producing nations, Brunei, Kuwait, and Qatar, ensures that the GNP level is some 10 per cent to 20 per cent higher than the GDP level. Similarly, labour income from its many sailors and other workers abroad makes GNP for the Philippines about 4 per cent higher than its GDP.

Comparison

Table 1.3 reports the top fifteen countries in terms of GNP level when the outcome for each nation in local currency is simply converted to the same international

Table 1.3 Top fifteen gross national product
(current $bn), 1999

Country	Size	% of world	Sum %
1 USA	9,163	29.8	30
2 Japan	4,395	14.3	44
3 Germany	2,091	6.8	51
4 UK	1,450	4.7	56
5 France	1,440	4.7	60
6 Italy	1,162	3.8	64
7 China	971	3.2	67
8 Brazil	730	2.4	70
9 Canada	615	2.0	72
10 Spain	589	1.9	74
11 Mexico	471	1.5	75
12 India	444	1.4	77
13 South Korea	402	1.3	78
14 The Netherlands	397	1.3	79
15 Australia	392	1.3	80
World	30,723		

standard currency, usually the US $, on the basis of the average exchange rate in the period of observation.[3] These are called current $. The total value of all goods and services produced in the world in 1999 was estimated to be $30,732 bn. Taken together, the top fifteen countries account for about 80 per cent of the world production value.

In terms of current $, the USA is by far the largest economy in the world, producing almost 30 per cent of all goods and services. This is more than twice as much as Japan, which is ranked second, which in turn is more than twice as large as Germany, which is ranked third. All other European countries in the production top fifteen, that is UK (fourth), France (fifth), Italy (sixth), Spain (tenth), and the Netherlands (fourteenth), are not listed in the population top fifteen. In fact, of the fifteen largest countries in terms of population listed in Table 1.2 only seven make it to the top fifteen in terms of income level. Having a large population is therefore not at all synonymous with having a large production value. A striking example is provided by the Netherlands which has a small population of 16 million people (ranked fifty-fifth), but a production value of $397 bn, only 10 per cent below the value produced by the 1 billion inhabitants of India. Australia is another relatively small country in terms of population, but large in terms of production value.

---

[3] Henceforth the $ sign always refers to the US $.

Purchasing power

The ranking of production value in Table 1.3 is deceptive because it tends to overestimate production in the high-income countries relative to the low-income countries. To understand this we have to distinguish between *tradeable* and *non-tradeable* goods and services. As the name suggests, tradeable goods and services can be transported or provided in another country, perhaps with some difficulty and at some costs. In principle, therefore, the providers of tradeable goods in different countries compete with one another fairly directly, implying that the prices of such goods are related and can be compared effectively on the basis of observed (average) exchange rates. In contrast, non-tradeable goods and services have to be provided locally and do not compete with international providers. Think, for example, of housing services, getting a haircut, or going to the cinema.

Since (i) different sectors in the same country compete for the same labourers, such that (ii) the wage rate in an economy reflects the average productivity of a nation (see also Chapter 3), and (iii) productivity differences between nations in the non-tradeable sectors tend to be smaller than in the tradeable sectors, converting the value of output in the non-tradeable sectors on the basis of observed exchange rates tends to underestimate the value of production in these sectors for the low-income countries. For example, on the basis of observed exchange rates, getting a haircut in the USA may cost you $10 rather than the $1 you pay in Tanzania, while going to the cinema in Sweden may cost you $8 rather than the $2 you pay in Jakarta, Indonesia. In these examples the value of production in the high-income countries relative to the low-income countries is overestimated by a factor of 10 and 4, respectively.

To correct for these differences, the United Nations International Comparison Project (ICP) collects data on the prices of goods and services for virtually all countries in the world and calculates 'purchasing power parity' (ppp) exchange rates, which better reflect the value of goods and services that can be purchased in a country for a given amount of dollars. Reporting ppp GNP levels therefore gives a better estimate of the actual value of production in a country.

Figure 1.2 illustrates the impact on the estimated value of production after correction for purchasing power. Two top income countries from Table 1.3 do not make it to the ppp top fifteen of Figure 1.2, namely the Netherlands (which drops to nineteenth place) and Australia (which drops to sixteenth place). They are replaced by Russia and Indonesia. The USA is still the largest economy, but now 'only' produces 21.6 per cent of world output, rather than 30 per cent. The estimated value of production for the low-income countries is much higher than before. The relative production of China (ranked second) is more than three times as high as before (rising from 3.2 per cent to 10.8 per cent), similarly for India (rising from 1.4 per cent to 5.4 per cent), Russia (rising from 1.2 per cent to 2.5 per cent), and Indonesia (rising from 0.4 per cent to 1.3 per cent).[4] The drop in the estimated value of output is particularly large for Japan (falling from 14.3 per cent to 7.8 per cent), reflecting the high costs of living in Japan.

---

[4] These percentages are not listed in Figure 1.2. More details are provided on the book's website.

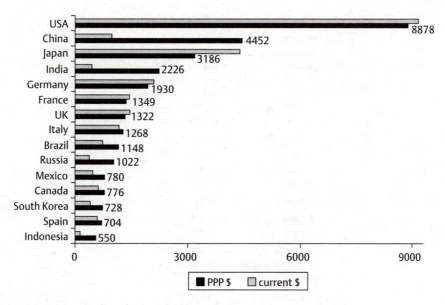

Fig. 1.2 Gross national product; ranked according to ppp

1.4 Income per capita

For an individual inhabitant of a country the total production value of the country is hardly relevant. More important is the production value per person, that is per capita. It should be noted that income per capita gives an idea of the well-being for the 'average' person in the country, but gives no information on the distribution of the income level within the country. If Jack and Jill together earn $100 the average income level is $50, which holds if they both earn $50 *and* if Jack earns $1 while Jill earns $99. The average income level is therefore a poor indicator of the 'representative' situation in a country if the distribution of income is more uneven. In general, the income level is more evenly distributed in Europe and Japan than in the USA, where it is in turn more evenly distributed than in many low-income countries.

Table 1.4 gives the top fifteen countries in terms of income per capita, corrected for purchasing power. The average income level in the world was $6,870 per person. The highest income level, exactly six times the world average, was generated in the tiny country of Luxembourg. The lowest income level ($440 per capita) was measured in Sierra Leone, a small African nation. High income levels per capita are generated in North America (USA and Canada), Japan, and Australia. All other high income per capita countries in Table 1.4 are located in Europe. Figure 1.3 illustrates the ppp per capita income level for all 164 countries for which data are available. It shows clustering of income levels with low values in Africa, intermediate values in Latin America and South-East Asia, and high values in moderate climatic zones, as emphasized by Bloom

Table 1.4 Top fifteen gross national income per capita (ppp $), 1999

Country	Size	% of world average
1 Luxembourg	41,230	600
2 USA	31,910	464
3 Switzerland	28,760	419
4 Norway	28,140	410
5 Iceland	27,210	396
6 Belgium	25,710	374
7 Denmark	25,600	373
8 Canada	25,440	370
9 Japan	25,170	366
10 Austria	24,600	358
11 The Netherlands	24,410	355
12 Australia	23,850	347
13 Germany	23,510	342
14 France	23,020	335
15 Finland	22,600	329
World	6,870	

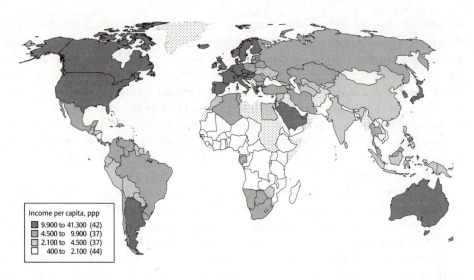

Income per capita, ppp
- 9.900 to 41.300 (42)
- 4.500 to 9.900 (37)
- 2.100 to 4.500 (37)
- 400 to 2.100 (44)

Fig. 1.3 Gross national income per capita

and Sachs (1998). A clear exception to this observation is provided by the oil producing nations in the Middle East (e.g. United Arab Emirates, Bahrain, Saudi Arabia).

1.5 International trade

As the title of this book suggests, the interactions between nations (mainly the international trade flows), their underlying forces, and the implications of (trade) policy are our primary focus of attention. Before we continue it should be noted that the comparison problems between countries discussed in sections 1.3 and 1.4 arising from the distinction between tradeable and non-tradeable goods do not occur when investigating and comparing trade flows, which can readily be compared using the exchange rates. So what are the large trading nations? The left-hand side of Table 1.5 lists the top fifteen countries in terms of export value, while the right-hand side lists the top fifteen countries in terms of import value. The same countries appear on both lists, only in a slightly different order. The total value of world exports is $7,004 bn, more than 23 per cent of the value of world production. Note the small statistical discrepancy between the export and import value.

Although the USA is both the world's largest exporter and the world's largest importer, the gap between it and number 2, Germany, is relatively small. Taking into consideration that the USA's share of world production is 30 per cent (see Table 1.3), the USA's share of

Table 1.5 Top fifteen international trade ($bn), 1999

Country	Exports	% of world	Country	Imports	% of world
1 USA	956	13.7	USA	1,116	15.9
2 Germany	626	8.9	Germany	593	8.5
3 Japan	465	6.6	UK	396	5.7
4 France	382	5.5	Japan	380	5.4
5 UK	374	5.3	France	338	4.8
6 Italy	292	4.2	Italy	275	3.9
7 Canada	278	4.0	Canada	259	3.7
8 The Netherlands	249	3.6	The Netherlands	220	3.1
9 China	219	3.1	Hong Kong	203	2.9
10 Hong Kong	212	3.0	China	190	2.7
11 Belgium	194	2.8	Belgium	179	2.6
12 South Korea	172	2.5	Spain	169	2.4
13 Spain	164	2.3	Mexico	155	2.2
14 Mexico	148	2.1	South Korea	144	2.0
15 Singapore	139	2.0	Singapore	144	2.0
World	7,004		World	7,007	

world exports (13.7 per cent, see Table 1.5) is rather modest. Similarly, the share in world exports of Japan and China, both large countries, is below their respective shares in world production. In contrast, all other countries in Table 1.5 have a larger share in world exports than in world production. To some extent this can be explained by the artificiality of drawing borders between nations on the globe. For example, if an American firm in Boston sells goods 5,000 km away in Los Angeles, this is not counted as exports because both cities are located in the USA. Compare this to a Dutch firm in Rotterdam, the world's largest harbour, selling goods to a Belgian consumer in Antwerp less than 100 km away, which of course is part of Dutch exports. Consequently, many countries in Table 1.5 are relatively small, high-income open economies: such as Canada, the Netherlands, Hong Kong, Belgium, and Singapore.

Exports relative to imports

Figure 1.4 illustrates the difference between the export value of goods and services and their import value for 158 countries. It also depicts a 45-degree line where exports are equal to imports and the trade balance is zero (see also the next section). Although a country's export value is generally roughly in line with its import value, the deviations between the two are clearly more substantial than the deviations between GDP and GNP illustrated in Figure 1.1. Japan had the largest trade balance surplus ($85 bn), followed by France ($44 bn) and Germany ($33 bn). The USA had by far the largest trade balance deficit ($160 bn), followed by Brazil ($32 bn) and Russia ($29 bn).

Exports relative to production

The reader may wonder how it is possible that small countries like Singapore, which has only 4 million inhabitants, and Hong Kong, which has only 7 million inhabitants, are able to reach the world's top fifteen in export and import value. The reason is that

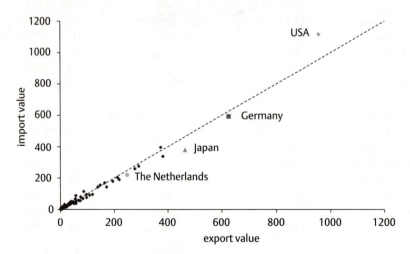

Fig. 1.4 Exports and imports of goods and services

countries may re-export goods and services they import to other countries, with only modest value added in the country itself. This is illustrated in Figure 1.5, which shows the top ten value of exports of goods and services relative to GDP. Note that Singapore, the highest ranked economy, exports a value of goods and services which is 70 per cent higher than the total value of production, which can be explained by re-exports. Six of the other countries in Figure 1.5, which are all small economies, also export more than the total production value.

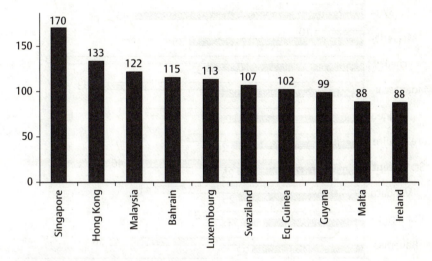

Fig. 1.5 Relative exports of goods and services

Box 1.2 **Tariffs as a source of government income**

In the rest of this book we will analyse the forces underlying international trade flows, their welfare impact for different agents in the economy, and the consequences of policy measures restricting trade flows. In general we will argue not only that international trade flows lead to efficiency gains and welfare improvements for a country as a whole, but also that policy measures restricting trade flows deteriorate welfare and reduce efficiency, sometimes in unexpected and covert ways. In view of these conclusions, supported by almost all international economists, the question arises *why* countries impose (welfare deteriorating) trade restrictions. We will discuss the more complicated distribution effects of trade restrictions, which may help to explain these phenomena, in the sequel. In this box, however, we want to point at the problems facing the governments of many developing nations which do not have an efficient tax collecting system available. After all, this requires detailed information on the inhabitants of the country, their income level, specific circumstances that may be relevant for an individual, and many public servants to gather and process the information. Nonetheless, the government of any nation requires funds to perform its basic duties, such as protecting the country, providing law, order, and education, etc. In the absence of an efficient tax collecting apparatus it is therefore tempting to collect government revenue by imposing tariffs on the (relatively easily controlled) imports of goods and services into the country. This is illustrated in Figure 1.6 which ranks countries in terms of generated import duties relative to the value of imports and also lists import duties relative to tax revenue. It shows not only that the countries imposing high tariffs are generally developing nations, but also that some countries are highly dependent on import duties for their tax revenue (for example 60 per cent for the Seychelles and 53 per cent for Madagascar).

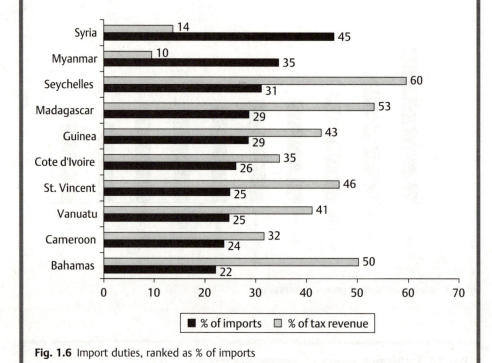

Fig. 1.6 Import duties, ranked as % of imports

1.6 **The balance of payments**

The balance of payments records a country's transactions with other countries. It is based on the rules of double-entry bookkeeping, with matching credit and debit entries. By definition the balance of payments is therefore equal to zero. We distinguish between two main parts of the balance of payments, namely the current account and the capital account, each with several subdivisions as summarized in Figure 1.7.

The balance of payments

Current account

Merchandise

Services
} Trade balance

Investment income

Unilateral transfers

Capital account

Long-term capital

Foreign direct investment

Portfolio investment

Short-term capital

Private non-monetary

Private monetary institutions

Official reserves

Fig. 1.7 The balance of payments

The transactions on the current account are income related, pertaining to produced merchandise (goods), provided services (also known as invisibles), investment income, and unilateral transfers. Exports are recorded as credit items ($+$) and imports as debit items ($-$). The sum of the merchandise and services balance is called the trade balance. It was discussed in section 1.5 and illustrated in Figure 1.4. More important, however, is the current account balance which also includes investment income and unilateral transfers. The reason is that investment income, such as dividend payments, reflects the remuneration for the use of capital, a factor of production, by another country. It is therefore essentially the payment for trade in (capital) services. Unilateral transfers, such as foreign aid to a developing nation, remittances, or military aid, are included as they represent income transfers to another country and not claims on another country. As a result, the current account balance measures the net change in claims on the outside world, which is recorded on the capital account.

The transactions on the capital account are asset related. An increase in claims on foreigners is a *capital outflow* and appears as a debit. An increase in claims by foreigners on our country is a *capital inflow* and appears as a credit. If the claim is longer than one year it is called long-term capital, for example foreign direct investment and long-term portfolio investment, such as securities and loans. Otherwise it is called short-term capital. Sometimes the classification is difficult. Purchasing foreign stocks is a short-term capital flow, unless you buy so much of the company that it becomes a foreign direct investment. Changes in official reserves may refer to changes by the central banking system in gold stocks, IMF credits, Special Drawing Rights, or foreign exchange reserves. As mentioned above, the balance of payments is zero by definition such that:

(1.2)   current account balance + capital account balance = 0

Suppose there is a surplus on the current account. This implies, roughly speaking, that the value of our exports (credit) is higher than the value of our imports (debit), that is the current account represents a net credit item. By the rules of accounting this must be matched by a net debit item on the capital account, and therefore a net capital outflow.

(1.3)   surplus current account ⇔ net capital outflow

The principle underlying the balance of payments is exactly the same as an individual's budget constraint.[5] If the income you earn this month (export of labour services, your only factor of production) is higher than the money you spend on consumption (import of goods and services), this will increase your claims on the outside world (for example by an increase of the balance on your chequing account). If your income is less than your consumption spending this month this will decrease your claims on the outside world.

1.7 Dynamics and globalization

In the previous sections we briefly discussed data on land area, population, income, and international trade using the most recent observation available. In this section we sketch the evolution over time of some of these variables in the recent past.

Capital flows

As is clear from equation (1.3), analysing a country's current account balance over a somewhat longer period of time gives a good idea of the net change in claims on the rest of the world. This is illustrated in Figure 1.8 for a selection of countries, where the current account balance is measured relative to GDP. Note that the scale on the vertical axis is not the same for the various panels in Figure 1.8. The USA, which used to be a net creditor, has accumulated such large current account deficits over the past two decades that it is now the world's largest debtor. Considering the size of the US economy, the recent current account deficit of roughly 4 per cent is rather large.

The current account balance for the UK is of the same order of relative magnitude as for the USA, with a less clear trend. The current account balance tends to be somewhat larger for smaller countries, such as Australia, which has a consistent capital inflow, and the Netherlands, which has a consistent capital outflow (thus building up net claims on the rest of the world). Over the past two decades Japan has had the largest capital outflow in absolute terms. This capital tends to be invested in the South-East Asian region, such as the Philippines. Note the abrupt break in the capital inflow into the Philippines at the end of the twentieth century as a result of the Asian crisis. In terms of relative magnitude, the oil producing nations, such as Kuwait and Saudi Arabia, are in a class of their own, with years in which 60 per cent of GDP was recorded as a capital outflow. In the case of Kuwait the impact of the Gulf War is immediately evident (the current account deficit was 240 per cent of GDP in 1991).

---

[5] In fact, budget constraints are additive, so we can do this for individuals in a country.

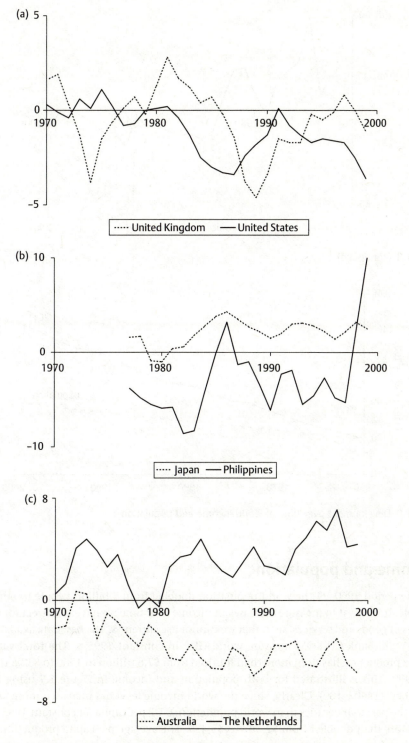

Fig. 1.8 Current account balance, selected countries (% of GDP)

(*continued overleaf*)

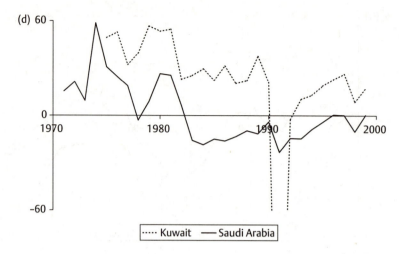

Fig. 1.8 (continued)

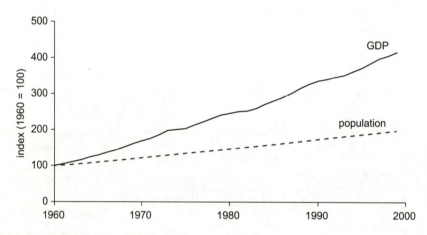

Fig. 1.9 Development over time of world income and population

Income and population

In the period 1960–99 the world population doubled from 3 billion people to 6 billion people. If we want to measure increases in income over time we have to correct for rising prices of goods and services, such that we cannot use current $. The best data available on the World Bank CD-ROM measure world GDP in constant 1995 $. The total value of world production has risen more than fourfold from $7.8 trillion in 1960 to $32.5 trillion in 1999. This is illustrated for both population and income in Figure 1.9 using index numbers (1960 = 100). Clearly, since the world income level has increased more rapidly over the past four decades than world population, GDP per capita (at constant 1995 US $) has more than doubled from $2,587 to $5,439. The average per capita production level has therefore increased at a rate of about 1.9 per cent per year.

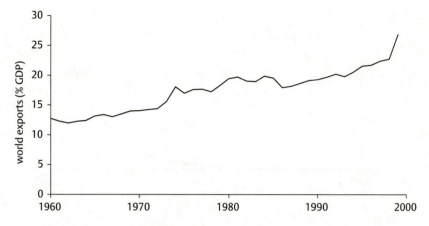

Fig 1.10 World exports relative to world income

International trade

The growing world population, which is becoming richer than ever before, is interacting more intensively than ever before as well. Technology improvements have not only made swift transport of goods and services at low prices available, but also enabled rapid communication with other people around the globe by telephone, fax, and the internet. This, in turn, has made it possible to trade services between nations which could not be traded before. Many airlines, for example, are now using the brainpower of software engineers in India to assist them in providing their services. One way to measure this increased interaction between nations is to look at the development of the exports of goods and services relative to income. As illustrated in Figure 1.10, this has risen from 12.5 per cent of GDP in 1960 to 26.9 per cent of GDP in 1999.

Globalization?

The phenomenon of increased interaction on a global scale is frequently referred to as 'globalization'. Unfortunately, this is not a very practical term because people may use it to refer to a wide range of empirical observations: for example, the tendency illustrated above that a larger share of income is traded internationally, or the fact that more and more firms are producing in different countries, thus becoming multinationals (see Chapter 15). Many people use the term in a derogatory sense when discussing social and cultural developments, for example lamenting the fact that the local restaurants disappear and are replaced by McDonald's, Burger King, and Pizza Hut around the globe. I give some numbers to illustrate that the supposed increased international interaction is not a figment of the imagination. On a global scale the number of fax machines per 1,000 people has risen from 3.8 in 1989 to 12.3 in 1997. The number of internet hosts per 10,000 people has risen from 8.6 in 1994 to 94.4 in 1999. Expenditures on information and communication technology as a percentage of global GDP has risen from 5.7 per cent in 1992 to 6.9 per cent in 1999. International telecommunications per subscriber have

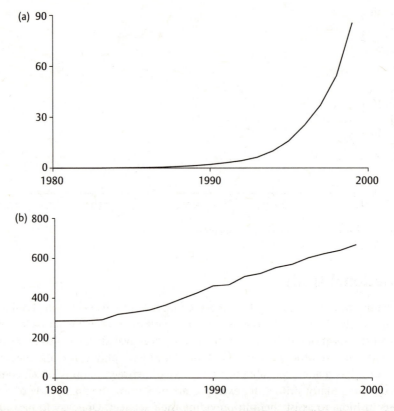

Fig. 1.11 Aspects of globalization (a) mobile phones (per 1000 people) (b) international tourism arrivals (millions)

gone from 52 minutes in 1981 to 129 minutes in 1999. Expenditures on international tourism have risen from $110 bn in 1980 to $416 bn in 1999. The number of internet users has increased from 45,000 in 1990 to 241 million in 1999. Finally, as illustrated in Figure 1.11, the number of international tourism arrivals has risen from 286 million in 1980 to 668 million in 1999, and the number of mobile phones per 1,000 people has increased from 0.1 in 1984 to 86 in 1999.

1.8 Trade connections in the world economy

To conclude the first chapter, we want to give an impression of the most important international trade connections in the world economy. The World Bank identifies seven global regions, namely (i) East Asia and Pacific (EAP; including China and Indonesia), (ii) (East) Europe and Central Asia (ECA; including Russia and Turkey), (iii) Latin America and the Caribbean (LAC; including Brazil and Mexico), (iv) Middle East and North Africa

Table 1.6 Intra- and interregional trade flows, 1997 (% of world total)

From	To									
	EAP	ECA	LAC	MNA	SAS	SSA	NAm	EUR	AAs	Total
EAP	1.36	0.15	0.18	0.11	0.13	0.08	2.19	1.61	4.09	9.90
ECA	0.16	1.38	0.05	0.12	0.03	0.02	0.20	2.37	0.13	4.47
LAC	0.16	0.08	1.06	0.08	0.02	0.03	2.82	0.77	0.27	5.30
MNA	0.20	0.10	0.06	0.07	0.04	0.01	0.28	0.88	0.50	2.13
SAS	0.07	0.04	0.02	0.02	0.02	0.01	0.25	0.33	0.16	0.92
SSA	0.08	0.03	0.04	0.01	0.00	0.05	0.330	0.53	0.11	1.18
NAm	1.29	0.26	2.87	0.32	0.11	0.13	6.07	3.39	2.95	17.38
EUR	1.40	3.07	1.06	1.11	0.35	0.57	3.83	27.68	2.83	41.91
AAs	4.82	0.25	0.60	0.19	0.21	0.14	4.16	2.76	3.67	16.81
Total	9.54	5.34	5.94	2.04	0.90	1.04	20.14	40.33	14.72	100.00

Source: own calculations, based on data provided by Jeroen Hinloopen (University of Amsterdam).
EAP = East Asia and Pacific; ECA = Europe and Central Asia; LAC = Latin America and Caribbean;
MNA = Middle East and North Africa; SAS = South Asia; SSA = Sub-Saharan Africa; NAm =
North America; EUR = Western Europe; AAs = AustralAsia. Totals may not sum due to rounding.

(MNA; including Egypt), (v) South Asia (SAS; including India), (vi) Sub-Saharan Africa (SSA; including Nigeria and South Africa), and (vii) the high-income countries. For the purposes of this section we have subdivided the group of high-income countries into three subgroups, namely North America (NAm), Western Europe (EUR), and AustralAsia (AAs, including Japan and Australia), leading to a total of nine global regions.[6]

Table 1.6 summarizes the international trade connections within and between the nine global regions. It states, for example, that 1.36 per cent of the world export flows are from countries in East Asia and the Pacific (EAP) to other countries in East Asia and the Pacific. Similarly, 3.85 per cent of the world export flows are from Western Europe to North America, etc. Figure 1.12 illustrates the information of Table 1.6 by rounding the numbers to the nearest integer and depicting only the thirty trade flows that are non-zero.

Figure 1.12 leads to several conclusions. First, South Asia scarcely participates in the global economy as none of its bilateral trade flows is large enough to be depicted in the figure. A similar observation holds for Sub-Saharan Africa, which almost only trades with Western Europe. Second, and in contrast to the first observation, Western Europe is a spider in the web of global international trade connections. Not only because it is the only global region with sizeable trade flows to every other region (with the exception of South Asia), but also because no less than 28 per cent of the world trade flows are from countries in Western Europe to other countries in Western Europe (intra-regional trade flows). Third, we note that the other high-income regions (North America and AustralAsia) also have large *intra*-regional trade flows (6 per cent and 4 per cent, respectively). Fourth, the largest *inter*-regional trade flows are from the high-income global

---

[6] The website of the book specifies exactly to which global region a country belongs.

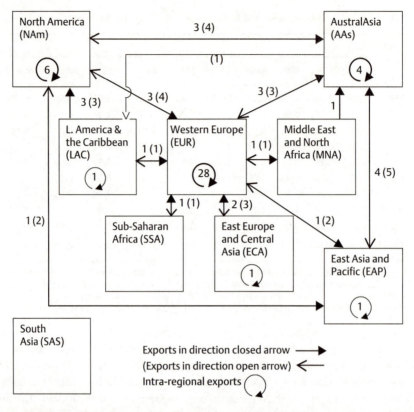

Fig 1.12 Global regions and international trade flows (% of world total)
Source: see Table 1.6.

regions to the other high-income regions joined by East Asia and the Pacific (with a population of 1.75 billion people). Fifth, and finally, Latin America (LAC), the Middle East and North Africa (MNA), and East Europe and Central Asia (ECA) hold an intermediate position, with connections to some other regions in their direct vicinity.

1.9 **Conclusions**

This chapter presents basic, but essential, information on the structure of the world economy. We give an impression of the importance of various countries using different measures. In terms of land area Russia is the largest country, while some relatively unknown African nations are also important. In terms of population China and India stand out, as do Asian nations in general. In terms of income, using either GDP or GNP, North America, Japan, and many European nations are important. This holds even when current dollars, which tend to overestimate the importance of high-income countries, are corrected for purchasing power. Japan and nations from North America and Europe also hold top positions with respect to income per capita. The differences in this respect are enormous: the highest ranking country is estimated to have an income per capita more than 100 times that of the lowest ranking country. International trade flows are dominated by relatively small European and South-East Asian countries. In general, the different rankings change the composition of important countries considerably. Only three countries, namely China, the USA, and Mexico, make it to the top fifteen lists in terms of land area, population, total income, *and* export value of goods and services.

When discussing the accounting principles of the balance of payments, we emphasized that a surplus on the current account, which is roughly a higher export than import value of goods, services, and investment income, translates into an outflow of capital, that is an increase in claims on the outside world. The opposite holds if there is a deficit on the current account. In dynamic terms, the world population is growing rapidly, doubling from 3 to 6 billion in four decades, but the world income level is growing even more rapidly. As a consequence, income per capita has also doubled in four decades. In the same time period, international trade flows have increased even more rapidly, such that world exports relative to world income have also doubled, reaching about 27 per cent in 1999. Whether this development should be called 'globalization' is questionable, as the term seems to have different meanings to different people.

With this information in the back of our heads we are ready to embark on our journey into international economics, which values the consistency of a general equilibrium approach. Clearly, we will not be able to 'explain' all empirical observations above, although international economists do work on all these issues. We will concentrate on explanations of international trade flows, and discuss how the insights derived there can be helpful for tackling important policy problems. Many other topics touched upon above will also be explored, such as capital flows, multinationals, geographic concentration, development, and growth. Along the way we will present more detailed empirical information on specific topics to raise new questions and guide us in our search.

Chapter 2

Opportunity Costs

Objectives/key terms

Productivity table	Constant returns to scale
Opportunity costs	Absolute costs
Balassa index	Revealed (comparative) advantage

The classical driving forces behind international trade flows are technological differences between nations. If another country can produce a good more cheaply than we ourselves can make it (opportunity costs), it is better to import this good from abroad. This will increase our welfare.

2.1 Introduction

Adam Smith[1] (1723–90) will provide us with the starting point of our analysis. On the peculiar notions of the costs and benefits of international trade prior to Adam Smith, for example considering the role of merchants, the reader is encouraged to consult Douglas Irwin's (1996) *Against the Tide: An Intellectual History of Free Trade*. It suffices for our present purposes to note that various authors advocated a policy of free trade, usually without providing a proper analytical background for this policy prescription, already before the publication of Smith's (1776) influential masterpiece *An Inquiry into the Nature and Causes of the Wealth of Nations*. The emergence of a doctrine of free trade at the time was largely a reaction to the Mercantilist literature of the seventeenth century, which advocated state regulation of trade to promote wealth and growth, maximize employment, achieve a favourable balance of trade, and protect the home industry. As Thomas Mun (1664) put it:[2] 'The ordinary means therefore to encrease our wealth and treasure is by Forraign Trade, wherein wee must ever observe this rule; to sell more to strangers yearly than wee consume of theirs in value.' It is, of course, immediately obvious that not all countries can be 'successful' by applying this Mercantilist maxim, since one country's trade surplus must by necessity be a trade

---

[1] Obviously, Adam Smith had a large impact on almost all aspects of economic analysis. We restrict ourselves here to his main contributions in international trade theory.   [2] See Allen (1965: 6).

Fig. 2.1 Adam Smith (1723–1790)

Scottish philosopher, considered by many to be the founder of modern economic science as we know it. Famous for the 'invisible hand', that is how people pursuing their own self-interest actually benefit society as a whole, and the advantages of increasing 'specialization' (the pin factory example). Major publications are *The Theory of Moral Sentiments* (1759) and *An Inquiry into the Nature and Causes of the Wealth of Nations* (1776).

deficit for the rest of the world. The general preoccupation at the time of accumulating bullion, that is gold and silver, was deemed necessary to allow a nation to maintain military forces abroad. The fact that soldiers do not actually consume gold and silver, but rather food, clothes, and shelter, was already pointed out by Smith.

If a free trade doctrine was already advocated by others prior to the *Wealth of Nations*, why do we pay so much attention to Adam Smith's analysis? First, because that's what it is, an *analysis* of economic reasons for advocating a policy of free trade. Second, because many people still needed to be convinced of the benefits of international trade, as illustrated for example by the work of James Steuart's (1767) *An Inquiry into the Principles of Political Oeconomy*. Third, because Smith was able to put many different arguments and elements together in a coherent and systematic framework, organized using a few general principles, and thus providing a new way of thinking about political economy. After a few years, this had a large impact on the profession. As Irwin (1996: 75) put it:

While drawing upon the work of others, Smith created such a compelling and complete case for free trade that commercial policy could no longer be seriously discussed without contending with his views, and herein lies one of Smith's foremost contributions to economics.

Although Adam Smith argued on many occasions quite strongly against the trade policy prescriptions of the Mercantilists, and passionately advocated free trade flows and eliminating trade barriers, it is fair to point out that he also saw room for some limits on those trade flows under special circumstances. One important example is the production of strategic goods, such as weapons, for which a strong dependence on imports was unwarranted in Smith's view.

2.2 **Smith's argument for free trade**

Summarizing Smith's argument for free trade, it runs roughly as follows. First, he emphasizes the *opportunity costs* in regulations in general (IV. ii. 3):[3]

No regulation of commerce can increase the quantity of industry in any society beyond what its capital can maintain. It can only divert a part of it into a direction into which it might not otherwise have gone; and it is by no means certain that this artificial direction is likely to be more advantageous to the society than that into which it would have gone of its own accord.

This aspect of the analysis, that regulations, for example promoting the interests of the shoemakers, imply that resources, such as capital and labour, are drawn away from other sectors of the economy, is probably Smith's most important contribution in this respect. Until then, the 'successfulness' of such regulations was measured for example by the increasing production of shoes, or by the increase in profits for the shoemakers. Smith pointed out that there was a cost to this increase, now known as opportunity costs, because the extra capital and labour used for shoe production might have been more advantageously employed in some other sector.

Second, he applies the opportunity cost principle to individuals in a society (IV. ii. 11):

It is the maxim of every prudent master of a family, never to attempt to make at home what it will cost him more to make than to buy. The taylor does not attempt to make his own shoes, but buys them of the shoemaker. The shoemaker does not attempt to make his own cloaths, but employs a taylor. The farmer attempts to make neither the one nor the other, but employs those different artificers. All of them find it for their interest to employ their whole industry in a way in which they have some advantage over their neighbours, and to purchase with a part of its produce, or what is the same thing, with the price of a part of it, whatever else they have occasion for.

His general conclusion is therefore that each individual is specializing in the production of those goods and services in which s/he has some advantage.

Third, he applies the same opportunity cost principle to international commercial policy (IV. ii. 12):

What is prudence in the conduct of every private family, can scarce be folly in that of a great kingdom. If a foreign country can supply us with a commodity cheaper than we ourselves can make it, better buy it of them with some part of the produce of our own industry, employed in a way in which we have some advantage. The general industry of the country, being always in proportion to the capital which employs it, will not thereby be diminished, no more than that of the above-mentioned artificers; but only left to find out the way in which it can be employed with the greatest advantage.

This leads to the conclusion that international trade flows reflect the fact that goods and services can sometimes be imported at lower cost from abroad than they can be produced at home. This increases the consumption opportunities for a nation, and is

---

[3] The reference numbers for Adam Smith follow the Glasgow convention of book, section, paragraph.

therefore beneficial for the nation as a whole, just as the specialization of the artificers, the shoemaker and the tailor, is advantageous at the individual level.[4]

The above observations, coupled with the labour theory of value, lead Joseph Schumpeter to conclude in his seminal *History of Economic Analysis* (1954: 374) that 'Adam Smith, ... seems to have believed that under free trade all goods would be produced where their absolute costs in terms of labour are lowest'. It is time to turn to a brief modern analysis of this proposition.

2.3 Analysis of absolute cost advantages

In general, to convince modern economists of the validity of an argument, one must be precise. This implies that one must specify the exact circumstances in a small (general equilibrium) economic model under which the conclusion is valid. Although some economists, and presumably many non-economists, lament the modern approach, for example because it implies that a lot of the richness of Smith's analysis (the eloquence of his writing, the examples he uses) is lost in the process, the advantages are substantial. First, and most importantly, because cheating is not allowed. You are forced to think your analysis through in detail and get your story right. The importance of this aspect cannot be stressed too much, because it is easy (and tempting) to sweep some of the loose ends and the details of the analysis (intentionally or unintentionally) under the mat in a purely verbal approach. Second, knowing the exact circumstances under which a conclusion is valid frequently points the way to a more general approach under which the conclusion is still valid, or to circumstances under which we may arrive at different conclusions.

To show a specific set of circumstances such that under free trade all goods will be produced where their absolute costs in terms of labour are lowest, as Schumpeter expressed Smith's view, assume that there are 2 countries, USA and Japan, producing 2 goods, food and cars, using 1 factor of production, labour (international economists refer to this setting as a $2 \times 2 \times 1$ model). The production function in both countries and for both goods exhibits constant returns to scale, indicating that if we double the amount of inputs in an industry (that is, labour), the output level (that is, production) will also double. We assume that there are many firms in both countries, each behaving perfectly competitively, that is each firm wants to maximize profits, taking the price levels in the output and input markets as given. Taken together, the assumptions of constant returns to scale and perfect competition imply that if a good is produced in equilibrium, the price level in the output market must be equal to the unit cost of production, see Box 2.1.

---

[4] An important forerunner of Adam Smith in terms of opportunity costs was Henry Martyn, see also Chapter 9, who in (1701) argued (Irwin 1996: 57): 'Things may be imported from India by fewer hands than as good would be made in England, so that to permit the consumption of Indian manufactures is to permit the loss of few men's labour ... a law to restrain us to use only English manufactures, is to oblige us to make them first, is to oblige us to provide for our consumption by the labour of many when that of few might be sufficient.'

Box 2.1 **Constant returns to scale and perfect competition**

In neoclassical economics we frequently combine the technological assumption of constant returns to scale with the behavioural assumption of perfect competition. This implies a simple, but important, relationship between the costs of production and the equilibrium price of a good on the market place.

Under constant returns to scale, knowing the (minimum) costs of producing one unit of a good, say c, gives us enough information to determine the (minimum) costs of producing an arbitrary number of goods, even if there are many different inputs into the production process. More specifically, if the firm wants to produce x units of a good, its costs are cx.

Under perfect competition, the firm takes the unit costs of production c as a parameter, that is it assumes that it has no control over the unit cost level, which will depend in particular on the level of technology (the production function) and the cost of the inputs (for example the wage rate). Similarly, the firm will treat the price it can fetch for a unit of output, say p, as a parameter beyond its control determined on the market place. If a firm sells x units of a product its total revenue will be px. The firm's profits π, total revenue minus total costs, can therefore be written as:

$$(2.1) \qquad\qquad \pi = px - cx = (p - c)x$$

Since the firm's objective function is to maximize profits and, as argued above, it treats the price p and the unit cost of production c as parameters, we can logically distinguish between three different possibilities:

- $p < c$. If the price p of the good on the market place is smaller than the unit cost of production c, profits are obviously maximized by not producing any units of the good: $x = 0$.

- $p = c$. If the price p of the good on the market place is equal to the unit cost of production c, profits are zero independently of the level of production; the production level x is undetermined at the firm level since the firm always maximizes profits independently of the scale of production (which in equilibrium can then be determined by other economic forces, such as the equality of total supply and demand for the good).

- $p > c$. If the price p of the good on the market place is larger than the unit cost of production c, profits are maximized at the firm level by producing an infinite number of goods ($x = \infty$), which also leads to infinite profits. Although this possibility may appeal to the entrepreneurs among the readers, an infinite production level cannot be reached in any economy with a finite number of inputs, implying that this logical possibility cannot be an economic equilibrium and therefore has to be discarded.

Summarizing the above arguments, we can conclude that under perfect competition and constant returns to scale: $p \leq c$, where $x > 0 \Rightarrow p = c$ and $p < c \Rightarrow x = 0$.

Chapter 2 tool: productivity table

To specifically point out the tools used in international economic analysis we usually draw attention to them in separate tool-boxes. A rather simple tool used in this chapter is the productivity table, summarizing the state of technology in both countries, see Table 2.1. Since the production functions use only 1 input (labour) and exhibit constant returns to scale, they can be summarized using a table specifying how much labour is required to produce 1 unit of either good in either country. The left-hand side of Table 2.1 gives these labour requirements in general terms, where a_F^{US} is the number of units of labour required in the USA to produce 1 unit of food, a_C^J is the number of units of labour required in Japan to produce 1 car, etc. These are measured in flows of labour services over a certain time period, for example the number of men required to work 40 hours per week during 8 weeks to produce 1 unit of output. The right-hand side of Table 2.1 gives an example using specific numbers for the unit labour requirements.

Table 2.1 Productivity table; labour required to produce 1 unit of output

	General specification		Example	
	Food	Cars	Food	Cars
USA	a_F^{US}	a_C^{US}	2	8
Japan	a_F^J	a_C^J	3	6

As is clear from Smith's arguments, the production functions must differ between the two countries for international trade flows to arise, that is the driving force behind such flows, according to Smith, are differences in technology. The discussion below focuses on the example (occasionally using the general specification in parentheses). In Table 2.1 we assume that Japan requires 3 units of labour to produce 1 unit of food, whereas the USA requires only 2 units of labour. Similarly, Japan needs 6 units of labour to produce 1 car, whereas the USA needs 8 units of labour. Since Japan is more efficient in the production of cars and the USA is more efficient in the production of food it would be beneficial for the world as a whole, according to Adam Smith, if the USA were to import cars from Japan, in exchange for food.

Let's see how this works exactly. Suppose the USA produces 1 car less. This frees up 8 (i.e. a_C^{US}) units of labour. These 8 units of labour can be used in the USA to produce $8/2 = 4$ (i.e. a_C^{US}/a_F^{US}) units of food. In modern terminology, the opportunity costs of producing a car in the USA are 4 units of food. The USA has now produced 1 car less and 4 units of food more. Suppose, however, that it wants to consume the same number of cars as before. It must then import 1 car from Japan. We will assume that the exchange of goods between countries is costless. This is not a particularly plausible assumption (international trade clearly involves costs of transportation, insurance, risk, etc.), which will only be relaxed much later in the analysis to focus attention sharply on the underlying forces determining international trade flows.

To produce 1 extra car, Japan needs 6 (i.e. a_C^J) units of labour. These labourers must come from the food sector, where production therefore drops by $6/3 = 2$ (i.e. a_C^J/a_F^J) units of food, reflecting the opportunity costs of producing a car in Japan. It is important to note that this hypothetical reallocation of labour between sectors in both countries results in the USA producing 1 car less, but 4 units of food more, while Japan produces 2 units of food less, but 1 car more. The total world production of cars therefore remains unchanged, while food production rises by 2 units. These 2 extra units of food reflect the potential gains from specialization if both countries concentrate in the production of the good they produce most efficiently, namely cars for Japan and food for the USA. In principle, both countries might gain, for example if they exchange 3 units of food for 1 car, in which case both countries can consume 1 unit of food more than before.

We will analyse the determination of the division of the gains from trade between the two countries, the determination of the terms of trade, and the extent of specialization in more detail in Chapter 3. For now it suffices to note that we have given precise conditions under which mutually beneficial gains from trade may arise if each country specializes in the production of the good it produces more efficiently.

2.4 Application: Japan and the USA

A proper econometric test of the various theories put forth in this book is clearly beyond our scope, but it is important to realize that it is ultimately the friction between theory and facts that leads to new economic insights. So now that we have a simple theory underlying international trade flows, a common-sense check to see if this theory makes any sense, also in today's world, is simply gathering some statistical information, more readily available now than in Adam Smith's days, and confront the theory with these data.

First, we stick as closely as we can to the example given in the text. This requires us to gather information about the labour productivity in Japan and the USA, both for the food sector and the car sector. To this end we use the International Standard Industrial Classification (ISIC) revision II data on production and employment, reported for various industries. As an indicator of labour productivity we use total value added in a sector, divided by total employment in that sector (we get back to some limitations of this procedure at a later stage). Since there is no 'car' sector in the data set, we use 'transport equipment' instead. Table 2.2 gives the results of these calculations for food and transport equipment, both for the USA and Japan.

Table 2.2 Value added per employed person
per year (US $, 1990)

	Food (311/2)	Transport equipment (384)
USA	82,337	77,582
Japan	48,273	81,928

Data sources: for value added Unido (*International
Yearbook for Industrial Statistics*, 1996); for exchange
rates IMF (*International Financial Statistics Yearbook*, 1999);
for employment International Labour Organization
(*Yearbook of Labour Statistics*, 1999); for trade data OECD
(foreign trade by commodities). (Category in parentheses.)

Table 2.3 Exports and imports; food and transport equipment
(million US $, 1998)

	Food (0 + 22 + 29 + 4)	Transport equipment (78 + 79)
Export from USA to Japan	9,286	8,018
Import in USA from Japan	419	34,682

Source: see Table 2.2. (Category in parentheses.)

Apparently the assumption in the example of Table 2.1, where the USA has a
higher productivity in the food sector and Japan has a higher productivity in the
car sector, is supported by the data in Table 2.2 (the reader of course realizes that the
example was constructed after the data was collected). According to Adam Smith it
will therefore be beneficial if the USA specializes in the production of food, to be exported
to Japan in exchange for cars. To verify this prediction, we must gather information on
trade flows between the two countries, and immediately encounter another empirical problem: the trade data are available using the Standard International Trade
Classification (SITC), which does not correspond perfectly with the ISIC classification
we used to estimate the labour productivities in Table 2.2. To circumvent this
shortcoming we aggregate several categories in the SITC trade data into one 'food'
category. Similarly for the 'transport equipment' category, still consisting mostly of
cars proper. The results are reported in Table 2.3.

It is clear that Adam Smith's basic prediction is supported by this example: the USA,
which is more efficient in food production, exports a lot of food ($9.3 bn) to Japan and
imports virtually no food ($0.4 bn) from Japan. In fact, the 'food' category is the USA's
largest export category. Similarly, Japan, which is more efficient in car production,
exports a lot of cars ($34.7 bn, the second largest category after machinery) to the USA,
while importing in comparison only a small number of cars ($8 bn) from the USA.

2.5 Problems with absolute cost advantage and the example

We have illustrated international trade flows arising from absolute cost advantages using two developed nations, the USA and Japan, as an example. Arguably, when comparing two such similarly developed nations, one country may be more efficient in the production of some goods, while the other country is more efficient in the production of some other goods. This raises the question whether there is room in this framework for beneficial international trade flows between developed and less developed nations, such as the USA and Ecuador. As the well-known historian Paul Kennedy (1995), criticizing the case for free trade more than 200 years after Adam Smith, put it (italics mine):[5] 'What if there is *nothing* you can produce more cheaply or efficiently than anywhere else, except by constantly cutting labour costs?' The suggestion is that less developed nations cannot compete on the international scene, and that they do not benefit from the international exchange of commodities. Whether this suggestion is true or not is analysed and answered in Chapter 3.

The point above is an analytic question which can be satisfactorily answered. The prediction of international trade flows in accordance with absolute cost advantages as suggested in section 2.4 for food and cars, however, is less convincing when extended to the other sectors of the economy. An overview for the USA and Japan is given in Table 2.4. As illustrated in the table by the shaded sectors, the prediction of net trade flows is in accordance with absolute costs advantage for only 11 of the 21 sectors. This is, to put it mildly, not a very impressive score, although it should be noted that if the differences in productivity are very large the net trade flow is generally in accordance with absolute cost advantage. This is illustrated in Figure 2.2 by calculating exports and imports for different categories as a percentage of total exports and imports and calculating the difference as an indication of net trade flows.[6] The most noteworthy exception is the 'machinery' sector. In Part III of this book we will argue that this is related to aggregation problems; the term machines refers to many differentiated goods. There are several important reservations to be made with respect to the calculations underlying Tables 2.2–2.4 to which we will return later in the book. One problem, however, is directly related to the comparison of value added per person in the two different nations underlying the construction of these tables, and as such lies at the heart of the 'comparative advantage' analysis of Chapter 3.

[5] Paul Kennedy also wrote almost two centuries after David Ricardo, which shows, as the analysis in Chapter 3 will clarify, that he should have done his homework more carefully.

[6] This procedure mitigates the problems that arise from calculating net trade flows resulting from large trade imbalances, such as the current account deficit for the USA.

Table 2.4 USA and Japan; value added, imports and exports, various sectors

ISIC	Industry	Trade (million US $)		Value added/person	
		Export to Japan	Import from Japan	USA	Japan
314	Tobacco	1,870	19	461,224	179,812
322/3	Wearing apparel and leather products	699	97	494,643	192,873
311/2	Food products	9,286	419	82,337	48,273
385	Professional and scientific equipment	4,220	6,574	77,039	47,216
321	Textiles	570	647	20,480	14,889
382/3	Machinery	16,738	58,161	155,308	113,687
313	Beverages	281	36	139,735	114,445
353/4	Petroleum and coal products	725	276	485,714	429,688
324	Footwear	117	2	29,114	26,987
355	Rubber products	331	1,613	66,010	61,421
356	Plastic products	820	1,320	43,831	42,372
341/2	Paper and printing products	1,111	417	77,826	78,237
361/2/9	Non-metallic mineral products	490	1,125	95,733	97,969
384	Transport equipment	8,018	34,682	77,582	81,928
381	Fabricated metal products	524	2,123	20,091	21,825
332	Furniture	342	131	14,095	15,913
390	Other manufacturing industries	4,213	8,490	44,737	51,182
372	Non-ferrous metals	559	502	62,057	77,722
351/2	Chemicals	4,993	4,977	224,747	285,621
331	Wood products	1,599	10	26,000	37,913
371	Iron and steel	378	3,469	67,516	114,927

Sources: see Table 2.2; shaded sectors have net exports in accordance with absolute advantage.

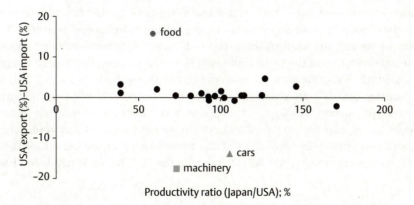

Fig. 2.2 Japan–USA exports and productivity, various sectors

2.6 **Measuring trade advantages:
the Balassa index I[7]**

We have seen that it is beneficial for a country to specialize in the production of those goods which it can produce more efficiently than another country, and to export these goods in exchange of imports of goods it can produce less efficiently. As such it provides a small and simple explanation for international trade flows. Subsequently, sections 2.4 and 2.5 'tested' the theory by looking at the trade flows between Japan and the USA in relation to labour productivity. We can, however, also turn the question around, by first empirically investigating which countries are exporting which goods and then wondering which theory, or theories, may explain this export pattern. Since the idea is that investigating a country's actual exports 'reveals' the country's strong sectors, the first step in this procedure is known as establishing a country's 'revealed comparative advantage'.[8] The index most frequently used in this respect was pioneered by Liesner (1958), but refined and popularized by Bela Balassa (1965, 1989), and is therefore known as the *Balassa index.*

Many countries are, for example, producing and exporting cars. To establish whether a country, say Japan, holds a particularly strong position in the car industry, Balassa argued that one should compare the share of car exports in Japan's total exports with the share of car exports in a group of reference country's total exports. The Balassa index is therefore essentially a normalized export share. More specifically, if BI_j^A is country A's Balassa index for industry j, this is equal to:

$$(2.2) \qquad BI_j^A = \frac{\text{share of industry } j \text{ in country A exports}}{\text{share of industry } j \text{ in reference country exports}}$$

If $BI_j^A > 1$ country A is said to have a revealed comparative advantage in industry j, since this industry is more important for country A's exports than for the exports of the reference countries.

Before actually calculating the Balassa index, we have to decide which exports to which countries to include and which countries to use as 'reference' countries. In this chapter we restrict attention to the exports of twenty-eight *manufacturing* sectors for the member countries of the Organization for Economic Cooperation and Development (OECD), which is also the group of reference countries, see Tables 2.5 and 2.6. This has the advantage that data are available for a long time period (1970–96), including information on production, employment, etc. The next chapter will report on exports of European Union countries to Japan, and explain the advantages of that approach.

Figure 2.3 illustrates the evolution of the Balassa index in the period 1970–96 for the two sectors with the highest Balassa index for the USA, Japan, Finland, and Italy. In

---

[7] This section is based on Ottens (2000) and Hinloopen and van Marrewijk (2001).

[8] The 'comparative' part of this name also reflects the developments in the next chapters.

Table 2.5 Manufacturing sectors in the Ottens database

Food	Wood products	Petrol and coal products	Non-ferrous metals
Beverages	Furniture	Rubber products	Metal products
Tobacco	Paper	Plastic products	Non-electrical machinery
Textiles	Printing and publishing	Pottery and china	El. machinery
Wearing apparel	Industrial chemicals	Glass and products	Transport equipment
Leather and products	Other chemicals	Non-metal products	Professional goods
Footwear	Petroleum refineries	Iron and steel	Other manufacturing

Table 2.6 Sectors with highest Balassa index, 1996

Australia		*Germany*		*Norway*	
Non-ferrous metals	5.60	Industrial chemicals	1.24	Non-ferrous metals	6.48
Food	3.91	Metal products	1.23	Petroleum refineries	6.14
Austria		*Greece*		*Portugal*	
Wood products	2.78	Wearing apparel	8.07	Footwear	13.32
Paper and products	1.94	Non-metal products	5.68	Pottery, china, etc.	7.83
Belgium		*Iceland*		*Spain*	
Other maunfacturing	4.56	Food	13.44	Footwear	3.60
Glass and products	2.04	Non-ferrous metals	5.25	Non-metal products	3.51
Canada		*Italy*		*Sweden*	
Wood products	6.46	Footwear	5.62	Paper and products	3.79
Paper and products	3.38	Leather and products	4.87	Wood products	3.49
Denmark		*Japan*		*United Kingdom*	
Furniture and fixtures	4.97	Electrical machinery	1.77	Beverages	2.01
Food	4.12	Professional goods	169	Printing and publishing	1.94
Finland		*The Netherlands*		*United States*	
Paper and products	7.83	Tobacco	4.31	Tobacco	2.73
Wood products	5.15	Petroleum Refineries	3.66	Professional goods	1.40
France		*New Zealand*			
Beverages	3.42	Food	9.20		
Glass and products	1.68	Leather and products	4.20		

Source: Ottens (2000). The numbers indicate the Balassa index in 1996.

all cases the Balassa index is above 1, as it should be for the strong export sectors. Apparently, the USA has a revealed comparative trade advantage for tobacco and professional goods and Japan for electrical machinery and professional goods. Note the fairly small value of the highest Balassa index for both countries (about 2 to 3). This can be attributed to the fact that both countries have a large industrial base, exporting a wide variety of goods, which makes it more difficult to achieve high values for the Balassa index. This contrasts with the much larger highest values for countries with a smaller industrial base, such as Italy (about 6–8) and Finland (about 8–11). Italy's highest ranking sectors are footwear (Italian shoes) and leather and products (e.g. handbags for the Italian fashion industry). Finland's highest ranking sectors are paper

and products and wood products. This must have something to do with the easy availability of factor inputs, that is wood from the large Finnish forests, as will be extensively
discussed in Part II of this book.

In general, sectors with a high comparative advantage tend to sustain this advantage
for a fairly long time. Tobacco, for example, is always the sector with the highest Balassa
index in the USA. The same holds for footwear in Italy and paper and products in Finland.
Changes over extended periods of time are, however, also possible. The Balassa index
for leather and products in Italy has clearly increased in the period of investigation. This
sector was ranked fourth in Italy in 1981 and second from 1984 onwards. Similarly,

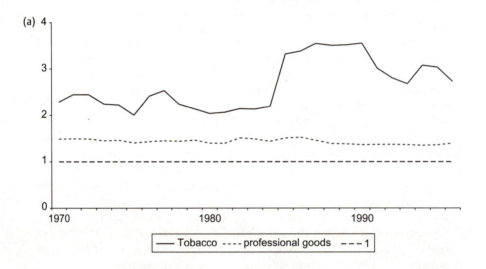

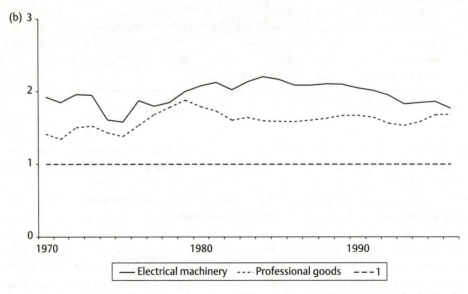

Fig. 2.3 Highest Balassa index, selected countries: (a) United States, (b) Japan, (c) Finland, (d) Italy

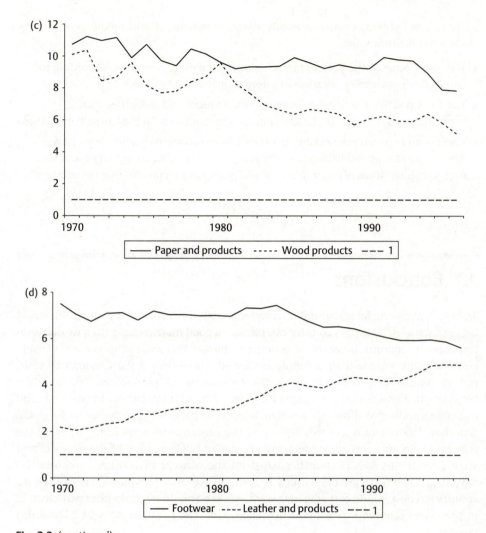

Fig. 2.3 (continued)

the highest ranking sector in Japan from 1970 to 1979 was pottery and china, not electrical machinery.

Table 2.6 gives an overview of the two sectors with the highest Balassa index in 1996 for the twenty OECD countries in the Ottens database. In general, the highest Balassa index for large countries is lower than for small countries. Note that paper and products and wood products are the two highest ranking sectors for Finland, Sweden, *and* Canada, all of which have extensive forests available. Also note that the labour intensive footwear industry is the highest ranking sector for Spain, Portugal, and Italy. Ottens also investigates the changes in the distribution of the Balassa index and the relationships between comparative advantage, employment and labour productivity. His main conclusions are:

- The mean value of the Balassa index is slowly increasing over time. According to Ottens this points to an increase in international specialization.

- There is a positive relationship between employment and industries with a comparative advantage. Specialization therefore tends to be in the 'correct' industries.

- There is no clear-cut relationship between labour productivity and comparative advantage. This probably indicates the importance of other factors of production, such as capital or natural resources, in also determining comparative advantage.

2.7 Conclusions

The classical driving forces behind international trade flows are technological differences between nations. If another country can produce a good more cheaply than we ourselves can make it (opportunity costs), it is better to import this good from abroad. We substantiated this argument in a simple framework based on constant returns to scale, perfect competition, with labour as the only factor of production. Specialization according to absolute cost advantages increases total output in the world economy, and therefore in principle allows for a welfare improvement for all participants in the global economy. We not only discussed some of the problems of empirically verifying the concept of absolute cost advantages, but also gave a brief overview of the strong export sectors for twenty OECD countries based on the concept of revealed (comparative) advantage, known as the Balassa index. In addition, we raised the question what to do if a country has no absolute cost advantages whatsoever. Should it refrain from participating in the global economy, as is frequently suggested? The next chapter will address this question.

Chapter 3
Comparative Advantage

Objectives/key terms

Comparative advantage	Production possibility frontier (ppf)
Autarky	Terms of trade
Gains from trade	World ppf

To determine a country's strong sectors based on technology differences only relative (or comparative) costs are important. Comparative costs are also vital for determining the terms of trade. International trade leads to welfare gains irrespective of absolute costs. The per capita welfare level, however, depends on absolute cost differences, which also explains the large international differences in wage levels.

3.1 Introduction

An important issue associated with the theory of absolute cost advantages as set forth in Chapter 2, which continues to puzzle thinkers up to this day as suggested by the Kennedy quote in section 2.5, now arises: how can you participate on the global market and gain from trading different goods and services if there is nothing you can produce more efficiently than anyone else? As we will see in Table 3.3 below, which gives empirical data for the European Union (EU) and Kenya, this is not merely a theoretical possibility; for all sixteen sectors of production for which we have data available, the EU is more productive than Kenya. So how can Kenya possibly trade with the EU? These problems were analysed in the first half of the nineteenth century in England by Robert Torrens, James Mill, and, most importantly, David Ricardo. All were in favour of free trade, and in the popular debate were particularly hostile towards the (in)famous Corn Laws, restricting grain imports into Britain. The most important contribution of this era was the theory of *comparative advantage*, also known as the *classical model*, or the *Ricardian model*. American Nobel laureate Paul Samuelson once even remarked that the theory of comparative advantage is 'one of the few ideas in economics that is true without being obvious'.

3.2 Classical economics and comparative advantage

As indicated in section 3.1, at the beginning of the nineteenth century various people were working on the same problem at the same time, namely how a country which is less efficient than another country in all sectors of production can still trade with other countries. They were all close to reaching the same conclusion. As Irwin (1996: 89) put it: 'Mill and Torrens were on the verge of an even more important insight', by which he means the theory of comparative advantage. After a quote from Torrens involving Poland, Irwin (1996: 90) concludes: 'this formulation lacks only the comparison of the cost ratios in both countries...whereby the theory is stated in its entirety. David Ricardo...provided this finishing touch in his *On the Principles of Political Economy and Taxation* in 1817.' In that work David Ricardo discusses a famous example of England and Portugal exchanging wine and cloth to complete the theory of comparative advantage, for which he therefore receives almost full credit (Ricardo 1817, ch. VII):[1]

England may be so circumstanced that to produce the cloth may require the labour of 100 men for one year; and if she attempted to make the wine, it might require the labour of 120 men for the same time. England would therefore find it her interest to import wine, and to purchase it by the exportation of cloth.

To produce the wine in Portugal might require only the labour of 80 men for one year, and to produce the cloth in the same country might require the labour of 90 men for the same time. It would therefore be advantageous for her to export wine in exchange for cloth. This exchange might even take place notwithstanding that the commodity imported by Portugal could be produced there with less labour than in England. Though she could make the cloth with the labour of 90 men, she would import it from a country where it required the labour of 100 men to produce it, because it would be advantageous to her rather to employ her capital in the production of wine, for which she would obtain more cloth from England, than she could produce by diverting a portion of her capital from the cultivation of vines to the manufacture of cloth.

Thus England would give the produce of the labour of 100 men for the produce of the labour of 80. Such an exchange could not take place between the individuals of the same country. The labour of 100 Englishmen cannot be given for that of 80 Englishmen, but the produce of the labour of 100 Englishmen may be given for the produce of the labour of 80 Portuguese, 60 Russians, or 120 East Indians.

Ricardo therefore argues that it is beneficial for Portugal to specialize in the production of wine and exchange the wine for cloth from England, even though it would require less Portuguese labour to produce this cloth than English labour. The details of this reasoning

---

[1] See Allen (1965: 63–4). Some economists question the contribution of Ricardo, see e.g. Chipman (1965: 480), or even suggest that James Mill rather than David Ricardo came up with the example (Thweatt 1976). Since his contemporary James Mill gives full credit to David Ricardo on at least two occasions (Irwin 1996: 91), I think it is fair to conclude that Ricardo does deserve most credit.

Fig. 3.1 David Ricardo (1772–1823)

Born in London, the third son of a Jewish family emigrated from Holland, he married the daughter of a Quaker and was disinherited by his parents. Ricardo nonetheless accumulated a fortune as a stock-jobber and loan contractor. As Blaug (1986: 201) puts it: 'Ricardo may or may not be the greatest economist that ever lived, but he was certainly the richest.' His fame today rests mainly, of course, on his contributions to the theory of comparative advantage.

will be further explained in the next section. The essence of the argument was summarized by James Mill in 1821 as follows:[2]

When a country can either import a commodity or produce it at home, it compares the cost of producing at home with the cost of procuring from abroad; if the latter cost is less than the first, it imports. The cost at which a country can import from abroad depends, not upon the cost at which the foreign country produces the commodity, but upon what the commodity costs which it sends in exchange, compared with the cost which it must be at to produce the commodity in question, if it did not import it.

3.3 Analysis of comparative advantage

The analytic set-up of the Ricardian model is almost identical to that in Chapter 2. Assume that there are 2 countries, the European Union (EU) and Kenya, producing 2 goods, food and chemicals, under constant returns to scale using 1 factor of production, labour (again a $2 \times 2 \times 1$ model). There are many firms in both countries, each behaving perfectly competitively. As in Chapter 2, if a good is produced in equilibrium, the price level in the output market must be equal to the unit cost of production (see Box 2.1).

Table 3.1 gives the productivity table, summarizing the state of technology in both countries. The left-hand side of Table 3.1 gives the labour requirements in general terms, where a_F^{EU} is the number of units of labour required in the EU to produce 1 unit of food, a_C^K is the number of units of labour required in Kenya to produce 1 unit of chemicals, etc. The right-hand side of Table 3.1 gives an example using specific numbers for the unit labour requirements.

[2] Irwin (1996: 91).

Table 3.1 Productivity table; labour required to produce 1 unit of output

	General specification		Example	
	Food	Chemicals	Food	Chemicals
EU	a_F^{EU}	a_C^{EU}	2	8
Kenya	a_F^K	a_C^K	4	24

As is clear from the table, the EU is more efficient in the production of both goods; it requires 2 rather than 4 units of labour to produce one unit of food and 8 rather than 24 units of labour to produce one unit of chemicals. Based on a theory of absolute cost advantages Kenya would not be able to trade with the EU. However, the theory of comparative cost advantages argues that only relative, or comparative, costs are important for determining a nation's production advantages. In the example we see that Kenya is twice as inefficient as the EU in producing food (requiring 4 units of labour, rather than 2) but three times as inefficient as the EU in producing chemicals (requiring 24 units of labour, rather than 8). It should therefore specialize in the production of food, and export this to the EU in exchange for chemicals.

Let's see how this works exactly.[3] Suppose Kenya produces 1 unit of chemicals less. This frees up 24 (i.e. a_C^K) units of labour. These 24 units of labour can be used in Kenya to produce $24/4 = 6$ (i.e. a_C^K/a_F^K) units of food. The opportunity costs of producing chemicals in Kenya are 6 units of food. Kenya has now produced 1 unit of chemicals less and 6 units of food more. Suppose, however, that it wants to consume the same quantity of chemicals as before. It must then import 1 unit of chemicals from the EU. To produce 1 extra unit of chemicals, the EU needs 8 (i.e. a_C^{EU}) units of labour. These labourers must come from the food sector, where production therefore drops by $8/2 = 4$ (i.e. a_C^{EU}/a_F^{EU}) units of food, reflecting the opportunity costs of producing chemicals in the EU. Now note that this hypothetical reallocation of labour between sectors in both countries results in Kenya producing 1 unit of chemicals less, but 6 units of food more, while the EU produces 4 units of food less, but 1 unit of chemicals more. The total world production of chemicals therefore remains unchanged, while food production rises by 2 units. These 2 extra units of food reflect the potential gains from specialization if both countries concentrate in the production of the good for which they have a comparative advantage, that is the good they produce *relatively* most efficiently, namely chemicals for the EU and food for Kenya. In principle, therefore, there is room for both countries to gain from trading with each other. It is time to see what determines the terms of trade and the division of gains from trade in the classical setting.

---

[3] The reader may note that the reasoning to follow is exactly the same as in Chapter 2. The conclusion to derive below therefore may seem obvious in retrospect. It illustrates one of the advantages of the demand for rigour in the modern analytic approach in economics.

3.4 **Production possibility frontier and autarky**

If we want to determine the terms of trade if two Ricardian type countries are trading goods with each other, we have to determine the equilibrium relationships in the economy. Although this is not too complicated in the Ricardian model, it is instructive to start the analysis from a situation of *autarky*, that is if the two countries are *not* trading any goods. This is done most easily using the production possibility frontier.

To determine the production possibility frontiers for the EU and Kenya for the example of Table 3.1, we have to specify the available factors of production in each country. It suffices to specify the number of workers available since labour is the only factor of production, say 200 labourers for the EU and 120 labourers for Kenya. This implies that the EU can produce a maximum of $200/2 = 100$ units of food if it produces no chemicals at all, or $200/8 = 25$ units of chemicals if it produces no food at all. Similarly, Kenya can produce a maximum of $120/4 = 30$ units of food, or a maximum of $120/24 = 5$ units of chemicals. This is summarized in Table 3.2.

Chapter 3 tool: Production possibility frontier (ppf)

The tool introduced in this chapter is that of the production possibility frontier (or curve). It is defined as *all possible combinations of efficient production points given the available factors of production and the state of technology*. The production possibility frontier therefore gives all production combinations for which it is not possible to produce more of some good without reducing the production of some other good. In our two-good setting of food and chemicals it either depicts the maximum amount of food one can produce for a given amount of chemical output or, equivalently, the maximum amount of chemicals the economy can produce for a given level of food production. An example for the Ricardian model is depicted in Figure 3.2, where point C is a production point beyond the scope of the production possibility frontier for the Kenyan economy (for lack of labourers or technology), while it is below, and therefore not part of, the production possibility frontier for the EU economy. Note, in particular, that the EU economy could produce more food without producing less chemicals at point D, or more chemicals without producing less food at point E. More examples will follow in the next chapters. Note that:

- The production possibility frontier is a technical specification; it does not depend on any type of market competition.

- The production possibility frontier depends on the available factors of production; if more labourers are available, more goods can be produced.

- The production possibility frontier depends on the state of technology; if new production techniques become available, more goods may be produced using the same amount of factors of production.

This is actually all the information we need to completely calculate the production possibility frontiers for Kenya and the EU in a Ricardian model, since there are constant returns to scale and there is only one factor of production. If the EU currently produces 100 food and 0 chemicals (which is a point on the production possibility frontier) and wants to produce 1 unit of chemicals, it has to transfer 8 labourers from the food sector to the chemicals sector. These 8 labourers could have produced $8/2 = 4$ units of food, so food production drops to $100 - 4 = 96$, which gives us another point on the production possibility frontier. Similarly, if the EU wants to produce another unit of chemicals (2 rather than 1) food production drops again by 4 units (to 92). These changes are therefore *equiproportional*, such that the Ricardian production possibility frontiers are *straight lines*. All we really have to do, therefore, is calculate the maximum production points and connect these with a straight line. This is illustrated using the information of Table 3.2 in Figure 3.2.

We can now determine the equilibrium price of chemicals in terms of food (which we take as our measurement unit, known as the numéraire) for both countries, provided we are willing to make one simple and very weak assumption: *both countries want to consume*

Table 3.2 Total labour available and maximum production levels

	Total labour available	Maximum production Food	Chemicals
EU	200	100	25
Kenya	120	30	5

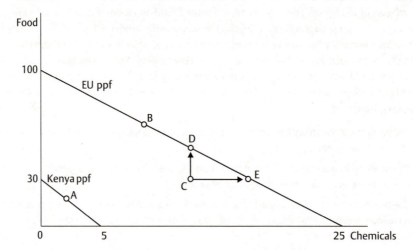

Fig. 3.2 Ricardian production possibility frontiers for the EU and Kenya

at least some units of both goods. Why does this assumption suffice to determine the price of chemicals in terms of food? Well, recall Box 2.1 and take the EU as an example:

- If the price of chemicals is more than 4 food, entrepreneurs want to produce only chemicals and no food. Since the economy wants to consume at least some food, this cannot be an equilibrium price.
- If the price of chemicals is less than 4 food, the entrepreneurs want to produce only food and no chemicals. Since the economy wants to consume at least some chemicals this also cannot be an equilibrium price.
- The price of chemicals is therefore 4 units of food in autarky in the EU.

Similar reasoning for Kenya leads to the conclusion that the price of chemicals is 6 units of food in autarky. This implies that the production possibility frontier coincides with the economy's budget line generated by the production levels in autarky for both countries. The consumers in both countries therefore choose the optimal consumption point along the production possibility frontier in autarky, while the entrepreneurs adjust their production levels along the ppf to accommodate the wishes of the consumers, say point A for Kenya and point B for the EU in Figure 3.2.

Conclusion

The autarky price ratio in a Ricardian model is exclusively determined by the technical coefficients of the productivity table; the price of chemicals in terms of food equals $a_C^{EU}/a_F^{EU} = 8/2 = 4$ in the EU and $a_C^K/a_F^K = 24/4 = 6$ in Kenya. Opportunities for trade between nations arise whenever the relative, or comparative, productivity ratios differ. They do not depend on absolute productivity levels.

3.5 Terms of trade and gains from trade

Determining the price of chemicals in terms of food in autarky in both countries does not allow us to determine exactly the terms of trade if the two countries decide to open up opportunities to trade with each other as this requires more detailed information on the demand structure of the economies than the simple assumption made in section 3.4. We can, however, determine the range within which the terms of trade can vary, and we can demonstrate that both countries may gain from trade. To start with the former, the autarky price of chemicals in terms of food is 4 in the EU and 6 in Kenya. The terms of trade can only vary within this range, endpoints included. If the price falls below 4 both countries want to produce only food, which cannot be an equilibrium, and if the price rises above 6 both countries want to produce only chemicals, which also cannot be an equilibrium.

As for the gains from trade, we can distinguish three separate cases, (i) if the terms of trade is strictly in between 4 and 6 both countries will gain, (ii) if the terms of trade is

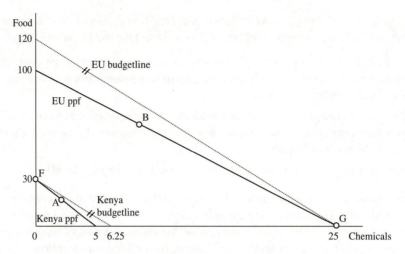

Fig. 3.3 The terms of trade is 4.8 units of food per unit of chemicals

4 only Kenya will gain while welfare in the EU will not change, and (iii) if the terms of trade is 6 only the EU will gain while welfare in Kenya will not change. Possibility (i) is illustrated in Figure 3.3, where we assume that the terms of trade is 4.8 units of food per unit of chemicals in the trading equilibrium. At that price Kenya will produce only food (30 units at point F) and will purchase abroad the required amount of chemicals at a price of 4.8 (to a maximum of 30/4.8 = 6.25 units). Similarly, at that price the EU will produce only chemicals (25 units at point G) and will purchase the amount of food it wants (to a maximum of 25 × 4.8 = 120 units).

How can we decide that if the terms of trade is 4.8 units of food per unit of chemicals both countries will gain from trade? Quite simply because at those terms of trade the production decisions of the entrepreneurs allow the consumers to choose a consumption point *beyond* the old autarky optimum (point A for Kenya and point B for the EU) because the budget line has pivoted outwards (around point F for Kenya and around point G for the EU). By revealed preference the consumption point chosen on the new budget line must be preferred to the old consumption point at autarky. So *if* a price of 4.8 is a trading equilibrium both countries will gain from trade (and similar reasoning holds for any other price strictly in between 4 and 6). The '*if*' above reflects the fact that a price of 4.8 can only be an equilibrium price if the consumers of the EU and Kenya combined at that price want to consume the total world production of both goods (30 units of food and 25 units of chemicals) given their income levels.[4]

Possibility (ii), that is Kenya will gain and EU welfare will remain unchanged if the terms of trade is 4, is illustrated in Figure 3.4. The way the autarky production points are chosen in Figure 3.2 makes it unlikely that a terms of trade higher than 4 is an equilibrium trading price, simply because it implies that the EU will specialize completely in the production of chemicals and food production will drop drastically. A plausible outcome in this set-up in

---

[4] Equivalently, the 'trade triangles' have to coincide. This is discussed further in the sequel.

Box 3.1 **Comparative costs, absolute costs, and international wages**

This chapter argues that differences in comparative costs are crucial for determining international trade flows and gains from trade. Absolute cost advantages, however, are crucial for determining a country's per capita welfare level, and thereby explain differences in international wages. To be concrete, take the framework of section 3.4, more specifically the example in Table 3.1, as the point of departure. Assume that the EU specializes in the production of chemicals, that Kenya specializes in the production of food, that the exchange rate is 1, and take the wage rate in Kenya as the numéraire. In a perfectly competitive economy with constant returns to scale the price of a product is equal to the cost of production, see Box 2.1. Since food is produced in Kenya, the Kenyan wage is 1, and it takes 4 units of Kenyan labour to produce 1 unit of food, the price of food must be 4 ($= 4 \times 1$). Let w_{EU} be the EU wage. Since the EU produces chemicals and it requires 8 units of EU labour to produce 1 unit of chemicals, the price of chemicals must be $8 \times w_{EU}$.

Now note that the EU can, in principle, also produce food. If it were to do this, and in view of the fact that it requires 2 units of EU labour to produce 1 unit of food, the price would be $2 \times w_{EU}$. Since we have assumed that only Kenya produces food, this price must be higher than the actual food price ($= 4$, see above). We conclude therefore that $2 \times w_{EU} > 4$, or $w_{EU} > 2$. Similarly, Kenya can, in principle, also produce chemicals. If it did, the price would be 24 ($= 24 \times 1$), since it requires 24 units of Kenyan labour to produce 1 unit of chemicals and the Kenyan wage is 1. Since Kenya does not actually produce chemicals, this price must be higher than the price currently prevailing ($= 8 \times w_{EU}$, see above). We conclude therefore that $8 \times w_{EU} < 24$, or $w_{EU} < 3$. Combining this information we can conclude that the EU wage rate is at least twice as high as the Kenyan wage rate, and at most three times as high. (As with the terms of trade, to calculate the wage rate exactly requires information of the demand structure to determine the trading equilibrium.) Evidently, this difference in the international wage rates depends on the difference in absolute costs in the two countries, that is on the difference in productivity levels. The EU per capita welfare level, based on this wage difference, therefore also depends on the difference in absolute cost levels, and is primarily based on its own productivity.

---

which the production levels of the EU are much larger than in Kenya is therefore that the terms of trade will be the same after opening up to trade as the autarky equilibrium price in the EU, namely 4 units of food per unit of chemicals. This implies that the EU budget line does not change, such that point B is still the optimal consumption point in the EU and welfare in the EU does not change. Kenya, however, completely specializes in the production of food and can trade this at the most beneficial terms of trade with the EU (up to a maximum of $30/4 = 7.5$ units of chemicals). The entrepreneurs in the EU simply adjust their production decisions along the production possibility frontier to accommodate the Kenyan wishes (who choose some point on their new budget line) and clear world markets. Note in particular that *Kenyan welfare rises* as a result of trading with the EU, while EU welfare remains unchanged, even though *Kenya is less efficient* in the production of both goods. Possibility (iii), if the terms of trade is 6 EU welfare will rise and Kenyan welfare will not change, is similar to possibility (ii) discussed above.

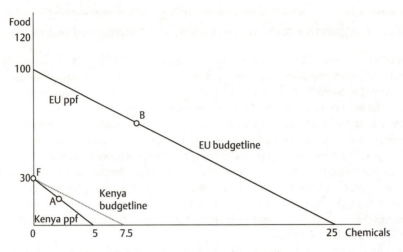

Fig. 3.4 The terms of trade is 4 units of food per unit of chemicals

3.6 Application: Kenya and the EU

Calculating the value added per worker in various sectors of the economy for the EU and Kenya in a similar fashion as used in section 2.4 for the USA and Japan we arrive at Table 3.3. Lack of data for some sectors implies that the number of observations has dropped to 16 sectors. For those 16 sectors, the EU has considerably higher productivity than Kenya. Based on the theory of absolute advantage, the EU should only be exporting to Kenya, and not import anything at all. However, as is evident from the table, the EU does import goods from Kenya, which could be based on trade in accordance with comparative advantage.

As can be calculated from Table 3.3 (see also the questions in the study guide) the EU indeed has a comparative advantage in the production of chemicals, as assumed in Table 3.1, which is the EU's second largest exporting sector. Similarly, Kenya has a comparative advantage in the production of food, which is by far its largest export sector. Net trade flows for these two products are in accordance with the theory of comparative advantage. As illustrated in Table 3.3 by the shaded sectors, the prediction of net trade flows is in accordance with comparative advantage for only five of the sixteen sectors. The theory of comparative advantage does better in terms of explanatory power than the theory of absolute advantage. Of the total trade flows (imports + exports) in Table 3.3, absolute advantage explains about 47.8 per cent of those flows, and comparative advantage explains about 68.4 per cent. If the differences in relative productivity[5] are

---

[5] Let VA_i^K be value added per worker in sector i in Kenya, similarly for the EU with superscript EU, and let a bar denote the country-wide average value added per worker, then the relative productivity ratio (Kenya/EU) used in Figure 3.5 is calculated as: $(VA_i^K/\overline{VA}^K)/(VA_i^{EU}/\overline{VA}^{EU})$.

Table 3.3 Kenya and EU; value added, imports and exports, various sectors

ISIC	Industry	Trade (1,000 US $)		Value added/person	
		Export to EU	Import from EU	Kenya	EU4
322/3	Wearing apparel and leather products	15,027	5,350	663	193,017
311/2	Food products	783,658	120,997	233	45,341
385	Professional and scientific equipment	1,361	42,577	5,306	33,092
321	Textiles	11,805	64,422	83	17,347
382/3	Machinery	8,977	310,198	981	116,668
313	Beverages	118	5,278	559	107,718
324	Footwear	273	2,363	262	19,477
355	Rubber products	378	8,368	717	46,370
356	Plastic products	30	29,027	229	30,673
341/2	Paper and printing products	34	29,301	343	47,402
361/2/9	Non-metallic mineral products	11,088	14,096	423	97,593
384	Transport equipment	4,067	94,096	124	55,413
381	Fabricated metal products	2,105	22,851	227	18,368
332	Furniture	268	3,336	49	15,344
351/2	Chemicals	11,024	173,129	452	154,537
331	Wood products	2,146	908	91	31,472

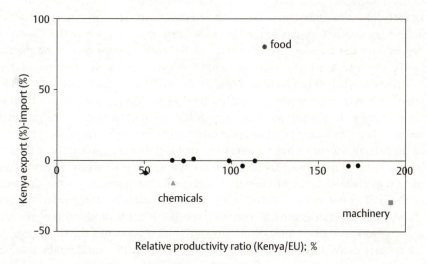

Fig. 3.5 Kenya–EU exports and productivity, various sectors

very large, the net trade flow is generally in accordance with comparative cost advantage. This is illustrated in Figure 3.5 by calculating exports and imports for different categories as a percentage of total exports and imports, using the difference as an indication of net trade flows. The most noteworthy exception is again (as in Chapter 2) the 'machinery' sector.

3.7 **More countries and world ppf**

The exposition in sections 3.4 and 3.5 uses two final goods and two countries. Both restrictions can be relaxed quite easily, as long as we continue to restrict ourselves to the analysis of only one production factor. Dornbusch, Fischer, and Samuelson (1977), for example, analyse a setting with many goods ranked from high to low in terms of comparative advantage, say for the EU. If we use the index i to identify a good and there are N goods, $i = 1, \ldots, N$, then the EU will have the highest comparative advantage for good 1, the second highest for good 2, etc. Dornbusch et al. show that there is a critical good, say n, such that the EU will produce the goods $1, \ldots, n$ and the other country produces the goods $n + 1, \ldots, N$.[6] Both countries therefore produce the range of goods for which its comparative advantage is highest.

Figure 3.6 illustrates the other case, in which there are two goods and more than two countries. This also allows us to discuss another concept, that of the world production possibility frontier. Suppose, to be concrete, that there are four countries, labelled A, B, C, and D, each able to produce two goods, food and chemicals. The top panel illustrates the production possibility frontiers of the four individual countries, where the slope of the ppf depends on the comparative advantage of the countries for producing food and chemicals. The bottom panel depicts the world production possibility frontier, that is all combinations of efficient production points for the world as a whole (but without factor mobility). The maximum world production level of food, F_{max} say, obtains if all four countries only produce food. Since country A has the flattest slope of its production possibility frontier, indicating that its opportunity costs for producing food are highest, it will be the first country to stop producing food, that is close to F_{max} the slope of the world ppf is equal to the slope of country A's ppf. Once point E_0 is reached country A will have completely specialized in the production of chemicals. Since country B has the second flattest slope of its ppf, country B will be the second country to start producing chemicals. This process continues until all countries specialize in the production of chemicals at C_{max}. The various dashed lines connecting F_{max} and C_{max} depict the world ppf.

Once we have derived the world ppf it is easy to determine the world production point in a free trading equilibrium. Suppose, for example, that the relative price of chemicals is equal to p_{c0}/p_{f0}. Then the maximum value of world production is obtained at point E_0,

---

[6] In some cases, the other country may also produce good n.

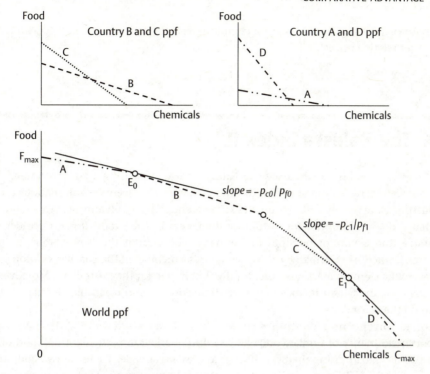

Fig. 3.6 Four countries and world ppf

Box 3.2 Comparative advantage and the organization of firms

It should be noted that the principles underlying an efficient production process in the international economy also hold at the firm level. A company employing 2,000 people should steer its workers to those labour activities they perform relatively most efficiently. The wage rate paid to an individual worker depends on absolute costs, see Box 3.1. The vivid example sometimes used here is that of a hospital employing a brain surgeon who also happens to be the world's fastest typist. This brain surgeon should nonetheless leave the typing work to her secretary, as she has a comparative advantage performing surgery (assuming that the typist cannot perform this activity). To assist her in making this choice, the wage she can earn as a brain surgeon is higher than the wage she can earn as a typist.

---

that is country A will produce chemicals and the other three countries will produce food. Country A will therefore export chemicals in exchange for food with the other three countries. Next, suppose that the relative price of chemicals is equal to p_{c1}/p_{f1}. Then the maximum value of world production is obtained at point E_1, that is country D will produce food and the other three countries will produce chemicals. Country D will therefore export food in exchange for chemicals with the other three countries. Similarly, for other relative prices.

3.8 **The Balassa index II**[7]

In Chapter 2 we briefly discussed the Balassa index, measuring a country's weak and strong sectors by using normalized export shares, for twenty-eight manufacturing industries using twenty OECD countries as a reference. The disadvantage of this approach is that it does not control for disturbing influences in the export flows. Consider, for example, the export of potatoes to Germany, either from the Netherlands or from Australia. Since, like Germany, the Netherlands is a member of the European Union (EU), access to the German market is easier for the Dutch than for the Australians. Moreover, as a neighbour the Dutch incur much lower transport costs to reach the German market than do the Australians.

To circumvent these difficulties Hinloopen and van Marrewijk (2001) analyse the export performance of similar countries to a third market; in particular the export of EU countries to Japan, using the EU countries also as a reference. There are two additional reasons for this selection: access to the relatively homogeneous Japanese market is, in principle, the same for all EU countries and the Japanese market is large enough to generate substantial export flows for a representative array of products.

The authors, who analyse the statistical properties of the distribution of the Balassa index, use monthly Eurostat data for twelve countries (EU-12) and ninety-eight industries at the two-digit level. We are, however, interested in the strong and weak sectors for the EU countries. In 1996, the most recent year analysed, the EU-12 exported Euro 32 bn to Japan and imported Euro 51.5 bn. This EU trade deficit is slowly decreasing. Table 3.4 shows the three sectors for each country with the highest Balassa index in 1994, the year in the middle of the sample period, as well as the export value for these sectors, and the share of the sector in the total exports of the country to Japan.

The sector with the highest comparative advantage in France, for example, is the aircraft industry. With almost 500 million Euro in export value it represents a sizeable share of French exports to Japan (almost 12 per cent). Clearly, this sector benefits from intermediate deliveries, mainly from Spain, Germany, and the UK, to the Airbus industry in Toulouse. A quick look at the top three industries in Table 3.4 shows that many sectors are fairly traditional, for example carpets and jewellery (diamonds) in Belgium, flowers in Holland, cars in Germany, silk and wool in Italy, (pork) meat in Denmark, and cork in Portugal.

In many cases the top ranking industries represent a substantial share of a country's exports to Japan; from high to low: Danish meat (46.78 per cent), German cars (37.48 per cent), Belgian jewellery (33.66 per cent), Greek tobacco (31.18 per cent), Irish chemicals

----

[7] This section is based on Hinloopen and van Marrewijk (2001).

Table 3.4 Top three export industries, measured by the Balassa index

	Export	Share	BI	Import	Share	Balance
France						
Aircraft	467,665	11.85	6.16	65,395	1.29	402,270
Chemical	171,089	4.33	3.74	27,456	0.54	143,633
Toys	139,625	3.54	3.73	99,970	1.97	39,655
Belgium						
Carpets	38,478	2.49	9.83	88	0.00	38,390
Jewellery	519,449	33.66	8.64	63,614	2.21	455,835
Zinc	2,072	0.13	6.37	173	0.01	1,899
The Netherlands						
Flowers	126,415	9.26	18.37	2,073	0.04	124,342
Sugars	21,654	1.59	8.69	128	0.00	21,526
Cocoa	20,096	1.47	6.98	89	0.00	20,007
Germany						
Industrial plants	213	0.00	2.85	—	—	—
Cereals	30,472	0.33	2.82	18	0.00	30,454
Cars	3,492,975	37.48	2.12	3,133,060	20.48	359,915
Italy						
Silk	59,019	1.73	6.63	2,775	0.08	56,244
Paper yarn	27,172	0.80	5.08	364	0.01	26,808
Wool	271,479	6.38	4.90	1,228	0.04	216,251
UK						
Nickel	49,087	1.28	5.41	8,229	0.07	40,858
Lead	318	0.01	4.86	29	0.00	289
Live animals	29,907	0.78	4.32	2,531	0.02	27,376
Ireland						
Org. chem.	256,485	28.69	4.21	10,780	1.20	245,705
Edible	8,442	0.94	3.39	24	0.00	8,418
Pharma.	160,574	17.96	3.18	9,055	1.01	151,519
Denmark						
Meat	626,190	46.78	17.98	—	—	—
Prepared meat	17,619	1.32	11.27	2,090	0.23	15,529
Fur	7,726	0.58	6.59	—	—	—
Greece						
Tobacco	24,699	31.18	142.70	—	—	—
Fruit	18,269	23.06	47.64	—	—	—
Other animals	836	1.06	16.11	29	0.00	807
Portugal						
Cork	17,201	15.53	187.10	118	0.02	17,083
Pulp	8,757	7.90	111.50	—	—	—
Ores	16,482	14.88	64.93	—	—	—

Table 3.4 (continued)

	Export	Share	BI	Import	Share	Balance
Spain						
Ores	27,116	3.65	18.46	—	—	—
Fish	89,157	12.01	11.76	3,145	0.15	86,012
Pulp	3,663	0.49	8.06	—	—	—

Source: Hinloopen and van Marrewijk (2001). Data are for 1994; values in thousand Euro; BI = Balassa Index; balance = export value − import value.

(28.69 per cent), and Portuguese cork (15.53 per cent). To illustrate that a top ranking industry in terms of the Balassa index, which after all is a relative measure, does not have to be an important sector for a nation, we can look at the exports of German complete industrial plants (0.00 per cent), English lead (0.01 per cent), or Belgian zinc (0.13 per cent).

When the Balassa index exceeds one, the sector is identified as a sector with comparative advantage and one would generally expect net exports to be positive. In this respect, however, we have to be cautious since the comparative advantage is calculated with regard to a set of reference countries which excludes Japan and, as mentioned above, the EU-12 countries have a trade deficit with Japan. Thus, to verify if net exports are indeed positive, Table 3.4 also gives the value of imports from Japan, the share in total imports, and the trade balance for each of the top three ranking industries. In all cases in Table 3.4 net exports are indeed positive.[8]

3.9 Conclusions

To determine a country's strong (export) sectors on the classical basis of technology differences, as well as its terms of trade, only comparative costs are important. International trade leads to welfare gains irrespective of absolute costs. Using empirical data on the EU and Kenya we concluded that the theory of comparative costs is somewhat better than the theory of absolute costs in determining international trade flows. Note, however, that the per capita welfare level largely depends on absolute cost differences, rather than comparative cost differences. This may explain the large international differences in the wage rate, namely as the result of productivity differences. The analysis can be generalized quite easily to incorporate more goods and more countries. The incorporation of more than one factor of production, however, is more complicated. This issue is addressed in Part II of this book.

---

[8] Table 3.4 shows a fair number of minuses, indicating that import data are not available. In most cases those trade flows are effectively zero.

Part Two

Neoclassical Trade

Part II (Neoclassical Trade) analyses comparative advantage in perfectly competitive economies with identical technologies as a result of differences in factor abundance. It also discusses the (distributional) welfare implications of trade policy, such as tariffs, quotas, and voluntary export restraints, for the classical and neoclassical models of Parts I and II.

Chapter 4
Production Structure

Objectives/key terms

Production functions	Isoquants
Cost minimization	Factor intensity
Constant returns to scale	Unit costs

The neoclassical driving forces behind international trade flows are differences in factor endowments between nations. The conclusions depend to a large extent on the production structure of the economy, based on identical technology, constant returns to scale, and perfect competition. This chapter briefly reviews the micro-economic foundations and main implications of this production structure.

4.1 Introduction

The classical theory of absolute and comparative cost advantages discussed in Chapters 2 and 3 focuses attention on technological differences between nations to explain international trade flows. At this point we may note at least three problems associated with the theory of comparative advantage.

First, the largest technological differences between nations presumably arise when these nations are very different in their state of economic development. Indeed, the technological differences discussed in Chapter 2 for the USA and Japan were much smaller than the differences between the EU and Kenya discussed in Chapter 3. Even if we acknowledge that only the relative differences are influential in determining comparative advantage, we would still expect substantial trade flows between nations with large differences in technology. However, as we saw in Chapter 1, there are only very small trade flows between developed and less developed nations.[1]

Second, the empirical discussion in Chapter 3 on the explanatory power of the theory of comparative advantage for the trade flows between the EU and Kenya was only

---

[1] Moreover, we will argue in this part of the book that a large proportion of the trade flows that do arise between developed and less developed nations result from a different underlying force for trade.

moderately supportive of this theory. Some of the difficulties were discussed at the end of Chapter 3. The feeling does arise, however, that other economic forces may be useful for explaining some of the trade flows not explained by the theory of comparative advantage.

Third, the focus on only one factor of production in the theory of comparative advantage seems too restrictive and precludes the analysis of many interesting issues. In getting some intuitive feel for the empirical validity of the theory of comparative advantage, we had to mould the data in a straitjacket. In particular, because we attributed *all* value added in a final goods sector to only one factor of production: labour. Clearly, some sectors, such as oil refineries, are much more capital intensive than other sectors, such as hairdressers. A larger part of the value added in the oil refinery is used to remunerate the capital investments involved than for the hairdresser. Similarly, some sectors, such as electronics firms, use more highly educated labourers than other sectors, such as domestic services. Differences in remuneration therefore may reflect differences in years of education and skills. This is in line with the finding in section 2.6 that there is no clear-cut relationship between revealed comparative advantage as measured by the Balassa index and labour productivity. To analyse these and other distributional economic aspects of production and trade flows requires the distinction of at least two different factors of production.

These observations bring us to the core of international trade theory: factor abundance theory, or the neoclassical theory of international trade, to be discussed in this chapter and the next four chapters.

4.2 **Neoclassical economics**

A proper understanding of the forces behind international trade and capital flows cannot be obtained without thoroughly studying the foundations of neoclassical economics. For many practical applications and problems an understanding of the small general equilibrium model known as the neoclassical model provides valuable economic intuition for the most important forces playing a role in production and consumption decisions. The foundations for the neoclassical model were laid by Eli Hecksher and his pupil Bertil Ohlin, two Swedish economists. Undoubtedly the most influential publication in this respect is Bertil Ohlin's (1933) *Interregional and International Trade*. After a brief discussion of some simplifications and the definition of a region, Ohlin (1933, ch. I) remarks:[2]

We have evidently pushed the analysis one step further, to an inquiry under what circumstances relative commodity prices will actually be different in two isolated regions. The starting point for such an investigation is the fact that all prices, of goods as well as of industrial agents, are ultimately, in each region, at any given moment, determined by the demand for goods and the possibilities of producing them. Behind the former lie two circumstances to be considered as known data in the

---

[2] See Allen (1965: 173).

Fig. 4.1 Paul Samuelson (1915–)

Born in Gary, Indiana, he has contributed from his MIT offices to virtually all parts of economic analysis. By applying and developing the neoclassical apparatus of optimization to the problems of consumers and producers, his influence on the mindset of today's economist cannot be overestimated. For International Economics in particular his importance is for the development of factor abundance theory.

problem of pricing: (1) the wants and desires of consumers, and (2) the conditions of ownership of the factors of production, which affect individual incomes and thus demand. The supply of goods, on the other hand, depends ultimately on (3) the supply of productive factors, and (4) the physical conditions of production.

Ohlin is thus well aware that the circumstances under which relative commodity prices in two isolated regions differ depend on an interplay between demand and supply conditions, each in turn depending on various other factors. Before we can derive any definite conclusions, therefore, we have to specify these demand and supply conditions. We will elaborate on various details in the next three chapters. In this chapter, we provide some of the production structure preliminaries of neoclassical economics. First, however, we give an overview of the most important results of the neoclassical model.

Each serious student of international economics must be familiar with the four main results of neoclassical trade theory, namely:

- The *factor price equalization* proposition (Samuelson 1948, 1949), see Chapter 5. This result argues that international free trade of final goods between two nations leads to an equalization of the rewards of the factors of production in the two nations.

- The *Stolper–Samuelson* proposition (Stolper and Samuelson 1941), see Chapter 5. This result argues that an increase in the price of a final good increases the reward to the factor of production used intensively in the production of that good.

- The *Rybczynski* proposition (Rybczynski 1955), see Chapter 6. This result argues that an increase in the supply in a factor of production results in an increase in the output of the final good that uses this factor of production relatively intensively.

- The *Heckscher–Ohlin* proposition (Ohlin 1933), see Chapter 7. This result argues that a country will export the good which intensively uses the relatively abundant factor of production.

The precise formulation of these results and the conditions under which they can be derived will be the topic of Part II of this book. It is important to keep the final conclusion (the Heckscher–Ohlin proposition) to be derived in Chapter 7 clearly in mind: the neoclassical driving forces behind international trade flows are based on differences in factor endowments between nations, that is a country will export those goods and services which intensively use its abundant factors of production. In a sense the other results, and the discussions in Chapters 4–6, only pave the way for the Heckscher–Ohlin proposition. Before we continue, we must point out that most technical details and the precise conditions under which the four main results of neoclassical trade theory can be derived were analysed and specified by Paul Samuelson. Instead of the term 'neoclassical trade theory' or 'factor abundance theory' the term 'HOS theory' (short for Heckscher–Ohlin–Samuelson) is also often used.

4.3 General structure of the neoclassical model

The general structure of the neoclassical model, to be used throughout Part II, can be summarized as follows.

- There are two countries, Austria (index A) and Bolivia (index B), two final goods, manufactures (index M) and food (index F), and two factors of production, capital (index K) and labour (index L). This is, therefore, a $2 \times 2 \times 2$ model. When appropriate, we will point out if the results to be derived below can be generalized to a setting with more goods, more countries, and more production factors.

- Production in both sectors is characterized by constant returns to scale. The two final goods sectors have different production functions.

- The state of technology is the same in the two countries, such that the production functions for each sector are identical in the two countries. Any trade flows arising in the model therefore do not result from Ricardian type differences in technology.

- The input factors capital and labour are mobile between the different sectors within a country, but are not mobile between countries.

- All markets are characterized by perfect competition. There are no transport costs for the trade of final goods between nations, nor any other impediments to trade.

- The demand structure in the two countries is the same (identical homothetic preferences). This assumption is only important for Chapter 7.

- Finally, the available amounts of factors of production, capital K and labour L, may differ between the two nations. These differences in factor abundance will give rise to international trade flows.

By imposing strong restrictions on the production structure (constant returns to scale) and the market structure (perfect competition) of the economy, the neoclassical model in general does not require strong restrictions on the functional form of the production functions to derive its four basic propositions. This is in contrast with the theories of absolute and comparative advantage discussed in previous chapters and with the new trade theories and geographical economic theories to be discussed in later chapters, all of which use simple specific functional forms to get the main points across as clearly as possible. As explained in the preface, for expository balance and clarity we will use only the simplest (Cobb–Douglas) production function to derive the main results of neoclassical economics. The remainder of this chapter will briefly review the main implications of the production structure of the neoclassical model.

4.4 **Production functions**

As indicated in section 4.3, there are two final goods, manufactures and food, with Cobb–Douglas production functions, different for the two sectors but identical in the two countries for each sector. We let M denote the production level of manufactures, K_m the amount of capital used in the manufacturing sector, and L_m the amount of labour used in the manufacturing sector. Similarly for food. Production is given by:

$$(4.1) \qquad M = \underbrace{K_m^{\alpha_m}}_{\substack{capital \\ input}} \underbrace{L_m^{1-\alpha_m}}_{\substack{labour \\ input}}; \; F = \underbrace{K_f^{\alpha_f}}_{\substack{capital \\ input}} \underbrace{L_f^{1-\alpha_f}}_{\substack{labour \\ input}}; \quad 0 < \alpha_m, \alpha_f < 1$$

For reasons to be explained further below the parameter α_m (α_f) is a measure of the capital intensity of the production process for manufactures (respectively food). Clearly, since we assumed these two parameters to be strictly in between 0 and 1, both capital and labour are indispensable inputs for both final goods sectors; at least some of both inputs is required to produce any output.

An important implication of the neoclassical production function specified in equation (4.1) is the ability to substitute one input for another, that is to produce the same level of output with different combinations of inputs. For example, if $\alpha_m = 0.5$ the entrepreneur is able to produce 1 unit of manufactures using 1 unit of capital and 1 unit of labour, or using 2 units of capital and 0.5 units of labour, or using 0.5 units of capital and 2 units of labour, etc. In principle, an infinite number of possible combinations is available to produce the same level of output. All possible efficient combinations of capital and labour able to produce a certain level of output is called an *isoquant*. This is illustrated for the isoquant $M = 1$ for three possible values of α_m in Figure 4.3.

Chapter 4 tool: Isoquant

If there are two or more inputs needed and/or available to produce a final good we call the set of all *efficient* input combinations an *isoquant*, see Figure 4.2.

The isoquant can be derived from the production function. Taking equation (4.1) as an example, the same level of output can be produced using many different combinations of capital and labour. Figure 4.2 illustrates this for the isoquant $M = 1$, where the shaded area shows all input combinations producing at least 1 unit of manufactures. The input combination at point A, therefore, enables the entrepreneur to produce 1 unit of manufactures. However, to produce 1 unit of manufactures the entrepreneur could use either less labour at point B than at point A, or less capital at point C than at point A, such that point A is not an efficient input combination to produce 1 unit of manufactures. As such, point A is not part of the $M=1$ isoquant. In contrast to points B and C, which both are part of the $M=1$ isoquant.

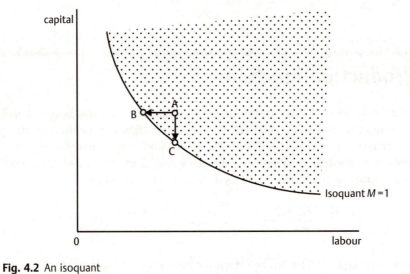

Fig. 4.2 An isoquant

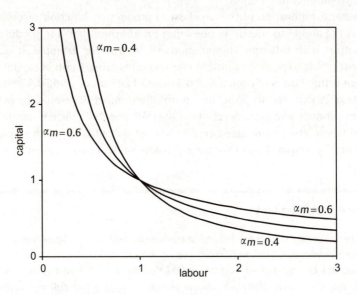

Fig. 4.3 Isoquant $M=1$ and the capital intensity parameter α_m

Note that, if very little of an input is used, it becomes harder to substitute this input for another input. This is illustrated in Table 4.1 for 10 combinations of capital and labour producing 1 unit of manufactures if $\alpha_m = 0.5$. Starting with 1 unit of capital and labour, the input of labour is gradually reduced by steps of 0.1 unit. To continue producing 1 unit of manufactures this implies that the required extra input of capital increases rapidly, from 0.171 to 20.442. The extent to which additional capital is needed to substitute for labour depends, of course, on the value of the parameter α_m. This is also illustrated in Figure 4.3, which shows that for higher levels of the capital intensity parameter α_m the isoquant is tilted towards the capital axis.

Table 4.1 Substitution possibilities ($\alpha_m = 0.5$)

L_m	K_m	Extra capital
1.0	1.000	—
0.9	1.171	0.171
0.8	1.398	0.226
0.7	1.707	0.310
0.6	2.152	0.444
0.5	2.828	0.677
0.4	3.953	1.124
0.3	6.086	2.133
0.2	11.180	5.095
0.1	31.623	20.442

Box 4.1 **Capital per worker**

The neoclassical model discussed in this part of the book argues that countries will export the final goods making intensive use of the relatively abundant factor of production. Since we distinguish between two main types of factors of production, capital and labour, the empirical question arises to what extent countries differ in their capital and labour endowments. This question is not so easy to answer because it requires us to aggregate many different varieties of capital and labour into one aggregate measure, see also Box 4.3 for a different approach. The construction of a consistent data set that can be compared for a large number of countries is therefore complicated and involves a lot of work. The most widely used data set was initiated by Lawrence Summers and Alan Heston, see their 1991 paper for a description and the National Bureau of Economic Research (NBER) website (http://www.nber.org) for updates.

As Table 4.2 shows, with a total value of $4,271 bn (1990, in 1985 constant $), the USA is estimated to have the largest capital stock. Japan has the second largest capital stock and West Germany the third largest. Since the West German workforce of 31 million people is considerably smaller than the American workforce of 123 million, the capital stock per worker is higher in West Germany ($50,116) than in the USA (34,705), despite the higher total American capital stock. The distribution of the capital stock per worker is illustrated in Figure 4.4 for the sixty countries for which data are available. Swiss workers had the highest capital stock per worker available ($73,459). Workers from Sierra Leone had the lowest capital stock per worker ($223).

Table 4.2 Total captial stock ranking

	Capital stock ($bn)	Workers (m)	Capital stock per worker ($)
1 USA	4,271	123	34,705
2 Japan	2,852	78	36,480
3 W. Germany	1,539	31	50,116
4 France	925	26	35,600
5 Italy	740	23	31,640
6 India	645	331	1,946
7 UK	601	28	21,179
8 Canada	566	13	42,745
9 Spain	386	14	27,300
10 Mexico	361	28	12,900
11 South Korea	321	18	17,995
12 Australia	298	8	37,854
13 Iran	258	17	15,548
14 Switzerland	248	3	73,459
15 Poland	232	20	11,890
16 Taiwan	229	9	25,722
17 The Netherlands	202	6	32,380
18 Turkey	185	24	7,589
19 Sweden	175	4	39,409
20 Belgium	152	4	36,646

Source: NBER website, data for 1990 in constant 1985 $.

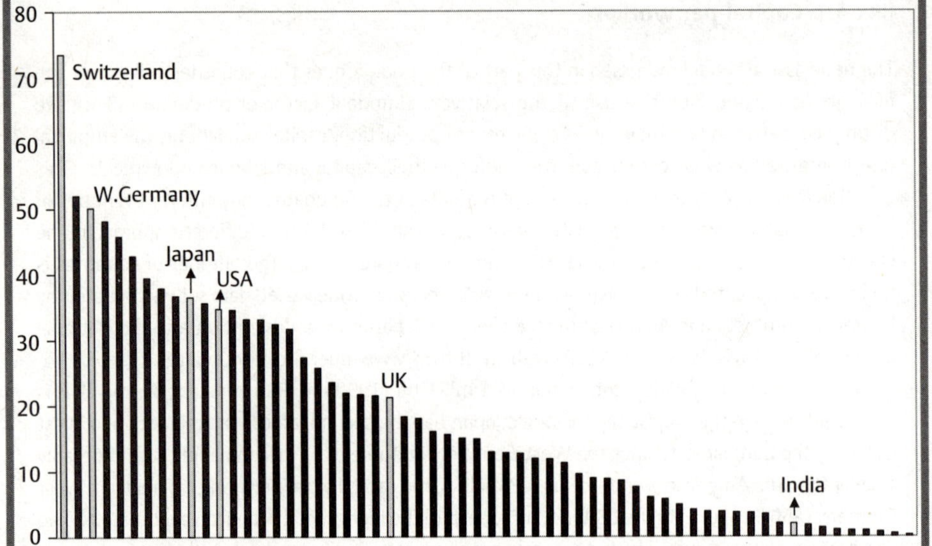

Fig. 4.4 Capital stock per worker × 1000 $

4.5 **Cost minimization**

The objective function for the entrepreneurs inhabiting our economic models is quite simply profit maximization. Although some objections can be raised against this objective function, one of the strongest arguments in its favour is the fact that entrepreneurs not striving towards profit maximization will be driven out of business by those who do. This certainly holds in perfectly competitive economies characterized by constant returns to scale, as analysed here, where the best a firm can do is ensuring that it does not make a loss (a nicer term is 'excess profits are zero'). The entrepreneur can actually break its production decision down into two steps. First, for any arbitrary level of production determine how this output level is achieved at minimum cost. Second, taking the outcome of the first step into consideration, determine the optimum output level. This second step is actually already discussed in Box 2.1. It is therefore time to analyse in somewhat more detail the first step, that of cost minimization. In this section we restrict attention to analysing the problem of producing 1 unit of output at minimum cost. Section 4.7 below will discuss this problem for arbitrary levels of output.

The problem facing an entrepreneur in the manufactures sector trying to minimize the costs for producing 1 unit of output is illustrated in Figure 4.5. Recall that the production function is given in equation (4.1), which implies that the entrepreneur can choose between two different inputs: capital K_m and labour L_m. As discussed in section 4.4 many different combinations of capital and labour are available to produce 1 unit of

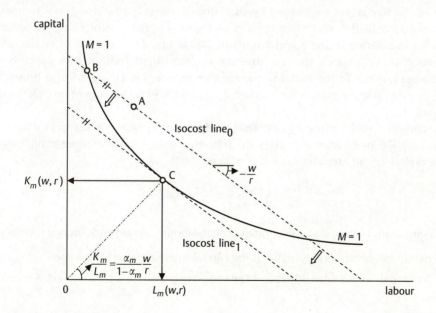

Fig. 4.5 Unit cost minimization

manufactures. This is illustrated by the isoquant $M = 1$ in Figure 4.5. There are three points, A, B, and C, explicitly stated in Figure 4.5. All three points can produce 1 unit of output. Point A, however, is not part of the isoquant $M = 1$, since the same level of output can be produced using either less labour or less capital (or a little less of both inputs) than the amount used at point A, which is therefore not an efficient input combination to produce 1 unit of output.[3]

Since the entrepreneur can choose between two different inputs, we first have to determine the level of costs associated with a certain input combination, before we can determine how to minimize the level of these costs. In this respect the assumption of perfect competition, which also applies to the input markets, is most convenient. The entrepreneur simply takes the price level of labour, the wage rate w determined on the labour market, and the price level of capital, the rental rate r determined on the capital market, as given. If the firm therefore hires L_m labour and K_m capital, total costs associated with this input combination are

$$\text{(4.2)} \qquad \text{costs} = \underbrace{wL_m}_{\substack{\text{labour} \\ \text{cost}}} + \underbrace{rK_m}_{\substack{\text{capital} \\ \text{cost}}}$$

Obviously, different input combinations of capital and labour can give rise to the same cost level. From equation (4.2) it is clear that such isocost combinations are straight lines in labour–capital space, with a slope equal to $-w/r$. This is illustrated for two isocost lines in Figure 4.5, with points A and B part of the same isocost line. Graphically, the cost minimization problem facing the entrepreneur is quite simple: move the dashed isocost line down to the south-west (in the direction of the arrows) as far as possible, with the restriction that at least one of the input combinations on the isocost line is able to produce 1 unit of manufactures (part of the $M = 1$ isoquant). The solution to this procedure applied to Figure 4.5 gives point C as the optimal input combination, using $K_m(w, r)$ units of capital and $L_m(w, r)$ units of labour. This notation makes explicit the fact that the optimal input combination depends on the wage rate w and the rental rate r, see also section 4.6. Figure 4.5 also illustrates the optimal relative input combination K_m/L_m. This plays an important role in the sequel.

Technical Note 4.1 explicitly calculates the solutions $K_m(w, r)$ and $L_m(w, r)$ for the cost minimization problem, which gives the following optimal *relative* input combination (the capital–labour ratio) for manufactures and food:

$$\text{(4.3)} \qquad \frac{K_m}{L_m} = \frac{\alpha_m}{1 - \alpha_m} \frac{w}{r}; \quad \frac{K_f}{L_f} = \frac{\alpha_f}{1 - \alpha_f} \frac{w}{r}$$

It is important to note that the optimal capital–labour ratio depends on two factors.

- The capital–labour ratio is higher if the capital intensity parameter α rises.
- The capital–labour ratio is higher if the wage–rental ratio w/r rises (section 4.6).

---

[3] It is part of another isoquant, producing a higher output level of manufactures (not illustrated).

Box 4.2 **Capital intensity parameter and the cost share of capital**

A simple and useful mnemonic for the capital intensity parameter α in the production function of equation (4.1) is the fact that it represents the share of total costs paid for the use of capital in the production process. This can be readily seen from equation (4.3) which can be rewritten as

$$\frac{(1 - \alpha_m)}{\alpha_m} rK_m = wL_m$$

Using this in the definition of total costs gives

$$rK_m + wL_m = rK_m + \left(\frac{1 - \alpha_m}{\alpha_m} rK_m\right) = \frac{rK_m}{\alpha_m} \Rightarrow \underbrace{\frac{\overbrace{rK_m}^{cost\ of\ capital}}{rK_m + wL_m}}_{total\ cost} = \alpha_m$$

Similarly, the total wage bill represents a share $1 - \alpha_m$ of total costs. We will return to this when discussing the demand side of the neoclassical model in Chapter 7.

For ease of exposition, and without loss of generality, we henceforth impose the following:

Assumption: the production of manufactures is relatively more capital intensive than the production of food for all w/r ratios, that is $\alpha_m > \alpha_f$.

4.6 Impact of wage rate and rental rate

As argued above, and derived in Technical Note 4.1, the optimal input of labour and capital depends on the wage–rental ratio. Three issues are important. First, the cost minimizing input combination depends only on the wage–rental *ratio*, not on their absolute levels. This is intuitively obvious, as an equiproportional change in the wage rate and the rental rate does not change the *slope* of the isocost lines in Figure 4.5, and therefore does not affect the cost minimizing input combination. An equiproportional change in input prices does, however, change the cost level, as derived in Technical Note 4.2. Second, an increase in the price of an input reduces the demand for that input, that is an increase in the wage rate reduces the demand for labour, while an increase in the rental rate reduces the demand for capital. This is illustrated for $\alpha_m = 0.5$ in Figure 4.6: as the wage rate rises the demand for labour falls. Third, and linked to the previous two observations, if the price of an input factor rises there is a substitution away from the more expensive input towards the other input. Thus, if the wage rate rises the demand for

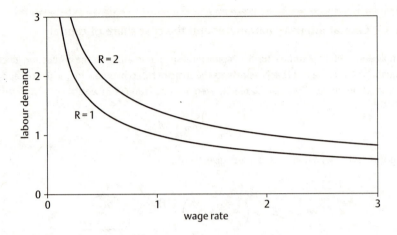

Fig. 4.6 Demand for labour as a function of the wage rate, $\alpha_m = 0.5$

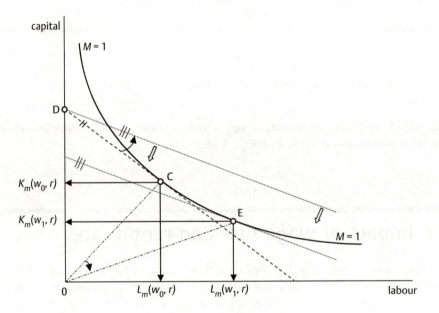

Fig. 4.7 Impact of lower wage on cost minimizing inputs

capital rises, and if the rental rate rises the demand for labour rises. This too is illustrated in Figure 4.6, where there is an increase in the demand for labour for any given level of the wage rate if the rental rate increases from $r = 1$ to $r = 2$.

These observations are explained in Figure 4.7, analysing the impact of a lower wage rate on the cost minimizing input combination. Initially, the wage rate and rental rate are identical to those analysed in Figure 4.5, thus leading to the cost minimizing input combination at point C. Suppose, then, that the wage rate falls from w_0 to w_1. As a result, the isocost line rotates counter-clockwise around point D. Consequently, production costs are no longer minimized at point C but, repeating the procedure described in section 4.5, at point E, using $K_m(w_1, r) < K_m(w_0, r)$ units of capital and $L_m(w_1, r) > L_m(w_0, r)$ units of labour. Thus, there has been a substitution away from the now relatively more expensive capital towards the cheaper labour. This substitution effect is summarized in the lower capital–labour ratio at point E compared to point C. The actual cost level achieved for all possible combinations of wage rates and rental rates is derived in Technical Note 4.2.

4.7 **Constant returns to scale**

As mentioned in section 4.3 the production processes are characterized by constant returns to scale (CRS), that is if we increase the use of both factors of production by the same multiplicative factor κ, the output produced also increases by that factor κ:

$$(4.4) \qquad \underbrace{(\kappa \cdot K_m)^{\alpha_m}}_{\substack{increase \\ capital}} \underbrace{(\kappa \cdot L_m)^{1-\alpha_m}}_{\substack{increase \\ labour}} = \kappa^{\alpha_m + 1 - \alpha_m} K_m^{\alpha_m} L_m^{1-\alpha_m} = \underbrace{\kappa \cdot}_{\substack{increase \\ production}} (K_m^{\alpha_m} L_m^{1-\alpha_m})$$

Clearly, this results from the fact that we imposed the powers of the two inputs capital and labour to sum to unity in the production function $(\alpha_m + (1 - \alpha_m) = 1)$.[4] The two main reasons for imposing constant returns to scale are ease of exposition (see Box 2.1 on the combination of perfect competition and constant returns to scale) and a replication argument; if the current mix of inputs produces 4 units of output, one should be able to double the output to 8 units simply by replicating the current production process (thus doubling the use of all inputs). Imposing constant returns to scale in the production process gives us two important simplifications, namely (i) for the structure of the isoquants and (ii) for the cost minimization process.

Structure of the isoquants

For any constant returns to scale production process it suffices to derive only one isoquant. Quite literally, one can say 'if you have seen one isoquant you have seen them all'. This is illustrated in Figure 4.8 for $\alpha_m = 0.5$ and three isoquants. First, take an arbitrary point, such as point A, on the isoquant $M = 1$. By the constant returns to scale property of the production process we know that if we double the use of both inputs we double the output of the production process. Graphically, if we draw a straight line from the origin through point A, we can double the use of both inputs by measuring the distance from the origin to point A and adding this distance from point A along the line earlier drawn

---

[4] If their sum exceeds unity there are increasing returns to scale, see Part III of the book. If their sum falls short of unity there are decreasing returns to scale.

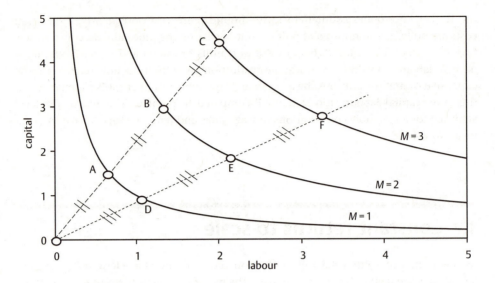

Fig. 4.8 Constant returns to scale and isoquants, $\alpha_m = 0.5$

through the origin and point A. We thus arrive at point B. Since doubling the use of inputs doubles the output produced, point B must be part of the $M = 2$ isoquant. Similarly, by tripling the use of inputs from point A we arrive at point C, which must be part of the $M = 3$ isoquant. We can repeat this procedure for another point on the $M = 1$ isoquant, such as point D. Doubling the inputs leads to point E, which must be part of the $M = 2$ isoquant, and tripling the inputs leads to point F, which must be part of the $M = 3$ isoquant. Repeating this procedure for all other points on the $M = 1$ isoquant shows that all isoquants are radial blow-ups of the $M = 1$ isoquant. Thus, once we have drawn one isoquant, we have in principle drawn them all after rescaling the inputs.

Cost minimization

Imposing constant returns to scale in the production process considerably simplifies the cost minimization problem. In section 4.5 and Technical Note 4.1 we solved the cost minimization problem for producing 1 unit of manufactures. Due to constant returns to scale, this suffices to determine the cost minimization problem for all levels of output. As argued above, all isoquants are radial blow-ups of one another. This implies in particular that the slope of an isoquant is the same for any ray through the origin. This is illustrated in Figure 4.9 and shown in Technical Note 4.3. Clearly, point A in Figure 4.9 minimizes the cost of producing 1 unit of manufactures for the wage–rental ratio drawn in the figure (equal to 1 in the example). Since a doubling of inputs (from point A to point B) doubles the output to 2 units of manufactures and the slope of the isoquant at point B is equal to the slope of the isoquant at point A, point B minimizes the cost of producing 2 units of manufactures. Similarly, point C minimizes the cost of producing 3 units of manufactures, etc. At the wage–rental ratio drawn in Figure 4.9, the cost minimizing input combination is a radial blow-up from the origin through point A. An increase or

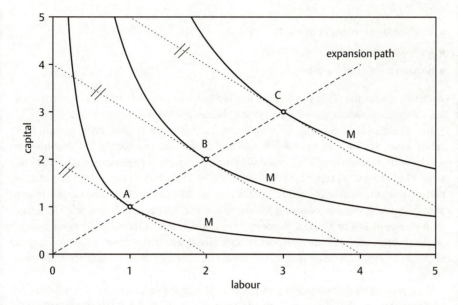

Fig. 4.9 Constant returns to scale and cost minimization, $\alpha_m = 0.5$, $w = r = 1$

Box 4.3 **Primary products exporters**

Sections 4.4–4.7 have discussed the main properties of the neoclassical production functions by distinguishing between just two factor inputs and two final goods. In reality one can, of course, identify several thousand different factors of production and final goods. For example, many types of capital goods, such as printing presses, desks, and computers, or many types of labour, such as unskilled labour, engineers, and accountants. Empirical research usually tries to find some middle ground in between the 2 factors of production and 2 final goods used in the exposition of the book and the thousands one can identify in reality by distinguishing a limited number of each, say in between 5 and 10 factors of production and in between 5 and 800 final goods.

The website of the International Trade Centre (ITC, see http://www.intracen.org), the joint UNCTAD/WTO organization, provides a good example of the empirical approach. To classify international trade flows, it distinguishes five factors of production and 257 final goods, based on the three-digit level of SITC classification Rev. 3. As we have argued in section 4.2 and will clarify in the next chapters, the intensity with which different final goods use the production factors has important ramifications for international trade flows. The ITC therefore aggregates the 257 final goods into five broader categories based on the intensity of the five factors in the production process:

- primary products
- natural-resource intensive products

- unskilled-labour intensive products
- technology intensive products, and
- human-capital intensive products.

We briefly discuss the world's main exporters in relative and absolute terms for each of these five categories in special interest boxes in this chapter and the next four chapters.

The ITC classifies 91 goods as 'primary' products, incorporating meat, dairy, cereals, fruit, coffee, sand, minerals, oil, natural gas, iron ore, copper ore, etc. For the 151 countries for which the ITC provides data, total exports of primary products in 1998 were equal to $816 bn, some 17 per cent of all exports. The left-hand side of Table 4.3 lists the top ten exporters of primary products in absolute terms. With a value of $80 bn the USA is the world's largest primary products exporter, shipping for example wheat, maize, soya beans, and cigarettes. With a value of $49 bn Canada, shipping for example wheat, is the second largest primary products exporter, while France, shipping grapes, wheat, and bovine meat, is the third largest. With the exception of Saudi Arabia, the other large primary products exporters are all in Europe.

Since primary products represent 13 per cent of American exports, the USA is below the world average in relative terms. The right-hand side of Table 4.3 lists the top ten world exporters of primary products in relative terms, all of which are located in the Middle East and Africa. Note that the export of primary products is virtually the only source of foreign exchange for all these countries, as even Uganda, ranked tenth, depends for 97 per cent of its exports on primary products. Also note the very small absolute size of the trade flows for these countries. The top three are Burundi (mostly coffee), Iraq (oil), and Yemen (oil).

Table 4.3 Top ten primary products exporters, 1998

No.	Top 10 in absolute terms			Top 10 in relative terms		
	Country	Exports		Country	Exports	
		Value	%		%	Value
1	United States	80	13	Burundi	100	0.0
2	Canada	49	25	Iraq	100	0.0
3	France	46	16	Yemen	99	0.0
4	The Netherlands	40	25	Mauritania	99	0.0
5	Germany	36	7	Chad	98	0.0
6	Australia	30	60	Guinea-Bissau	98	0.0
7	Saudi Arabia	29	86	Equatorial Guinea	97	2.1
8	United Kingdom	29	11	Gabon	97	1.9
9	Russian Federation	24	49	Nigeria	97	1.7
10	Belgium	23	14	Uganda	97	1.4

Source: WTO/UNCTAD International Trade Centre website http://www.intracen.org; value in bn US $. The % shares are relative to the country's total exports.

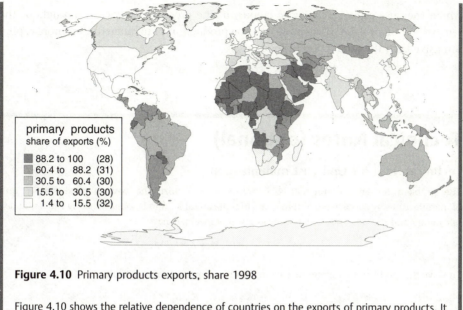

Figure 4.10 Primary products exports, share 1998

Figure 4.10 shows the relative dependence of countries on the exports of primary products. It indicates clearly that Africa, the Middle East, and South America are the world's top primary products exporters in relative terms.

decrease of the scale of production therefore takes place along the expansion path drawn in the figure. Thus, once we have solved the cost minimization problem for producing 1 unit of manufactures, we have automatically solved this problem for all other output levels.

4.8 **Conclusions**

This chapter briefly reviews the microeconomic foundations and main implications of the neoclassical production structure. There are two factors of production, capital and labour, which can be partially substituted for one another in the production process. As a result of constant returns to scale, the isoquants (depicting efficient combinations of capital and labour for producing a given output level) are radial blow-ups of one another. As a result, the final goods producer equiproportionally adjusts the cost-minimizing inputs of capital and labour to change the output level for a given wage rate and rental rate. The cost-minimizing capital–labour input mix depends on (i) the wage–rental ratio, and (ii) a parameter measuring the capital intensity of the production process. The latter parameter can therefore be used to classify the final goods based on the intensity with which they use capital (relative to labour) in the production process; throughout the remainder of Part II we will assume that the production of manufactures is more capital intensive than the production of food.

Technical Notes (optional)

Technical Note 4.1 Unit cost minimization

The problem for an entrepreneur who wants to minimize the cost of producing 1 unit of manufactures by choosing the input quantities of capital K_m and labour L_m, taking the rental rate of capital r and the wage rate of labour w as given is specified as:

(4.A1) $$\min_{K_m, L_m} wL_m + rK_m \quad s.t. \quad M = K_m^{\alpha_m} L_m^{1-\alpha_m} \geq 1$$

To solve this problem we define the Lagrangean Γ, using the Lagrange multiplier λ:

(4.A2) $$\Gamma = wL_m + rK_m + \lambda(1 - K_m^{\alpha_m} L_m^{1-\alpha_m})$$

Derive the two first order conditions $\partial\Gamma/\partial K_m = \partial\Gamma/\partial L_m = 0$ for an optimum and note

(4.A3) $$w = (1 - \alpha_m)\lambda K_m^{\alpha_m} L_m^{-\alpha_m} \quad \text{and} \quad r = \alpha_m \lambda K_m^{-(1-\alpha_m)} L_m^{1-\alpha_m}$$

Taking the ratio of these two conditions and simplifying determines the optimal capital–labour ratio K_m/L_m for the production of manufactures, which depends in a simple way on the wage–rental ratio w/r and the capital-intensity parameter α_m

(4.A3) $$\frac{K_m}{L_m} = \frac{\alpha_m}{1 - \alpha_m}\frac{w}{r}$$

This relationship between the optimal use of capital and labour can be substituted in the production function to derive the actual amount of capital and number of labourers you need to produce 1 unit of manufactures at minimum cost.

(4.A4) $$M = K_m^{\alpha_m} L_m^{1-\alpha_m} = \left(\frac{\alpha_m}{1 - \alpha_m}\frac{w}{r}L_m\right)^{\alpha_m} L_m^{1-\alpha_m} = 1$$

Simplifying this, denoting the optimal choice of labourers $L_m(w, r)$ since it depends on the wage rate w and the rental rate r, and repeating the procedure for the optimal choice of capital $K_m(w, r)$ gives:

(4.A5) $$L_m(w, r) = \left(\frac{\alpha_m}{1 - \alpha_m}\frac{w}{r}\right)^{-\alpha_m} \quad \text{and} \quad K_m(w, r) = \left(\frac{\alpha_m}{1 - \alpha_m}\frac{w}{r}\right)^{1-\alpha_m}$$

The interpretation of these results is discussed in the main text. Replacing the index m with the index f in the above two equations will give the demand for labour and capital in the Food sector.

Technical Note 4.2 Duality

In Technical Note 4.1 we derived the optimal factor input mix of capital and labour to minimize the costs of producing 1 unit of manufactures, see equation (4.A5). For the entrepreneur it is, of course, important to know how high these minimum costs for producing 1 unit of manufactures really are.

We will denote these[5] by $c_m(w,r)$, as they depend on the wage rate w and the rental rate r. They can be derived by substituting the *optimal* (i.e. cost minimizing) factor inputs into the costs $wL_m + rK_m$:

$$(4.A6) \qquad c_m(w,r) = wL_m(w,r) + rK_m(w,r) = w\left(\frac{\alpha_m}{1-\alpha_m}\frac{w}{r}\right)^{-\alpha_m} + r\left(\frac{\alpha_m}{1-\alpha_m}\frac{w}{r}\right)^{1-\alpha_m}$$

After some algebraic manipulations the unit cost function can be simplified to

$$(4.A7) \qquad c_m(w,r) = \gamma_m r^{\alpha_m} w^{1-\alpha_m}, \quad \text{where } \gamma_m \equiv \alpha_m^{-\alpha_m}(1-\alpha_m)^{-(1-\alpha_m)}$$

(The symbol '$\equiv$' means 'is defined to be equal to'). Replacing the index m by the index f gives the unit cost function of food. Note that the structure of the unit cost function is similar to the structure of the production function. Both are Cobb–Douglas functions, with α as the power for capital in the production function and as the *price* of capital in the unit cost function, and $1-\alpha$ as the power of labour in the production function and as the *price* of labour in the unit cost function. This is no coincidence, but a phenomenon known as duality. Before we discuss this, note that

$$(4.A8) \qquad \begin{aligned} \frac{\partial c_m(w,r)}{\partial w} &= \left(\frac{\alpha_m}{1-\alpha_m}\frac{w}{r}\right)^{-\alpha_m} = L_m(w,r) \quad \text{and} \\ \frac{\partial c_m(w,r)}{\partial r} &= \left(\frac{\alpha_m}{1-\alpha_m}\frac{w}{r}\right)^{1-\alpha_m} = K_m(w,r) \end{aligned}$$

That is, if we differentiate the unit cost function with respect to the price of labour the outcome is identical to the unit cost minimizing number of labourers and if we differentiate the unit cost function with respect to the price of capital the outcome is identical to the unit cost minimizing amount of capital. This result is known as *Shephard's lemma*. We can thus arrive at the cost minimizing input combinations in two different ways. First, we can specify a production function and explicitly derive the cost minimizing input combination as we did in Technical Note 4.1. Second, we can use the dual approach, that is specify a unit cost function as in (4.A7) above and simply differentiate with respect to the wage rate and the rental rate to derive the optimal combination of labour and capital. Taking some technical restrictions into consideration these two approaches, specifying either a production function or a cost function, are *equivalent*. Depending on the problem to be analysed one approach may be more convenient than another. In this book we will not use the dual approach, see however Dixit and Norman (1980), and Brakman and van Marrewijk (1998) for various applications of the dual approach to international economics.

Technical Note 4.3 Slope of isoquants

By definition, an isoquant depicts all possible efficient input combinations to produce a certain level of output, say $M = \bar{M}$. Totally differentiating the production function (4.1) for this level of output gives

$$(4.A9) \qquad \alpha_m K_m^{\alpha_m-1} L_m^{1-\alpha_m} dK_m + (1+\alpha_m)K_m^{\alpha_m} L_m^{-\alpha_m} dL_m = d\bar{M} = 0$$

from which the slope on any point of the isoquant can be derived easily

$$(4.A10) \qquad \frac{dK_m}{dL_m} = \frac{1-\alpha_m}{\alpha_m}\frac{K_m}{L_m}$$

Clearly, the slope of an isoquant depends only on the capital–labour *ratio*. Thus, if we change both inputs equiproportionally by the factor κ, where $\kappa = 2$ at point B relative to point A and $\kappa = 3$ at point C relative to point A in Figure 4.9, the slope of the isoquant remains the same. The implications are discussed in the main text.

---

[5] The reader may note that these unit costs $c_m(w, r)$ are labelled unit costs c in Box 2.1.

Chapter 5
Factor Prices

Objectives/key terms

Factor price equalization   Stolper–Samuelson
Unit value isoquant/isocost line   Lerner diagram
Magnification effect   Globalization debate

We discuss the connections between the prices of final goods and the rewards to factors of production, in particular how trade between countries can lead to factor price equalization. We apply these results to discuss and evaluate the 'globalization' debate of the 1990s.

5.1 Introduction

The first two main results of neoclassical economics, namely (i) factor price equalization and (ii) Stolper–Samuelson, are related to an economy's factor prices. The results will be more precisely stated below, and discussed and derived in more detail in this chapter. We start the discussion with result (i), as result (ii) derives almost immediately from it. The term 'factor price equalization' refers to the idea that trade in final goods between two nations leads to an equalization of the rewards for the factors used to produce these goods. As Bertil Ohlin (1933, ch. II) put it:[1]

The most immediate effect of trade between a number of regions under the conditions which have been assumed to exist is that commodity prices are made to tally. ... Trade has, however, a far-reaching influence also on the prices and the combination and use of the productive factors, in brief, on the whole price system. ... In both regions ... the factor which is relatively abundant becomes more in demand and fetches a higher price, whereas the factor that is scantily supplied becomes less in demand and gets a relatively lower reward than before.

Carefully reading the above quote makes clear that Ohlin did not actually think that the rewards for the factors of production will be equalized between the two regions, just that there is a *tendency* for the rewards of the factors of production to become more equal

---

[1] See Allen (1965: 185–6).

Fig. 5.1 Harry Johnson (1923–1977)

Born in Toronto, Canada, Harry Johnson worked at the University of Cambridge (UK), the University of Chicago (USA), and the Graduate Institute of International Studies (Switzerland). He travelled all over the globe to lecture and give presentations. While travelling, and drinking large quantities of alcohol, he produced an enormous quantity of high-quality economic papers, books, pamphlets and journal articles, in particular in international economics and monetary economics. His work in international economics, using geometric rather than algebraic illustrations and proofs, focuses on policy relevant issues, welfare economics, tariffs in the face of retaliation, and the theory of second-best.

between the regions (to understand this the reader must realize that the factor of production relatively abundant in one country is relatively scarce in the other country). The term factor price equalization derives from Paul Samuelson's (1948, 1949) work on the formalization of Ohlin's ideas on the tendency of factor prices between nations to converge as a result of international trade in final goods, which shows that these factor prices will in fact become equal. It is this version of the idea, discussed also below, which became one of the cornerstones of the neoclassical economics framework. To be fair to Ohlin, however, in a more general setting, allowing for more final goods, more factors of production, and other complications, factor prices will not become equal as a result of trade in final goods, but there is a *tendency* for factor rewards to move closer together, just as Ohlin argued. This prompted Paul Samuelson (1971) to write an essay with the title 'Ohlin was right'.

5.2 **Factor price equalization**

Using the neoclassical production structure with two countries, two final goods, and two factors of production explained in more detail in Chapter 4, Samuelson's (1948, 1949) result can most usefully be stated as follows.

Factor price equalization proposition (FPE)

In a neoclassical framework with two final goods and two factors of production, there is a one-to-one correspondence between the prices of the final goods and the prices of the factors of production, provided both goods are produced. This implies

(i) *if the factor rewards (w, r) are known the prices of the final goods (p_m, p_f) can be derived, and*

(ii) *if the prices of the final goods (p_m, p_f) are known the factor rewards (w, r) can be derived.*

Reading the statement of the proposition above, the reader may justifiably wonder why it is called the factor price equalization proposition, since there is no mention of any equalization, nor even of countries involved in such an equalization process. The reason is that a simple application of the above proposition leads to the following:

Corollary

In a neoclassical framework with two countries, two final goods, and two factors of production, international trade of the final goods, which equalizes the prices of these goods in the two nations, also leads to an equalization of the rewards of the factors of production in the two nations, provided both final goods are produced in both nations and the state of technology in the two nations is the same.

The statement of the corollary makes two provisions, namely (i) both final goods must be produced in both nations, and (ii) the state of technology in the two nations must be the same. Provision (i) is also used in the FPE proposition. Clearly, if we want to apply that proposition, we also have to use the provision in the application. Why both goods must be produced in both countries will become clear in the discussion of the proposition in the sections below. Provision (ii), on the equality of the state of technology, is new because we now have the production functions in two countries to take into consideration. The reasoning in the corollary is quite simple. If international trade between Austria and Bolivia leads the prices of the final goods to be the same (recall that there are no transport costs or other impediments to trade), that is $p_{mA} = p_{mB}$ and $p_{fA} = p_{fB}$, then applying the FPE proposition leads us to conclude that the factor rewards, the wage rate and the rental rate, must also be equalized for the two countries, that is $w_A = w_B$ and $r_A = r_B$, if both countries produce both goods and the state of technology is the same (otherwise the same set of final goods prices could lead to a different set of factor prices, see also below).

5.3 The Lerner diagram

The FPE proposition makes two separate statements. It says that if the factor rewards (w, r) are known the prices of the final goods (p_m, p_f) can be derived. It also says that if the prices of the final goods (p_m, p_f) are known the factor rewards (w, r) can be derived. These two issues will be addressed in sections 5.4 and 5.5. The tool of analysis used in those sections is briefly discussed in this section.

Chapter 5 tool: Lerner diagram

The analysis below uses two intricately related tools of analysis, namely the unit value isocost line and the unit value isoquant, together forming the Lerner diagram. The *unit value isocost line* depicts all input combinations (L, K) giving rise to a cost level of 1 unit of measurement, taking the input prices (w, r) as given. This is illustrated in Figure 5.2. If you like big numbers, the unit of measurement could be $1 million or $1 billion, but this is simply a scale effect, so the same results are derived if the unit of measurement is $1. The *unit value isoquant* for a final good, say manufactures, is a regular isoquant, that is it depicts all efficient input combinations (L_m, K_m) giving rise to a certain production level of manufactures, with the provision that the *value* of this production level is 1 unit of measurement, taking the final goods price p_m as given. This is illustrated in Figure 5.3, and discussed further below. Note that each final good gives rise to its own unit value isoquant, depending on the production function and its own price level. Combining these tools gives you Figure 5.4, which is known as the Lerner diagram, named after Abba Lerner (1952).

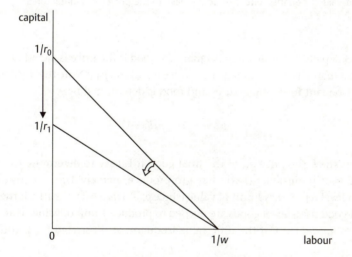

Fig. 5.2 Unit value isocost line; effect of an increase in rental rate r

Figure 5.2 depicts two unit value isocost lines, namely for the factor prices (w, r_0) and for the factor prices (w, r_1). Note that by definition the isocost line is given by

$$(5.1) \qquad\qquad\qquad rK + wL = 1$$

From equation (5.1) the intercepts of the unit value isocost line are easily calculated as $1/w$ for the labour axis and $1/r$ for the capital axis. Figure 5.2 depicts a situation in which the rental rate of capital rises from r_0 to r_1, causing a counter-clockwise rotation of the unit value isocost line around the point $(1/w, 0)$.

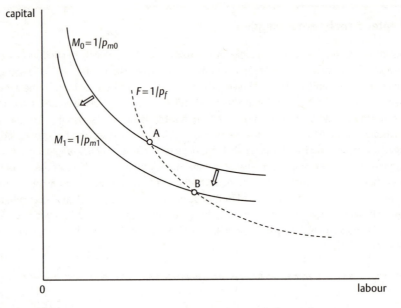

Fig. 5.3 Unit value isoquants: effect of an increase in the price of manufactures

Figure 5.3 depicts one unit value isoquant for food if the price is p_f and two unit value isoquants for manufactures, namely if the price is p_{m0} and p_{m1}. Note that by definition the unit value isoquant for manufactures and food is determined by

(5.2) $$p_m M = 1; \quad p_f F = 1$$

Thus, if you know the price p_m of the final good it is easy to determine the number of goods (and thus the isoquant) you have to produce, namely $1/p_m$, to ensure that this production level represents 1 unit of value (since $p_m \cdot (1/p_m) = 1$). Clearly, if the price level of the final good rises, fewer goods are needed to produce 1 unit of value. Thus a price *rise* results in an *inward* shift of the unit value isoquant, as illustrated for manufactures in Figure 5.3.

A final remark on Figure 5.3, depicting three different isoquants, may be useful. As drawn, the isoquants intersect at two locations, point A and point B. The reader will recall from the microeconomics class that two isoquants cannot intersect, since the same input combination cannot give rise to two different output levels if both combinations make efficient use of the resources. Nonetheless, the isoquants in Figure 5.3 do intersect. Is there an error in the figure? No, there is not. Note that at the two points of intersection A and B an isoquant for manufactures intersects with an isoquant for food. Since these are two different goods, there is no contradiction. The points A and B have no special interpretation, other than that apparently the same input combination produces the same value of output, namely 1, for both goods.

5.4 **From factor prices to final goods prices**

Now that we have briefly discussed the unit value isocost line and the unit value isoquants we are in a position to derive the FPE proposition once we realize the connections between these tools in a perfectly competitive economy. As already discussed in Box 2.1, *if* a good is produced under perfect competition the price of the good is equal to the cost of production. In other words, there are no (excess) profits, such that if an entrepreneur can generate a revenue of 1 unit of measurement, this entrepreneur also incurs a cost of 1 unit of measurement. The FPE proposition makes only one provision, namely that both goods must be produced. Thus for both final goods 1 unit of revenue must be equal to 1 unit of costs.

The connections between costs and revenue are illustrated in Figure 5.4. If the price of manufactures is p_m and the wage–rental ratio is w/r the entrepreneur minimizes production costs for the unit value isoquant of manufactures at point A. To be an equilibrium production point, the costs must be equal to the revenue, such that the unit value isocost line must be tangent at point A. Similar reasoning holds for the food sector at point B. Note also that, as assumed in Chapter 4, the relative capital intensity is higher in the manufactures sector than in the food sector, that is $K_m/L_m > K_f/L_f$ because $\alpha_m > \alpha_f$.

With these preliminaries, it is relatively easy to show the first part of the FPE proposition, that is if the factor rewards (w, r) are known the prices of the final goods (p_m, p_f) can be derived. Once the factor prices are known, the unit value isocost line is known and

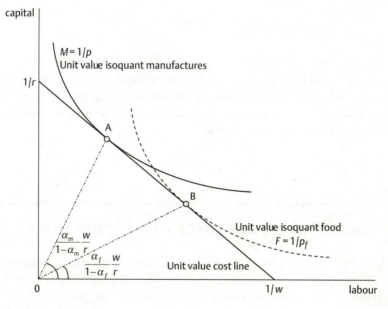

Fig. 5.4 The Lerner diagram

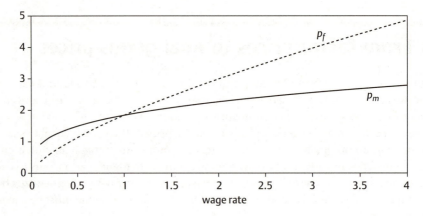

Fig. 5.5 Final goods prices as a function of the wage rate, $r=1$, $\alpha_m=0.7$, $\alpha_f=0.3$

we only have to determine which isoquant for either good is tangent to this unit value isocost line:

$$(w,r) \Rightarrow \text{isocost line} \Rightarrow \text{unit value isoquant} \Rightarrow (p_m, p_f)$$

The calculations were actually already performed in Technical Note 4.2, see equation (4.A7): if the market is characterized by perfect competition and production by constant returns to scale, then *if* a good is produced in equilibrium the price of the good is equal to the unit costs of production:

(5.3) $$p_m = \underbrace{\gamma_m}_{constant} r^{\alpha_m} w^{1-\alpha_m}; \quad p_f = \underbrace{\gamma_f}_{constant} r^{\alpha_f} w^{1-\alpha_f}$$

The constants γ_m and γ_f are defined in Technical Note 4.2. The relationship between the final goods prices and the input prices given in equation (5.3) is illustrated for changes in the wage rate in Figure 5.5. As an inspection of equation (5.3) shows, the price of food rises more quickly than the price of manufactures if the wage rate increases because $1 - \alpha_f > 1 - \alpha_m$. We return to this below.

5.5 From final goods prices to factor prices

Showing the second part of the FPE proposition, that is if the prices of the final goods (p_m, p_f) are known the factor rewards (w, r) can be derived, is a little bit more complicated. Conceptually, we can reverse the logic of section 5.4. First, the two unit value isoquants for manufactures and food can be determined from the identities $p_m M = 1$ and $p_f F = 1$.

Second, the unit value cost line can then be determined by deriving the line tangent to both unit value isoquants:

$$(p_m, p_f) \Rightarrow \text{unit value isoquant} \Rightarrow \text{isocost line} \Rightarrow (w, r)$$

However, in this case it is easier to invert equations (5.3) above to get:

(5.4) $\qquad w = \underbrace{\gamma_w}_{constant} [p_f^{\alpha_m} p_m^{-\alpha_f}]^{1/(\alpha_m - \alpha_f)}; \quad r = \underbrace{\gamma_r}_{constant} [p_m^{1-\alpha_f} p_f^{-(1-\alpha_m)}]^{1/(\alpha_m - \alpha_f)}$

See Technical Note 5.1 for a derivation of these equations and the definition of the parameter constants γ_w and γ_r. The structure of the equations is similar to those of the production functions and the unit cost functions. Note, however, that this time the difference in the capital intensity parameters $\alpha_m - \alpha_f$ plays a crucial role in determining the sign of the powers in the equation. In Chapter 4 we already assumed that the production of manufactures is relatively more capital intensive than the production of food, such that $\alpha_m - \alpha_f > 0$. Equation (5.4) gives us a first indication that this assumption is important for the results to be derived and discussed below.

Box 5.1 **More countries, more goods, and more factors I**

The two results discussed in this chapter, factor price equalization and Stolper-Samuelson, are derived in a framework with 2 countries, 2 goods, and 2 factors of production. This raises the question, of course, whether these results also hold in a more general setting. Ignoring the rather complex mathematical details of this more general setting, the answer is 'yes, sort of'. Factor price equalization, for example, does not hold in a strict sense (which would also be immediately refuted by empirical evidence). Instead, it is possible to distinguish so-called 'cones of diversification' for which FPE holds, leading to *groups* of countries with similar factor prices. The Stolper-Samuelson result holds in a weaker sense, that is a higher price for some final good 'on average' increases the rewards of the factors used intensively in the production of that good. The magnification effect (see section 5.8) holds quite generally, that is a higher price for some final good increases the relative reward to *some* factor of production ('friend') and reduces the relative reward of some other factor of production ('enemy').

5.6 **Stolper–Samuelson**

Now that we have developed the economic tools to analyse factor price equalization it is easy to derive the Stolper–Samuelson proposition, which relates the impact of a change in final goods prices to the rewards of the factors of production and the factor intensity of the production processes. In retrospect the basic reasoning is quite simple and widely applicable. However, when summarizing the impact of international trade for goods and factor prices, the production levels, and the international trade flows, Bertil Ohlin (1933, ch. II) argued:[2]

goods containing a large proportion of scantily supplied and scarce factors are imported, the latter hence becoming less scarce.... The price even of the factors which are made relatively less scarce may well rise in terms of commodities, for the total volume of goods increases, owing to the more efficient use of the productive facilities made possible through trade, and the *average* price of productive factors consequently rises in all regions.

As we will see below, the conclusion Ohlin draws here, that the average price of productive factors rises in all regions, is wrong. At least, it is wrong if this statement is interpreted as an indication that both the wage rate and the rental rate will rise against a 'suitable' combination of the prices of manufactures and food. The precise consequences were analytically derived for the first time by Wolfgang Stolper and Paul Samuelson (1941). Ohlin's remark above may be salvaged, as we will see in Chapter 7, if the statement is interpreted as an indication that the 'average' price of the wage rate and rental rate combined rises relative to the 'average' price of manufactures and food combined.[3] The formal link between the prices of final goods, the rewards to factors of production, and the relative intensity of the production process can be stated as follows.

Stolper–Samuelson proposition

In a neoclassical framework with two final goods and two factors of production, an increase in the price of a final good increases the reward to the factor of production used intensively in the production of that good and reduces the reward to the other factor, provided both goods are produced.

Using the assumption that the relative capital intensity for manufactures is higher than for food, the proposition thus leads to the following conclusions:

- If the price of manufactures rises, the rental rate will rise (because the production of manufactures is relatively capital intensive), and the wage rate will fall.
- If the price of food rises, the wage rate will rise (because the production of food is relatively labour intensive), and the rental rate will fall.

---

[2] See Allen (1965: 201–2).

[3] It seems clear to me that this is not what Ohlin meant.

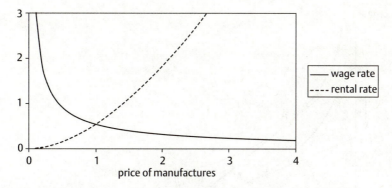

Fig. 5.6 Impact of changing the price of manufactures, $p_f = 1$, $\alpha_m = 0.7$, $\alpha_f = 0.3$

These conclusions, which are partly illustrated in Figure 5.6, show that the first interpretation of the Bertil Ohlin quote above must be wrong. Suppose, for the sake of argument, that the price of manufactures rises as a result of international trade. Then the wage rate will fall. If we realize that the price of food has not changed, it is clear that the wage rate has fallen relative to the price of *both* final goods. The reward to labour has therefore unambiguously fallen, that is a labourer can now buy less of both goods than before the change in the price of manufactures. Similarly, from the conclusions we know that the rental rate of capital has risen, such that capital owners can now buy more units of food (the price of which has not changed). Moreover, as we will see in section 5.8, the rental rate of capital has also risen relative to manufactures, such that capital owners can also buy more units of manufactures. The reward to capital has therefore unambiguously risen relative to both final goods. These distribution aspects of the neoclassical production structure are interesting and receive considerable attention in applications. Whether or not the gains to the capital owners outweigh the losses to the labourers in our hypothetical example will be discussed in Chapter 7.

5.7 **Graphical analysis**

We analyse the impact of an increase in the price of manufactures for the factor rewards w and r using the Lerner diagram. We can do this because the Stolper–Samuelson proposition states that both final goods are produced, such that the price of both goods must be equal to the cost of production. Initially, the price of manufactures is equal to p_{m0}. As we know from the FPE proposition, the price p_{m0} for manufactures together with the price p_f for food, which does not change, determines the wage rate w_0 and the rental rate r_0 through the points of tangency at A and B in Figure 5.7.

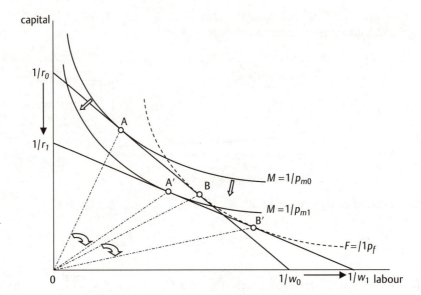

Fig. 5.7 Analysis of an increase in the price of manufactures

If the price of manufactures rises from p_{m0} to p_{m1}, the unit value isoquant for manufactures shifts *in*ward, as indicated by the open straight arrows, because fewer goods are needed to generate 1 unit of value as a result of the price rise. Using the FPE proposition again, we can derive the new wage rate w_1 and rental rate r_1 through the points of tangency at A′ for the new unit value isoquant of manufactures and B′ for the old unit value isoquant of food. It is clear from Figure 5.7 that the rental rate of capital r has increased (because $1/r$ had decreased) and the wage rate has fallen (because $1/w$ has risen).

Figure 5.7 is drawn in accordance with the assumption that the production of manufactures is relatively capital intensive; the slope of the line OA, which is equal to the capital–labour ratio of manufactures, is steeper than the slope of the line OB, which is equal to the capital–labour ratio of food. Similarly, after the price change OA′ is steeper than OB′. Note that the capital–labour intensity falls for the production of both final goods, as indicated by the open curved arrows; there is a substitution away from the more expensive capital towards the cheaper labour in both sectors of production. We can conclude that, as a result of the increase in the price of the relatively capital intensive manufactures, the rental rate of capital rises and the wage rate falls, in accordance with the Stolper–Samuelson proposition. We get similar conclusions in accordance with this proposition, as the reader may verify, for all other possible combinations (for example by changing the price of food).

Box 5.2 **An alternative (dual) approach**

The Stolper–Samuelson result can also be derived using the dual approach (see Technical Note 4.2), based on the fact that if food is produced in equilibrium the unit costs of production must be equal to its price, and similarly for manufactures. Recall:

(5.3) $$p_m = \gamma_m r^{\alpha_m} w^{1-\alpha_m}; \quad p_f = \gamma_f r^{\alpha_f} w^{1-\alpha_f}$$

Based on equation (5.3), reproduced above, we can draw isocost *curves* in (r, w)-space, that is combinations of rental rate and wage rate giving rise to the same costs for the production of one good. This is done in Figure 5.8 for both food and manufactures. Initially, the price of both goods is 1, leading to equilibrium at point E_1, the only combination of rental rate and wage rate at which both goods can be produced.

Since the production of manufactures is relatively capital intensive $(\alpha_m > \alpha_f)$, the isocost curve for the manufactures sector cuts that of the food sector from above in E_1.[4] Now suppose that the price of manufactures rises from 1 to 1.25. This shifts the combinations at which price is equal to unit costs *up* in Figure 5.8. The equilibrium moves to E_2, such that the rental rate rises and the wage rate falls, in accordance with the Stolper–Samuelson result.

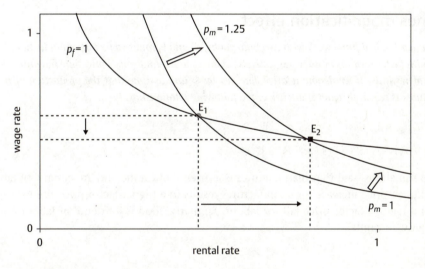

Fig. 5.8 Stolper–Samuelson in the dual approach, $\alpha_m = 0.6$, $\alpha_f = 0.3$

[4] Using Shephard's lemma, see Technical Note 4.2, it can also be shown that the slope of the isocost curve is equal to the capital–labour ratio.

5.8 **The magnification effect**

The Stolper–Samuelson proposition says that if, for example, the price of manufactures rises, then the reward to the factor of production used relatively intensively in the production of manufactures, in our case capital, rises, and the reward to the other factor falls. Both the price of manufactures and the rental rate of capital rise, but there is no indication which rises faster. This issue is addressed by Ronald Jones (1965), who shows that the price of the factor of production rises *more* in relative terms than the price of the final good, that is the rental rate rises faster than the price of manufactures. This can be seen in Figure 5.7 once we realize that the extent of the inward shift of the unit value isoquant is proportional to the price change of manufactures. The fact that the new unit value isoquant for manufactures cuts the line OA strictly above the line from $1/r_1$ to $1/w_0$, indicates that the relative change of the rental rate is larger than the relative change of the price of manufactures. Analytically, this can be verified by totally differentiating equation (5.4), see Technical Note 5.2.

Jones magnification effect

In a neoclassical framework with two final goods, M and F, and two factors of production, K and L, with factor rewards r and w, respectively, changes in the final goods prices are magnified in the factor rewards. If we denote relative changes by $\sim$ and assume that the production of manufactures is relatively capital intensive, the following relationships hold:

(i) *if $\tilde{p}_m > \tilde{p}_f$, then $\tilde{r} > \tilde{p}_m > \tilde{p}_f > \tilde{w}$*
(ii) *if $\tilde{p}_m < \tilde{p}_f$, then $\tilde{r} < \tilde{p}_m < \tilde{p}_f < \tilde{w}$.*

It is sometimes said that manufactures is a 'friend' of capital and an 'enemy' of labour, because a price increase for manufactures results in a higher factor price rise for capital and a relative factor price fall for labour. Similarly, food is a 'friend' of labour and an 'enemy' of capital.

Box 5.3 **Natural-resource intensive manufacturing exporters**

The ITC classifies twenty-one goods as 'natural-resource intensive' products, incorporating leather, cork, wood, lime, precious stones, pig iron, copper, aluminum, lead, etc. For the 151 countries for which the ITC provides data, total exports of natural-resource intensive manufactures in 1998 were equal to $248 bn, some 5 per cent of all exports. The left-hand side of Table 5.1 lists the top ten exporters of natural-resource intensive manufactures in absolute terms. With a value of $19 bn (mostly gold) the USA is the world's largest natural-resource intensive manufacturing exporter, closely followed by Germany and Belgium (mostly diamonds) with $17 bn each. With the exception of the Russian Federation, the other large exporters are all OECD countries.

Since natural-resource intensive manufactures represent only 3 per cent of American and German exports, they do not make it to the right-hand side of Table 5.1, listing the top ten world exporters of natural-resource intensive manufactures in relative terms. These are all located in Africa and Central Asia. The top three are the Democratic Republic of Congo (Zaire; diamonds and some cobalt), Gambia (diamonds), and the Central African Republic (diamonds). Note the small absolute size of these trade flows and the high dependence on the exports of natural-resource intensive manufactures for all these countries, ranging from 77 per cent for Congo to 42 per cent for tenth ranked Armenia. Figure 5.9 shows the relative dependence of countries on the exports of natural-resource intensive manufactures. These are clearly distributed in a haphazard way around the globe, presumably largely depending on the availability of exportable natural resources.

Table 5.1 Top ten natural-resource intensive manufacturing exporters, 1998

No.	Top 10 in absolute terms			Top 10 in relative terms		
	Country	Exports		Country	Exports	
		Value	%		%	Value
1	United States	19	3	Congo, Dem. Rep.	77	0.2
2	Germany	17	3	Gambia	74	0.0
3	Belgium	17	10	Central African Rep.	71	0.1
4	Canada	15	8	Zambia	66	0.1
5	Russian Federation	13	26	Sierra Leone	65	0.0
6	Italy	12	6	Eritrea	60	0.0
7	United Kingdom	12	4	Bahrain	59	0.1
8	South Korea	11	9	Niger	58	0.1
9	France	9	3	Kyrgyzstan	49	0.2
10	Australia	9	18	Armenia	42	0.0

Source: WTO/UNCTAD International Trade Centre website http://www.intracen.org; value in bn US $. The % shares are relative to the country's total exports.

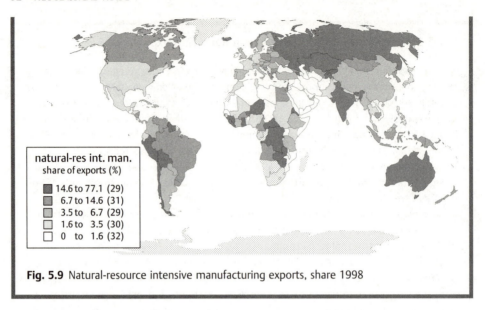

Fig. 5.9 Natural-resource intensive manufacturing exports, share 1998

5.9 Application: globalization, low wages, and unemployment

The neoclassical factor abundance model, and in particular the Stolper–Samuelson result, has been at the heart of a heated trade policy debate in the last decade of the twentieth century on the impact of 'globalization' for wages and unemployment in the high-income countries, see Lawrence and Slaughter (1993), Wood (1994), and Collins (1998). For a survey see Wood (1998). In Chapter 1 we already pointed out that the term 'globalization' tends to be confusing, as it has different meanings for different people. In this particular debate it refers to increased imports and competition for the OECD countries from 'low-wage' countries in Asia, Latin America, and Africa.

Empirical observations

Two quite different empirical observations in Europe and America formed the basis for the debate, which distinguishes between two types of labour: high-skilled labour (so-called white-collar workers) and low-skilled labour (so-called blue-collar workers). The American problem is suggested in Figure 5.10. Initially, the wages for the white-collar and blue-collar workers are rising roughly equally fast. This changes in the 1980s (since 1984), when the wages of the white-collar workers start to rise relative to the blue-collar workers. In the same time period, as also illustrated in Figure 5.10, imports of goods and services

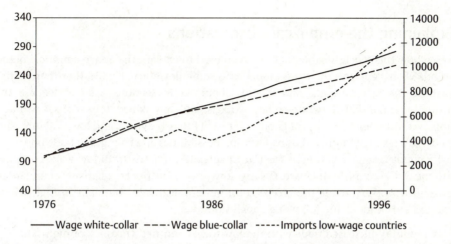

Fig. 5.10 Smaller wage increases for blue-collar workers in USA. Wage index for white-collar and blue-collar workers (1976 = 100): left-hand scale. Imports from low-wage countries (Africa, Latin America and ASEAN): right-hand scale, $ millions

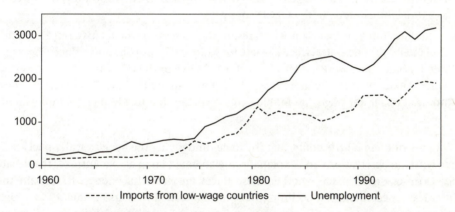

Fig. 5.11 Rising unemployment in France. Unemployment ×1000; imports from low-wage countries (Africa, Latin America, and ASEAN), $ millions

from low-wage countries are rising, although the relationship with the development of the relative wages is not very clear. In the public debate the declining relative wage of blue-collar workers was widely attributed to imports and competition from low-wage countries.

The European problem is suggested for France in Figure 5.11. In the 1970s French unemployment starts to rise rapidly, from 600,000 in 1974 to more than 3 million in 1994. Simultaneously, imports from low-wage countries rise from about $600 million in 1974 to about $2 billion in 1997. As a result of this simultaneous occurrence, the high level of French unemployment, especially for low-skilled workers, was widely attributed in the public debate to imports and competition from low-wage countries.

Explaining the empirical observations

To see how the neoclassical model has been used to explain the above empirical observations we have to interpret the model with some flexibility. First, rather than distinguishing the factor inputs capital and labour, as in sections 5.2–5.8, we use the distinction high-skilled (white-collar) workers and low-skilled (blue-collar) workers. Moreover, there are two types of goods, high-skill intensive goods and low-skill intensive goods. As a result of improved transportation possibilities and changes in trade policy for major countries (such as China, see also Chapter 17), imports from low-wage countries into the OECD countries increase. Clearly, low-wage countries are relatively abundant in low-skilled workers, while the OECD countries are relatively abundant in high-skilled workers. This leads to the following conclusions:

- As a result of increased trade with the low-wage countries, the price of high-skill intensive goods rises relative to the price of low-skill intensive goods in the OECD countries (see Chapter 7), such that

- The OECD countries start to produce more high-skill intensive goods and less low-skill intensive goods. The fall in production of the low-skill intensive sector is interpreted as a *de-industrialization* in the OECD countries.

- According to the Stolper–Samuelson result, the increase in the relative price of high-skill intensive goods raises the wage rate for white-collar workers and reduces the wage rate for blue-collar workers. This is what we observe in the USA. In Europe, however, where labour markets are more rigid, the fall in demand for blue-collar workers does not lead to a lower wage rate for blue-collar workers, but to a higher unemployment level.

At present there is little doubt that the forces underlying the neoclassical model are in line with the observations and explanations elaborated upon above. Instead, the debate now focuses on the issue whether these forces are powerful enough to explain the empirical observations of a declining wage for low-skilled workers in America and high unemployment in Europe. To put these in a proper perspective, consider the following. The total import value from the low-wage countries of Figure 5.10 into the USA in 1999 was about $12 bn. Although this is a nice sum to have in your wallet, it is only 1 per cent of the USA's total imports of $1,116 bn in 1999. The latter, in turn, is only about 12 per cent of the USA's enormous GDP of $9,152 bn, such that imports from low-wage countries are only 0.13 per cent of American GDP.[5] This cannot possibly be held responsible for any actual developments in the relative wage rate of blue-collar workers in the USA. Instead, it is thought that technological changes and sector adjustments favouring white-collar workers relative to blue-collar workers are largely responsible for the empirical developments. Similarly, the rigid labour markets in Europe are largely responsible for the high unemployment levels in some European countries. The increased OECD trade levels with low-wage countries seem to have had limited influence in this respect.

[5] Variations in the selection of 'low-wage' countries can increase this percentage somewhat, never to exceed 1 per cent of American GDP.

5.10 **Conclusions**

There is a one-to-one connection between the prices of final goods and the rewards to the factors of production, that is if we know the price of food and manufactures we can derive the wage rate and the rental rate, and vice versa. If trade between nations equalizes the prices of food and manufactures, it therefore also equalizes the wage rate and the rental rate (factor price equalization). If the production of food is labour intensive and the price of food rises, this raises the wage rate and reduces the rental rate. The opposite holds if the price of manufactures rises (Stolper–Samuelson). Moreover, the changes in the factor prices are larger in relative terms than the changes in the final goods prices (magnification effect). We apply these results and the neoclassical model to better understand the 'globalization' debate of the 1990s, where it was argued that increased international trade with low-wage countries led to higher unemployment in Europe and a deterioration in the relative wage rate of blue-collar workers in the USA. Countries with a high share of exports of natural-resource intensive manufactures are distributed in a haphazard way around the globe, presumably largely depending on the availability of exportable natural resources.

Technical Notes (optional)

Technical Note 5.1 **Factor prices as a function of final goods prices**

We start by recalling the relationships between costs and prices

$$(5.A1) \qquad p_m = \gamma_m r^{\alpha_m} w^{1-\alpha_m} \quad \text{and} \quad p_f = \gamma_f r^{\alpha_f} w^{1-\alpha_f}$$

Now write the rental rate r as a function of the final goods price and the wage rate for both equations using the definition $\gamma_m \equiv \alpha_m^{-\alpha_m}(1 - \alpha_m)^{-(1-\alpha_m)}$ and similarly for γ_f

$$(5.A2) \qquad r = \alpha_m(1 - \alpha_m)^{(1-\alpha_m)/\alpha_m} p_m^{1/\alpha_m} w^{-(1-\alpha_m)} \quad \text{and} \quad r = \alpha_f(1 - \alpha_f)^{(1-\alpha_f)/\alpha_f} p_f^{1/\alpha_f} w^{-(1-\alpha_f)}$$

Since we have two equations determining the rental rate r, setting them equal to each other allows us to determine the wage rate w as a function of the final goods prices p_m and p_f, see below. A similar procedure gives the rental rate r as a function of the final goods prices p_m and p_f.

$$(5.A3) \qquad w = \gamma_w p_f^{\alpha_m/(\alpha_m-\alpha_f)} p_m^{-\alpha_f/(\alpha_m-\alpha_f)}, \quad \text{where } \gamma_w \equiv \left[\frac{\alpha_m(1 - \alpha_m)^{(1-\alpha_m)/\alpha_m}}{\alpha_f(1 - \alpha_f)^{(1-\alpha_f)/\alpha_f}}\right]^{-\alpha_m\alpha_f/(\alpha_m-\alpha_f)}, \quad \text{and}$$

$$(5.A4) \qquad r = \gamma_r p_m^{\frac{1-\alpha_f}{\alpha_m-\alpha_f}} p_f^{\frac{-(1-\alpha_m)}{\alpha_m-\alpha_f}}, \quad \text{where } \gamma_r \equiv \left[\frac{(1 - \alpha_m)\alpha_m^{\frac{\alpha_m}{1-\alpha_m}}}{(1 - \alpha_f)\alpha_f^{\frac{\alpha_f}{1-\alpha_f}}}\right]^{(1-\alpha_m)(1-\alpha_f)/(\alpha_m-\alpha_f)}$$

Technical Note 5.2 Jones magnification

Quite frequently in economic analysis the relationships between different economic forces are rather complex when stated in levels, but surprisingly simple when stated in relative changes. This fact is, for example, fruitfully used in the Jones (1965) analysis of the neoclassical model in general. Suppose the relationship between the variables z and v is of the type $z = av^\eta$ for some constant a and parameter η. For any variable z, let $\tilde{z}$ denote the relative change of z, that is $\tilde{z} \equiv dz/z$. Total differentiation of $z = av^\eta$ gives $dz = \eta a v^{\eta-1} dv$. Dividing the left-hand side by z and the right-hand side by av^η (which is the same as z) gives

(5.A5).
$$\frac{dz}{z} = \eta \frac{av^{\eta-1}dv}{av^\eta}, \quad \text{or} \quad \tilde{z} \equiv \frac{dz}{z} = \eta \frac{dv}{v} \equiv \eta\tilde{v}.$$

In relative changes, the relationship $z = av^\eta$ therefore reduces quite simply to $\tilde{z} = \eta\tilde{v}$. Applying this result to equation (5.4) gives

(5.A6)
$$\tilde{w} = \frac{\alpha_m}{\alpha_m - \alpha_f}\tilde{p}_f - \frac{\alpha_f}{\alpha_m - \alpha_f}\tilde{p}_m; \quad \tilde{r} = \frac{1-\alpha_f}{\alpha_m - \alpha_f}\tilde{p}_m - \frac{1-\alpha_m}{\alpha_m - \alpha_f}\tilde{p}_f$$

Now apply these relationships for example if the price of manufactures rises ($\tilde{p}_m > 0$) and the price of food remains the same ($\tilde{p}_f = 0$):

(5.A7)
$$\tilde{r} = \frac{1-\alpha_f}{\alpha_m - \alpha_f}\tilde{p}_m > \tilde{p}_m > 0 = \tilde{p}_f > -\frac{\alpha_f}{\alpha_m - \alpha_f}\tilde{p}_m = \tilde{w}$$

Thus the rental rate of capital rises more than the price of manufactures, which uses capital intensively, which rises more than the price of food ($=0$), which rises more than the wage rate (which actually falls relative to the price of both goods). This result, which holds more generally, is known as the *Jones magnification effect*.

Chapter 6
Production Volume

Objectives/key terms

Rybczynski result	Edgeworth Box
Contract curve	Sector-specific capital
Output magnification	Labour migration in Israel

We analyse the connection between the production levels of final goods and the available factors of production (Rybczynski effect). We apply this result to discuss the effect of immigration from Russia into Israel in the 1990s.

6.1 Introduction

After the discussion of the relationship between the prices of final goods and the rewards to factors of production in Chapter 5, we now turn to the relationship between the level of production of final goods (food and manufactures) and the available production factors (labour and capital). The third main result in neoclassical trade theory, which investigates this relationship, is named after the Polish economist Rybczynski, who provided the first analysis in 1955 in a production equilibrium (such that all available inputs are employed). The Rybczynski result lies at the heart of the Heckscher–Ohlin proposition, relating the direction of international trade flows and factor abundance, as we will see in the next chapter.

The tool used to demonstrate the Rybczynski effect in this chapter is called the Edgeworth Box.[1] Named after Francis Edgeworth, it elegantly combines various aspects of an efficient production equilibrium in one graphical framework, and as such is a useful tool of analysis also in other areas of economics, such as microeconomics and game theory. The factor price equalization result, discussed in Chapter 5, will also prove to be useful in the sequel.

---

[1] It is sometimes also called the Edgeworth–Bowley Box.

Fig. 6.1 Francis Edgeworth (1845–1926)

Born in Ireland, Edgeworth was educated in Dublin and Oxford, and worked initially in London and eventually at Oxford. After its foundation in 1891 he was editor of the *Economic Journal* for thirty-five years. He was the first to define the law of diminishing product in marginal, rather than average, terms. He was also the first to define a general utility function, depending on the quantity of all goods consumed and thus bringing substitutability and complementarity within reach. Moreover, he was the first to introduce indifference curves, the contract curve, and the core of an economy. Since all these concepts are still widely used in economics his influence is substantial.

6.2 Rybczynski

The connection between the available factors of production, the output levels of final goods, and the relative intensity of the production processes for a given set of final goods prices with a neoclassical production structure can be stated as follows.

Rybczynski proposition

In a neoclassical framework with two final goods, two factors of production, and constant prices of the final goods, an increase in the supply of one of the factors of production results in an increase of the output of the final good that uses this factor of production relatively intensively and a reduction in the output of the other final good, provided both goods are produced in equilibrium.

Using the assumption made in Chapter 4 that the production of manufactures is relatively capital intensive this leads to the following conclusions:

- If the available amount of labour rises, the output of food increases (because its production is labour intensive) and the output of manufactures falls.

- If the available amount of capital rises, the output of manufactures increases (because its production is capital intensive) and the output of food falls.

There are at least two points to note with respect to the Rybczynski proposition. First, the statement is made for *given* values of the final goods prices p_m and p_f. This is important to realize, since in a full general equilibrium framework we would expect an increase in the amount of a factor of production, which leads to output changes, also to affect the (relative) price level of final goods. The Rybczynski proposition can then be used as an indication for the direction of the price changes of final goods. We return to this issue below. Second, the reader of course realizes that, starting from some initial equilibrium with concomitant production levels, an increase in the available amount of a factor of production *in principle* allows the economy to produce more of *both* goods, by allocating some of the extra input to one sector and the rest to the other sector. The Rybczynski proposition states, however, that this is *not* what happens; the output of one final good rises and the output of the other final good *falls*. The remainder of this chapter will use the link between the two points above to show why this is true.

6.3 **The Edgeworth Box**

In Chapter 5 we introduced the Lerner diagram to analyse the links between the prices of final goods and the prices of factors of production in an economic equilibrium in which both goods are produced. This time we want to analyse the connections between the available factors of production and the quantity of output produced, for which a different tool is suitable: the Edgeworth Box.

The situation is illustrated in Figure 6.2. Panels *a* and *b* show different isoquants for manufactures and food. Obviously, an increase in the available amount of capital or labour leads to an increase in the output of the sector to which it is allocated. The question arises how to allocate the available capital and labour over the two final goods sectors, and how to show this problem clearly in one picture. Drawing the isoquants for the two goods from the same origin, as we did in Chapter 5 and as illustrated in panel 6.2*c*, is not very useful as it does not help us to allocate the inputs efficiently.

The important step in constructing the Edgeworth Box is the realization that in an economic equilibrium all available inputs must be used either in one sector or in the other, that is both the capital market and the labour market must be in equilibrium.

(6.1) $$K_m + K_f = K; \quad L_m + L_f = L$$

Once we know the total available amount of capital K, it suffices to know the capital input K_m to calculate the remaining use of capital $K_f = K - K_m$. Similarly, once we know how much labour L is available and the amount L_m used for manufactures, we also know how much is available for production of food, namely $L_f = L - L_m$. The Edgeworth Box uses this principle by transposing the origin for the isoquants of one of the final goods onto the total amount of capital K and labour L available for production, as explained in the Chapter 6 tool and illustrated in Figure 6.4.

Figure 6.4 illustrates the Edgeworth Box for the Cobb–Douglas production functions of equation (4.1), assuming that $K = L = 5$. The origin for manufactures is in the south-west corner, as usual. The dashed lines in the figure give three different isoquants for manufactures, each having the well-known curvature. The origin for food is located exactly on top of the total available amount of capital and labour (in this case 5), and rotated 180 degrees. The amount of labour used for food is thus measured from right to left, as indicated by the arrow in Figure 6.4, and the amount of capital used for food is measured

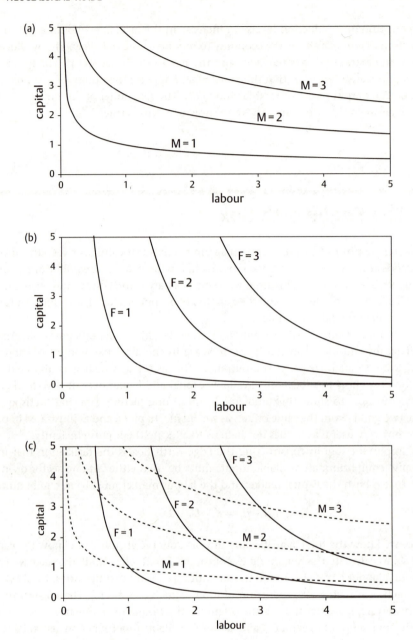

Fig. 6.2 Isoquants for manufactures and food, $\alpha_m = 0.7$, $\alpha_f = 0.3$

Chapter 6 tool: Edgeworth Box

The Edgeworth Box is constructed using the field of isoquants for manufactures and food illustrated on the left-hand side of Figure 6.3 (using the isoquants $M = 2$ and $F = 1$ as an example). The origin and axes of one of the goods, in this case food, is turned around 180 degrees and placed exactly on the total amount of capital *K* and labour *L* available in the economy. The result is illustrated in Figure 6.4 and further discussed in the main text.

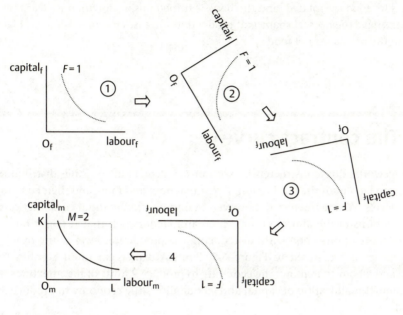

Fig. 6.3 Construction of the Edgeworth Box

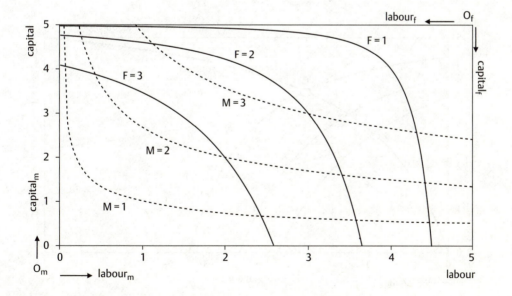

Fig. 6.4 The Edgeworth Box, $K = L = 5$, $\alpha_m = 0.7$, $\alpha_f = 0.3$

from top to bottom, as indicated by the other arrow in Figure 6.4. There are also three isoquants for food drawn in the figure. At first sight, their curvature may seem strange and they may appear to be increasing in the wrong direction, but once it is realized that the axes for food are rotated (and the book is turned upside down), it is clear that these isoquants have the normal shape and production increases if more capital and labour is put into the production of food.

6.4 The contract curve

The Edgeworth Box constructed in section 6.3 depicts all possible distributions of capital and labour for the production of manufactures and food, and their concomitant output levels. We are interested, however, in finding *efficient* input combinations, that is distributions of the allocation of capital and labour such that it is not possible to produce more of one good without reducing the production level of the other good. This concept is illustrated in Figure 6.5. Point A depicts an input combination of capital and labour that allows the economy to produce 2 units of manufactures. At the same time, this allocation of capital and labour allows the economy to produce 3 units of food.

Point A in Figure 6.5 is not an efficient input allocation. Keeping the output level of manufactures fixed, that is restricting ourselves to the isoquant $M=2$, we could produce more units of food. This is illustrated in Figure 6.5 by point B, where the economy

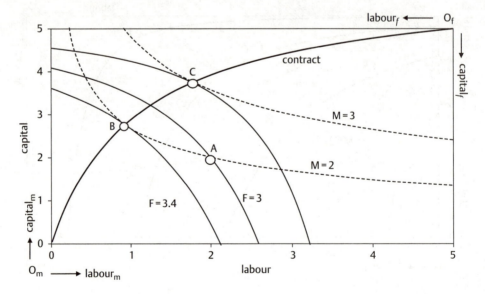

Fig. 6.5 The contract curve, $K=L=5$, $\alpha_m=0.7$, $\alpha_f=0.3$

produces 2 units of manufactures and simultaneously produces 3.4 units of food. If, starting from point B, we want to produce more units of food, we have to reduce the production of manufactures. Similarly, if we want to increase the production of manufactures, we have to reduce the production of food. Point B is thus an efficient input allocation. Graphically, it is characterized by the tangency of the isoquants for the production of manufactures and food. Point C in Figure 6.5 is another efficient input allocation. The curve connecting all efficient input combinations in the Edgeworth Box is called the *contract curve*. It is analytically derived in Technical Note 6.1.

In Figure 6.5 the contract curve is drawn above the diagonal connecting the two origins O_m and O_f. This is because the production of manufactures is relatively capital intensive. The extent of the curvature of the contract curve depends on the difference in the degree of capital intensity. This is illustrated for four different cases in Figure 6.6. If the capital–labour intensity is the same for the two final goods, that is if $\alpha_m = \alpha_f$ (in which case the two production functions are identical), the contract curve coincides with the diagonal connecting the two origins. The larger the difference in capital intensity, the more pronounced the curvature of the contract curve and, as we will see in the next chapter, the more pronounced the curvature of the production possibility frontier.

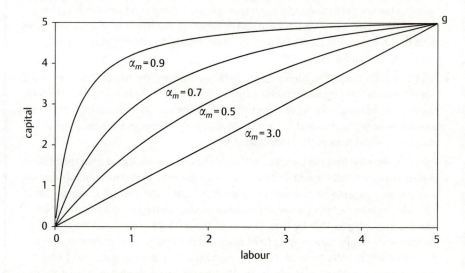

Fig. 6.6 Contract curves for different values of α_m, $\alpha_f = 0.3$

Box 6.1 **Sector-specific capital**

A special case of the neoclassical model arises when we allow for sector-specific factors of production. Also adding a time dimension, a rapidly adjusting factor of production and a slowly adjusting factor of production, we can distinguish between the short term, the intermediate term, and the long term. Obviously, adjusting the allocation of factors of production after some exogenous change, say an increase in the price of manufactures, requires time to move capital and labour from one sector to the other. Let's assume that labour is easier to reallocate than capital, which we refer to as sector-specific (in the short run and intermediate run, but not in the long run). We discuss the reallocation of factors of production using Figure 6.7, which depicts the value marginal product of labour (VMPL) for manufactures (bottom left origin) and food (bottom right origin), *given* the distribution of capital. In equilibrium a sector's VMPL is equal to the wage rate The distance between the two origins is equal to the total labour force, the allocation of labour to manufactures is measured from the left-hand origin and the allocation of labour to food from the right-hand origin. In both sectors the marginal product of labour (and VMPL) declines as more labour is used.

- Point E_0 depicts the initial equilibrium, in which the wage rate for manufactures w_{m0} is equal to the wage rate in the food sector w_{f0}.

- Points E_0 and E_1 depict the short-term (Ethier) equilibrium, *given* the allocation of capital and labour to the two sectors, after an increase in the price of manufactures. Nothing changes for the food sector, such that the wage rate remains w_{f0}. The higher price of manufactures shifts the VMPL curve ($p_m \times MPL$) in that sector up, leading to a higher wage rate w_{m1} for manufactures than for food.

- Point E_2 depicts the medium-term (Neary 1978) equilibrium. The higher short-term wage rate in the manufacturing sector leads to a reallocation of labour from food (where the wage rate starts to increase) to manufactures (where the wage rate starts to decline) until a new equilibrium (with equal wages) is reached. Obviously, this increases the production of manufactures and reduces the production of food.

- Point E_3 depicts the long-run (neoclassical) equilibrium. At the initial equilibrium point E_0 we implicitly assumed that the rental rate of capital was the same in the two sectors. However, after the price increase for manufactures (raising the value) and the reallocation of labour from food to manufactures (raising the marginal product of capital), the rental rate for manufactures is higher than for food. Over time, this will lead to a reallocation of capital from food to manufactures, leading to an upward shift of VMPL for manufactures and a downward shift of VMPL for food. These changes in turn require a reallocation of labour, which requires a reallocation of capital, etc. The process continues until both the wage rate and the rental rate are the same in the two sectors. Point E_3 depicts the ultimate long-run equilibrium. Note that in the intermediate term (point E_2) the wage rate is *higher* than at the initial equilibrium, while in the long run (point E_3) we have drawn the wage rate to be *lower* than at the initial equilibrium. When looking at Figure 6.7 this seems to be an arbitrary decision on our part, depending on the extent of the shifts in the VMPL curves as a result of the reallocation of capital. This is, however, not the case as the long-run equilibrium is determined by the neoclassical model and we know from the Stolper–Samuelson result that an increase in the price of manufactures (which is capital intensive) raises the reward to capital (rental rate) and reduces the reward to labour (wage rate). For the labourers, the impact of the price change is therefore beneficial in the short run and intermediate run, but detrimental in the long run.

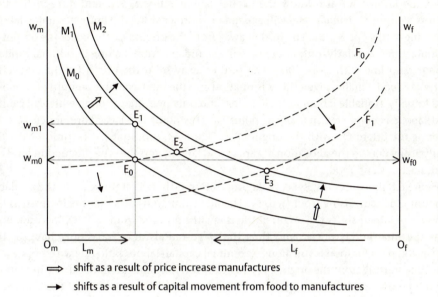

⇒ shift as a result of price increase manufactures

→ shifts as a result of capital movement from food to manufactures

Fig. 6.7 Sector-specific capital

6.5 The distribution of labour and capital

We are now in a position to derive the distribution of capital and labour in the economy and the concomitant production levels of manufactures and food. Moreover, we can illustrate this graphically in the Edgeworth Box and demonstrate the Rybczynski proposition stated in section 6.2. The basic reasoning involves three main steps.

- Given the prices of the final goods p_m and p_f, we can determine the wage rate w and the rental rate r using the factor price equalization proposition of Chapter 5, provided both goods are produced in equilibrium.
- If we know the wage rate w and the rental rate r, we can derive the optimal (cost-minimizing) capital–labour ratios for both goods K_m/L_m and K_f/L_f. It is important to realize that these capital–labour ratios do not change as long as the final goods prices p_m and p_f do not change.

- Using the full employment conditions, equation (6.1), and the capital–labour ratios K_m/L_m and K_f/L_f we can derive the equilibrium allocation of capital and labour in the two sectors, and thus the production levels in both sectors.

This is illustrated in Figure 6.8. Once the final goods prices, and thus the wage–rental ratio, are known we also know the capital–labour ratios K_m/L_m and K_f/L_f in the two sectors. Output of *manufactures* will expand or contract along the optimal capital–labour ratio line with slope K_m/L_m. The further away from the origin O_m, the larger the output of manufactures. Similarly, output of *food* will expand or contract along its optimal capital–labour ratio line with slope K_f/L_f. The further away from the origin O_f, the larger the output of food. Finally, given this information and the total available amount of capital K and initially available labour L_0 there is one, and only one, allocation in which all capital and labour is employed, namely at point E_0. This point is on the contract curve connecting the origin O_m with the origin O_f in Figure 6.8 (not drawn). Technical Note 6.2 analytically derives the allocation of capital and labour, and thus the production levels of manufactures and food.

Figure 6.8 illustrates the Rybczynski proposition if there is an increase in the available amount of labour, rising from L_0 to L_1. The first thing to note is that the increase in the amount of labour shifts the origin of the isoquants for food from O_f to O'_f. Second, note that the final goods prices, and thus the wage–rental ratio, have not changed, the expansion path for food is still along its optimal capital–labour ratio line with slope K_f/L_f, this time starting from the origin O'_f. Thus, as before, the allocation of capital and labour for the production of the two goods is determined by the intersection of the expansion paths, at point E_1. This point is on the contract curve connecting the origin O_m with the origin O'_f in Figure 6.8 (not drawn).

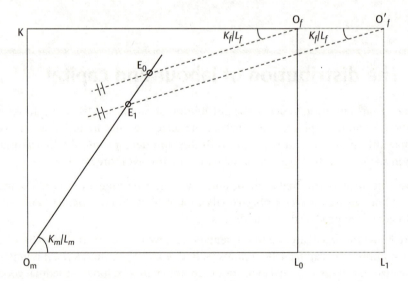

Fig. 6.8 The Rybczynski proposition; expansion of labour

How can we conclude that the output level for food has increased and for manufactures has fallen, as required by the Rybczynski proposition? Quite simply, by measuring the distance of the allocation point from the origin. Since the line from O_m to E_0 is longer than from O_m to E_1, the output of manufactures has *decreased*. Similarly, since the line from O_f to E_0 is shorter than from O'_f to E_1, the output of food has *increased*. These conclusions are linked to the capital–labour intensity of the two sectors, as summarized in the Rybczynski proposition.

The proposition is also easy to understand if we let λ_m be the share of the labour force in manufactures, that is $\lambda_m = L_m/L$, and take the ratio of equation (6.1) to get (see Technical Note 6.2):

(6.2)
$$\underbrace{\frac{K}{L}}_{\substack{economy \\ cap.\ int}} = \lambda_m \underbrace{\frac{K_m}{L_m}}_{\substack{manuf. \\ cap.\ int}} + (1 - \lambda_m) \underbrace{\frac{K_f}{L_f}}_{\substack{Food \\ cap.\ int}}$$

Equation (6.2) shows clearly that the economy-wide capital–labour ratio K/L is equal to the weighted average of the sectoral capital–labour ratios K_m/L_m and K_f/L_f. Since the latter do not change for given final goods prices, a change in the available amount of one of the production factors, which changes the economy-wide capital–labour ratio K/L, can only be accommodated by changing the share of labour in manufactures λ_m. Obviously, an increase in the economy-wide capital–labour ratio must lead to an increase in the share of labour allocated to the capital intensive sector, and vice versa for a decrease in the economy-wide capital–labour ratio. That, in a nutshell, is the Rybczynski proposition.

Finally, it is worthwhile to point out that Jones (1965) also shows that there is a magnification effect in output space, as was shown in Chapter 5 for the prices of factors of production. More specifically, given that the production of manufactures is capital intensive, the following relationships hold:

(i) if $\tilde{K} > \tilde{L}$, then $\tilde{M} > \tilde{K} > \tilde{L} > \tilde{F}$

(ii) if $\tilde{K} < \tilde{L}$, then $\tilde{M} < \tilde{K} < \tilde{L} < \tilde{F}$

Box 6.2 **Unskilled-labour intensive manufacturing exporters**

The ITC classifies thirty-one goods as 'unskilled-labour intensive manufacturing' products, incorporating pipes, various textiles, clothing, glass, pottery, ships, furniture, footwear, and office supplies. For the 151 countries for which the ITC provides data, total exports of unskilled-labour intensive manufactures in 1998 were equal to $610 bn, some 13 per cent of all exports. The left-hand side of Table 6.1 lists the top ten exporters of unskilled-labour intensive manufactures in absolute terms. With a value of $78 bn China is the world's largest unskilled-labour intensive manufactures exporter, including ships, shoes, and wearing apparel, followed by Italy with a value of $48 bn (including furniture, footwear, and pullovers). The other large exporters are all OECD countries.

Despite the fact that unskilled-labour intensive manufactures represent a sizeable 43 per cent of Chinese and 24 per cent of Italian exports, neither country makes it to the right-hand side of Table 6.1, listing the top ten world exporters of unskilled-labour intensive manufactures in relative terms. The majority of these are located in Asia. The top three are Nepal (carpets),

Bangladesh (clothing and textiles), and Pakistan (cotton and textiles). Note the small absolute size of these trade flows and the high dependence on the exports of unskilled-labour intensive manufactures for all these countries, ranging from 89 per cent for Nepal to 62 per cent for tenth ranked Albania. Figure 6.9 shows the relative dependence of countries on the exports of unskilled-labour intensive manufactures. These are clearly concentrated in South-East Asia and Central Europe.

Table 6.1 Top ten unskilled-labour intensive manufacturing exporters, 1998

| No. | Top 10 in absolute terms | | | Top 10 in relative terms | | |
| | Country | Exports | | Country | Exports | |
		Value	%		%	Value
1	China	78	43	Nepal	89	0.3
2	Italy	48	24	Bangladesh	86	4.4
3	Germany	45	9	Pakistan	83	5.8
4	United States	45	7	Cambodia	82	0.6
5	France	30	10	Haiti	78	0.2
6	South Korea	28	22	Sri Lanka	69	2.8
7	Japan	25	7	Liberia	68	0.9
8	Taiwan	23	20	Laos	67	0.1
9	United Kingdom	22	8	Mauritius	64	1.1
10	Belgium	21	13	Albania	62	0.2

Source: WTO/UNCTAD International Trade Centre website http://www.intracen.org; value in bn US $. The % shares are relative to the country's total exports.

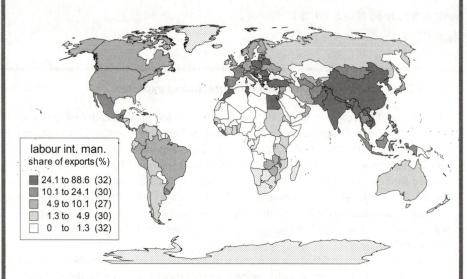

labour int. man.
share of exports (%)

- 24.1 to 88.6 (32)
- 10.1 to 24.1 (30)
- 4.9 to 10.1 (27)
- 1.3 to 4.9 (30)
- 0 to 1.3 (32)

Fig. 6.9 Unskilled-labour intensive manufacturing exports, share 1998

6.6 **Application: Russian immigrants in Israel**

To see how the Rybczynski result can be useful for understanding empirical changes in production we discuss the study of Gandal, Hanson, and Slaughter (2000), who analyse the impact of Russian immigration into Israel in the 1990s. In late 1989 the Soviet Union relaxed emigration restrictions, which induced many Russian Jews to emigrate to Israel. From 1989 to 1996 some 670,000 Russian Jews arrived, increasing the Israeli population by 11 per cent and the labour force by 14 per cent. A notable aspect of this large influx of labour into Israel was the change in skills composition of the labour force. Gandal et al. distinguish between four different types of labour: LTH (less than highschool), HG (high-school graduate), SC (some college), and CG (college graduate). As illustrated in Figure 6.10, compared to the rest of the Israeli population the Russian immigrants had high education levels in the period 1989–96, with much higher shares in the SC and CG categories.

Despite the large influx of workers, particularly of workers with a high education level, there was no noticeable evidence of depressed wages, while the relative wage of high-skilled workers slightly increased (rather than decreased, as might be expected from the high-skill composition of arriving Russians). Gandal et al. point to two forces for explaining these observations. First, since Israel is a small open economy with limited influence on the world price of final goods, the Rybczynski result can be used to understand the constant wage rate, provided Israel increases the (relative) production in sectors requiring high education levels in the production process. Second, if changes in technology in general favour the demand for high education levels, this may explain the

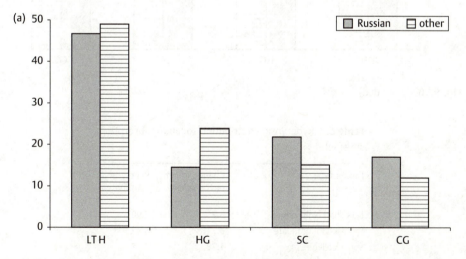

Fig. 6.10 Labour skills composition of Russian immigrants and other Israeli workers (a) 1980, (b) 1989, (c) 1996. LTH = less than high school, HG = high school, SC = some college, CG = college graduate

(*continued overleaf*)

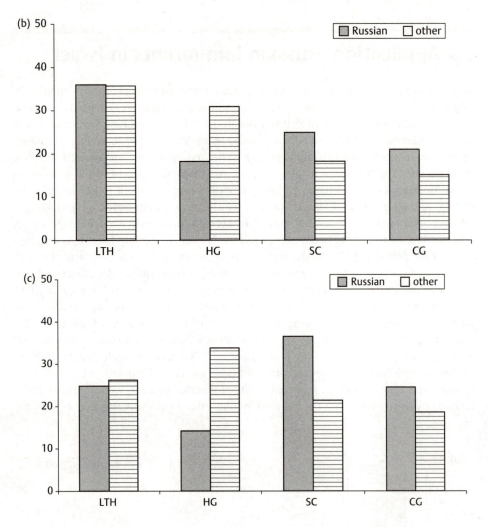

Fig. 6.10 (continued)

Table 6.2 Rybczynski contribution to labour absorption in Israel

Labour type	Change in net factor supply	Rybczynski contribution
Less than high-school	3.25	7.90
High-school graduate	3.71	5.32
Some college	1.78	3.62
College graduate	2.86	2.93

Source: Gandal, Hanson, and Slaughter (2000); change in net factor supply is the change in the factor's share of Israeli employment, corrected for global technology changes.

Box 6.3 **More countries, more goods, and more factors II**

The Rybczynski result discussed in this chapter holds in a weaker sense in a more general setting allowing for more countries, more goods, and more factors of production. An increase in the available amount of a factor of production 'on average' increases the production of goods using this factor intensively in the production process. The magnification effect holds generally, that is an increase in a production factor increases the production level of *some* good ('friend') and reduces the production level of some other good ('enemy').

(small) increase in skill premium in the wage rate. The authors find empirical support for these two explanations in a framework with five factors of production (capital and the four types of labour) and nineteen sectors of production. Table 6.2 reports the estimated Rybczynski contribution to labour absorption in Israel, that is the extent to which a change in a factor's supply can be explained from a change in the composition of output, which ranges from about half for the LTH category to almost completely for the CG category.

6.7 **Conclusions**

We analyse the connection between the production levels of final goods and the available factors of production using the Edgeworth Box. The set of all efficient allocation combinations, leading to maximum output of one good given the output level of the other good, is called the contract curve. The curvature of the contract curve is determined by the difference in capital intensity in the production processes of final goods. For given prices of the final goods, an increase in the available amount of capital leads to an increase in the production of (capital intensive) manufactures and a reduction in the production of food. The opposite holds for an increase in the available amount of labour (Rybczynski effect). We apply this result to discuss the effect of immigration from Russia into Israel in the 1990s. In accordance with the Rybczynski effect, the influx of relatively highly educated Russian workers led to a change in the output composition of final goods production in the direction of high-skill intensive sectors. Countries with a high share of exports in unskilled-labour intensive manufactures are concentrated in South-East Asia and Central Europe.

Technical Notes (optional)

Technical Note 6.1 Determination of the contract curve

To determine the contract curve in the Edgeworth Box it is clear that the slopes of the isoquants must be the same. For the Cobb–Douglas production functions of equation (4.1) these are (see Technical Note 4.3)

$$(6.A1) \qquad \frac{dK_m}{dL_m} = \frac{1 - \alpha_m}{\alpha_m} \frac{K_m}{L_m}; \qquad \frac{dK_f}{dL_f} = \frac{1 - \alpha_f}{\alpha_f} \frac{K_f}{L_f}$$

Setting these two slopes equal to each other and realizing that $K_f = K - K_m$ and $L_f = L - L_m$ gives the following relationship between K_m and L_m

$$(6.A2) \qquad K_m = \frac{\alpha_m (1 - \alpha_f) K L_m}{\alpha_f (1 - \alpha_m) L + (\alpha_m - \alpha_f) L_m}$$

This is the contract curve. Note that if the capital intensity is the same in the two final goods sectors, that is if $\alpha_m = \alpha_f$, the contract curve reduces to a straight line equal to the diagonal of the Edgeworth Box.

Technical Note 6.2 The distribution of capital and labour

Given the total available factors of production capital K and labour L, and the prices of the final goods, and therefore of the wage rate and the rental rate, we can determine the share of labourers working in each sector as follows. Take the ratio of equation (6.1), and let λ_m be the share of the labour force in manufactures, that is $\lambda_m = L_m / L$

$$(6.A3) \qquad \frac{K}{L} = \frac{K_m}{L} + \frac{K_f}{L} = \frac{L_m}{L} \frac{K_m}{L_m} + \frac{L_f}{L} \frac{K_f}{L_f} = \lambda_m \frac{K_m}{L_m} + (1 - \lambda_m) \frac{K_f}{L_f}$$

Now substituting the optimal capital–labour ratios in both sectors as a function of the wage–rental ratio gives

$$(6.A4) \qquad \frac{K}{L} = \lambda_m \frac{\alpha_m}{1 - \alpha_m} \frac{w}{r} + (1 - \lambda_m) \frac{\alpha_f}{1 - \alpha_f} \frac{w}{r}$$

We use this equation to determine the share of labourers in manufactures λ_m

$$(6.A5) \qquad \lambda_m = \frac{(1 - \alpha_m)(1 - \alpha_f)}{\alpha_m - \alpha_f} \frac{(K/L)}{(w/r)} - \frac{\alpha_f (1 - \alpha_m)}{\alpha_m - \alpha_f}$$

This completely determines the distribution of capital and labour over the two final goods sectors. Finally, this distribution of capital and labour can be used to determine the production level for manufactures.

$$(6.A6) \qquad M = K_m^{\alpha_m} L_m^{1 - \alpha_m} = \left(\frac{K_m}{L_m} \right)^{\alpha_m} L_m = \left(\frac{\alpha_m}{1 - \alpha_m} \frac{w}{r} \right)^{\alpha_m} \lambda_m L$$

Similarly, for food.

Chapter 7
Factor Abundance

Objectives/key terms

Heckscher–Ohlin result	Homothetic demand
Rybczynski lines	Marginal rate of substitution (MRS)
Marginal rate of transformation (MRT)	Leontief paradox
Autarky	International trade
General equilibrium	Missing trade

We analyse the connection between the direction of international trade flows and the factor intensity of the production process. Countries tend to export goods making intensive use of the abundant factors of production (Heckscher–Ohlin result). We show the implications of the neoclassical model for a range of countries and discuss some empirical tests of the model.

7.1 Introduction

The fourth and last main result of the neoclassical trade model to be analysed in this book is the Heckscher–Ohlin proposition. Although the principle of the result is not difficult to comprehend, a complete understanding does require knowledge of all aspects of the neoclassical trade model, that is the production structure, the demand structure, and the equilibrium relationships between them. In short, it requires an understanding of the general equilibrium structure of the model. So far, we have not used any assumptions about the demand structure; the factor price equalization proposition, the Stolper–Samuelson proposition, and the Rybczynski proposition are all only dependent on the supply structure of the economy.

The Heckscher–Ohlin proposition relates the abundance of the factors of production in a region or country and the international trade flows of goods and services. As Ohlin (1933, ch. I) remarked in his *Interregional and International Trade*:[1]

Australia has more agricultural land, but less labour, capital, and mines than Great Britain; consequently Australia is better adapted to the production of goods which require great quantities of

---

[1] See Allen (1965: 170).

Fig. 7.1 Bertil Ohlin (1899–1979)

Bertil Ohlin was a Swedish economist who studied at Lund and Stockholm, worked mostly at the Stockholm School of Economics, and was politically active as a member of parliament for thirty-three years and as the leader of the Swedish liberal party. He became well known after his dispute with John Maynard Keynes on the transfer problem, considering the German reparations payments after the First World War. (It was Ohlin, not Keynes, who was right on most issues, see Brakman and van Marrewijk (1998).) His most important work, however, was on the theory of factor abundance, with the publication of *Interregional and International Trade* in 1933, inspired by the work of his old teacher Eli Heckscher. It won him the Nobel prize in economics in 1977.

agricultural land, whereas Great Britain has an advantage in the production of goods requiring considerable quantities of other factors. If both countries produced their own total consumption, agricultural products would be very cheap in Australia, but manufactured articles relatively dear, whereas the reverse would be the case in Great Britain, where owing to the scanty supply of land each acre would have to be intensely cultivated with much labour and capital to provide the necessary amount of food. The utmost economy would have to be exercised with land, and owing to the tendency to diminishing returns the yields of wheat, etc., from the last units of capital and labour would be very small. In Australia, on the other hand, the abundance of land would lead to an extensive method of cultivation, very little labour and capital being expended on each acre; hence the yield from each unit of capital and labour would be great.

Ohlin therefore argues that in autarky, that is if there are no international trade flows, the price of agricultural goods in Australia will be low compared to Great Britain because the production of agricultural goods is relatively land intensive (compared to the production of manufactured goods) and Australia has an abundant supply of agricultural land. This connection results from the fact that the abundant supply of agricultural land leads to a low price for the factor services of land, which are a substantial part of the costs of production of agricultural goods, thus leading to low prices for those goods. Moreover, since the price of agricultural goods is lower in Australia than in Great Britain in autarky, Australia will export those goods if international trade is allowed.

The final result, which can be summarized as 'Australia will export those goods which intensively use the relatively abundant factor of production', is simple to comprehend and intuitively appealing. As is clear from the detailed analysis in the preceding chapters, and the care to be taken in the sequel of this chapter, given the simplicity of the Heckscher–Ohlin proposition it is remarkable how much structure we have to impose on the economy before we can actually conclude that this connection between factor abundance, the capital–labour intensity in the production of final goods, and the direction of international trade flows exists.

7.2 **Heckscher–Ohlin**

We can state the main result of neoclassical trade theory, linking the available factors of production, the relative intensity of the production processes, and the direction of international trade flows as follows.

Heckscher–Ohlin proposition

In a neoclassical framework with two final goods, two factors of production, and two countries which have identical homothetic tastes, a country will export the good which intensively uses the relatively abundant factor of production.

Using the assumption made in Chapter 4 that the production of manufactures is capital intensive thus leads to the following conclusions.

- If a country is relatively capital abundant, it will export manufactures (because its production is capital intensive).
- If a country is relatively labour abundant, it will export food (because its production is labour intensive).

In the demonstration of the Heckscher–Ohlin result below we will use the previous results, in particular the factor price equalization proposition and the Rybczynski proposition. Evidently, the direction of international trade flows in the neoclassical trade model stems from the supply structure of the economy. Indeed, one can argue that the supply side of the economy over the centuries has received much more attention than the demand side of the economy, at least within international economics. Nonetheless, as is evident from the Ohlin quote in section 4.1, we must take the influence of the demand structure into consideration in a general equilibrium setting before we can draw any definite conclusions about the direction of international trade flows. Essentially, this problem is 'solved' by eliminating all demand bias, as explained in the next section.

7.3 **Demand**

Exports of goods and services from one country to another can be viewed as excess supply flows. After all, such exports can be defined as the difference between the quantity of goods produced and consumed within a nation.

(7.1) $$\text{exports} = \text{production} - \text{consumption}$$

International trade flows therefore represent the outcome of the interplay between the supply structure and the demand structure of the economy. The supply structure determines the production level of goods and services in the economy. For the neo-classical trade model, this has been discussed at length in the previous three chapters. The demand structure of the economy determines the consumption level of goods and services in the economy. It will be discussed in this section.

As is immediately evident from equation (7.1), a relationship between the supply structure of an economy and international trade flows can only be derived if we some-how eliminate differences in demand structure between nations. The neoclassical trade model therefore makes the following:

Assumption: all consumers in all countries have identical homothetic preferences.

Rather than discussing what identical homothetic preferences are exactly, we will define a utility function for all consumers in accordance with the assumption above and briefly discuss the main implications of this function, see also Box 7.1. In economics we assume that consumers, that is you, I, and everyone else, try to maximize the utility derived from their income earned (through work or ownership of capital goods), by a suitable choice of consumption of goods and services, in accordance with our preferences. Since we have to pay for our consumption goods and we have a limited income level, this problem can be stated mathematically as a maximization problem. Let C_m be the consumption level of manufactures, let C_f be the consumption level of food, and let I be the income level. Then the consumer's problem involves maximization of the utility function U below (with parameter δ_m), subject to the budget constraint $I = p_m C_m + p_f C_f$:

$$(7.2) \qquad U = C_m^{\delta_m} C_f^{1-\delta_m}; \quad 0 < \delta_m < 1$$

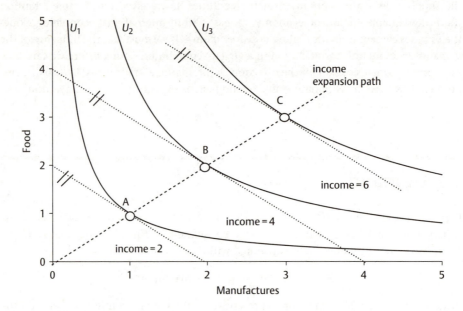

Fig. 7.2 Consumer optimization problem, $p_m = p_f = 1$, $\delta_m = 0.5$

Box 7.1 **Homothetic demand**

The utility function specified in equation (7.2) is an example of a homothetic utility function. As illustrated in Figure 7.2, it gives rise to iso-utility curves that are radial blow-ups of one another, just like the isoquants are radial blow-ups if the production function exhibits constant returns to scale. So why do we distinguish between these two different concepts? Because it is customary to think of preferences as an ordinal concept. It is meaningful to speak of a doubling in output, as is the case if we double all inputs in a constant returns to scale production process, but not of a doubling of utility if we double the consumption levels. We cannot say we are 'twice as happy' if we consume twice as many of all goods, just that we prefer this consumption level over some other consumption combination.

The concept of the utility function is therefore a tool for explaining the optimal choices of consumers; it is a translation of the consumer's preference structure. The numbers attached to the iso-utility curves depicted in Figure 7.3 are arbitrary, only their magnitude is important. More specifically, it must be true that $U_1 < U_2 < U_3$, which holds for the numbers 1, 2, and 3, but also for the numbers 1, 6, and 400. If a utility function is homothetic, the iso-utility curves are radial blow-ups, as in Figure 7.3, and the two conclusions emphasized in the main text (C_m/C_f is a function of p_m/p_f and the distribution of income is not important) still hold.

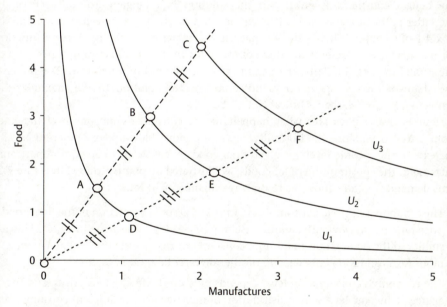

Fig. 7.3 Homothetic iso-utility curves are radial blow-ups

The problem is illustrated in Figure 7.2 for $p_m = p_f = 1$ and $\delta_m = 0.5$. The line 'income = 2' depicts the budget constraint for the consumer if her income level is 2. Any consumption combination on this line or below (to the south-west) is feasible from a budget point of view. The consumer chooses the consumption combination giving maximal utility. Graphically, this occurs at the point of tangency of the budget constraint with an iso-utility curve, that is a curve depicting all consumption combinations giving rise to the same level of utility. In Figure 7.2 this occurs at point A, where the budget constraint is tangent to the U_1 iso-utility curve.

Remark 1: The Marginal Rate of Substitution (MRS) is the absolute value of the slope of an iso-utility curve, that is MRS $= |dC_f/dC_m| = (\partial U/\partial C_m)/(\partial U/\partial C_f)$. It is a measure for the ease with which the consumer can substitute one good for another on the margin and still achieve the same utility level. If consumers take the final goods prices as given, utility maximization implies: MRS $= p_m/p_f$.

Since the utility function (7.2) is of the Cobb–Douglas type, like the production functions (4.1), the reader of course realizes that the consumer's maximization problem is quite similar to the producer's problem of cost minimization. In the former problem, the budget constraint is given and the solution is a tangent iso-utility curve. In the latter problem the isoquant is given and the solution is a tangent isocost line. In Box 4.1 of Chapter 4, it was shown that the parameter α_m in the production function for manufactures represents the share of total cost in the manufacturing sector paid to the capital owners. Similarly, the parameter δ_m in the utility function (7.2) represents the share of income spent on manufactures as the solution to the maximization problem ($p_m C_m = \delta_m I$, see Technical Note 7.1).

Figure 7.2 also illustrates what happens if the consumer's income level increases from 2 to 4 or 6. Since the iso-utility curves are radial blow-ups of one another, any increase in the income level, for given final goods prices, leads to an equiproportional increase in the consumption of all goods, as illustrated by points B and C in Figure 7.2. This demand structure allows us to draw two main conclusions:

- The economy's optimal consumption ratio C_m/C_f is only a function of the final goods price ratio p_m/p_f. Obviously, an increase in p_m/p_f leads to a decrease in C_m/C_f. This is similar to the observation that under constant returns to scale the capital–labour ratios K_m/L_f and K_f/L_f only depend on the wage–rental ratio w/r.

- The economy's consumption level depends only on the final goods prices, and the aggregate income level I. The distribution of income over the different consumers in the economy is not relevant for determining the aggregate consumption levels.

The second observation is also clear from Figure 7.2. Suppose the aggregate income level is 8. If this income level is equally divided over 2 consumers, they both consume at point B. The aggregate consumption level is then 2B. If one of the consumers receives 6 income and the other consumer receives 2 income, then the first consumer consumes at point C and the second at point A. Aggregate income is then $A + C = 2B$. Similarly, for any other distribution of income.

7.4 **The production possibility frontier**

We will illustrate and discuss the Heckscher–Ohlin proposition in the sequel using the production possibility frontier (ppf) introduced in Chapter 3. To do that we will first have to discuss some of the properties of the ppf in the neoclassical production structure. Recall that the frontier depicts all efficient production combinations in final goods space, that is the maximum output of food for any given feasible production level of manufactures. Similarly, in Chapter 6 we showed that the contract curve in the Edgeworth Box depicts all efficient input combinations. Since the contract curve was derived explicitly, see Technical Note 6.1, it is not hard to calculate all efficient output combinations, which is the ppf.[2] The result is depicted in Figure 7.4.

As the reader can see, in contrast to the Ricardian ppf of Chapter 3, which is a straight line, the ppf in the neoclassical trade model is curved. This arises from the difference in the degree of capital intensity between the two final goods sectors, which makes one sector more responsive to changes in capital input and the other sector more responsive to changes in labour input. As with the contract curve in the Edgeworth Box (illustrated in Figure 6.6), the larger the difference in capital intensity, the more pronounced the curvature of the ppf, as illustrated in Figure 7.5.

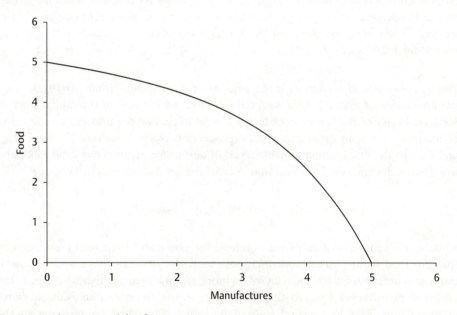

Fig. 7.4 Production possibility frontier; $K = L = 5$; $\alpha_m = 0.8$; $\alpha_f = 0.1$

---

[2] The contract curve gives K_m as a function of L_m. The inputs for food can be calculated using $K_f = K - K_m$ and $L_f = L - L_m$. Using the production functions, the output levels can be determined. It is not possible to write the production possibility frontier as an explicit function.

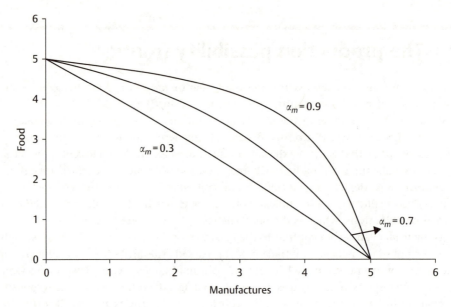

Fig. 7.5 Production possibility frontiers; impact of changing α_m; $\alpha_f = 0.1$

Remark 2: The Marginal Rate of Transformation (MRT) is the absolute value of the slope of the production possibility frontier |dF/dM|. It is a measure for the ease with which the producers can technically substitute the production of one good for another on the margin. If factor markets are perfectly competitive, and MC denotes marginal costs of production, the following relationship holds: MRT = MC$_m$/MC$_f$.

The ppf of course also changes if the amount of the available inputs changes. Since the production of manufactures is capital intensive, an increase in the capital stock K, for a fixed value of the labour stock L, has a larger impact on the maximum production of manufactures than on the maximum production of food. Indeed, if we let M_{max} and F_{max} be the maximum attainable levels of output for manufactures and food, and use relative changes (see Technical note 5.2) for the production functions, we get

$$(7.3) \qquad \tilde{M}_{max} = \alpha_m \tilde{K} + (1 - \alpha_m)\tilde{L}; \quad \tilde{F}_{max} = \alpha_f \tilde{K} + (1 - \alpha_f)\tilde{L}$$

Since $\alpha_m > \alpha_f$, the maximum production level for manufactures increases more rapidly than for food if the capital stock increases. Similarly, since $1 - \alpha_f > 1 - \alpha_m$ the maximum production level for food increases more rapidly than for manufactures if the labour stock increases. The fact that an increase in the amount of an available factor of production leads to a biased shift of the ppf is illustrated for increases in the capital stock in Figure 7.6.

Figure 7.6 also illustrates another aspect of changes in output that will be useful in the discussion below. Recall that the Rybczynski proposition relates changes in the available amount of a factor of production and changes in output for given final goods prices. We

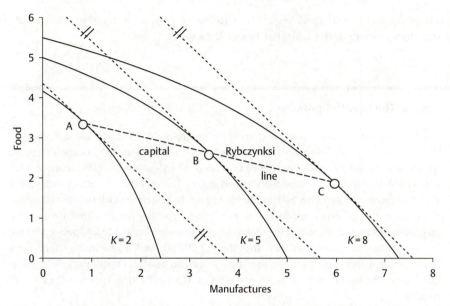

Fig. 7.6 Impact of a change in capital on the ppf and the Rybczynski line, $L = 5$, $\alpha_m = 0.8$, $\alpha_f = 0.2$

Chapter 7 tool: Rybczynski lines

The Rybczynski proposition states that an increase in the available amount of one of the factors of production for given final goods prices leads to an increase in the output of the good that uses this factor intensively, and a fall in the output of the other good, provided both goods are produced. Moreover, the proof of the Rybczynski proposition in Chapter 6, using the Edgeworth Box, made it clear that the changes are equiproportional, that is a doubling in the change of the factor of production leads to a doubling of the changes in output. In final goods space this equiproportionality leads to straight lines (called Rybczynski lines) connecting output changes starting from some equilibrium. Since there are two factors of production, capital and labour, there are two Rybczynski lines, a capital Rybczynski line and a labour Rybczynski line. This is illustrated in Figure 7.6 and further discussed in the main text.

---

can illustrate the proposition in final goods space, for example by increasing the capital stock, as in Figure 7.6. If the capital stock is 2, the economy produces at point A for some ratio of final goods prices. For the same final goods prices, but a higher capital stock of 5, the economy produces at point B. The output of the capital intensive manufactures has increased, that of the labour intensive food has decreased. Similarly, if the capital stock is 8 for that final goods price ratio, the economy produces at point C. Since the changes in the Rybczynski proposition are equiproportional, the points A, B, and C are on a straight line. It is called the capital Rybczynski line and traces out all changes in output for changes in the capital stock from 2 to 8, for given final goods prices and labour stock (equal to 5 in Figure 7.6). If we analyse changes in the labour stock, we can derive a similar labour Rybczynski line.

Box 7.2 **The Leontief paradox**

The first, and most famous, empirical study of the neoclassical trade model was performed by Wassily Leontief (1956). Using trade data and factor intensities for the USA, Leontief computed the amount of capital and labour required to produce $1 million worth of US exports in 1951 and $1 million worth of US import-competing goods. Thinking that the USA was a capital abundant country, he expected to show, on the basis of the Heckscher–Ohlin result discussed in this chapter, that US export production is more capital intensive than US import competing production. Instead, he found that the capital–labour ratio was roughly $13,000 per worker year in the export sector, which was *lower* than the $13,700 per worker year in the import competing sector. It appeared, therefore, that the USA was, on balance, importing capital services from abroad through its trade of goods and services. This has become known as the Leontief paradox.

Various explanations have been suggested to solve the Leontief paradox. First, it could be that there is a demand bias, in which case the USA would consume more capital intensive products than other countries, see Chapter 17. Second, there could be a so-called factor-intensity reversal, in which case, for example, the production of manufactures is more capital intensive in the rest of the world while the production of food is more capital intensive in the USA, making it impossible to estimate the foreign factor intensities using US data, as Leontief did. More important, however, seems to be the third explanation, put forward by Jaroslav Vanek (1959), who argued that the 2 × 2 × 2 framework is too restrictive and we should

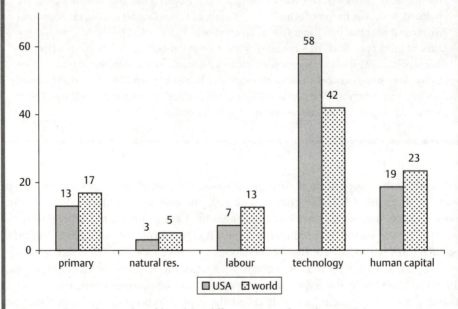

Fig. 7.7 Share of US and world trade in different types of goods 1998 (%)

distinguish between more types of goods and more factors of production. Theoretical work by Vanek showed that in a more general setting a weaker version of the Heckscher–Ohlin result holds, that is a country tends to export goods and services which 'on average' make intensive use of the abundant factors of production. See section 7.9 for an empirical discussion.

Figure 7.7 illustrates the argument that we should take more factors of production into consideration. Various special interest boxes in Chapters 4–8 briefly discuss the ICT data distinguishing between five types of products: primary, natural-resource intensive, unskilled-labour intensive, technology intensive, and human-capital intensive. Figure 7.7 shows that (i) by far the largest share of US exports is in technology intensive and human-capital intensive products, and (ii) when compared to the world average the USA has a revealed comparative advantage only in technology intensive products (discussed further in Box 7.3). Neither observation is controversial.

7.5 Structure of the equilibrium

The Heckscher–Ohlin result concentrates on the structure of international trade flows in a trading equilibrium. It is therefore useful to review the general equilibrium structure of the neoclassical trade model, as summarized in Figure 7.8.

There are five types of economic agents, namely (i) labourers, (ii) capital owners, (iii) consumers, (iv) producers of manufactures, and (v) producers of food. Note that these are functional distinctions; the same person could be a producer of manufactures, a capital owner, and a consumer at the same time. Also note that Figure 7.8 distinguishes between two types of flows; namely the flows of goods and services, indicated by closed-point arrows, and money flows, indicated by open-point arrows. These two flows always move in opposite directions.

- The *labourers* supply their services to produce either manufactures or food. In return they receive a remuneration called the wage rate. Since labour is perfectly mobile between the two sectors, the wage rate is the same in the two sectors.

- The *capital owners* supply their services to produce either manufactures or food. In return they receive a remuneration called the rental rate. Since capital is perfectly mobile between the two sectors, the rental rate is the same in the two sectors.

- Both labourers and capital owners earn an income, which they use to spend on manufactures and food as *consumers*. Since production takes place under perfect competition and constant returns to scale, there are no profits generated in the economy. The only income available for consumption is therefore generated by supplying labour services and capital services.

- The *producers of manufactures* hire labour services on the labour market, for which they pay the wage rate, and capital services on the capital market, for which they pay the

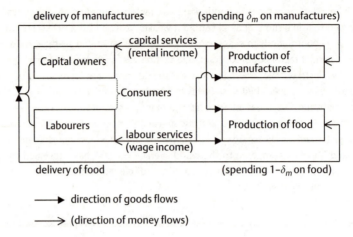

delivery of manufactures (spending δ_m on manufactures)

delivery of food (spending $1-\delta_m$ on food)

$\longrightarrow$ direction of goods flows

$\longrightarrow$ (direction of money flows)

Fig. 7.8 Equilibrium structure

rental rate. They use these services in the most efficient way to produce manufactures, which they sell to consumers at the price p_m.

- Similarly, for the *producers of food*.

The economy is in equilibrium if six conditions are fulfilled, namely (i) consumers maximize their utility, (ii) producers maximize their profits, (iii) all labourers are employed, (iv) all capital is used, (v) the supply of manufactures is equal to the demand for manufactures, and (vi) the supply of food is equal to the demand for food. In the next two sections we will distinguish between two types of equilibria:

- The *autarky equilibrium*, in which the above six equilibrium relationships hold at the national level; there is no cross-border activity whatsoever.

- The *international trade equilibrium*, in which the above six relationships hold at the global level for the final goods markets, and at the national level for the factors of production. There is therefore no impediment to cross-border trade for final goods (at zero transport costs), while capital and labour services cannot move across borders.

7.6 Autarky equilibrium

Figure 7.9a illustrates the autarky equilibrium if there is an equal supply of capital and labour ($K=L=5$), the cost share of capital in manufactures is 0.8 ($\alpha_m=0.8$), the cost share of capital in food is 0.2 ($\alpha_f=0.2$), and the share of income spent on manufactures is 0.6 ($\delta_m=0.6$). As Figure 7.9 shows, the ppf is tangent to the income line generated by the autarky production point; that is the Marginal Rate of Transformation

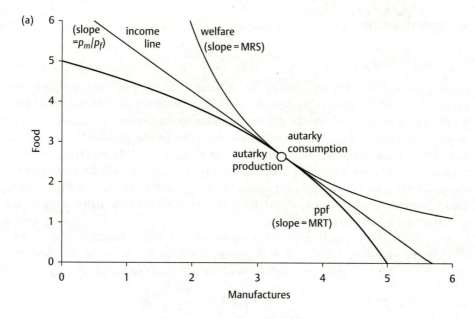

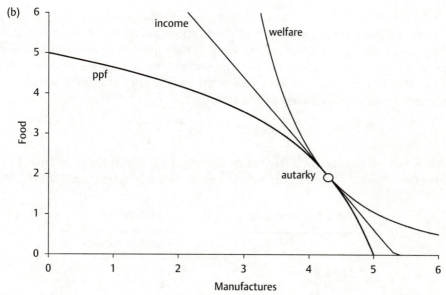

Fig. 7.9 Autarky production and consumption (a) $K = L = 5$, $\alpha_m = 0.8$, $\alpha_f = 0.2$, $\delta_m = 0.6$; (b) $K = L = 5$, $\alpha_m = 0.9$, $\alpha_f = 0.2$, $\delta_m = 0.8$

MRT is equal to the final goods price ratio p_m/p_f because producers maximize profits and markets are perfectly competitive. Similarly, the iso-utility curve is tangent to the income line generated by the production point; that is the Marginal Rate of Substitution MRS is equal to the final goods price ratio p_m/p_f because consumers maximize utility and take prices as given. The autarky equilibrium is therefore characterized by (the sub-index 'au' refers to autarky):

$$(7.4) \qquad MRT_{au} = \left(\frac{p_m}{p_f}\right)_{au} = MRS_{au}$$

Clearly, given the restrictions facing the economy (no international contacts), the autarky equilibrium achieves the best possible outcome; at the equilibrium production point, which is also the equilibrium consumption point, welfare is maximized. The autarky equilibrium depends, of course, on the value of the parameters, the capital and labour stock available, the production functions, the utility function, etc. This is illustrated in Figure 7.9b, with a higher value for the capital intensity parameter for manufactures ($\alpha_m = 0.9 > 0.8$), which results in a more curved ppf, and a higher share of income spent on manufactures ($\delta_m = 0.8 > 0.6$), which results in a higher demand for manufactures relative to food.

Given the Cobb–Douglas production functions and utility function, the autarky equilibrium wage–rental ratio and final goods price ratio can be explicitly calculated, see Technical Note 7.2 (also for a definition of the parameter γ_{au}).

$$(7.5) \qquad \left(\frac{w}{r}\right)_{au} = \underbrace{\gamma_{au}}_{constant} \frac{K}{L}; \quad \left(\frac{p_m}{p_f}\right)_{au} = \frac{\gamma_m}{\gamma_f} \left(\frac{w}{r}\right)_{au}^{-(\alpha_m - \alpha_f)}$$

Both the wage–rental ratio and the final goods price ratio are simple functions of the *relative* factor abundance K/L of the economy. If the capital stock increases relative to the labour stock, the wage–rental ratio rises since labour becomes relatively more scarce. This, in turn, results in a decrease of the relative price of manufactures, which uses capital relatively intensively (see Chapter 5).

$$\text{To summarize}: \qquad \frac{K}{L} \uparrow \Leftrightarrow \frac{w}{r} \uparrow \Leftrightarrow \frac{p_m}{p_f} \downarrow$$

Since we are particularly interested in the effect of differences in relative factor abundance, Table 7.1 specifies the autarky equilibrium for 'Austria' and 'Bolivia'. The

Table 7.1 Autarky values for 'Austria' and 'Bolivia'

	Austria	Bolivia
Capital K	7	3
Labour L	3	7
Share of income δ_m spent manufactures	0.6	0.6
Capital parameter α_m manufactures	0.8	0.8
Capital parameter α_f food	0.2	0.2
Wage–rental w/r	1.83	0.34
Price manufactures/price food; (p_m/p_f)	0.70	1.92
Welfare level	2.96	2.67
Production of manufactures	4.03	2.42
Production of food	1.87	3.10

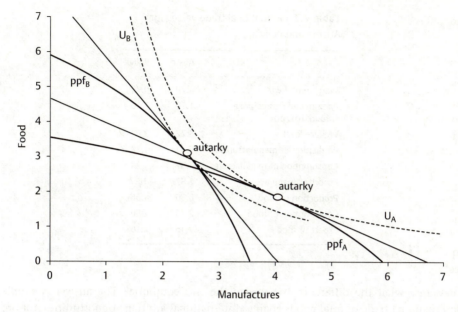

Fig. 7.10 Autarky equilibrium

values *above* the double line in Table 7.1 are *exogenously specified* parameters. All values *below* the double line in Table 7.1 are *endogenously determined* by the conditions of the autarky equilibrium. Austria is capital abundant relative to Bolivia $(7/3 > 3/7)$. Therefore, Austria's ppf is biased towards the production of manufactures, and it produces relatively more of manufactures in autarky. Note from Table 7.1 that the relative price of manufactures is higher in Bolivia in autarky, as illustrated in Figure 7.10.

7.7 International trade equilibrium

The international trade equilibrium is also characterized by utility maximization and profit maximization. Since the former leads to equality of the marginal rate of substitution and the final goods price ratio, and the latter leads to equality of the marginal rate of transformation and the final goods price ratio, the international trade equilibrium is summarized by (the sub-index 'tr' refers to trade):

$$(7.6) \qquad MRT_{tr} = \left(\frac{p_m}{p_f}\right)_{tr} = MRS_{tr}$$

Since the same equalities between the marginal rate of substitution, the price ratio, and the marginal rate of transformation hold in the autarky equilibrium, the question

Table 7.2 International trade values for
Austria and Bolivia

	Austria	Bolivia
Wage–rental w/r	0.79	0.79
Price manufactures/price food; (p_m/p_f)	1.16	1.16
Welfare level	3.22	2.92
Production of manufactures	5.44	1.38
Consumption of manufactures	3.57	3.24
Export of manufactures	1.87	− 1.87
Production of food	0.60	4.66
Consumption of food	2.75	2.50
Export of food	− 2.16	2.16

may arise what the difference is between the two equilibria? The answer is simple, international trade of final goods enables international arbitrage opportunities not previously available. The crucial aspect is to realize that although the autarky equilibrium is efficient given the imposed restriction of no trade, which leads to $MRT = p_m/p_f = MRS$ in both countries, it is not efficient if international trade is possible because the autarky prices are different in the two countries. Thus, in autarky $MRT = p_m/p_f = MRS$ holds *within* countries, but not *between* countries. It is this aspect which makes international trade and gains from trade possible.

The international trade equilibrium is summarized in Table 7.2 and illustrated in Figure 7.11.[3] International arbitrage opportunities arising from the costless trade of final goods ensures that the prices of food and manufactures must be the same in the two countries in the international trade equilibrium; the relative price with trade is in between the two autarky equilibrium prices

$$(7.7) \qquad \left(\frac{p_m}{p_f}\right)^{Austria}_{au} < \left(\frac{p_m}{p_f}\right)_{tr} < \left(\frac{p_m}{p_f}\right)^{Bolivia}_{au}$$

For Austria the relative price of manufactures rises in trade relative to autarky. The production of manufactures therefore increases (and that of food falls); the production shifts from point aut_A in Figure 7.11 to point pr_A. Simultaneously, the higher relative price for manufactures in Austria results in a substitution away from manufactures on the consumption side in Austria; the consumption ratio C_f/C_m rises from the ratio in point aut_A to the ratio in point co_A. In the international trade equilibrium, the production point pr_A for Austria no longer coincides with the consumption point co_A for Austria. There is, of course, a link between these two points, since the total value of

---

[3] We have made it easy for ourselves to calculate the equilibrium because both countries produce both goods in the international trade equilibrium. This is not necessary, see below and the study guide.

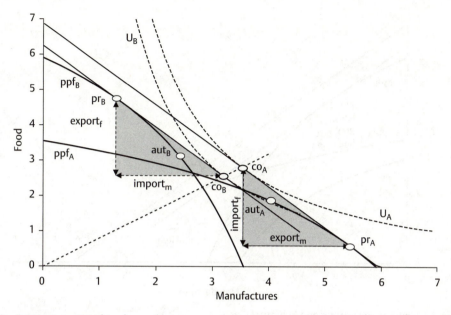

Fig. 7.11 International trade equilibrium

the expenditures on consumption cannot exceed the total value of income generated by the production level in the economy.[4] That is, the consumption point must be on the income line generated by the production point of Austria, with a slope equal to the international price ratio p_m/p_f, see Figure 7.11. Clearly, Austria now produces more manufactures than it consumes. It will therefore export manufactures in exchange for imports of food. Finally, we note that the welfare level achieved by Austria rises; the new consumption point co_A is on a higher iso-utility curve than at point aut_A.[5]

In Bolivia opposite changes take place. The relative price of manufactures falls, such that Bolivia produces less manufactures and more food. Simultaneously, the consumption mix in Bolivia moves in the direction of manufactures. Bolivia therefore produces more food than it consumes, which it will export in exchange for imports of manufactures. This allows Bolivia also to reach a higher welfare level. On a global scale the international trade flows improve efficiency. The world production of manufactures rises by 5.7 per cent from 6.45 to 6.82, and the world production of food rises by 5.8 per cent from 4.97 to 5.26. Note also that the international trade equilibrium requires that the excess demand for manufactures by Bolivia, that is its imports of manufactures, must be equal to the excess supply of manufactures by Austria, that is its exports of manufactures. The two *trade triangles* in Figure 7.11 must coincide.

Figure 7.12 proves the Heckscher–Ohlin proposition using Rybczynski lines. Let's again concentrate on Austria. Note that the global capital–labour ratio K/L is equal to $(7+3)/(3+7) = 1$. This is lower than Austria's capital–labour ratio, which is 7/3. If we

---

[4] At least if there is no international borrowing or lending in the period under consideration, or if the values are measured in present value terms.

[5] The same conclusion follows from revealed preference.

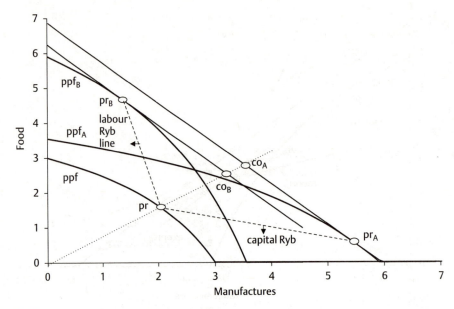

Fig 7.12 International trade and Rybczynski lines

now take away capital from Austria until its capital–labour ratio is equal to the global capital–labour ratio (in this case until its capital stock is 3), its output level will move along the capital Rybczynski line for given final goods prices until it reaches production point pr. In Figure 7.12 the ppf if $K=L=3$ is also drawn, and labelled ppf. At point pr the demand for food is equal to the supply of food. Moving in the opposite direction, thus adding capital, we know that at given final goods prices the demand for food increases because the income level increases and (from the Rybczynski proposition) the supply of food decreases because food is labour intensive. Thus Austria, which is capital abundant, must import the labour intensive food, and thus export the capital intensive manufactures. A similar conclusion can be reached for Bolivia exporting the labour intensive food using the labour Rybczynski line. Note that, to avoid cluttering the diagram, the distribution of capital and labour over the two countries was chosen such that Bolivia's labour Rybczynski line reaches the same production point pr. In general, of course, this is not the case.

Box 7.3 **Technology intensive manufacturing exporters**

The ITC classifies seventy-one goods as 'technology intensive manufacturing' products, incorporating various chemicals, medicaments, plastics, engines, generators, machines, tools, pumps, telecommunications and photo equipment, optical equipment, and aircraft. For the 151 countries for which the ITC provides data, total exports of technology intensive manufactures in 1998 were equal to $2,022 bn, some 42 per cent of all exports. This makes technology intensive manufactures by far the largest of the five categories identified by the ITC in terms of international trade flows. The left-hand side of Table 7.3 lists the top ten exporters of technology

Table 7.3 Top ten technology intensive manufacturing exporters, 1998

No.	Top 10 in absolute terms			Top 10 in relative terms		
	Country	Exports		Country	Exports	
		Value	%		%	Value
1	United States	354	58	Singapore	76	77
2	Germany	240	48	Ireland	70	43
3	Japan	212	56	Malta	69	1
4	United Kingdom	137	53	Philippines	69	20
5	France	124	43	Taiwan	59	70
6	Singapore	77	76	United States	58	354
7	The Netherlands	74	46	Switzerland	58	45
8	Italy	73	37	Japan	56	212
9	Taiwan	70	59	Malaysia	55	40
10	Belgium	54	33	United Kingdom	53	137

Source: WTO/UNCTAD International Trade Centre website http://www.intracen.org; value in bn. US $. The % shares are relative to the country's total exports.

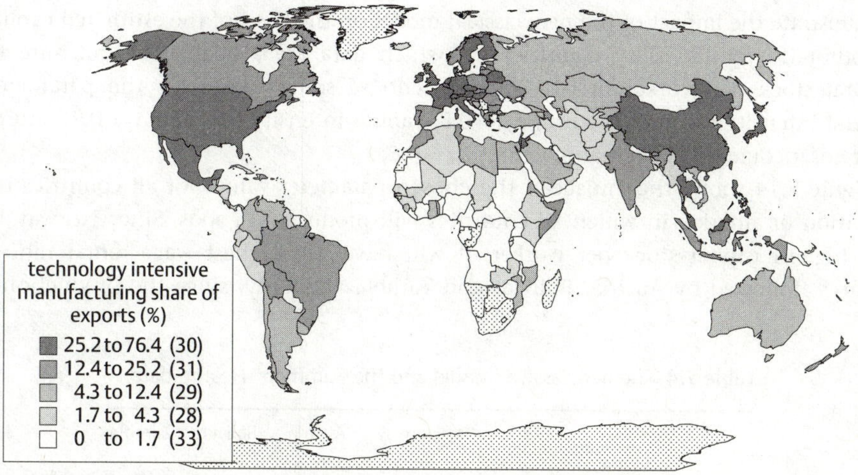

Fig. 7.13 Technology intensive manufacturing exports, shares 1998

intensive manufactures in absolute terms. With an impressive value of $354 bn the USA is the world's largest technology intensive manufactures exporter, including semiconductors, computers, and aircraft. The USA is followed by Germany ($240 bn; medicine and machinery) and Japan ($212 bn; semiconductors). With the exception of Taiwan, the other large exporters are all OECD countries.

For the first time since we started to discuss the factor intensity of exports in these special interest boxes (see Chapters 4–6) some of the world's ten largest exporters in absolute terms also make it to the list of the world's ten largest exporters in relative terms. As the right-hand side of Table 7.3 indicates, this holds for Singapore, Taiwan, USA, Japan, and the UK. The top three in relative terms is formed by Singapore (computer chips and semiconductors), Ireland (computers and computer chips), and Malta (semiconductors). Figure 7.13 shows the relative dependence of countries on the exports of technology intensive manufactures. These are clearly concentrated in the rich OECD countries.

7.8 Application: the Summers–Heston data

We can use the empirical capital–labour ratio estimated for a range of countries in the Summers–Heston database, see Box 4.1, to better illustrate the functioning of the neo-classical model (and to show that complete specialization is possible). The illustrations below will use the observations for all countries for which data are available, but the discussion will focus on four relatively small countries: Norway, Austria, Bolivia, and Zambia. Of these four countries Norway had the highest capital per worker ($48,100), followed by Austria ($34,600), Bolivia ($570), and Zambia ($130), see Table 7.4. To illustrate the impact of the neoclassical model on the basis of the estimated capital–labour ratio for the sixty countries for which data are available, we measure the capital stock per worker in $10,000 and choose some values for the parameters; capital intensity for manufactures $\alpha_m = 0.8$, capital intensity for food $\alpha_f = 0.2$, and the share of income spent on manufactures $\delta_m = 0.6$.

Figure 7.14 shows the impact of the chosen parameter values for all countries in a situation of autarky, in which all countries will produce all goods. Since Norway has the highest capital stock per worker, it will have the highest wage–rental ratio in autarky, followed by Austria, Bolivia, and Zambia. Similarly, since the production of

Table 7.4 The neoclassical model and the Summers–Heston data

	Norway	Austria	Bolivia	Zambia
Capital per worker	4.81	3.46	0.57	0.13
Autarky wage–rental	2.95	2.12	0.35	0.08
Autarky price manufactures/food	0.52	0.64	1.88	4.46
Autarky production manufactures	2.65	2.04	0.48	0.15
Autarky production food	0.59	0.56	0.39	0.29
Trade wage–rental	1.20	1.04	1.04	0.54
Trade price manufactures/food	0.98	0.98	0.98	0.98
Trade production manufactures	3.52	2.56	0.25	0.00
Trade production food	0.00	0.14	0.70	0.67

Note: Capital stock per worker $\times$ $10,000, parameters: $\alpha_m = 0.8$; $\alpha_f = 0.2$; $\delta_m = 0.6$.

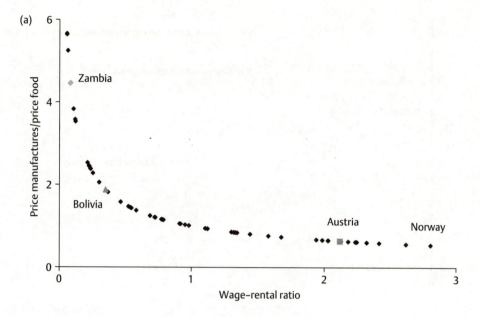

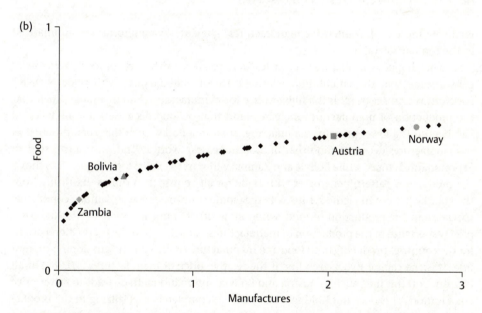

Fig. 7.14 Autarky values

manufactures is capital intensive and Norway is capital abundant, the relative price of manufactures is lowest in autarky in Norway, followed by Austria, Bolivia, and Zambia. Both observations are illustrated in Figure 7.14*a*. The impact of the capital stock per worker on the production of food and manufactures per worker in autarky is shown in Figure 7.14*b*. Clearly, as the capital stock per worker increases countries produce

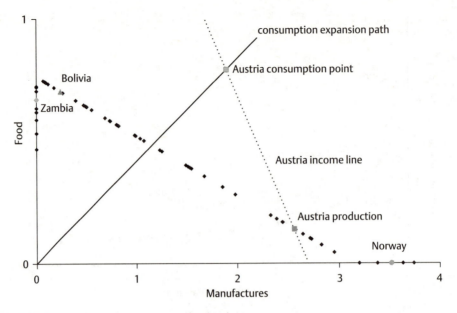

Fig. 7.15 Free trade production per worker levels

relatively more capital intensive manufactures. The autarky equilibrium is summarized in the top part of Table 7.4.

So what happens if all these countries start to trade with each other at zero costs? Let's assume that the equilibrium relative price of manufactures with trade is 0.98.[6] For Norway and Austria this is a higher price for manufactures than in autarky, such that the production of manufactures increases (and that of food decreases). For Bolivia and Zambia this is a lower price for manufactures than in autarky, such that their production of manufactures decreases (and that of food increases). Norway and Austria will start to export manufactures, while Bolivia and Zambia will start to export food. Figure 7.15 shows the production pattern per worker with trade for all countries. It differs drastically from the autarky pattern in Figure 7.14*b*. Note that some countries, such as Zambia, completely specialize in the production of food, while some other countries, such as Norway, completely specialize in the production of manufactures. Also note that the production pattern for the countries producing both food and manufactures is on a downward sloping straight line. It is the capital Rybczynski line if the relative price of manufactures is 0.98. For all countries on this line, such as Austria and Bolivia, international trade leads to factor price equalization. This does not hold for the countries completely specializing in the production of one good, such as Norway and Zambia, where the wage rate and rental rate must clear the local factor markets. Note, however, from Table 7.4 that, as suggested by Ohlin, there is a tendency for factor prices to become more equal as a result of international trade (the wage–rental ratio falls in Norway and rises in Zambia).

Figure 7.15 also shows the consumption expansion path. All countries below this line will export manufactures, those above will export food. We have also drawn the

---

[6] This value would result if all countries were perfectly integrated (capital and labour mobility).

income line generated by the production level per worker for Austria. The point of intersection with the consumption expansion path determines the Austrian consumption point. Clearly countries with a high capital stock per worker, such as Austria, will be able to generate more income per worker and consume more of both food and manufactures than countries with a low capital stock per worker. Differences in the capital stock per worker can therefore partially explain differences in welfare, see also Chapter 16.

7.9 **The case of the missing trade**

The first thorough analysis of the more general neoclassical trade model (more countries, more goods, and more factors) was performed by Bowen, Leamer, and Sveikauskas (1987). This section, however, discusses the more recent study of Daniel Trefler (1995), who analyses trade flows between thirty-three countries together accounting for 76 per cent of world exports and 79 per cent of world GNP. Trefler distinguishes nine factors of production: capital, cropland, pasture, and six labour categories (professional and technical workers, clerical workers, sales workers, service workers, agricultural workers, and production, transport, and unskilled workers).

The empirical success of the more general neoclassical trade model is modest: when the predicted sign of the net factor content of trade is weighted by size the model explains about 71 per cent. As Trefler (1995: 1031) puts it, this is 'uncomfortably close to the coin-toss alternative of 50 percent'. The important contribution of Trefler's work rests in the way he continues, by providing a detailed analysis of the deviations between empirical trade flows and predicted trade flows. He shows, in particular, that the factor service trade is much smaller than its factor-endowments prediction, a phenomenon referred to by him as 'the case of the missing trade'.

Trefler investigates several alternative hypotheses which may explain the case of the missing trade in conjunction with the neoclassical trade model, finding empirical support for two additions, namely (i) differences in technology and (ii) demand bias:

(i) The neoclassical model analysed in Part II of this book assumes that countries have access to the same technology. Trefler argues, however, that there are technology differences between countries, and that incorporating these differences (in a neutral way) increases the goodness-of-fit from 71 to 78 per cent. Obviously, we have already discussed the impact of technology differences on international trade in the classical model of Part I of this book.

(ii) It is generally observed that consumers display a bias toward domestically produced goods, see Armington (1969). Allowing for Armington-type demand bias in the neoclassical model increases the goodness-of-fit from 71 to 87 per cent. The impact of demand differences on international trade is further discussed in Chapter 17. Incorporating both technology differences and Armington demand in the model increases the goodness-of-fit even further to 93 per cent.

7.10 Conclusions

We analyse the connection between the direction of international trade flows and the factor intensity of the production process in the general equilibrium structure of the neoclassical trade model. In autarky, countries with a high capital–labour ratio will have a high wage–rental ratio (since labour is relatively scarce) and a low relative price for the capital intensive good. Allowing for free trade of final goods at no costs equalizes the final goods prices in the two countries, as well as the wage rate and the rental rate (provided both goods are produced in both countries; FPE proposition). Since the relative price of the capital intensive good rises compared to autarky for the capital abundant country (which raises the rental rate and reduces the wage rate; Stolper–Samuelson proposition), this country starts to produce more capital intensive goods, which will be exported in exchange for the labour intensive good. The opposite holds for the labour abundant country (Heckscher–Ohlin proposition). As a result of improved efficiency at the global level, welfare increases in both countries in the international trade equilibrium compared to autarky. The model performs reasonably well empirically, provided we also take into consideration technology differences (Part I of this book) and demand bias (see Chapter 17).

Technical Notes (optional)

Technical Note 7.1 Utility maximization

The problem for a consumer who wants to maximize utility, given the income level I and the prices of final goods p_m and p_f, by choosing the consumption levels C_m and C_f is specified as:

(7.A1)
$$\max_{C_m, C_f} C_m^{\delta_m} C_f^{1-\delta_m} \quad s.t. \quad I = p_m C_m + p_f C_f$$

To solve this problem we define the Lagrangean Γ, using the Lagrange multiplier λ:

(7.A2)
$$\Gamma = C_m^{\delta_m} C_f^{1-\delta_m} + \lambda[1 - p_m C_m - p_f C_f]$$

Derive the two first order conditions $\partial\Gamma/\partial C_m = \partial\Gamma/\partial C_f = 0$ for an optimum and note

(7.A3)
$$\lambda p_m = \delta_m C_m^{\delta_m - 1} C_f^{1-\delta_m}; \quad \lambda p_f = (1 - \delta_m) C_m^{\delta_m} C_f^{-\delta_m}$$

Taking the ratio of these two conditions and simplifying determines the optimal spending ratio $p_m C_m / p_f C_f = \delta_m / (1 - \delta_m)$. Using this in the budget constraint gives

$$(7.A4) \qquad I = p_m C_m + p_f C_f = p_m C_m + \frac{1 - \delta_m}{\delta_m} p_m C_m = \frac{1}{\delta_m} p_m C_m \Rightarrow p_c C_m = \delta_m I$$

Thus, the share δ_m of income is spent on manufactures, and the share $1 - \delta_m$ on food.

Technical Note 7.2 Derivation of the autarky equilibrium

To derive the autarky equilibrium, we first note that the structure of the utility function ensures that the agents always want to consume a positive amount of both goods. Since these goods cannot be imported from abroad, both goods have to be produced in our own country. We can therefore use the factor price equalization proposition, the Stolper–Samuelson proposition, and the Rybczynski proposition whenever convenient, all of which require the economy to produce both goods in equilibrium. The demand for manufactures is given in equation (7.4) as a function of income I and price p_m. Since the only income generated in the economy in equilibrium derives from the supply of labour or capital, total income is given by

$$(7.A5) \qquad I = wL + rK = r\left(\frac{w}{r}L + K\right)$$

Furthermore, in Chapter 5 it was shown that there is a one-to-one correspondence between the rewards to factors of production and the price of final goods. In particular, if the wage rate w and the rental rate r are known, equation (5.3) gives the prices p_m and p_f. Using this equation, it follows that

$$(7.A6) \qquad \frac{r}{p_m} = \frac{r}{\gamma_m r^{\alpha_m} w^{1-\alpha_m}} = \frac{1}{\gamma_m}\left(\frac{w}{r}\right)^{\alpha_m - 1}; \quad \frac{p_m}{p_f} = \frac{\gamma_m}{\gamma_f} \frac{r^{\alpha_m} w^{1-\alpha_m}}{r^{\alpha_f} w^{1-\alpha_f}} = \frac{\gamma_m}{\gamma_f}\left(\frac{w}{r}\right)^{-(\alpha_m - \alpha_f)}$$

Using these results in the demand function for manufactures, we get

$$(7.A7) \qquad C_m = \delta_m \frac{I}{p_m} = \delta_m \frac{r}{p_m}\left(\frac{w}{r}L + K\right) = \delta_m \frac{1}{\gamma_m}\left(\frac{w}{r}\right)^{\alpha_m - 1}\left(\frac{w}{r}L + K\right)$$

This gives us the demand for manufactures as a function of the wage–rental ratio w/r. If both goods are produced, the Rybczynski analysis of Chapter 6 and the full employment conditions determine the production level of manufactures, also as a function of the wage–rental ratio w/r, see Technical Note 6.2. Equating demand for and supply of manufactures gives us, after some algebra, the autarky equilibrium wage–rental ratio

$$(7.A8) \qquad \left(\frac{w}{r}\right)_{au} = \gamma_{au}\frac{K}{L}; \quad \gamma_{au} \equiv \frac{(1 - \alpha_f) - \delta_m(\alpha_m - \alpha_f)}{\alpha_f + \delta_m(\alpha_m - \alpha_f)}$$

Chapter 8

Trade Policy

Objectives/key terms

Tariff/effective tariff	Quota
Voluntary export restraints (VER)	Harberger triangle
Double distortion	Offer curve
Trade indifference curves	'Optimal' tariff and retaliation

We analyse the impact of trade policy on the size of trade flows, focusing in particular on the distribution of winners (protected domestic producers) and losers (consumers, the country as a whole, and other countries). The distributional welfare aspects of trade policy make the demand for protection (lobbying) understandable.

8.1 Introduction

In the previous seven chapters we have presented and analysed various economic forces giving rise to international flows of goods and services. We also demonstrated that these flows are beneficial for all countries involved, leading to higher efficiency in the Ricardian model based on technology differences and in the Heckscher–Ohlin model based on differences in factor abundance. This view of international trade flows bene-fiting society and increasing efficiency contrasts with a variety of different views from pressure groups frequently popularized in the media, blaming international economics, globalization, international trade flows, and international factor movements for virtually anything a specific group may dislike either at home or abroad, such as unemployment, low wages, environmental degradation, low development levels, unfair competition, etc. This leads to high-profile trade disagreements in the media, such as car imports from Japan in the 1980s, or the 'wars' between the European Union and the United States, such as the 'steel war', the 'cheese war', the 'meat war', and the 'banana war'.

It is not possible to carefully evaluate the quality of the arguments of all pressure groups leading to a specific position and policy recommendation, not only because such arguments are frequently lacking, or contradicting and inconsistent when they do exist, even within one group, but also because new pressure groups pop up and old ones

Fig. 8.1 James Meade (1907–1995)

Meade studied and worked at both the University of Cambridge and Oxford University. He also worked at the London School of Economics and was active outside academia, for the League of Nations and for the British Cabinet Office, where he collaborated with Richard Stone on national income accounts for Britain. He incorporated the Keynesian framework in the textbook *An Introduction to Economic Analysis and Policy*, which appeared in 1936, only a few months after Keynes' *General Theory*. He systematically analysed internal and external balance in a general equilibrium framework. His work on trade policy and welfare analysis led to the 'theory of second best'. He shared the Nobel prize in economics in 1977 with Bertil Ohlin, see Chapter 7.

disappear at a rate that is impossible to keep up with.[1] It is clear, however, that the many pressure groups give rise to a demand, whether successful or not, for action by government officials to impose trade restrictions, to limit 'unfair' competition, to save domestic jobs or the environment, etc. To a limited extent, this chapter gives some reasons for the existence of pressure groups or lobby groups. The majority of this chapter, however, analyses the consequences of imposing trade restrictions for production, consumption, and international trade flows. Arnold Harberger (1954), for example, argued that the monopoly power distortions in the United States impose a cost on society in the order of a few tenths of a per cent of GNP. A couple of years later, he estimated the costs of trade restrictions for the Chilean economy to be about 2.5 per cent of GDP, see Harberger (1959). How did he arrive at these estimates, and how accurate are they?

8.2 **Tariffs, quotas, and other trade restrictions**

Once a government body is convinced, for whatever reason, of the necessity to impose trade restrictions, there is an endless list of policy options to choose from. Suppose the European Commission decides that the domestic production of computers is of vital interest to the European Union, perhaps for security or strategic reasons, and decides to protect the computer industry from the hard and cold winds of global competition. Here are some options available to the European Commission:

- Impose a 100 Euro tax per imported computer (specific tariff)
- Impose a 12 per cent tax per imported computer (*ad valorem* tariff)
- Restrict the number of imported computers (quota)
- Subsidize the production of European computers

---

[1] The American economist Paul Krugman analyses the arguments of many influential pressure groups in an accessible style, see (at the time of writing) http://www.mit.edu/krugman/www/. Check the web links from www.oup.com/uk/marrewijk for the most up-to-date URL.

- Subsidize the export of European computers
- Require a 'minimum content' before a computer may be labelled 'European'
- Prohibit the sale or import of computers to or from certain countries for safety reasons

All these policy measures will affect production, consumption, and trade flows in a different way. Clearly, therefore, we cannot provide an in-depth analysis of each policy measure in this introductory textbook. Instead, we restrict ourselves to providing a rather detailed analysis of the impact of tariffs on the international economic system, dealing more cursorily with the impact of some other trade restrictions (also in the study guide).

Despite the numerous eye-catching trade disputes mentioned in section 8.1, trade restrictions, such as tariffs, have been falling on a global scale for a long time. This has undoubtedly contributed to the rapid increase in international trade and capital flows. To a large extent, the fall in trade restrictions can be attributed to the work of the General Agreement on Tariffs and Trade (GATT), a multilateral organization which has now transformed itself into the World Trade Organization (WTO), see Chapter 12. The GATT finished a long series of multilateral trade negotiation rounds in the complicated Uruguay Round, which lasted from 1986 to 1994. As illustrated in Figure 8.2, these successive GATT rounds substantially reduced the average tariff rates, to approximately 15 per cent of the 1930 value.

Calculating an average tariff rate, as is done in the data underlying Figure 8.2, is actually quite complicated. We will not go into too much detail here, but an obvious first candidate for calculating an average tariff is, of course, weighing the imports of the various goods and services into the country by the value of the import flows. There are at least two disadvantages to that method. First, if a tariff on a specific good, say cheese, is

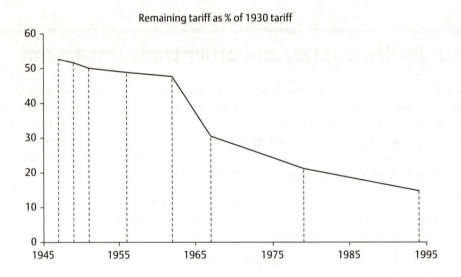

Fig. 8.2 Tariff reductions in successive GATT rounds

Source: Bowen, Hollanda, and Uiaene (1998). Vertical lines indicate the end year of successive rounds; from left to right. First, Second, Third, Fourth, Dillon, Kennedy, Tokyo, Uruguay.

Table 8.1 Calculating the effective tariff rate

Good	World price	Tariff (%)	Domestic price ($)
Finished product	100	20	120
Raw material	60	10	66
Available for processing stage	40	$(100 \times (54 - 40)/40 = 35)$	54

very high, this may completely stop all imports of cheese into the country. This is called a *prohibitive* tariff. When import shares are used to calculate the average tariff, the prohibitive tariff for cheese imports receives a weight of zero, thus leading to a low estimate of average tariffs despite the fact that the tariff on cheese is so high as to stop all imports of cheese. Second, we should be careful to specify which activity we are protecting when calculating the impact of a combination of tariff rates. For this purpose, the *effective tariff rate* can be calculated, see Table 8.1.

Suppose the production of a final good is a simple process, requiring only the availability of some raw material and a processing stage to make the finished product. If the value of the finished product on the world market is $100 and our country imposes a 20 per cent tariff on the import of finished products, one could say that the tariff protection is 20 per cent. However, if the world market price for the raw material is $60, and our country imposes only a 10 per cent tariff on the import of raw materials, this implies that the entrepreneurs in our country can be remunerated for the processing stage to the extent of $100 \times 1.20 - $60 \times 1.10 = 54. If our country imposes no tariffs at all, there would only be $100 - $60 = 40 available for the processing stage of the production process. The effective rate of protection for the production process is therefore $100 \times (54 - 40)/40 = 35$ per cent, which is considerably higher than the nominal rates of 10 per cent and 20 per cent officially imposed by our country. The effective rate of protection is more cumbersome to calculate in a more complicated production process. In general, however, the effective rate of protection is higher the larger the share of raw materials in the production process, the lower the tariff on raw materials, and the higher the tariff on finished goods. Developed countries indeed have a tendency to put lower tariffs on the imports of raw materials than on the imports of finished products, leading to higher effective tariffs for the processing stage than the nominal tariffs suggest.

8.3 Tariffs and partial equilibrium

Small country

We start our analysis of tariffs with an explanation of the estimate of the costs of trade restrictions for Chile, as calculated by Harberger (1959). The basic consequences of imposing a tariff on a specific good, within a partial equilibrium framework, is illustrated in Figure 8.3, which gives the domestic demand and supply schedule for a specific good for the home country. We assume that the home country is a *small country*, that is its (net) demand is so small that the country is not able to influence the price for the good on the world market, such that the *world price is given*. Moreover, we assume that the country imposes an *ad valorem* tariff t.

If the home country were not engaged in international trade, the market would clear at the price p_2 to ensure that domestic demand q_2 is equal to domestic supply. If the country, however, does not impose any tariff at all, the price for the good would be determined on the world market, equal to p_0. Since at the world price p_0 the quantity supplied q_0 is lower than the quantity demanded q_4, the difference $q_4 - q_0$ must be imported from abroad.

What happens if the home country imposes an *ad valorem* tariff of t? First of all, since the home country is small and cannot affect world prices, the world price p_0 of the good remains unchanged. When those goods are imported into the home country, however,

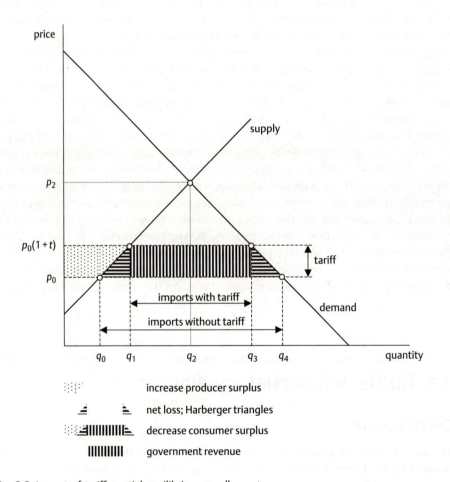

Fig. 8.3 Impact of tariff; partial equilibrium, small country

the *ad valorem* tariff has to be paid, which increases the domestic price level to $p_0(1 + t)$. Second, as a result of the increase in domestic price, home production increases from q_0 to q_1, and consumer demand falls from q_4 to q_3. Imports from abroad thus decrease from $q_4 - q_0$ to $q_3 - q_1$. Since domestic production has increased and imports have fallen, some people might argue that imposition of the tariff has the desired effect of protecting home production and jobs. These issues should be addressed in a general equilibrium setting, see the next section. Is the imposition of the tariff, within the structure of the partial equilibrium model, a good idea? No, it is not. To arrive at this conclusion, we have to investigate the welfare effects of the tariff, where we will distinguish between three types of agents, namely the producers, the government, and the consumers.

● Welfare for the domestic producers, as measured by the producer surplus, has *increased*. The size of this increase is measured left of the supply curve from the old price p_0 to the new price $p_0(1 + t)$, as indicated by the area ⣿ in Figure 8.3.

● Welfare for the government, as measured by the government revenue, has *increased*. The size of the government revenue is equal to the difference between the domestic price $p_0(1 + t)$ and the world price p_0, multiplied by the size of the imports $q_3 - q_1$, as indicated by the area ▐▌▐▌▐▌ in Figure 8.3.

● Welfare for the consumers, as measured by the consumer surplus, has *decreased*. The size of this decrease is measured left of the demand curve from the old price p_0 to the new price $p_0(1 + t)$, as indicated by the area ▐▌▐▌▐▌▬ in Figure 8.3.

This analysis clarifies that there are winners and losers within the home country as a result of the imposition of the tariff, creating a conflict of interests within the country and thus explaining the frequently heated debates on imposing trade restrictions. The domestic producers are in favour of the tariff, as it increases the producer surplus. This explains why producers organize themselves into lobbying groups trying to convince government officials of the need to impose trade restrictions. Focusing attention strictly on revenue, the government is also in favour of the tariff. Within a broader perspective, the government will, of course, have to weigh the interests of the various groups within the country. Raising funds for the government to finance, for example public schools, the construction of highways, and the like, is, however, a formidable problem for many developing nations, making the imposition of tariffs as an easy way to generate such funds an attractive option, see Box 1.2. The big losers are, however, the consumers, who are faced with a large decrease in the consumer surplus. The consumers more than completely finance the increase in producer surplus and the increase in government revenue. The difference is a net welfare loss to the home country, as measured by the so-called Harberger triangles indicated by the area ◢ ◣ in Figure 8.3. When estimating the welfare loss of trade restrictions in Chile, Harberger (1959) essentially estimated the size of these triangles. Note, finally, that the loss of the imposition of the tariff, the sizeable decrease in consumer surplus, is spread across many consumers, while the benefits, the increases in producer surplus and government revenue, are enjoyed by a limited number of producers and the government. This makes it much harder for consumers to organize themselves and defend the benefits of free trade, since there are many consumers and the interest of each individual consumer for this good

---

Box 8.1 **Quota equivalence and the attractiveness of VERs**

The discussion in this chapter focuses attention on the analysis of tariffs. There are three reasons for this. First, there are many different types of trade restrictions and we cannot analyse them all in the same detail. Second, tariffs continue to present an important and visible obstacle to international trade flows, despite the reductions achieved over the years as a result of GATT/WTO efforts. Think, for example, of the role import duties play for tax collection in developing countries, see Box 1.2. Third, and most importantly, the impact of other trade restrictions, such as quota and voluntary export restraints (VERs), is largely *equivalent* to the impact of tariffs, at least in the framework analysed in this chapter. (This remark does not hold for the retaliation analysis at the end of this chapter.)

Consider, for example, the impact of imposing an import quota in the partial equilibrium framework analysed in Figure 8.3. If the size of this quota is equal to $q_3 - q_1$ the domestic market will clear at the price $p_0(1 + t)$, and it is argued that the impact of a quota equal to $q_3 - q_1$ is equivalent to imposing a tariff t. This holds clearly for the loss in consumer surplus, the rise in producer surplus, and the net efficiency loss (the two Harberger triangles). The only distribution effect where the equivalence between tariffs and quota is questionable concerns the revenue the government will collect if it imposes a tariff. Who collects the potentially sizeable government revenue if a quota is imposed, rather than a tariff? To save the equivalence argument it is argued that the government can auction the import quota, and thus collect all this revenue. In practice, this does not occur, such that entrepreneurs who, through lobbying, historical accident, or otherwise, are able to get the licence to import the good with the quota restriction can earn large profits.

The distribution of the tariff revenue can also explain the potential attractiveness of the so-called 'voluntary' export restraint for an exporting country. Suppose this country, let's say Japan, is convinced that a large importing country, say, the USA is about to impose trade restrictions on the import of one of its goods, say cars. Obviously, Japan will be opposed to any trade restrictions on the import of cars into the USA. Convinced of the inevitability of American action, Japan may decide to 'voluntarily' limit the export of cars to the American market. The effect is equivalent to the USA imposing an import quota, except for the fact that the Japanese exporters are able to reap the tariff-equivalent government revenue. This makes a VER more attractive than an import quota.

---

is limited, than for the producers to organize vocal lobbying groups, since the interests of each producer are large. There is thus an organizational bias *against* free trade.

Large country

The arguments above specifically stipulated that home is a small country. Apparently this is important, but why? The essential point is to realize in the above analysis that, other things being equal, the imposition of a tariff reduces imports of the good into the home country, from $q_4 - q_0$ to $q_3 - q_1$, see Figure 8.3. If home is a *large* country, however, other things are not equal and the reduction in imports, which is a decrease in net demand by the home country on the world market, results in a lower price for the good on the world market. In Figure 8.4 this fall in the world price level as a result of the imposition of the tariff is indicated by the drop from p_0 to p_1. Essentially, then, the imposition of the tariff implies that the large home country uses its monopsony power to improve its terms of trade, as it can now import the good more cheaply.

The rest of the analysis is similar.

- Producer welfare increases, as indicated by the area ⬚⬚⬚ in Figure 8.4.
- Government revenue increases, as indicated by the area ‖‖‖‖‖ in Figure 8.4.
- Consumer welfare falls, as indicated by the area ⬚⬚⬚≣‖‖‖‖‖≣ in Figure 8.4.

The main difference with the preceding analysis, in which home was a small country and could not influence the terms of trade, is that part of the government revenue, namely the area ⁄⁄⁄⁄⁄ in Figure 8.4, is not paid for by the domestic consumers but by the foreign producers. The net welfare gain for the home country is therefore the difference

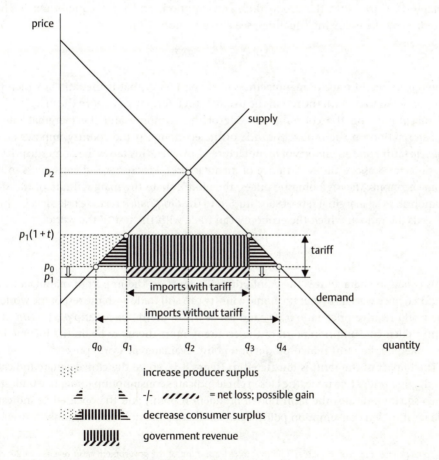

Fig. 8.4 Impact of tariff; partial equilibrium, large country

between the part ✱✱✱✱✱✱ of government revenue paid for by the foreign producers and the efficiency loss triangles ◢   ◣ , which is potentially positive.

8.4 Tariffs and general equilibrium

We will now analyse the impact of a tariff in a general equilibrium setting. To do that, we use the neoclassical model explained in Chapters 4–7. We assume that the home country is relatively labour abundant, such that under free trade it will import the capital intensive manufactures, and export the labour intensive food. Moreover, we assume in this section that the home country is *small* and cannot influence its terms of trade. The price of manufactures relative to the price of food is therefore given. Section 8.7 below will analyse the general equilibrium impact of imposing a tariff if the home country is large.

If the home country engages in free trade, identified by the sub-index *tr*, the analysis in Chapter 7 shows that the production, consumption, and trade equilibrium is characterized by the following equalities, see also equation (7.6).

$$(8.1) \qquad MRS_{tr} = \frac{p_m}{p_f} = MRT_{tr}$$

The (given) world price of manufactures relative to food, that is the ratio at which the economy can trade with the rest of the world, is therefore equal to both the marginal rate of substitution on the consumption side of the economy and the marginal rate of transformation on the production side of the economy. If the country imposes an *ad valorem* tariff *t* on the imports of manufactures, however, this raises the domestic price of manufactures above the world price of manufactures. Producers and consumers in the home economy, facing domestic prices, therefore equate the marginal rate of transformation and the marginal rate of substitution to the *tariff ridden* relative price level, which exceeds the ratio at which the economy can trade with the rest of the world.

$$(8.2) \qquad MRS_{tariff} = \frac{p_m(1+t)}{p_f} = MRT_{tariff} > \frac{p_m}{p_f}$$

This equation characterizes the equilibrium if a tariff on the import of manufactures is imposed once we realize that the home country can still trade with the rest of the world at the world relative price ratio p_m/p_f, and *not* at the domestic price ratio $p_m(1+t)/p_f$. The tariff ridden consumption point of the economy must therefore be on the income line generated by the tariff ridden production point, evaluated at world prices.[2]

The impact of the tariff is illustrated in Figure 8.5, where the closed square indicates production under free trade, the closed circle indicates consumption under free trade, the open square indicates the tariff ridden production point, and the open circle indicates the tariff ridden consumption point. Let's summarize the main conclusions.

---

[2] To be precise, this requires either a lump sum redistribution of the government tariff revenue to the consumers, or government consumption preferences identical to private consumers.

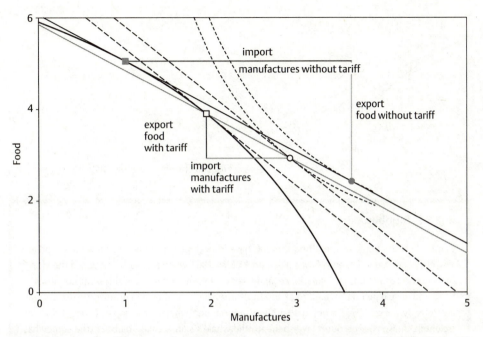

Fig. 8.5 Impact of tariff in general equilibrium. Closed square = production without tariff, closed circle = consumption without tariff, open square = production with tariff, open circle = consumption with tariff; economy structure as described in chapters 4–7, $\alpha_m = 0.8$, $\alpha_f = 0.2$, $\delta_m = 0.6$, $K = 3$, $L = 7$, $p_m/p_f = 1$

- As in the partial equilibrium approach of section 8.3, the production of manufactures increases because the relative price of manufactures rises, but it is clear that there is a simultaneous reduction in the production of food. This represents the opportunity costs of trade restrictions, as already identified by Adam Smith, see Chapter 2.
- There is a reduction of income generated by the economy (evaluated at world prices).
- The income loss and the deviation from world prices leads to a reduction in welfare (this is further explained below).
- The tariff leads to a reduction in the volume of trade.

The imposition of the tariff actually imposes a double distortion on the economy, as is implicit in equation (8.2) and made explicit in Figure 8.6. First, because the domestic price level deviates from the price level at which the economy can trade with the rest of the world, the economy produces at a sub-optimal production point, leading to an income loss. This reduction in income leads, of course, to a lower welfare level. Note, however, that at the income level generated by the tariff ridden production point, the economy could consume at the open triangle in Figure 8.6, lowering the welfare level from U_3 to U_2. Second, the tariff also leads to a sub-optimal consumption point because the domestic price level deviates from the world price level, leading to consumption at the open circle and further reducing the welfare level from U_2 to U_1.

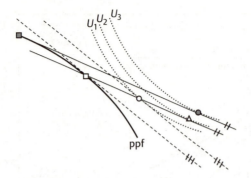

Fig. 8.6 Tariffs: a double distortion

Box 8.2 **Blubber**

Can trade restrictions, or the lifting thereof, have important consequences for a good's price? Yes, they can. A good example was given on 11 May 2001 when Norway announced the lifting of its export restrictions on 'blubber' to Japan. For environmental reasons almost all countries in the world have banned the hunting of and trade in whales. The only two noteworthy exceptions are Norway (since 1993, arguing that there are enough whales) and Japan (since 1987, for 'scientific' reasons). The outer layer beneath the whale's skin is called blubber (the somewhat friendlier Dutch name for this is 'whale bacon'; the word 'blubber' actually means 'mud' in Dutch). Blubber is not eaten in Norway, while it is considered a healthy delicacy, and eaten raw, in Japan. In the 1980s Norway banned the export of blubber. After the announcement of the lifting of the ban on exports to Japan, the price of blubber in Norway rose from 0.1 cent to 57 krona per kilogram in one day, an almost 600-fold increase overnight.

Information source: NRC Handelsblad (2001c).

Chapter 8 tool: The offer curve

Before we can continue with analysing the impact of imposing a tariff if the home country is large, such that it has market power and can influence its terms of trade, we have to introduce another economic tool of analysis, already used by Alfred Marshall, called the offer curve. Figure 8.7 depicts free trade production and consumption combinations for six different relative price levels of manufactures.[3] Going from top to bottom, we see that as the relative price of manufactures increases, the economy will produce more and more manufactures, until the economy is completely specialized in the production of manufactures. Simultaneously, we see that the consumption ratio of food to manufactures increases from top to bottom, because the relative price of manufactures is rising, and that the distance from the origin is determined by the income level of the economy generated by the production point.

Figure 8.7 also draws the trade triangles at the different price levels, which make the inequality between production and consumption at the national level possible. Going again from top to bottom, we see that the economy initially exports food in exchange for imports of manufactures if the relative price of manufactures is very low. Once the relative price level

[3] The structure of the economy is explained in Chs. 4–7; $\alpha_m = 0.8$, $\alpha_f = 0.2$, $\delta_m = 0.6$, $K = 7$, $L = 3$.

of manufactures exceeds the autarky price (0.695), the economy starts to export manufactures in exchange for imports of food. The figure clearly demonstrates the connections that exist between the relative price of manufactures and the export–import combination the economy is willing to offer to the rest of the world at that price level.

Figure 8.8 depicts five of the six export–import combinations the economy is willing to offer to the rest of the world as illustrated in Figure 8.7. Point A in Figure 8.8, for example, depicts the export of manufactures the economy offers in exchange for the import of food if the relative price of manufactures is equal to 2. This relative price ratio is, of course, given by the slope of the line from point A to the origin in Figure 8.8. The five dots in Figure 8.8 give the export–import combinations for five different relative price levels. The offer curve, also depicted in Figure 8.8, connects these five points by depicting all possible export–import combinations for all possible relative price levels.

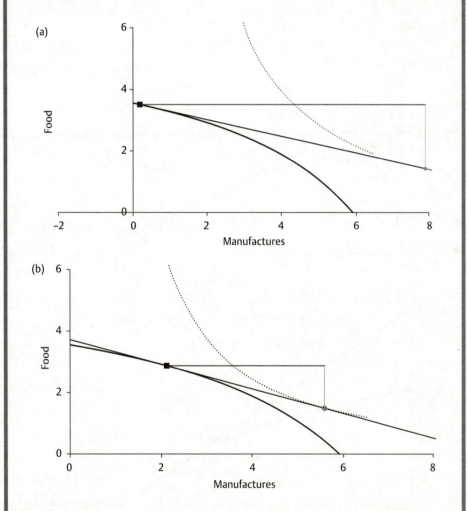

Fig. 8.7 Production (square), consumption (circle), and relative price of manufactures (a) $p_m/p_f = 0.27$, (b) $p_m/p_f = 0.4$, (c) $p_m/p_f = 0.5$, (d) $p_m/p_f = 0.695$, (e) $p_m/p_f = 1$, (f) $p_m/p_f = 2$

(continued overleaf)

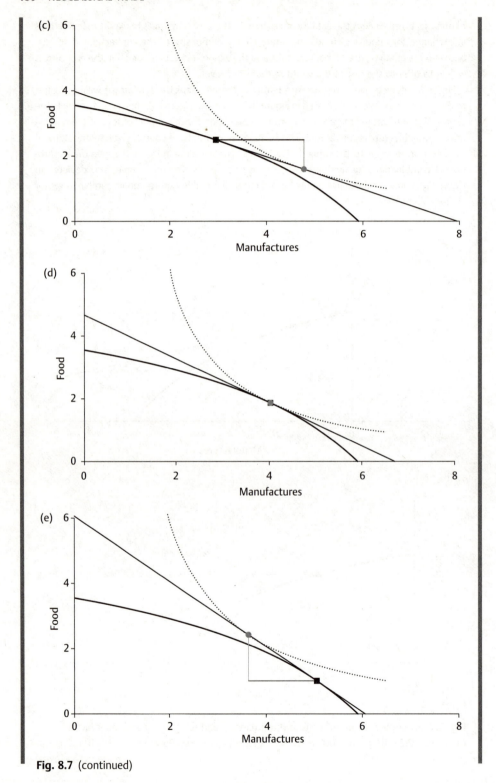

Fig. 8.7 (continued)

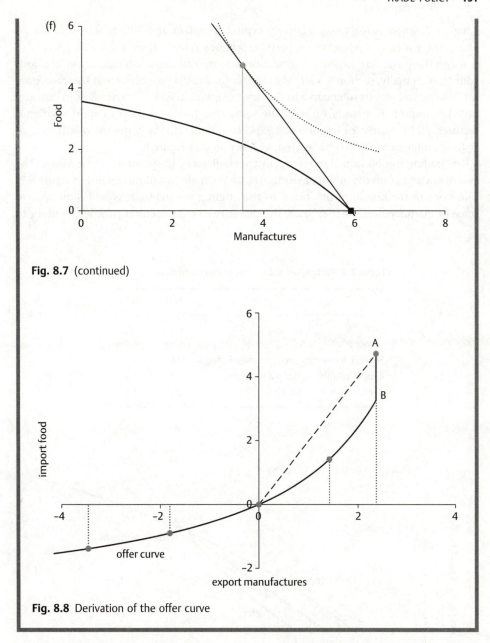

Fig. 8.7 (continued)

Fig. 8.8 Derivation of the offer curve

8.5 **General equilibrium with offer curves**

Combining the offer curve of a country with the offer curve from the rest of the world allows us to determine the trading equilibrium in the economy, and the concomitant exports and imports. To illustrate this, we will use the economic structure also used in

Chapter 7, where Austria was relatively capital abundant and Bolivia relatively labour abundant. For ease of reference we partly reproduce Table 7.1, see Table 8.2.

Using the procedure explained in section 8.5, we can derive an offer curve for both countries. Actually, section 8.5 already did this for Austria. We can repeat the procedure for Bolivia, and plot its offer curve in the same diagram. It will be convenient to measure Bolivia's import of manufactures in the same direction as Austria's export of manufactures, and similarly for imports and exports of food. This switches the orientation of Bolivia's offer curve relative to Austria, as illustrated in Figure 8.9.

The trading equilibrium of the two countries is given by the point of intersection of the two offer curves (not the origin), as indicated by the trade equilibrium point in Figure 8.9. The slope of the line from this point to the origin gives the trade equilibrium relative price of manufactures. At that price, the quantity of manufactures Austria is willing to

Table 8.2 Parameter values for Austria and Bolivia

	Austria	Bolivia
Capital K	7	3
Labour L	3	7
Share of income δ_m spent on manufactures	0.6	0.6
Capital intensity α_m for manufactures	0.8	0.8
Capital intensity α_f for food	0.2	0.2

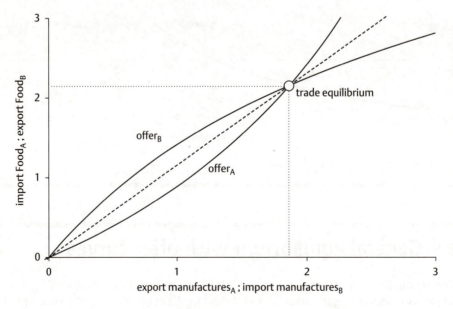

Fig. 8.9 Determination of trade equilibrium with offer curves

offer in exchange for imports of food is equal to the quantity of manufactures Bolivia is demanding in exchange for exports of food. The world markets for both goods are thus in equilibrium.

8.6 The 'optimal' tariff?

Given the preliminaries of sections 8.5 and 8.6, we can now analyse the impact of imposing a tariff if the home country is large and can influence its terms of trade. Recall that the partial equilibrium analysis of section 8.3 suggests that a large country might gain from trade under certain circumstances. As we will see below, this result carries over to a general equilibrium analysis.

If the country is able to benefit from imposing a tariff, this benefit must arise from the ability to influence its terms of trade, since section 8.4 demonstrates that for any *given* terms of trade imposing a tariff always leads to a welfare loss. The analysis in section 8.4 also shows that for any given terms of trade, imposing a tariff reduces the volume of trade, see Figure 8.5. Since the offer curve derived in section 8.5 depicts the combination of exports and imports for all possible terms of trade, and imposing a tariff reduces the volume of trade for any given terms of trade, we can conclude that the imposition of a tariff leads to an inward rotation of the offer curve. For the equilibrium derived in the previous section, see Table 8.2 and Figure 8.9, this inward rotation is illustrated in Figure 8.10 if the capital abundant Austria imposes a 40 per cent

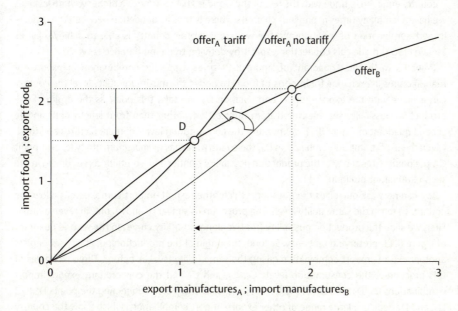

Fig. 8.10 Trade equilibrium if Austria imposes a 40 per cent tariff

tariff on the imports of food. Figure 8.10 also shows Austria's offer curve if it does not impose a tariff, which would lead to the free trade equilibrium point C. After the tariff is imposed by Austria, the tariff ridden trade equilibrium point at which the export of manufactures by Austria is equal to the import of manufactures by Bolivia is at point D in Figure 8.10.

Figure 8.10 allows us to draw at least two conclusions. First, a tariff imposed by a large country also leads to a reduction in the volume of trade, as indicated by the arrows in Figure 8.10. Second, by imposing a tariff a large country can indeed exercise its monopsony power for food (and at the same time its monopoly power for manufactures), leading to an improvement in its terms of trade. In Figure 8.10 this follows from the fact that the slope of a line from the origin to the tariff ridden equilibrium point D is steeper than the slope of a line drawn from the origin to the free trade equilibrium point C (both lines are not drawn in the figure). The tariff thus leads to a higher relative price of manufactures, which is Austria's export good and represents an improvement in Austria's terms of trade. The question remains whether or not Austria's welfare level has improved. To answer that question we make use of trade indifference curves, which essentially translate a country's preferences and production possibilities into export–import indifference curves. This is explained in detail in Box 8.3.

Box 8.3 **Trade indifference curves**

A country engaged in trade with the rest of the world is able to achieve a higher welfare level, as we have seen many times in previous chapters. There is thus a connection between the export–import combination of a nation and the welfare level this country is able to achieve. James Meade (1952) made this connection explicit by deriving trade indifference curves.

Point D_4 in the first quadrant of Figure 8.11 gives a specific combination of exports of manufactures in exchange for imports of food. To derive the maximum utility level the country can achieve with the export–import combination D_4, we take this point as the origin of the production possibility set, measured from right to left, rather than from left to right. In the second quadrant of Figure 8.11 we measure the consumption levels of manufactures and food. Given the export–import combination D_4, the country reaches its maximum utility level at point C_4, the point of tangency of the production possibility frontier and iso-utility curve$_4$ drawn in the second quadrant of Figure 8.11.

We can now ask ourselves the question, which other export–import combinations allow the country to reach the same utility level? The procedure is similar to above, only in reverse order. First, we slide the production possibility frontier along iso-utility curve$_4$ in the second quadrant of Figure 8.11, preserving tangency. Second, the origin of the production possibility set depicts another export–import combination giving the same utility level as before. Three examples of this procedure, the consumption levels C_3, C_2, and C_1 and the concomitant export–import combinations D_3, D_2, and D_1, are given in Figure 8.11. The curve connecting the points D_4, D_3, D_2, and D_1 depicts a large range of other export–import combinations which allow the country to reach the same utility level. It is labelled trade indifference curve$_4$.

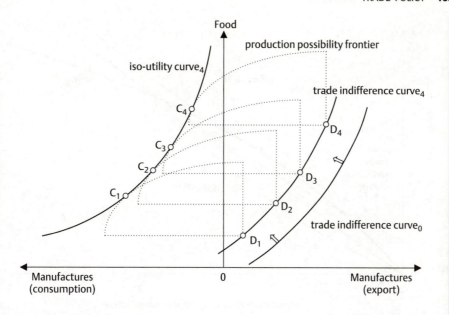

Fig. 8.11 Derivation of trade indifference curves

Three final remarks should be made. First, note that the trade indifference curve simultaneously reflects the curvature of the iso-utility curve and of the production possibility frontier. Second, we can in principle repeat this procedure for any arbitrary iso-utility curve, leading to an infinite number of trade indifference curves in the first quadrant of Figure 8.11. We have drawn one other example, labelled trade indifference curve$_0$. Third, note that the welfare level the economy can reach increases in the north-west direction in the first quadrant of Figure 8.11. In particular, trade indifference curve$_0$ depicts a lower welfare level than trade indifference curve$_4$.

Figure 8.12 depicts two trade indifference curves. One curve is tangent at point C to the price line from the origin to point C, which depicts the free trade equilibrium. Tangency at that point is ensured by the perfectly competitive behaviour of the economic agents and the absence of distortions. The other trade indifference curve is tangent at point D to the offer curve of Bolivia. As explained in Box 8.2, the trade indifference curve tangent at point D represents a higher welfare level for Austria. Can the government of Austria manipulate the international economic conditions to reach point D? The answer is yes, as also drawn in Figure 8.12. If the government of Austria imposes a tariff on the imports of food, this leads to an inward rotation of its offer curve and a concomitant change of the international trade equilibrium point. By carefully choosing its tariff rate, the government of Austria can in principle ensure that its tariff ridden offer curve intersects Bolivia's offer curve at point D. Given the offer curve of Bolivia, the highest possible welfare level Austria can achieve is at point D. The tariff rate that ensures that Austria's tariff ridden offer curve intersects Bolivia's offer curve at point D is therefore known as the 'optimal' tariff. It is derived formally in Technical Note 8.1. If the country is large, in

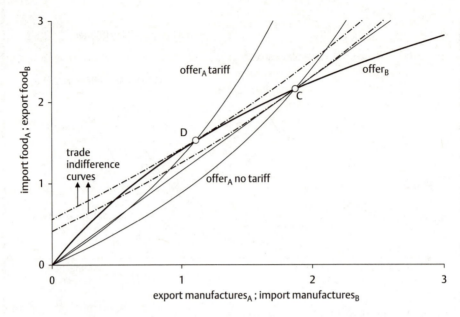

Fig. 8.12 The 'optimal' tariff

the sense that it can influence its terms of trade, this optimal tariff is always positive within this framework. See, however, the next section and Chapter 17.

8.7 Optimal tariffs and retaliation

In the analysis in the preceding section, the government of Austria is very smart. In fact, the government knows a lot and is able to perform extremely complicated calculations. It knows the production structure of its own economy, the preferences of its consumers, and the economic behaviour of its inhabitants. This allows the government of Austria to calculate the production and consumption points for all possible relative prices of manufactures, and thus the concomitant export and import decisions at those prices. Using all this information, the government of Austria can then derive its own offer curve. In addition, the government can manipulate this offer curve by calculating the impact of imposing a tariff on the import of food for the above production, consumption, export, and import decisions. But that is not all. The government of Austria also knows all of this information on production, technology, preferences, consumption, exports, and imports for the economy of Bolivia, which allows it to derive Bolivia's offer curve. Finally, then, the government of Austria is able to combine all of this information into determining the point of tangency of its own trade indifference curves with Bolivia's offer curve, which enables it to calculate the 'optimal' tariff.

The above observations on the formidable informational requirements and supposed ability of the government of Austria to process detailed economic information in determining the optimal tariff, raises two important questions. First, do we really think any government in the world has this information available, and is capable at the same time of performing the required calculations? The answer undoubtedly must be negative, putting the entire reasoning process of a country able to determine the optimal tariff into question. Second, even if we allow the government of Austria, within the setting of this economic structure, to be so smart as to calculate the optimal tariff, why shouldn't the same hold for the government of Bolivia?

The second question is addressed in Figure 8.13. If both countries engage in free trade, the trade equilibrium occurs at point C, the intersection of the two offer curves if neither country imposes a tariff on imports. As explained in the previous section, if Austria is very smart it can calculate the point of tangency of Bolivia's offer curve and its trade indifference curves to determine the optimal tariff which will rotate its own offer curve inwards to ensure that the trade equilibrium moves from point C to point D to maximize its own welfare. If the government of Bolivia is as smart as the government of Austria, it will follow a similar procedure to calculate its own optimal tariff which will rotate its own offer curve inwards to ensure that its own welfare is maximized at the point of tangency of its own trade indifference curves and Austria's offer curve. In Figure 8.13 this is given by point E. Country B's optimal tariff is therefore calculated to rotate Bolivia's offer curve inward to move the trade equilibrium from point C to point E.

Where does all of this cleverness of Austria and Bolivia lead to? Austria performs complicated calculations to try to move the international equilibrium from point C to point D. Bolivia performs complicated calculations to try to move the international

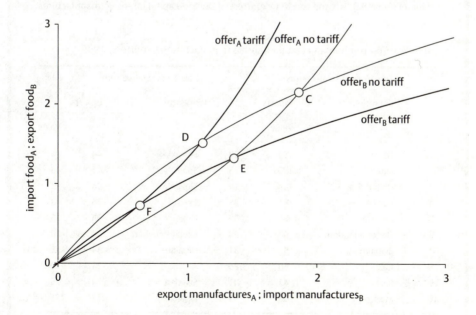

Fig. 8.13 Tariffs and retaliation

equilibrium from point C to point E. The end result is that neither country gets what it wants, because the intersection of the two tariff ridden offer curves occurs at point F. As drawn in Figure 8.13, this leads to lower trade and welfare levels for both countries. One can imagine that numerous game-theoretic manoeuvres have been analysed by international economists within this framework, assuming that both countries move simultaneously in calculating 'optimal' tariffs in a sequence of steps, or that one country moves before the other country retaliates in a series of alternating steps in calculating 'optimal' tariffs, etc. In all cases, the end result of all this cleverness is the same. The international equilibrium moves in the wrong direction, leading to lower welfare levels for both countries than is achieved at the free trade equilibrium at point C in Figure 8.13. Traditionally, this is why we think there is an important role for multilateral trade negotiations, first in the GATT and now in the WTO (see Chapter 12), for moving the international economy into the direction of free trade, and away from retaliation and trade wars which reduce welfare for all countries involved.

Box 8.4 Human-capital intensive manufacturing exporters

The ITC classifies forty-three goods as 'human-capital intensive manufacturing' products, incorporating synthetic colours, pigments, perfumes, cosmetics, rubber and tyres, tubes, pipes, various types of steel and iron, cutlery, televisions, radios, cars, watches, and jewellery. For the 151 countries for which the ITC provides data, total exports of human-capital intensive manufactures in 1998 were equal to $1,127 bn, a sizeable 23 per cent of all exports. The left-hand side of Table 8.3 lists the top ten exporters of human-capital intensive manufactures in

Table 8.3 Top ten human-capital intensive manufacturing exporters, 1998

No.	Top 10 in absolute terms			Top 10 in relative terms		
	Country	Exports		Country	Exports	
		Value	%		%	Value
1	Germany	163	32	Slovakia	44	4
2	Japan	125	33	Spain	41	43
3	United States	114	19	Slovenia	38	3
4	France	81	28	Canada	36	72
5	Canada	72	36	Finland	35	15
6	United Kingdom	61	24	Czech Republic	34	10
7	Belgium	51	31	Ukraine	34	3
8	Italy	50	25	Austria	34	19
9	Spain	43	41	Sweden	34	25
10	Mexico	36	31	Japan	33	125

Sources: WTO/UNCTAD International Trade Centre website http://www.intracen.org; value in bn US $.
The % shares are relative to the country's total exports.

absolute terms. With a value of $163 bn Germany is the world's largest human-capital intensive manufactures exporter, followed by Japan ($125 bn) and the USA ($114 bn). In all three cases automobiles and parts for automobiles form the main component of these exports. The other large exporters are also OECD countries.

As indicated by the right-hand side of Table 8.3, three countries in the list of the world's ten largest exporters of human-capital intensive manufactures in absolute terms also make it to the list of the world's ten largest exporters in relative terms, namely Spain, Canada, and Japan. The top three in relative terms is formed by Slovakia, Spain, and Slovenia. Automobiles and automobile parts are again the main component in all three cases. Figure 8.14 shows the relative dependence of countries on the exports of human-capital intensive manufactures. These are concentrated in the rich countries, plus central Europe, Brazil, and Argentina.

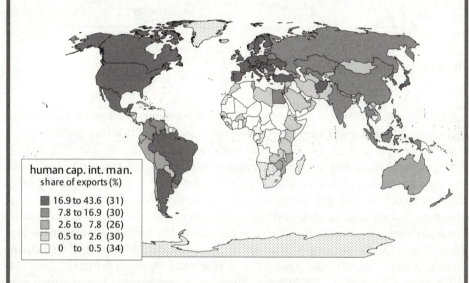

human cap. int. man.
share of exports (%)

- 16.9 to 43.6 (31)
- 7.8 to 16.9 (30)
- 2.6 to 7.8 (26)
- 0.5 to 2.6 (30)
- 0 to 0.5 (34)

Fig. 8.14 Human-capital intensive manufacturing exports

8.8 Tariffs in the USA

For some important countries, such as the USA, the average tariff rate has reached historically low levels, as illustrated in Figure 8.15. At the beginning of the nineteenth century the tariff revenue was very high, about 50 per cent of the value of imports. In this period the southern part of the USA wanted to import cheap foreign manufactures (from Britain) while the northern part of the USA demanded protection of the domestic industry. The controversy over tariffs peaked in 1828 with the tariff of Abominations, when the southern congressmen made a strategic mistake by amending a bill to include

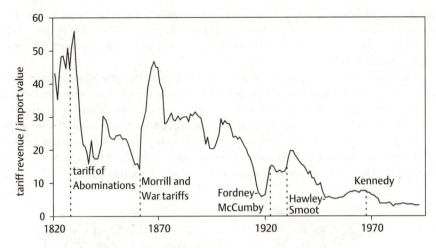

Fig. 8.15 USA average tariffs, 1821–1992

high tariffs on raw materials in the hope that their northern colleagues would reject it (because northern manufacturers used those raw materials), which they did not.

With a compromise law in 1833 the average American tariff rate started to decline, although not coming down as far as European tariffs. The decline stopped in 1861 when the Morrill tariff was passed, raising rates on iron and steel products, followed by other duties in 1862 and 1864, also designed to finance the Civil War. At the beginning of the twentieth century tariff rates came down considerably when the Wilson administration put many items on the 'free list'. This was reversed in the first recession after the First World War, when the Fordney–McCumber tariff was passed in 1922, intended to help the farmers. It was followed by the Hawley–Smoot tariff in 1930, which as Kenen (2000: 213) put it was 'once called the "Holy-Smoke Tariff" by a student with keener insight than memory'. After the Second World War a series of multilateral GATT negotiations, for example in the American-inspired Kennedy Round, eventually resulted in the current low average tariff rates, also for other countries in the world (see Figure 8.2).

8.9 Conclusions

We analyse the impact of trade policy on the size of trade flows and the distribution of welfare effects. In general, there are both winners and losers of imposing trade restrictions, which makes the demand for protection (lobbying) understandable. Among the winners are protected domestic producers and, in terms of tariff revenue, the government. The main losers are the domestic consumers, who pay for the increased profits of domestic producers and the tariff revenue, the country as a whole, in terms of an efficiency loss (Harberger triangles), and the foreign producers. The main difference between tariffs and quota rests in the question who receives the tariff-equivalent government revenue. The foreign country can try to reap this benefit by establishing a 'voluntary' export restraint. Imposing a tariff always leads to a net welfare loss for a small country, which cannot influence its terms of trade. Within a neoclassical framework, a large country, which can influence its terms of trade, might benefit from a net welfare gain by imposing an 'optimal' tariff based on its monopoly power. This argument breaks down under a system of retaliation leading to tariff wars, which clarifies the necessity of multilateral trade negotiations (WTO, see Chapter 12).

Technical Notes (optional)

Technical Note 8.1 Derivation of the 'optimal' tariff

Using the standard optimal pricing rule for a monopolist $p(1 - 1/\varepsilon) = MC$, see Technical Note 9.1 in the next chapter, the 'optimal' tariff t_A for Austria can quite easily be derived as a function of the foreign excess demand elasticity ε_B^d once we realize that Austria acts as a monopolist, its marginal costs are its own price p_A, the price it charges indirectly through the tariff it imposes is the foreign price p_B, with elasticity $\varepsilon = \varepsilon_B^d$, and the two prices are related through $p_B = (1 + t_A)p_A$. Simple substitution gives:

$$\left. \begin{array}{r} p_B(1 - 1/\varepsilon_B^d) = p_A \\ p_B = (1 + t_A)p_A \end{array} \right\} \Rightarrow t_A = \frac{1}{\varepsilon_B^d - 1} \quad \text{('optimal' tariff)}$$

Part Three

New Trade

Part III (New Trade) investigates the impact of imperfect competition, economies of scale, and product differentiation on the structure of the international economy and the size and type of its trade flows. This 'new trade' approach is the fruitful result of incorporating elements of the industrial organization literature in international economics. Part III also analyses the impact of new trade theory on (strategic) trade policy, discusses the main international organizations, and applies the economic insights on the structure of the world economy learned in Parts I–III to an investigation of the process of (European) economic integration.

Chapter 9
Imperfect Competition

Objectives/key terms

Monopoly/oligopoly   Mark-up pricing
Cournot competition   Reaction curves
Pro-competitive effect of trade   Reciprocal dumping

Acknowledging that many firms have market power, we discuss the effect of international trade, which increases competition, on production, consumption, and welfare.

9.1 Introduction

So far we have analysed perfectly competitive markets, that is markets in which the firms do not perceive they have any market power. More specifically, they do not think they can influence the price at which the market clears. All firms individually, therefore, take the market clearing price as given in their profit maximization problem. Each firm determines how much it will produce at any given price level. The actions of all firms together determine the market supply. This is confronted with the demand of consumers to determine the price at which the market actually clears. Collectively, the firms therefore *do* influence the market clearing price. If there are many firms, the impact of any individual firm on the market clearing price is negligible, hence the assumption that each firm takes this price as given.

In many cases the assumption of perfect competition is a reasonable approximation. At the Dutch flower auction, for example, each night hundreds of growers deliver the flowers cut, selected, and packed that day to the auction to be sold off early the next morning at whatever price will clear the market. In many other cases, however, perfect competition is not a reasonable approximation. There may, for example, be only one company that delivers water to your house, or only one telephone company, or one electricity company, etc. If so, this company obviously has market power and will realize that an increase in its production level will reduce the market clearing price. Or, equivalently, it will realize that if it raises the price level, the demand for its goods or services will fall. Alternatively, there may be only a few companies, rather than one.

Fig. 9.1 Joseph Stiglitz (1942–)

Like Samuelson, Joe Stiglitz was born in Gary, Indiana. He received his Ph.D. from MIT when he was only 24 years old. He has moved around from one prestigious university to another, never staying very long. Recently, he was chief economist of the World Bank before moving to Stanford University. His many contributions to economics focus on imperfect competition and the importance of costly information. Outside his own field the most influential contribution has undoubtedly been 'Monopolistic competition and optimum product diversity', published jointly with Avinash Dixit in the *American Economic Review* in 1977, see Chapter 10.

There are at the moment, for example, only two companies producing large wide-body commercial aircraft for the global market, namely the American Boeing company and the European Airbus consortium. Both companies realize that they have market power, and that their actions will influence the other company. They take this into consideration when determining the optimal strategy, see also Chapter 11.

If a firm does not take the price level on the market as given, but strategically interacts with other firms and the market to maximize its profits, we are no longer in the realm of 'perfect competition'. Instead, we say such a market is characterized by 'imperfect competition', a poorly chosen term indeed, certainly in those cases in which it gives a better description of the market. The world of perfect competition is attractive; it is well defined, its behavioural assumptions are clear and easy to understand, it leads to powerful conclusions, and in most cases it substantially increases our knowledge and understanding of the workings of an economy. In contrast, the world of imperfect competition is a mess. Since there is an unlimited number of ways in which one can deviate from the 'perfect' world, there are many different 'imperfect' models, some of astounding complexity, leading to many different outcomes and policy prescriptions. To top things off, imperfect competition is hard to model in a general equilibrium setting, certainly in conjunction with production under increasing returns to scale (see the sequel). No wonder (international) economists have shied away from imperfect competition for a long time.

This does not mean that there has been no attention for the connections between monopoly power and international trade flows. Already in 1701 Henry Martyn wrote a clear and concise tract, entitled *Considerations upon the East India Trade*, opposing monopoly restraints on the East India trade and restrictions on manufactured imports from India. Instead, such trade should be open to all merchants, not just to those licensed by the government:[1]

In an open trade, every merchant is upon his good behavior, always afraid of being undersold at home, always seeking out for new markets in foreign countries; in the meantime, trade is carried on with less expense: This is the effect of necessity and emulation, things unknown to a single company.

---

[1] See Irwin (1996: 57).

Martyn therefore opposes monopoly power in trade flows, arguing that competition among companies improves efficiency. Nonetheless, there may be good reasons why there are only a few firms, or one, in an industry. Many of the examples given above, such as power companies, telecommunications, or aircraft production, require large initial investments before production of goods and services can start; the construction of a power plant, the wiring of a city, or the development of a new aircraft and construction of a factory to build these aircraft. After the initial investment, which can be seen as a fixed cost, production can start, involving high or low production costs. The larger the size of the firm, as measured by the production level, the lower the costs of production per unit of output, because the large initial fixed investment costs can be spread across more goods. In other words, there are increasing returns to scale at the firm level. As we will argue in the next chapter, this is incompatible with perfect competition. The consequences of increasing returns to scale are analysed in more detail in the following chapters. This chapter analyses the impact of market power, and not the impact of increasing returns to scale, such that all production functions in this chapter exhibit constant returns to scale.

9.2 **Monopoly**

Suppose that there is only one firm active on a specific market. This firm is called a monopolist. Like any other firm, it will be interested in maximizing its profits, probably camouflaged in its brochures as a commitment to efficiency, service to society, and eagerness to deliver high-quality goods and services to its customers. Since it is the only firm active in the market, it will of course realize that its actions have a large impact on the market. In particular, the firm will realize that there is a negative relationship between the price charged for its products and the quantity sold on the market. The monopolist's profit maximization problem is therefore more sophisticated than the problem facing a perfectly competitive firm which treats the output price as a parameter. A monopolist must not only gather information about its own production processes and cost structure, but also about the market for its product and the responsiveness of this market to changes in the price charged by the monopolist. It is time for a quick review of the monopolist's profit maximization problem.

Figure 9.2 illustrates the monopolist's problem. The market demand curve is given by the downward sloping solid line. It is assumed to be linear, which implies that the marginal revenue (MR) curve is also linear, with the same intercept and a slope twice as steep (see Chapter 9 tool). The marginal revenue curve is steeper than the demand curve because the firm has to lower its price if it wants to sell more goods, which also lowers the revenue on the initial output. We assume that the firm's marginal costs (MC) are constant, as indicated by the dashed horizontal line in Figure 9.2.

To maximize its profits, the firm will set its marginal costs equal to its marginal revenue, as indicated by point A. It will therefore produce the monopoly output indicated

---

Chapter 9 tool: Microeconomics and markets

The tools to be used in this chapter are taken from standard microeconomic theory. If a firm perceives it has market power, it will use this market power to the best of its advantage. We will analyse the case of a pure monopoly (one firm), of oligopoly (a few firms), and of monopolistic competition (many firms with individual market power, see Chapter 10). Let p be the price of a good, and q the quantity produced. If the demand curve is linear, that is $p = a - bq$ for some positive parameters a and b, it follows that revenue R (price times quantity) equals

$$R = pq = (a - bq)q = aq - bq^2$$

This, in turn, implies that marginal revenue MR (increase in total revenue if more output is produced) is equal to $MR = dR/dq = a - 2bq$.

We conclude, therefore, that if market demand is linear, then the marginal revenue curve is also linear; with the same intercept and a slope twice as steep as the demand curve.

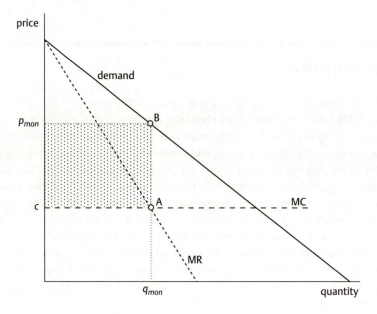

Fig. 9.2 Optimal output for a monopolist

by q_{mon} in Figure 9.2. To determine the price the firm will charge at this output level, we have to go back to the demand curve, see point B, which gives us price level p_{mon}. The most important thing to note about Figure 9.2 is that the price charged by the monopolist is *higher* than the marginal cost of production. In determining the optimal price for its products, the monopolist thus charges a *mark-up* over the marginal cost of production.

This mark-up depends on the price elasticity of demand $\varepsilon \equiv -(dq/dp)(p/q)$ as follows:

(9.1)
$$p\left(1 - \frac{1}{\varepsilon(q)}\right) = c(q)$$

where $c(q)$ is the marginal cost of production, see Technical Note 9.1. The deviation between price and marginal cost of production is in stark contrast to a perfectly competitive market, in which the market clearing price is always equal to the marginal cost of production. The fact that a monopolist's market power enables the firm to charge a higher price than the marginal cost of production also implies that the firm is able to make a profit. Since we assumed the marginal cost of production to be constant, the firm's profits are represented by the shaded rectangle in Figure 9.2 as $(p_{mon} - c)q_{mon}$, that is price minus cost times quantity sold.[2]

9.3 Monopoly in general equilibrium: autarky

As explained in section 9.1, we focus on the consequences of market power in this chapter. Section 9.2 argued, in a partial equilibrium setting, that the most important implication of monopoly power is the fact that the price charged on the output market is a mark-up over the marginal cost of production. We now discuss the impact of monopoly power in autarky in a simple general equilibrium setting, based on James Markusen's (1981) analysis. The main assumptions are as follows:

- There is a single producer of manufactures; this is a monopoly market.
- There are many producers of food; the market is perfectly competitive.
- The markets for factors of production (capital and labour) are also perfectly competitive (the monopolist of manufactures therefore has no monopsony power on its input markets).
- All firms maximize profits.
- All consumers maximize utility, taking the final goods prices as given.

Without going into any further detail as to how the autarky equilibrium is determined exactly, we can draw some important conclusions based on the properties that must hold in this equilibrium. First, we know that the Marginal Rate of Transformation must be equal to the ratio of marginal costs, see Chapter 7. Second, we know that the price charged by the monopolist is a mark-up over the marginal cost of production, see equation (9.1). Third, we know that the Marginal Rate of Substitution must be equal to

[2] The shaded area represents operating profits. This may be required to recuperate the initial (fixed cost) outlays if there are increasing returs to scale, see Chapter 10.

the ratio of final goods prices, see again Chapter 7. Fourth, we know that market clearing in autarky implies that production must be equal to consumption in equilibrium. Combining this information leads to the following important conclusion:

$$(9.2) \qquad MRT = \frac{MC_m}{MC_f} = \frac{p_m(1 - 1/\varepsilon_m)}{p_f} < \frac{p_m}{p_f} = MRS$$

where ε_m is the price elasticity of demand for manufactures.

The autarky equilibrium if there is a monopoly for manufactures is illustrated in Figure 9.3, see point Mon. Note that point Mon is in accordance with the four remarks made above. Perfect competition in the factor markets implies that the production point is efficient, that is it must be on the production possibility frontier. Since the monopolist for manufactures charges a higher price than the marginal cost of production, the marginal rate of transformation deviates from the final goods price ratio, which in turn is equal to the marginal rate of substitution, see equation (9.2). Moreover, at the income level generated by the economy at point Mon, the consumers also want to consume at point Mon, such that production equals consumption in both sectors.

As is clear from Figure 9.2, the fact that there is a monopoly in manufactures implies that the economy is not producing at the social optimum; the utility level achieved at point Mon is equal to U_{mon}, which is strictly below the utility level U_{opt} which the economy can achieve in autarky at point Opt. The monopoly in manufactures, leading to a mark-up of price over marginal costs, therefore leads to a sub-optimal autarky equilibrium in which the production of manufactures is too low.

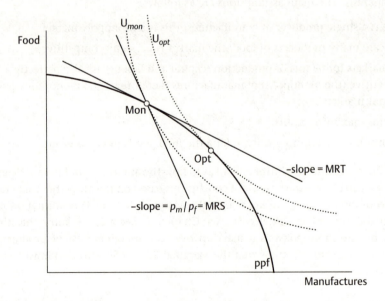

Fig. 9.3 Autarky equilibrium with monopoly for manufactures

9.4 **Oligopoly**

Market power can, of course, also arise if there are only a few firms, rather than one, active in a market. This is called an oligopoly. If there are just two firms, say an Austrian firm (sub-index A) and a Bolivian firm (sub-index B), the market is called a duopoly. That case has already been analysed by Augustin Cournot (1838). He assumes that the two firms produce identical goods, such that there is only one market demand curve, and that both firms maximize their profits, *given* the demand curve and the output level of their opponent. Determining the equilibrium production levels, and concomitant price level, in this market is somewhat more involved than if there is only one firm. As in section 9.2, we impose a linear demand curve, see however Technical Note 9.2.

Let p be the market price and $q = q_A + q_B$ be the total output in the market. We focus on the problem for the Austrian firm. Similar observations hold for the Bolivian firm. The basic problem for the Austrian firm is quite similar to the problem facing a monopolist. However, given the linear market demand $p = a - bq$ and the fact that total output is the sum of the Austrian firm's and Bolivian firm's output, it follows that the Austrian firm's profits π_A depend on the Bolivian firm's output level as follows:

$$(9.3) \qquad \pi_A = (p - c)q_A = [(a - c) - b(q_A + q_B)]q_A$$

where c is the marginal cost of production. Observe that

(i) Given the output level q_{B0} of the Bolivian firm, the Austrian firm maximizes profits π_A through a suitable choice of its output level, at say q_{A0}.
(ii) If the Bolivian firm changes its production level from q_{B0} to q_{B1}, the Austrian firm's profit maximization problem in point (i) is affected, which leads to a *different* optimal choice of its output level, say q_{A1}.
(iii) In general, therefore, each different output level of the Bolivian firm leads to a different optimal output level for the Austrian firm. The collection of all optimal output responses by the Austrian firm to the Bolivian firm's output level is called the *Austrian firm's reaction curve*.

This is illustrated in Figure 9.4. First, given that the Bolivian firm produces q_{B0} units of goods, the Austrian firm's optimal output choice must determine the optimal output combination on the dashed horizontal line generated by point q_{B0}. Since the Austrian firm maximizes profits, this dashed line must be tangent to one of its isoprofit curves, some of which are also drawn in Figure 9.4. The optimal production level for the Austrian firm, given that the Bolivian firm produces q_{B0}, is therefore equal to q_{A0}. Second, if the Bolivian firm increases its output level from q_{B0} to q_{B1}, this reduces the price level in the market and the Austrian firm's profitability. Consequently, the Austrian firm's optimal response is then a reduction in output, from q_{A0} to q_{A1}. Third, similar reactions by the Austrian firm to changes in the output level of the Bolivian firm are given by the dots in Figure 9.4. Connecting all such dots gives the reaction curve of the Austrian firm. Fourth, note that if the output level of the Bolivian firm is equal to zero, the Austrian firm's

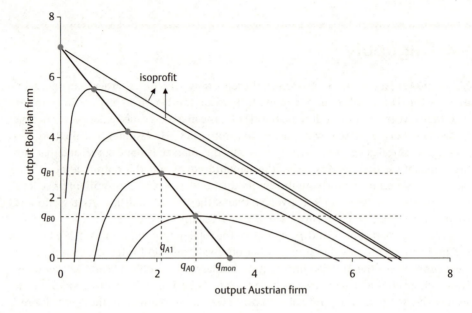

Fig. 9.4 Derivation of Austrian firm's reaction curve, $a = 8$, $b = c = 1$

problem reduces to that of a monopolist. Clearly this leads to the maximum attainable profits for the Austrian firm, at point q_{mon} in Figure 9.4. The isoprofit curves of the Austrian firm in Figure 9.4 increase as they approach q_{mon}.

As already remarked above, the Bolivian firm faces a similar problem as the Austrian firm. This means that, taking the output level q_A as given, the Bolivian firm will derive its optimal (profit maximizing) output level q_B. If we vary the Austrian firm's output level, we can derive all optimal responses by the Bolivian firm, which then obviously gives the Bolivian firm's reaction curve. This is illustrated in Figure 9.5, which also gives the Austrian firm's reaction curve and an isoprofit curve for each firm. Note that the isoprofit curve for the Bolivian firm is vertical at the point of intersection with its reaction curve because the Bolivian firm maximizes its profits at that point. The Cournot equilibrium is reached at the point of intersection of the two reaction curves, as indicated by point C in Figure 9.5. Why? Because, as the reader may wish to verify, it is the only point in the figure for which the Austrian firm maximizes its profits given the output level of the Bolivian firm, while simultaneously the Bolivian firm maximizes its profits given the output level of the Austrian firm. The duopoly price p_{duo} and quantity for each firm q_{duo} are derived in Technical Note 9.2, as given in equation (9.4).

$$(9.4) \qquad q_{duo} = \frac{a-c}{3b} = q_A = q_B; \quad p_{duo} = \frac{a+2c}{3} < \frac{a+c}{2} = p_{mon}, \text{ because } a > c$$

Note, in particular, that the duopoly price is *lower* than the monopolistic price, which implies that the duopoly output level for the market ($2q_{duo}$) is higher than the monopoly output level. Apparently, more competition, as measured by an increase in the number of firms, leads to a lower price level. In fact, if the Austrian firm operates in a market

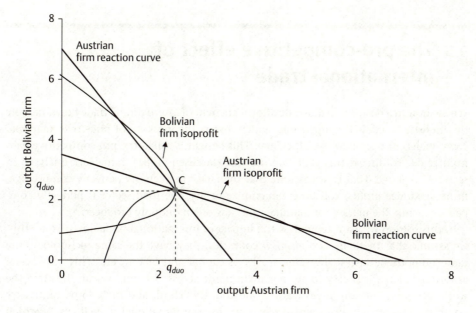

Fig. 9.5 Cournot equilibrium

with more than one firm, the following result holds in general, see again Technical Note 9.2:

$$(9.5) \qquad p \left(1 - \underbrace{\frac{q_A}{q}}_{\substack{market \\ share}} \frac{1}{\varepsilon(q)} \right) = c(q_A)$$

Equation (9.5) indicates that the marginal-revenue-equals-marginal-cost rule which the Austrian firm applies leads to a mark-up of price over marginal cost depending on:

- The price elasticity of demand $\varepsilon(q)$ prevailing in the market
- The Austrian firm's market share q_A/q

More specifically, the higher the price elasticity of demand the lower the mark-up, and the lower the Austrian firm's market share the lower the mark-up. In the limit, as the number of firms in the Cournot model becomes arbitrarily large and the Austrian firm's market share becomes arbitrarily small, the mark-up disappears and the price becomes equal to the marginal cost of production, as in the perfectly competitive model. One of the main attractions of the Cournot model is therefore that it reduces to the monopoly model if there is only one firm and to the perfectly competitive model if there are arbitrarily many firms.

9.5 The pro-competitive effect of international trade

We are now in a position to illustrate another benefit of international trade flows, namely the increase in market competition, which lowers the mark-up of price over marginal costs, which in turn increases efficiency. This benefit is called the pro-competitive gain from trade. To discuss this effect we use the Markusen (1981) framework analysed in section 9.3 above. That is, we assume that the factor markets are perfectly competitive, firms maximize profits, consumers maximize utility, the food sector is perfectly competitive, while the market for manufactures has one monopoly producer.

In this section we want to analyse the impact of international trade flows. To do this, we assume that there are two *identical* countries; they have the same technology, the same homothetic tastes, the same stocks of capital and labour, etc. This has several advantages. First, it is easy to get our main point across. Second, we can illustrate the world economy by only investigating one country. Third, and most importantly, we neutralize any other reasons which may give rise to international trade flows, or which may lead to gains from trade; since technology is the same there is no Ricardian reason to trade, and since the capital–labour ratio is the same there is no Heckscher–Ohlin reason to trade.

The pro-competitive gains from trade are illustrated in Figure 9.6. In autarky both countries produce at the same distorted production and consumption point Mon, as discussed in section 9.3. In autarky, the manufactures firm is a monopolist, which implies

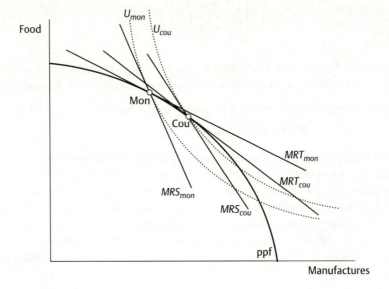

Fig. 9.6 Pro-competitive gains from trade

that the marginal rate of transformation is below the marginal rate of substitution, see equation (9.2). If trade of final goods is allowed, however, the monopoly producers for manufactures in both countries are confronted with an extra competitor, namely the previous monopolist in the other country. The market for manufactures has therefore become a duopoly, rather than a monopoly, in both countries. As described in section 9.4, and analogous to our reasoning in section 9.3, we can therefore conclude:

$$(9.6) \qquad MRT_{duo} = \frac{MC_m}{MC_f}\bigg|_{duo} = \frac{p_m(1 - 1/2\varepsilon_m)}{p_f} < \frac{p_m}{p_f}\bigg|_{duo} = MRS_{duo}$$

As in the autarky equilibrium with a monopoly summarized in equation (9.2), the marginal rate of transformation is below the marginal rate of substitution in the trade equilibrium with a duopoly. Note, however, that in a duopoly firms only take the effect of their share of the market into consideration when determining the optimal production level, see equation (9.5). The wedge between the marginal rate of transformation and the marginal rate of substitution has therefore *reduced* from $1 - 1/\varepsilon_m$ to $1 - 1/2\varepsilon_m$ (because each firm in our example controls half the market). Consequently, the Cournot international trade equilibrium is illustrated by point Cou in Figure 9.6, in which the wedge between the marginal rate of transformation and the marginal rate of substitution has reduced, leading to more efficient production and higher welfare. This is known as the pro-competitive effect of international trade.

Remark. Note that the monopoly firms in both countries have a strong incentive to lobby with their respective governments *against* international trade flows. If they are successful in producing barriers to such flows, their profits will rise.

9.6 'Reciprocal dumping'

The power of the pro-competitive gains from trade is nicely illustrated in the Brander (1981) and Brander and Krugman (1983) 'reciprocal dumping' approach. It is based on the Cournot competition model of sections 9.4 and 9.5, and therefore assumes a symmetric situation with two identical countries, but it allows for international trade to take place at positive transport costs. As we will see shortly, the model predicts that there is 'pointless' and costly trade in homogeneous products between the two countries, which nonetheless can increase welfare. The GATT 1994 defines 'dumping' as the sale of export below normal value. The term 'normal value' is operationalized either as (i) the comparable price of the product in the exporting country, (ii) the comparable price for export to a third country, or (iii) the cost of production in the country of origin plus a reasonable addition for selling cost and profit.[3] Since the firms in the model to be developed below

---

[3] The normal value minus the export price is the margin of dumping. It must exceed 2 per cent to be actionable, in which case the importing country can levy an anti-dumping duty if the imports cause, or are likely to cause, injury to the domestic industry.

Box 9.1 Iceberg transport costs

'Iceberg' transport costs, introduced by Paul Samuelson (1952), imply that only a fraction of the goods shipped between locations actually arrives at the destination. The fraction that does *not* arrive represents the cost of transportation. The parameter T, defined as the number of goods that need to be shipped to ensure that 1 unit arrives per unit of distance, represents the transport costs. Suppose, for example, that the unit of distance is equal to the distance from Naaldwijk (a small town in the centre of the Dutch horticultural agglomeration) to Paris, and that 107 flowers are sent from Holland to France, while only 100 arrive unharmed in Paris and can be sold. Then $T = 1.07$. It is as if some goods have melted away in transit, hence the name iceberg costs. This way of modelling the transport costs without introducing a transport sector is very attractive in combination with the Chapter 10 price setting behaviour of producers, see Chapter 14.

---

sell goods in the other country at the same price as at home and do not recuperate the costs of transportation, it is called the 'reciprocal dumping' model.

We illustrate the reciprocal dumping model for linear demand functions using 'iceberg' transport costs, see Box 9.1. The parameter $T \geq 1$ denotes the number of goods that need to be shipped to ensure that one unit of the good arrives in the other country. If the marginal cost of producing the good is c for both firms, the marginal cost of delivering the good in the other country is therefore $Tc > c$. Let q_{AA} be the Austrian firm's supply in Austria and q_{BA} be the Bolivian firm's supply in Austria. With a linear demand curve, the price p_A in Austria can be written as a function of the total quantity supplied:

$$(9.7) \qquad\qquad p_A = a - b(q_{AA} + q_{BA})$$

Autarky

In autarky, the Austrian firm is a monopolist in Austria. As illustrated in Figure 9.7, the price is determined by the equality of marginal cost and monopoly marginal revenue at point A, leading to monopoly price p_{mon} and monopoly output q_{mon}.

Trade

With free international trade, the Austrian firm faces competition from the Bolivian firm, despite the fact that the Bolivian firm has higher marginal costs of delivering goods to the market of Austria as a result of the transport costs T. This gives the Austrian firm a natural advantage in the domestic market. Nonetheless, as long as the price in Austria is above the Bolivian firm's marginal costs inclusive of transport costs Tc, the Bolivian firm will make a profit by selling goods in Austria's market. As shown in Technical Note 9.3, the reciprocal dumping equilibrium is given by:

(9.8) $$q_{AA} = \frac{a + Tc - 2c}{3b}; \quad q_{BA} = \frac{a + c - 2Tc}{3b}; \quad p_{rec} = \frac{a + c + Tc}{3}$$

Note that $q_{AA} > q_{BA}$, that is the Austrian firm's market share in Austria is larger than the Bolivian firm's market share as a result of its lower marginal costs. The situation is illustrated in Figure 9.7. With imports equal to q_{BA} the domestic market demand curve for the Austrian firm shifts inward (not drawn). The perceived marginal revenue curve therefore shifts down from MR_{mon} to MR_{rec}. The Austrian firm's output level is determined by the equality of the new marginal revenue curve with the marginal cost of production at point B. The Bolivian firm's demand curve in Austria is shifted further inwards (by the extent of q_{AA}) and its output level is determined by equality of its perceived marginal revenue curve with its marginal costs inclusive of transport costs (not drawn). Since the Bolivian firm sells fewer units in Austria's market, its perceived elasticity of demand is higher than the Austrian firm's, leading to a lower mark-up over marginal costs (which are higher for the Bolivian firm than for the Austrian firm, leading to the same price in equilibrium).

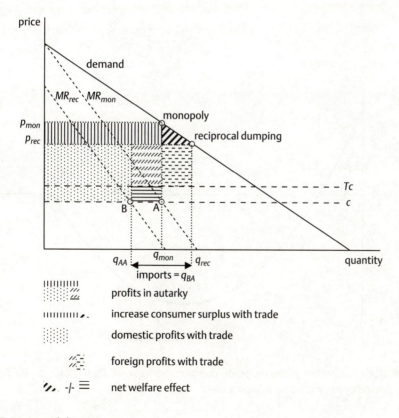

Fig. 9.7 Reciprocal dumping

Reciprocal dumping and welfare

Note that this symmetric model gives rise to 'reciprocal dumping' as a result of the difference in perceived elasticity of demand: the Bolivian firm incurs high transport costs to sell goods in Austria's market at a lower mark-up over marginal costs than at home, and similarly for the Austrian firm in Bolivia's market. Despite this seemingly pointless and costly international trade, the pro-competitive effect of trade, leading to lower prices, higher quantities, and smaller deviations between price and marginal costs, may increase the welfare level of both countries. Figure 9.7 illustrates the welfare changes using the partial equilibrium tools developed in Chapter 8. Since trade reduces prices there is an increase in consumer surplus. At the same time, the domestic firm's drop in profits at home is only partially compensated by an increase in profits abroad. In general, therefore, the welfare effect is ambivalent. As illustrated in Figure 9.8, however, for small and moderate transport costs the net welfare effects are positive. Only if transport costs are high (in this specific example if transport costs are 24 per cent; that is $T = 1.24$) is the net welfare effect negative. A further increase in transport costs eventually reduces this welfare loss as trade becomes too small and costly. Ultimately trade disappears (prohibitive transport costs).

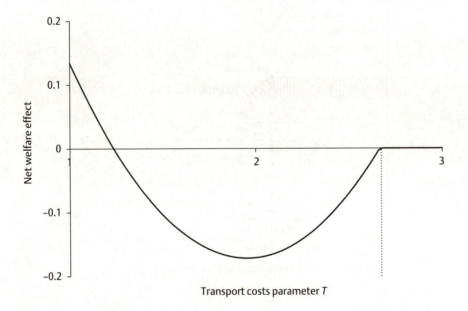

Fig. 9.8 Trade and welfare in the reciprocal dumping model, $a = 3.25$, $b = 0.65$, $c = 0.75$, the dashed line indicates prohibitive transport costs

9.7 **Application: the Twaron takeover**

Aramid fibres were made for the first time in the 1970s. These synthetic fibres are very strong and light, do not break or rust, and have a high chemical and heat resistance. They are used, for example, for friction and sealing, and the production of tyres, protective clothing, optical cables, and bulletproof vests. Until recently there were three firms producing aramid fibres, namely an American firm (DuPont, producing 18,000 tons under the brand name Kevlar), a Dutch firm (Acordis, producing 10,300 tons under the brand name Twaron), and a Japanese firm (Teijin, producing 1,400 tons under the brand name Technora). In 2000 the Japanese firm Teijin bought the aramid fibre component from the Dutch firm Acordis. The impact of the takeover in this oligopolistic market structure, which changed from three suppliers to two suppliers as a result of the takeover, can be estimated using the Cournot model of section 9.4. This is indicated in Table 9.1 for a demand structure with constant price elasticity (rather than the linear demand discussed in section 9.4). After calibrating the model to ensure that the above distribution of market shares results (i.e. DuPont has the lowest and Teijin the highest marginal costs), the table reports the impact of the takeover for two demand elasticities, namely $\varepsilon = 2$ and $\varepsilon = 1$.

The decrease in international competition as a result of the takeover increases the market clearing price by about 2–6 per cent, depending on the price elasticity of demand. All suppliers in the market benefit from the higher price, leading to higher operating profits. These rise for DuPont as a result of the higher price (an estimated effect of 6–8 per cent) and for the new combination Twaron/Technora as a result of the higher price and the better use of economies of scale (an estimated effect of 9–16 per cent).

Table 9.1 Implications of the Twaron takeover (%)

	Price elasticity of demand	
	$\varepsilon = 2$	$\varepsilon = 1$
Price rise after takeover	1.9	6.1
Rise in operating profits after takeover		
Kevlar	6.5	8.1
Twaron/Technora	9.5	15.6

9.8 **Conclusions**

Profit maximizing firms in an imperfectly competitive market will charge a mark-up of price over marginal costs. The size of the mark-up depends on the price elasticity of demand and on the degree of competition, such that an increase in the number of firms reduces the mark-up. In a general equilibrium setting, imperfect competition leads to a sub-optimal outcome (a deviation between MRS and MRT). Since international trade increases market competition, as foreign firms start to compete on the domestic market and vice versa, international trade improves economic efficiency (by diminishing the deviation between MRS and MRT), the so-called pro-competitive gains from trade. This 'reciprocal' dumping may even increase welfare if international trade is costly.

Technical Notes (optional)

Technical Note 9.1 Monopolist profit maximization

If a market's demand curve is given by $p(q)$, and a monopolist's cost function is given by $C(q)$, where q is the quantity of output, then the firm's profits π are given by

(9.A1)
$$\pi = p(q)q - C(q)$$

The first-order condition for profit maximization is

(9.A2)
$$p + \frac{dp}{dq}q = \frac{dC}{dq}$$

If we let $c(q)$ denote the marginal cost of production and, as is customary, measure the responsiveness of demand to price changes in relative terms, that is using the elasticity of substitution $\varepsilon(q) \equiv -(dq/dp)(p/q) > 0$, the first-order condition can be rewritten as

(9.A3)
$$p\left(1 - \frac{1}{\varepsilon(q)}\right) = c(q)$$

If demand is linear ($p = a - bq$), we have $\varepsilon(q) = (a - bq)/bq$ resulting in

(9.A4)
$$q_{mon} = \frac{a - c}{2b}; \quad p_{mon} = \frac{a + c}{2} > \frac{c + c}{2} = c, \text{ because } a > c$$

Technical Note 9.2 Cournot profit maximization

Suppose a market's demand curve is given by $p(q)$, where q is total output by all firms active in the market. If firm A is one of those firms, we can write market output as $q = q_A + q_{-A}$, where q_A is the output of firm A and q_{-A} is the output of all other firms. If firm A's cost function is given by $C(q_A)$, then firm A's profits π_A are given by

(9.A5)
$$\pi_A = p(q)q_A - C(q_A)$$

The first-order condition for profit maximization is

(9.A6)
$$p + \frac{dp}{dq}q_A = c(q_A)$$

where $c(q_A)$ is the marginal cost of production. Let $\varepsilon(q)$ be the price elasticity of demand, then the first-order condition can be rewritten as

(9.A7)
$$p\left(1 - \frac{q_A}{q}\frac{1}{\varepsilon(q)}\right) = c(q_A)$$

For a duopoly, linear demand curve $p = a - bq$, and $c(q) = c$, firm A's reaction curve is

(9.A8)
$$\frac{\partial \pi_A}{\partial q_A} = 0 \Rightarrow q_A = \frac{a-c}{2b} - \frac{1}{2} q_B$$

Similarly for firm B. The Cournot equilibrium is at the intersection of the reaction curves

(9.A9)
$$q_A = q_B = \frac{a-c}{3b}; \quad p_{duo} = \frac{a+2c}{3} < \frac{a+c}{2} = p_{mon}, \text{ because } a > c$$

Technical Note 9.3 Reciprocal dumping model

Since the model is symmetric for the two countries, we concentrate on Austria. With a linear demand curve, the price p_A can be written as a function of firm A's supply in Austria q_{AA} and firm B's supply in Austria q_{BA}:

(9.A10)
$$p_A = a - b(q_{AA} + q_{BA})$$

Assuming that marginal cost of production is equal to c for both firms, and that there are iceberg transport costs, such that marginal cost for firm B for delivery of goods in Austria is equal to Tc, the profit functions π are:

(9.A11)
$$\pi_A = [a - b(q_{AA} + q_{BA})]q_{AA} - cq_{AA}$$
$$\pi_B = [a - b(q_{AA} + q_{BA})]q_{BA} - Tcq_{BA}$$

First-order conditions for profit maximization, given the other firm's output level, are:

(9.A12)
$$(a - bq_{BA}) - 2bq_{AA} = c; \quad (a - bq_{AA}) - 2bq_{BA} = Tc$$

Solving these two linear equations gives:

(9.A13)
$$q_{AA} = \frac{a + Tc - 2c}{3b}; \quad q_{BA} = \frac{a + c - 2Tc}{3b}; \quad p_{rec} = \frac{a + c + Tc}{3}$$

Chapter 10

Intra-industry Trade

Objectives/key terms

Aggregation level	Grubel–Lloyd index
Intra-industry trade	(love-of-) Variety
Dixit–Stiglitz demand	Price elasticity of demand
Internal and external scale economies	Monopolistic competition
Mark-up pricing	Zero profits

We extend the analysis of imperfect competition by including economies of scale, which in conjunction with the size of the market determines the number of different types of goods and services available. Trade increases the extent of the market, thus making more types of goods available. This can be used to explain the empirical phenomenon of intra-industry trade (two-way trade in similar types of goods).

10.1 Introduction

The phenomenon of intra-industry trade is a prime example of a widely known and accepted empirical regularity in the search for a satisfactory theoretical foundation for many years. For a long time the empirical researchers were therefore clearly ahead of the theoretical researchers. What is intra-industry trade? It refers to the fact that many countries simultaneously export and import very similar goods and services; intra-industry trade is therefore trade within the same industry or sector. Germany, for example, exports many cars to France and simultaneously imports many cars from France as well. Why does Germany do this? This chapter seeks to give an answer to this question based on aspects of a nation's demand structure, as well as its supply structure.

The intra-industry trade phenomenon was first noted empirically when a group of European Countries formed the European Common Market, which has now grown into the European Union and currently consists of fifteen countries, see Chapter 13. It was soon realized that intra-industry trade is a general characteristic of international trade flows. Path-breaking empirical research in measuring the size and importance

Fig. 10.1 Avinash Dixit (1944–   )

Born in Bombay, India, where he studied mathematics and physics, Dixit continued his studies at the University of Cambridge, where he got his BA, and at MIT, where he got his Ph.D. before moving to Princeton in 1980. His theoretical work, characterizing market equilibrium and designing policies, covers various areas of economics, such as microeconomics, international economics, industrial organization, public economics, investment under uncertainty, and growth and development. Influential contributions are 'Monopolistic competition and optimum product diversity' published jointly with Joseph Stiglitz (see Chapter 9) in the *American Economic Review* in 1977, and two books, namely *Theory of International Trade*, with Victor Norman in 1980, and *Investment under Uncertainty*, with Robert Pindyck in 1994.

of intra-industry trade was performed by Pieter Verdoorn (1960), Bela Balassa (1966), and Herbert Grubel and Peter Lloyd (1975), see section 10.2.

Why did the realization that there is intensive intra-industry trade between nations embarrass theoretical economists? Because the theories of comparative advantage developed until then, based on Ricardian technology differences or Heckscher–Ohlin factor abundance, cannot explain this type of trade. Both types of models assume that firms in the same industry produce identical goods, such that consumers do not distinguish between the goods produced by different firms, nor care which firm produced the goods in making their demand decisions. A country will therefore either only export goods within the same industry, or only import these goods, but not simultaneously export and import goods within the same industry.

It was, of course, immediately realized that the goods and services produced by firms in the same industry are, in fact, not identical. Taking the simultaneous German exports of cars to France and imports of cars from France again as an example, everyone acknowledges that a Volkswagen Golf is not the same as a Peugeot 206. They are similar products, delivering similar services, produced using a similar technology, such that they are classified in the same industry, but they are not the same. A satisfactory theoretical explanation should therefore be able to distinguish between goods and services which are close, but imperfect substitutes. This requires a change in the demand structure of the economy, such that consumers demand many different varieties of similar, but not identical, products in the same industry.

Suppose that we are able to change the demand structure of the economy such that consumers have a preference for different varieties of similar products. Are we then able to explain intra-industry trade? Not yet, because we still have to explain why the domestic industry does not provide an arbitrarily large number of varieties to cater to the preferences of consumers. Going back again to the Germany–France car example, it is clear that Volkswagen has the ability and technology available to produce a car virtually identical to the Peugeot 206, and is thus able to fulfil demand for that type of product. Large initial investment costs, spread over several years, are required, however, before such a new type of car is designed, developed, tested, and can be produced. These large investment costs, giving rise to increasing returns to scale, are the primary reason for Volkswagen, or other German car manufacturers, to produce only a limited number

Box 10.1 **Dixit–Stiglitz monopolistic competition**

There is only one way for competition to be 'perfect'. In contrast, there is a bewildering range of models describing 'imperfect' competition, investigating many different cases and assumptions regarding market behaviour, the type of good, strategic interaction, preferences of consumers, etc. This was also the case with monopolistic competition, until Avinash Dixit and Joseph Stiglitz (1977) published 'Monopolistic competition and optimum product diversity' in the *American Economic Review*. This article was to revolutionize model building in at least four fields of economics: trade theory, industrial organization, growth theory, and geographical economics.[1]

The big step forward was to make some heroic assumptions concerning the symmetry of new varieties and the structural form, which allowed for an elegant and consistent way to model production at the firm level benefiting from internal economies of scale in conjunction with a market structure of monopolistic competition, without getting bogged down in a taxonomy of oligopoly models. These factors are responsible for the present popularity of the Dixit–Stiglitz model. Researchers in all fields now using the Dixit–Stiglitz formulation intensively were aware that imperfect competition is an essential feature of many empirically observed phenomena. The Dixit-Stiglitz model was therefore immediately accepted as the new standard for modelling monopolistic competition; its development was certainly very timely. In international trade theory, its introduction enabled international economists to explain and understand intra-industry trade, see Krugman (1979, 1980). In industrial organization it helped to get rid of many ad hoc assumptions, which hampered the development of many models, see Tirole (1988). The Dixit–Stiglitz model was also used to explore the role of intermediate differentiated goods in international trade models. This reformulation of the standard Dixit–Stiglitz model plays an important role in the link between international trade and economic growth, see Grossman and Helpman (1991*a*). Finally, the model is intensively used in Geographical Economics, see Brakman, Garretsen, and van Marrewijk (2001).

of different varieties. This also implies that a car manufacturer, being the only producer of a particular variety, has considerable market power, which it takes into consideration when maximizing profits.

These considerations clarify why it took some time, and considerable ingenuity, to provide a solid theoretical explanation of intra-industry trade flows, since such an explanation has to incorporate:

- Consumer preferences with a demand for different varieties of similar products;
- Increasing returns to scale in production, limiting the diversity in production which the market can provide;
- A market structure of imperfect competition consistent with the phenomenon of increasing returns to scale.

[1] The paper by Spence (1976) on a similar topic slightly predates Dixit and Stiglitz (1977), but had considerably less influence. See Neary (2001) for a discussion on Dixit–Stiglitz monopolistic competition.

The challenge is to incorporate these features in a simple general equilibrium setting, for which the industrial organization literature provided the most important stimulus with the Dixit and Stiglitz (1977) paper, see Box 10.1. The American economist Paul Krugman (1979, 1980) used the Dixit–Stiglitz variety specification combined with internal increasing returns to scale to analyse intra-industry trade in a Chamberlinian (1933) model of monopolistic competition. Simultaneously, Lancaster (1979) introduced consumer heterogeneity, where consumers are distinguished by their most preferred product characteristics, in which differentiated products cater to different tastes. In both cases, increasing returns to scale limit the extent of diversity that the market can provide. We restrict attention to the *Krugman* variety approach, not only because it is the easiest framework to work with, but also because it has had a bigger impact on the rest of the international trade literature, and serves as a good introduction to geographical economics and endogenous growth theory, see Chapters 14 and 16.

10.2 **Measuring intra-industry trade**

How do we measure intra-industry trade, the extent of trade in similar goods? Although various options are available, the measure most often used is the Grubel–Lloyd index, which is simple and intuitively appealing. Let Ex_i be the exports of industry i and let Im_i be the imports of industry i, then the Grubel–Lloyd index GL_i for industry i is defined as

(10.1)
$$GL_i = 1 - \frac{|Ex_i - Im_i|}{Ex_i + Im_i}$$

If a country only imports or only exports goods or services within the same industry, such that there is no intra-industry trade, the second term on the right-hand side of equation (10.1) is equal to 1 ($Ex_i/Ex_i = 1$ or $Im_i/Im_i = 1$), such that the whole expression reduces to 0. Similarly, if the exports of goods or services are exactly equal to the imports of those goods or services within the same industry ($Ex_i = Im_i$), the second term on the right-hand side of equation (10.1) is equal to zero, such that

---

Chapter 10 tool: Grubel–Lloyd index

The most widely used tool in international economics for empirically determining the extent of intra-industry trade was developed by Herbert Grubel and Peter Lloyd, and is therefore known as the Grubel–Lloyd index. It is a simple index, explained in detail in the main text, which varies between 0 (no intra-industry trade) and 1 (complete intra-industry trade), or between 0 and 100 in percentage terms.

the whole expression reduces to 1. The Grubel–Lloyd index therefore varies between 0, indicating no intra-industry trade, and 1, indicating only intra-industry trade.

Which share of international trade is intra-industry trade? We first illustrate this question using data for the Philippines and Japan given in Table 10.1, and then report the results of a more detailed study in Table 10.2. International trade data are grouped at the 'digit' level. The first row of Table 10.1 gives exports and imports between the Philippines and Japan at the 1-digit level, namely for SITC category 8 'miscellaneous manufactured products'. Since the exports are $383 million and the imports are $576 million, applying equation (10.1) shows that according to the Grubel–Lloyd index 80 per cent of the trade in category 8 is intra-industry trade, see the last column in Table 10.1.

Table 10.1 International trade between the Philippines (RP) and Japan; 1998

SITC		Exports from RP	Imports into RP	GL index
8	Miscellaneous manufactured articles	383,167	576,412	0.80
81	Prefabricated buildings	4,147	2,186	0.69
82	Furniture and parts thereof	42,332	6,155	0.25
83	Travel goods, handbags, and similar containers	4,804	67	0.03
84	Articles of apparel and clothing accessories	115,627	3,255	0.05
85	Footwear	13,283	920	0.13
87	Prof. scientific and controlling instruments	24,091	175,018	0.24
88	Photographic apparatus	72,174	123,333	0.74
89	Miscellaneous manufactured articles	106,709	265,477	0.57

Source: OECD (Foreign trade by commodities) × $1,000; GL index = Grubel–Lloyd index; RP = Republica ng Pilipinas, the Republic of the Philippines.

Table 10.2 Intra-industry trade, GL-index manufacturing sector 1995 (3-digit level, %)

Country	World	OECD 22	NAFTA	East Asia dev.	Latin America
Australia	36.6	17.5	16.0	39.2	41.6
Bangladesh	10.0	3.5	1.7	3.4	8.0
Chile	25.7	10.1	11.5	3.6	47.8
France	83.5	86.7	62.7	38.7	22.9
Germany	75.3	80.1	61.2	36.2	22.8
Japan	42.3	47.6	45.7	36.1	7.0
Malaysia	60.4	48.5	57.9	75.0	10.4
Hong Kong	28.4	20.2	25.2	19.9	13.6
UK	85.4	84.0	72.5	46.6	38.6
USA	71.7	74.0	73.5	41.4	66.0

Source: NAPES website, http://napes.anu.edu.au/

What are 'miscellaneous manufactured goods'? An indication is given in the other rows of Table 10.1, giving a breakdown at the two-digit level of category 8. Apparently, it consists of such diverse goods as prefabricated buildings, footwear, and photographic apparatus. The calculation in the above paragraph grouped all of this together at the one-digit level. The Grubel–Lloyd index of 80 per cent calculated above thus classifies trade of footwear in exchange for prefabricated buildings as intra-industry trade. This seems a bit far-fetched, and obviously leads to artificially high intra-industry trade estimates, such that it is preferable to analyse the goods classification and intra-industry trade at a more detailed level. For category 8 at the two-digit level in Table 10.1, the Grubel–Lloyd index of intra-industry trade varies from 0.03 for travel goods to 0.74 for photographic apparatus. The unweighted average of these eight two-digit categories is equal to 0.34, and the weighted average[2] is equal to 0.45. Both are considerably lower than the 0.80 value calculated at the one-digit level for category 8. We conclude, therefore, that analysing international trade flows at a lower, or more detailed, level of aggregation leads to a reduction in the estimated extent of intra-industry trade. The phenomenon of intra-industry trade, however, does not disappear if we do this, see Table 10.2.

Table 10.2 summarizes the extent of intra-industry trade in 1995 at the three-digit level for a selection of countries. Take the USA as an example. Averaged over all countries, no less than 71.7 per cent of US trade can be categorized as intra-industry trade. This is, however, unevenly distributed. US trade with the Asian newly indus-trialized countries (41.4 per cent intra-industry trade) and Latin America (66.0 per cent intra-industry trade) has a lower intra-industry trade component than US trade with the NAFTA countries (73.5 per cent) or the OECD countries (74.0 per cent). Similarly, the high overall level of intra-industry trade for France (83.5 per cent) is the combination of low intra-industry trade levels with respect to Latin America (22.9 per cent) and South-East Asia (38.7 per cent), and high intra-industry trade levels with respect to NAFTA (62.7 per cent) and the OECD (86.7 per cent). Table 10.2 also illustrates the lower intra-industry trade levels for developing nations (for example 10.0 per cent for Bangladesh), such that we may conclude that intra-industry trade is more prevalent among devel-oped nations and that similar developed nations are largely engaged in trading similar types of goods between themselves.

Figure 10.2 depicts the evolution of the Grubel–Lloyd index for Germany, Japan, and the USA over a period of thirty-five years (1961–96), measured at the two-digit level. All three countries have experienced an increase in the extent of intra-industry trade; for Germany from 41 to 73 per cent, for Japan from 25 to 43 per cent, and for the USA from 47 to 67 per cent. Similar developments have occurred in most other nations. Apparently, intra-industry trade is becoming more important over time.

---

[2] The sum of exports and imports as a share of the total is used as the relevant weight.

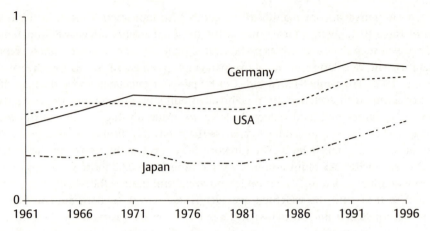

Fig. 10.2 Evolution of intra-industry trade
Source: Siebert (1999)

10.3 Dixit–Stiglitz demand

The Dixit–Stiglitz model of monopolistic competition acknowledges that consumers demand a large range of different varieties of similar, but not identical products. Think, for example, of a range of varieties for mobile telephones, automobiles, televisions, etc. Although each producer of any individual variety has monopoly power in supplying its own variety, there is of course strong competition between firms in producing varieties of similar products. The demand structure of the Dixit–Stiglitz model allows for this strong competition. Let c_i be the level of consumption of a particular variety i of manufactures, and let N be the total number of available varieties. The Dixit–Stiglitz approach uses a Constant Elasticity of Substitution (CES) function for the utility U derived from the consumption of manufactures as a function of the consumption c_i of the N varieties:[3]

$$(10.2) \qquad U = \left(\sum_{i=1}^{N} c_i^{\rho} \right)^{1/\rho} ; \quad 0 < \rho < 1$$

Note that the consumption of all varieties enters equation (10.2) symmetrically. This greatly simplifies the analysis in the sequel. The parameter ρ, discussed further below, represents the love-of-variety effect of consumers. If $\rho = 1$ equation (10.2) simplifies to $U = \sum_i c_i$ and variety as such does not matter for utility (100 units of one variety gives the same utility as 1 unit of 100 varieties). Products are then perfect substitutes (1 unit less of one variety can exactly be compensated by 1 unit more

---

[3] Many textbooks discuss the properties of the CES function. See also Brakman and van Marrewijk (1998), who compare it with the properties of other utility functions.

of another variety). We therefore need $\rho < 1$ to ensure that the product varieties are imperfect substitutes. In addition, we need $\rho > 0$ to ensure that the individual varieties are substitutes (and not complements) for each other, which enables price setting behaviour based on monopoly power, see Technical Note 9.1 and section 10.5.

It is worthwhile to dwell a little longer on the specification of (10.2). Suppose all c_i are consumed in equal quantities, that is $c_i = c$ for all i. We can then rewrite equation (10.2):

$$(10.2') \qquad U = \left(\sum_{i=1}^{N} c^{\rho} \right)^{1/\rho} = (Nc^{\rho})^{1/\rho} = N^{1/\rho}c = \underbrace{N^{(1/\rho)-1}}_{\text{love-of-variety}} \underbrace{\left[Nc \right]}_{\substack{\text{claim on} \\ \text{resources}}}$$

In many models, as in the model discussed here and in the endogenous growth model of Chapter 16, the term Nc in equation (10.2') corresponds to a claim on real resources, requiring labour (and/or capital) to be produced. The number of available varieties N therefore represents an externality, or the extent of the market. Since $0 < \rho < 1$, the term $(1/\rho) - 1$ is larger than 0. This implies that an increase in the extent of the market N, which requires a proportional increase in the claim on real resources Nc, increases utility U derived from consumption of N varieties by more than the increase in the claim on real resources (since the term $N^{(1/\rho)-1}$ rises it represents a bonus for large markets). In this sense an increase in the extent of the market, which increases the number of varieties N the consumer can choose from, more than proportionally increases utility, hence the term love-of-variety effect.

Now that we have briefly digressed on the love-of-variety effect it is time to go back to the problem in hand: how does the consumer allocate spending on manufactures over the different varieties? Let p_i be the price of variety i for $i = 1, \ldots, N$. Naturally, funds $p_i c_i$ spent on variety i cannot be spent simultaneously on variety j, as given in the budget constraint with income I in equation (10.3):

$$(10.3) \qquad \sum_{i=1}^{N} p_i c_i = I$$

In order to derive a consumer's demand, we must now solve a somewhat more complicated optimization problem, namely maximize utility derived from the consumption of manufactures given in equation (10.2), subject to the budget constraint of equation (10.3). The solution to this problem is (see Technical Note 10.1):

$$(10.4) \qquad c_j = p_j^{-\varepsilon}[P^{\varepsilon-1}I], \text{ where } P = \text{price index}, \ U = I/P, \varepsilon \equiv 1/(1-\rho) > 1$$

Note that the definition of the price index P apparently implies that $U = I/P$. The price index P thus gives an exact representation of the utility level derived from the consumption of manufactures; this utility increases if, and only if, the income level I increases faster than the price index P. Such a price index is called an exact price index, see Diewert (1981) for further details.

10.4 Demand effects; income, price elasticity ε, and the price index P

Section 10.3 derived the demand for manufacturing varieties. The demand for variety 1, for example, is influenced by four variables, see equation (10.4):

(i) the income level I

(ii) the price p_1 of good 1

(iii) some parameter ε, and

(iv) the price index P.

Let's go over these points in more detail.

Point (i) is straightforward. The higher the income level, the more the consumer spends on variety 1. In fact, this relationship is equiproportional: other things being equal a 10 per cent rise in the income level results in a 10 per cent increase in the demand for all varieties of manufactures.

Point (ii) is also straightforward, but very important. It is straightforward in the sense that we obviously expect that the demand for variety 1 is a function of the price charged by the firm producing variety 1. It is very important in view of *how* demand for variety 1 depends on the price p_1. Note that the last part of equation (10.4) is written in square brackets. It depends on the price index for manufactures P and the income level I. Both are macroeconomic entities which the firm producing variety 1 will take as given, that is it will assume to have no control over these variables (see below for a further discussion). In that case, we can simplify the demand for variety 1, by defining $\gamma \equiv [P^{\varepsilon-1}I]$, as $c_1 = \gamma p_1^{-\varepsilon}$. This in turn implies that the price elasticity of demand for variety 1 is constant and equal to the parameter $\varepsilon > 1$, i.e. $-(\partial c_1/\partial p_1)(p_1/c_1) = \varepsilon$. This simple price elasticity of demand is the main advantage of the Dixit–Stiglitz approach as it greatly simplifies the price setting behaviour of monopolistically competitive firms, see section 10.5. Figure 10.3 illustrates the demand for a variety of manufactures as a function of its own price for different values of ε. Note that the demand for a variety falls much faster as a result of a small price increase, say from 1 to 1.5, if the price elasticity of demand is high.

Point (iii) becomes clear after the discussion in point (ii). We have defined the parameter ε not only to simplify the notation of equation (10.4) as much as possible, but also because it is an important economic parameter as it measures the price elasticity of demand for a variety of manufactured goods. In addition, this parameter measures the elasticity of substitution between two different varieties, that is how difficult it is to substitute one variety of manufactures for another variety of manufactures. Evidently, the price elasticity of demand and the elasticity of substitution are related in the Dixit–Stiglitz approach, a point which has been criticized in the literature. Be that as it may, our intuitive explanations of some phenomena in the remainder of this book will sometimes be based on the price elasticity of demand interpretation of ε, and

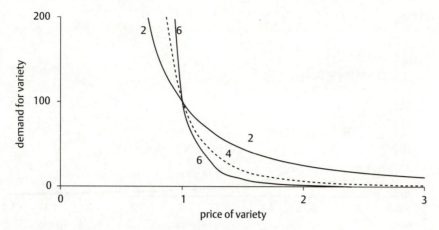

Fig. 10.3 Dependence of demand for a variety of manufactures on price and ε. Demand is given by $100\,p_i^{-\varepsilon}$, ε varies (2, 4, and 6)

sometimes on the elasticity of substitution interpretation, using what we feel is easiest for the problem at hand.

Point (iv), finally, indicates that the demand for variety 1 depends on the price index P. If the price index P increases, implying that 'on average' the prices of the manufacturing varieties competing with variety 1 are rising, then the demand for variety 1 is increasing (recall that $\varepsilon - 1 > 0$). The varieties are therefore economic substitutes of one another (if the price of a particular variety increases its own demand falls and the demand for all other varieties rises).

To finish our discussion of the demand structure of the core model we want to make a final remark concerning point (ii) above, where we argued that the (own) price elasticity of demand for the producer of variety 1 is equal to ε. Recall the specification of the demand function: $c_1 = p_1^{-\varepsilon}\lfloor P^{\varepsilon-1}I \rfloor$. We argued that the term in square brackets is treated as a constant by the producer because these are macroeconomic entities. Although this is true it overlooks a tiny detail: one of the terms in the specification of the price index of manufactures P is the price p_1. Thus, a truly rational producer would also take this minuscule effect on the aggregate price index into consideration.[4] For that reason it is often assumed that the number of varieties N produced is 'large', that is if our producer is one of 80,000 firms we can safely ignore this effect. This is illustrated in Figure 10.4 where we have plotted the demand curve facing the producer of a variety if she assumes she cannot influence the price index of manufactures, and the true demand taking this effect on the price index into consideration (details below Figure 10.4). Clearly, the assumption is a bad approximation if there are just two firms (panel *a*), but then nobody suggests you should use monopolistic competition in a duopoly. If there are twenty firms the approximation is already much better (panel *b*), if there are 200 firms the

---

[4] In fact, using (3.6) the exact price elasticity of demand for a specific variety can be derived. Illuminating in this respect is the analysis in the neighbourhood of p if $p_i = p$ for all other varieties, in which case $-(\partial c/\partial p)(p/c) = \varepsilon[1 - 1/N]$. The second term on the right-hand side is inversely related to the number of varieties N, approaching 1 if N becomes large.

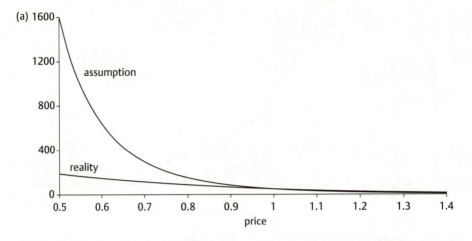

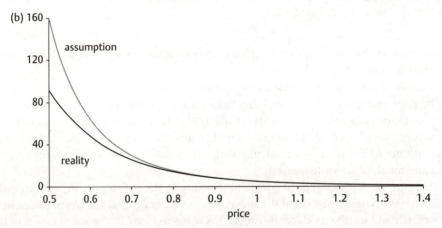

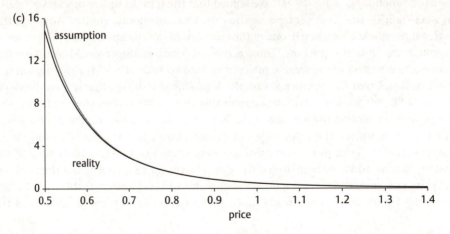

Fig. 10.4 Deviation between assumed demand and reality. (a) $N=2$, (b) $N=20$, (c) $N=200$, (d) $N=2000$, spending on manufactures $=100$, price of other firms $=1$, $\varepsilon=5$

(continued)

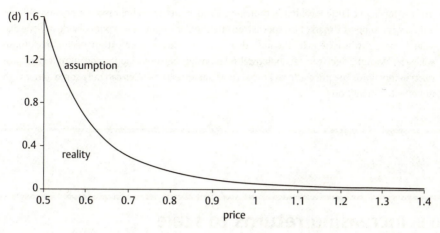

Fig. 10.4 (continued)

deviation is virtually undetectable (panel c), while it is unobservable if there are 2,000 firms (panel d). We can thus safely ignore this detail for a reasonably large number of varieties.

Box 10.2 **External and internal economies of scale**

The term 'Economies of Scale' or 'Increasing Returns to Scale' refers to a situation in which an increase in the level of output produced implies a decrease in the average costs per unit of output for the firm. It translates itself into a downward sloping average cost curve, see Figure 10.5. To identify the source of the fall in average costs Scitovsky (1954) distinguished between *internal* and *external* economies of scale. With internal economies of scale the decrease in average costs is brought about by an increase in the production level of the firm itself. The more the firm produces, the better it can profit from scale economies, and the higher its cost advantage over smaller firms. The market structure underlying internal scale economies must necessarily be one of *im*perfect competition as internal economies of scale imply market power. With external economies of scale, the decrease in average costs comes about through an output increase at the level of the industry as a whole, making average costs per unit a function of industry-wide output. Scitovsky distinguished here between *pure* and *pecuniary* external economies.

With *pure* (or *technological*) external economies an increase in industry-wide output alters the technological relationship between input and output for each individual firm. It therefore has an impact on the firm's production function. A frequently used example (dating back to Alfred Marshall) concerns information spillovers. An increase in industry output increases the stock of knowledge through positive information spillovers for each firm, leading to an increase in output at the firm level. The market structure can then be perfectly competitive since the size of the *individual* firm does not matter.

Pecuniary external economies are transmitted by the market through price effects for the individual firm, which may alter its output decision. Two examples, again based on Marshall, are the existence of a large local market for specialized inputs and labour market pooling. A large industry can support a market for specialized intermediate inputs and a pool of industry-specific skilled workers, which benefits the individual firm. Contrary to pure external economies these spillovers do not affect the technological relationship between inputs and output (the production function). The price effects crucial to pecuniary externalities can only come about with imperfect competition.

10.5 Increasing returns to scale

The Japanese companies Nikon and Canon, together with the Dutch ASM Lithography company, dominate the global market for chip machines, the vital tools for producing computer chips. The newest generation of ASM Lithography's machines, measuring $2\,m^2$ and weighing 7 tons, cost \$7 million apiece. To give an indication of the size of the (fixed) costs required for the equipment of one chip-making factory, Doug Dunn, chairman of ASM Lithography, remarked (NRC 2001*a*): 'It takes four years before a new factory is fully operational. It involves an investment of 2 billion dollars.' Clearly, then, chip makers are operative in a market with increasing returns to scale, implying that total costs increase, but costs per unit of output fall, as output expands. Numerous other sectors of the economy are also characterized by increasing returns to scale, usually because of initial investment costs before production can start; think of the automobile examples in section 10.1, or the shipping industry, or the aircraft industry, or setting up an internet site, or a law firm (where an initial investment in knowledge is required before legal services can be produced), etc.

We distinguish between external and internal increasing returns to scale, see Box 10.2. If there are increasing returns to scale, as in the examples given above, the firm will realize that its costs per unit of output fall if output expands. Internal returns to scale are therefore incompatible with perfect competition.[5] Therefore, if you think returns to scale are important, you must necessarily analyse a market of imperfect competition. In order not to overestimate the firm's power at the macroeconomic level, we will focus on a market of monopolistic competition.

Production in the manufacturing sector is characterized by internal economies of scale, which means that there is imperfect competition in this sector (see Box 10.2). The varieties in the manufacturing industry are all produced with the same technology. Internal economies of scale mean that each variety is produced by a single firm;

---

[5] If a firm takes the price of output *p* as given and the costs per unit of output *c* fall as output expands, the firm would want to make an infinite amount of goods if *c* falls below *p*, which cannot be an equilibrium.

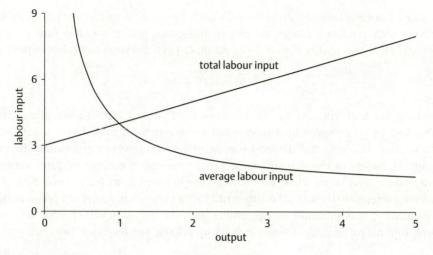

Fig. 10.5 Production function for a variety of manufactures

the firm with the largest sales can always outbid a potential competitor. The economies of scale are modelled in the simplest way possible:

(10.5) $l_i = f + mx_i$

where l_i is the amount of labour necessary to produce x_i of variety i. The parameters f and m describe, respectively, the fixed and marginal labour input requirement. The fixed labour input f in (10.5) ensures that as production expands less labour is needed to produce a unit of x_i, which means that there are internal economies of scale. This is illustrated in Figure 10.5, showing the total labour required to produce a certain amount of output, and the average amount of labour required to produce that amount of output.

10.6 **Optimal pricing and zero profits**

Each manufacturing firm produces a unique variety under internal returns to scale. This implies that the firm has monopoly power, which it will use to maximize its profits. We will therefore have to determine the price setting behaviour of each firm. The Dixit–Stiglitz monopolistic competition model makes two assumptions in this respect. First, it is assumed that each firm takes the price-setting behaviour of other firms as given, that is if firm 1 changes its price it will assume that the prices of the other $N-1$ varieties will remain the same. Second, it is assumed that the firm ignores the effect of changing its own price on the price index P of manufactures. Both assumptions seem reasonable if the number of varieties N is large, as also discussed in section 10.4.

For ease of notation we will drop the sub-index for the firm in this section. Note that a firm which produces x units of output using the production function in equation (10.5) will earn profits π given in equation (10.6) if the wage rate it has to pay is W.

$$(10.6) \qquad \pi = px - W(f + mx)$$

Naturally, the firm will have to sell the units of output x it is producing, that is these sales must be consistent with the demand for a variety of manufactures derived in section 10.3. Although this demand was derived for an arbitrary consumer, the most important feature of the demand for a variety, namely the constant price elasticity of demand ε, also holds when we combine the demand from many consumers with the same preference structure. If the demand x for a variety has a constant price elasticity of demand ε, maximization of the profits given in equation (10.6) leads to a very simple optimal pricing rule, known as mark-up pricing, see Technical Note 9.1.

$$(10.7) \qquad p(1 - 1/\varepsilon) = mW$$

The term 'mark-up pricing' is obvious. The marginal costs of producing an extra unit of output is equal to mW, while the price p the firm charges is higher than this marginal cost. How much higher depends crucially on the price elasticity of demand. If demand is rather inelastic, say $\varepsilon = 2$, the mark-up is high (in this case 100 per cent). If demand is rather elastic, say $\varepsilon = 5$, the mark-up is lower (in this case 25 per cent). Note that the firm must charge a higher price than marginal cost in order to recuperate the fixed costs of labour fW. Because the price elasticity of demand ε is constant, the mark-up of price over marginal cost is also constant, and therefore invariant to the scale of production.

Box 10.3 **The parameter ε as a measure of returns to scale?**

The parameter ε is directly related to the consumer's preferences, as defined in equation (10.2). In equilibrium, however, it is also used as a measure of economies of scale. One specific measure of economies of scale is: average costs divided by marginal costs; if marginal costs are lower than average costs an increase in production will reduce the cost per unit. We can calculate this measure for the equilibrium level of production. The production level is (eq. 10.8): $f(\varepsilon - 1)/m$, which requires $f\varepsilon$ labour, so the average costs are $f\varepsilon/(f(\varepsilon - 1)/m = m\varepsilon/(\varepsilon - 1)$. The marginal labour costs are simply m, so this measure of scale economies reduces to average costs/marginal costs $= \varepsilon/(\varepsilon - 1)$. For a low value of ε this measure of scale economies is high, and vice versa. In equilibrium it only depends on the elasticity of substitution parameter ε, and not on the parameters f and m of the production function. This peculiar result, in which the measure of scale economies is related to parameters not of the production function but of the utility function, is an artifact of the Dixit–Stiglitz model of monopolistic competition, which makes average costs over marginal costs an unsuitable measure of scale economies.

Now that we have determined the optimal price a firm will charge to maximize profits we can actually calculate those profits. This is where another important feature of monopolistic competition comes in. If profits are positive (sometimes referred to as excess profits) it is apparently very attractive to set up shop in the manufacturing sector. One would then expect that new firms enter the market and start to produce a different variety. This implies, of course, that the consumer will allocate her spending over more varieties of manufactures. Since all varieties are substitutes for one another, the entry of new firms in the manufacturing sector implies that profits for the existing firms will fall. This process of entry of new firms will continue until profits in the manufacturing sector are driven to zero. A reverse process, with firms leaving the manufacturing sector, would operate if profits were negative. Monopolistic competition in the manufacturing sector therefore imposes as an equilibrium condition that profits are zero. If we do that in equation (10.6) we can calculate the scale at which a firm producing a variety in the manufacturing sector will operate, see Technical Note 10.2.

(10.8)
$$x = \frac{f(\varepsilon - 1)}{m}$$

Equation (10.8), giving the scale of output for an individual firm, may seem strange at first sight. No matter what happens, the output per firm is fixed in equilibrium. The constant price elasticity of demand in conjunction with the production function is responsible for this result. It implies that the manufacturing sector as a whole only expands and contracts by producing more or fewer varieties, as the output level per variety does not change. Since the scale of production is constant, as given in equation (10.8), it is easy to determine (i) how much labour is needed to produce this amount of output using the production function, and (ii) how many varieties N are produced in the economy by dividing the total labour force L by the amount of labour required per variety (which gives $N = L/f\varepsilon$), see Technical Note 10.2. Evidently, a larger market, as measured by the available amount of labour L, is able to support a larger number N of varieties, thus giving consumers more varieties to choose from.

10.7 Explaining intra-industry trade

How does all of the above help us to understand intra-industry trade flows, and possible gains from such trade flows? Let us first summarize the main conclusions derived in sections 10.3–10.6:

- Consumers demand different varieties of similar goods. Other things being equal, the more varieties are available to cater to specific needs of the consumer, the higher the derived utility level.

- Consumer demand for any particular variety increases if (i) the price of the variety falls (with a constant price elasticity of demand ε), (ii) the price of any other variety increases, and (iii) the income level increases.

- Producers supply many different varieties of similar goods. Before production of any particular variety can start an initial investment cost is necessary (for invention of the variety, or to set up a production plant), such that there are internal increasing returns to scale. This gives market power to the individual producers.

- Producers maximize profits by choosing the optimal price level. Since the price elasticity of demand is constant, the mark-up of price over marginal costs is also constant.

- Firms enter and exit the market for producing new varieties until (excess) profits are equal to zero. In this setting, this results in a constant production level for each variety of manufactures, such that a change in total market supply is equivalent to a change in the number of varieties produced.

Given these preliminary results, it is straightforward to put two and two together and explain how intra-industry trade may arise, and what its benefits are. Consider two countries, Belgium and the Netherlands, with a demand and supply structure as laid out in sections 10.3–10.6. We will assume these countries are identical in all respects, except in the size of their labour force; more specifically, we assume Belgium has 5 million labourers, and the Netherlands has 7 million labourers. Since technology is the same for the two countries, there is no Ricardian basis for international trade. Since there is only one factor of production (labour) it is impossible even to identify relative factor abundance, such that there is no Heckscher–Ohlin basis for international trade. Nonetheless, international trade, of the intra-industry type, will arise in this model, and it will lead to gains from trade for both countries.

We start with a brief discussion of the autarky equilibrium. If we let the wage rate be the numéraire, all firms face the same marginal costs and the same price elasticity of demand. They therefore all charge the same price. If all workers are employed, the total income level is identical to the number of labourers, because firms enter and exit the market until profits are zero and the wage rate is the numéraire. As explained at the end of section 10.6, and emphasized above, the number of varieties produced in each country is proportional to the size of the market (as measured by the total labour force):

(10.9) $$N_{Belgium} = \frac{L_{Belgium}}{f\varepsilon}; \quad N_{Netherlands} = \frac{L_{Netherlands}}{f\varepsilon}$$

Suppose that the fixed costs f and the elasticity of substitution ε are such that 500 labourers are required in equilibrium for the production of one variety. As illustrated in Figure 10.6, Belgium will then produce and consume 10,000 varieties in autarky and the Netherlands will produce and consume 14,000 varieties in autarky.

What changes if these two countries start to trade with one another (at zero transport costs and in the absence of any other impediment to trade)? The answer is: virtually nothing and very much at the same time. The 'virtually nothing' part refers

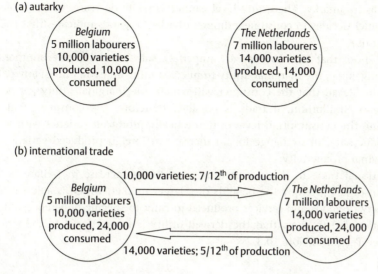

Fig. 10.6 Intra-industry trade in the Krugman model

to the fact that the price for a variety does not change, nor does production size for any variety, or the number of varieties produced. The 'very much' part refers to the fact that we now have intensive trade flows between the two nations, because the consumers have a preference for variety and therefore want to consume all varieties produced in both countries. The total number of varieties consumed therefore increases from 10,000 in Belgium and 14,000 in the Netherlands to 24,000 in both countries. Since demand is proportional to the size of the market, a Belgian producer will export 7/12 of total production to the Netherlands, while a Dutch producer will export 5/12 of total production to Belgium. These intensive trade flows of similar types of goods, produced using similar technologies in both countries, can be classified as intra-industry trade.

In the Ricardian model, as in the Heckscher–Ohlin model, there are gains from trade through more efficient production at a global scale. In Chapter 9, where we discussed the pro-competitive gains from trade, the pressure of international competition reduces the domestic distortions, and therefore leads to efficiency gains. In the Krugman model, none of these factors is operative. The reader will have noticed that the production levels have not changed at all in either country. Since the Dutch are exporting 5/12 of their production level of each variety, the level consumed of those varieties falls by 5/12. In exchange the Dutch are now consuming 7/12 of the Belgian production level of the varieties produced in Belgium. The total consumption level has not changed ($10,000 \times 7/12 - 14,000 \times 5/12 = 0$). All we are doing is exporting manufactures in exchange for the import of an equal amount of manufactures. Are there any gains from these trade flows? The answer is: yes. Two remarks are in order.

First, note that the wage rate, and thus the consumer's income level, has not changed in trade relative to autarky, nor has the price of domestically produced varieties. If trade is possible, therefore, the consumer can still consume the same combination of goods as in autarky. The utility level cannot possibly decrease, while the fact that the consumer decides to consume a different basket of goods indicates that the utility level must rise.

Second, note that the varieties are imperfect substitutes for one another. Other things being equal, the marginal utility from consuming an extra unit of any particular variety falls. Recall that the consumer will equate the marginal utility per dollar for all goods in equilibrium. If trade is possible, therefore, the consumer will benefit by reducing the consumption level of domestically produced varieties with low marginal productivity, in exchange for an increase in foreign produced varieties with a high marginal productivity.

International trade in this set-up thus leads to an increase in welfare because it allows consumers to enjoy the benefits of a larger market, which is able to sustain a large variety of goods and services produced to cater to specific preferences. Indeed, it is straightforward to show that the derived utility is proportional to the size of the market, see Technical Note 10.3.

10.8 An alternative interpretation: intermediate goods

So far, we have discussed the Krugman model of intra-industry trade, that is trade between countries of similar goods and services within the same industry, which is becoming more important, as measured by the Grubel–Lloyd index. The gains from trade in the Krugman setting derive from the ability to sustain a wider variety of goods and services in a larger market as a result of increasing returns to scale. A larger market therefore is better able to fulfil the preferences of consumers, who like variety. In short, the entire discussion and interpretation of the model is in terms of production and trade of *final* goods and services for the consumer market.

The Krugman interpretation of the model is illustrated in Figure 10.7. In autarky, country A produces N_A different varieties under increasing returns to scale and monopolistic competition. Similarly for country B. If the two countries engage in international trade with one another, the consumers in both countries purchase some goods from all domestic producers *and* import some goods from all foreign producers. The resulting trade flows are therefore intra-industry trade flows of final goods from producers to consumers.

The American economist Wilfred Ethier (1982) came up with an entirely different, and influential, interpretation of the same model. He pointed out (1982: 950–2) that: 'the largest and fastest growing component of world trade since World War II has been the exchange of manufactures between the industrialized economies. ... (I cannot resist the temptation to point out that producers' goods are in fact much more prominent in trade than are consumers' goods).' One of the objectives of the Ethier

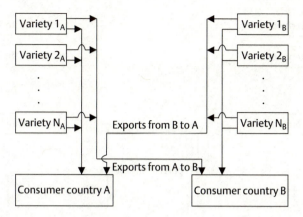

Fig. 10.7 The Krugman interpretation

article is therefore to explain the large intra-industry trade flows of *intermediate* goods, that is trade flows from one producer to another, rather than from producer to consumer.

Figure 10.8 illustrates how Ethier was able to explain those trade flows through a reinterpretation of the Krugman model. Instead of interpreting the various varieties produced in both countries as different final goods, he interpreted them as different, and new, intermediate goods in a complex final goods production process. This can refer to different types of capital goods, such as cars, printing machines, copiers, presses, etc., or to different types of services, such as accounting, engineering, cleaning, etc. The providers of intermediate goods, produced under increasing returns to scale, have market power and are operating in a market of monopolistic competition.

There is only one final good delivered to the consumers. The producers of the final good, say Y, combine the intermediate inputs from all variety producers in a perfectly competitive market, that is taking the prices of the intermediate goods providers as given, into the single output. The final good production function is similar to the utility function in the Krugman approach, see equation (10.2):

(10.10) $$Y = \left(\sum_{i=1}^{N} x_i^{\rho} \right)^{1/\rho} ; \quad 0 < \rho < 1$$

In this interpretation, the x_i refer to intermediate goods deliveries. The price elasticity of demand for intermediate goods by final goods producers is, of course, again a constant, equal to $\varepsilon \equiv /(1 - \rho)$. Once we impose a well-behaved utility function $U(Y)$ on top of this structure, the outcome is essentially the same as in the Krugman model. This time, as displayed in Figure 10.8, we have active international intra-industry trade flows of *intermediate goods* between nations.

It is also important to understand the difference of interpretation of an increase in the extent of the market in the Ethier model. First, recall that a larger market enables an increase in the number N of varieties produced. Second, remember that

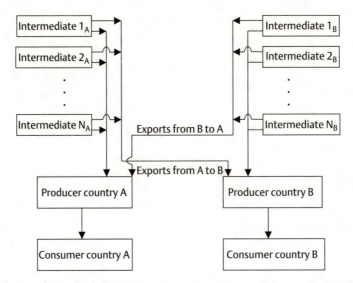

Fig. 10.8 The Ethier interpretation

the increase in the number of varieties leads to higher utility levels in the Krugman model through a love-of-variety effect. In a similar way, a larger market leads to an increase in the number of intermediate goods available to final goods producers, which increases their total output level through a positive production externality. The different intermediate goods are imperfect substitutes for one another. Therefore, the more there are available to the final goods producer, the more efficiently the production process is organized, and the higher the production level.

10.9 Conclusions

The empirically observed prevalence of intra-industry trade (two-way trade in similar products), measured using the Grubel–Lloyd index, is hard to explain on the basis of differences in factor abundance or technology. Using the Krugman model, an extension of the Dixit–Stiglitz model, we provide an analysis of imperfect competition under economies of scale, which in conjunction with the size of the market determines the number of different varieties of goods and services available to consumers (or firms in the intermediate product interpretation of Ethier). International trade increases the extent of the market, thus making more types of goods available. This raises welfare through a love-of-variety effect for final goods or raises production through increased specialization leading to positive production externalities. In both cases the model can be applied to better understand intra-industry trade of final goods and intermediate goods. The general structure of this model will be the basis of more applications in the sequel of the book.

Technical Notes (optional)

Technical Note 10.1 Dixit–Stiglitz demand

To maximize equation (10.2) subject to the budget constraint (10.3) we define the Lagrangean Γ, using the multiplier κ:

$$(10.A1) \qquad \Gamma = \left[\sum_{i=1}^{N} c_i^{\rho} \right]^{(1/\rho)} + \kappa \left[I - \sum_{i=1}^{N} p_i c_i \right]$$

Differentiating Γ with respect to c_j and equating to 0 gives the first order conditions:

$$(10.A2) \qquad \left[\sum_{i=1}^{N} c_i^{\rho} \right]^{(1/\rho)-1} c_j^{\rho-1} = \kappa p_j \quad \text{for} \quad j = 1, \ldots, N$$

Take the ratio of these first order conditions with respect to variety 1, note that the first term on the left-hand side cancels (as does the term κ on the right-hand side), and define $\varepsilon \equiv 1/(1-\rho)$ as discussed in the main text. Then:

$$(10.A3) \qquad \frac{c_j^{\rho-1}}{c_1^{\rho-1}} = \frac{p_j}{p_1} \quad \text{or} \quad c_j = p_j^{-\varepsilon} p_1^{\varepsilon} c_1 \quad \text{for} \quad j = 1, \ldots, N$$

Substituting these relations in the budget equation gives:

$$(10.A4) \qquad \sum_{j=1}^{N} p_j c_j = \sum_{j=1}^{N} p_j [p_j^{-\varepsilon} p_1^{\varepsilon} c_1] = p_1^{\varepsilon} c_1 \sum_{j=1}^{N} p_j^{1-\varepsilon} = p_1^{\varepsilon} c_1 P^{1-\varepsilon} = I, \quad \text{or} \quad c_1 = p_1^{-\varepsilon} P^{\varepsilon-1} I$$

$$P \equiv \left[\sum_{j=1}^{N} p_j^{1-\varepsilon} \right]^{1/(1-\varepsilon)}$$

This explains the demand for variety 1 as given in equation (10.4). The demand for the other varieties is derived analogously. The question remains why the price index P was defined as given in equation (10.A4). To answer this question we have to substitute the derived demand for all varieties in equation (10.2), and note along the way that $-\varepsilon\rho = 1 - \varepsilon$ and $1/\rho = -\varepsilon/(1-\varepsilon)$:

$$U = \left(\sum_{i=1}^{N} c_i^{\rho} \right)^{1/\rho} = \left(\sum_{i=1}^{N} (p_i^{-\varepsilon} P^{\varepsilon-1} I)^{\rho} \right)^{1/\rho} = IP^{\varepsilon-1} \left(\sum_{i=1}^{N} p_i^{-\varepsilon\rho} \right)^{1/\rho} = IP^{\varepsilon-1} \left(\sum_{i=1}^{N} p_i^{1-\varepsilon} \right)^{-\varepsilon/(1-\varepsilon)}$$

Using the definition of the price index P from equation (10.A4) this simplifies to:

$$(10.A5) \qquad U = IP^{\varepsilon-1} \left(\sum_{i=1}^{N} p_i^{1-\varepsilon} \right)^{-\varepsilon/(1-\varepsilon)} = IP^{\varepsilon-1} P^{-\varepsilon} = I/P$$

Technical Note 10.2 Equilibrium scale of production

Put profits in equation (10.6) equal to zero and use the pricing rule $p(1 - 1/\varepsilon) = mW$:

(10.A6)
$$px - W(f + mx) = 0; \quad px = fW + mWx; \quad \left[\frac{\varepsilon}{\varepsilon - 1}mW\right]x = fW + mWx$$

$$\left[\frac{\varepsilon}{\varepsilon - 1} - 1\right]mWx = fW; \quad x = \frac{f(\varepsilon - 1)}{m}$$

This explains equation (10.8). Now use the production function (10.5) to calculate the amount of labour required to produce this much output:

(10.A7)
$$l_i = f + mx = f + m\frac{f(\varepsilon - 1)}{m} = f + f(\varepsilon - 1) = f\varepsilon$$

Finally, determining the number N of varieties produced simply follows by dividing the total number of manufacturing workers by the number of workers needed to produce 1 variety: $N = L/l_i = L/f\varepsilon$.

Technical Note 10.3 Intra-industry trade and welfare

Since the price of all varieties is the same in equilibrium, the consumption level is the same for all varieties in equilibrium. From equation (10.2) it follows that the utility level is then equal to $U = N^{1/\rho}c$. The production level for any variety is given in equation (10.8) as $x = f(\varepsilon - 1)/m$. Dividing this by the number of people L gives the per capita consumption c. Finally, recall that the number of varieties is proportional to the labour force, that is $N = L/f\varepsilon$, and combine the above information to get:

(10.A8)
$$U = N^{1/\rho}c = \left(\frac{L}{f\varepsilon}\right)^{1/\rho}\frac{f(\varepsilon - 1)}{mL} = \gamma_U L^{1/(\varepsilon - 1)}; \quad \gamma_U \equiv \frac{\varepsilon - 1}{m}\left(\frac{1}{f\varepsilon}\right)^{1/\rho}$$

Chapter 11

Strategic Trade Policy

Objectives/key terms

Strategic trade   Non-equivalence
Brander–Spencer model   Bertrand competition
Eaton–Grossman model   Informational requirements

We analyse the impact of 'strategic' trade policy, designed to give domestic producers an advantage in a world characterized by imperfect competition.

11.1 Introduction

In Chapter 8 we discussed the effects of trade policy, that is tariffs, quotas, and the like, in a classical or neoclassical world of perfect competition. We concluded that trade restrictions are detrimental for small countries unable to influence the world price level, both in a partial and a general equilibrium setting. The analysis was somewhat less clear-cut for large countries, since their ability to influence the terms of trade suggested that a suitable restriction of trade (the 'optimal' tariff) would enable them to increase their welfare, be it at the cost of a deterioration of welfare in the other countries of the world. In a more general setting, taking retaliation by other countries through a suitable choice of their 'optimal' tariffs into consideration, we concluded again that free trade is the true optimal policy.

The optimal tariff argument is based on market power at the country level. Chapters 9 and 10 have discussed market power at the firm and industry level in a world of imperfect competition (monopoly, oligopoly, monopolistic competition), sometimes based on increasing returns to scale. This suggests, of course, that the analysis of trade policy in a world based on the models of Chapters 9 and 10 is more involved and potentially leaves more room for beneficial government intervention. As we will elaborate below, both suggestions are true in principle. An omniscient government *could* indeed potentially make the right 'strategic' choices by promoting the interests of certain sectors. This so-called strategic trade policy argument, see sections 11.4 and 11.5, received a lot of attention for a fairly brief period of time, as explained in section 11.6. We also explain

Fig. 11.1 Jagdish Bhagwati (1934–   )

Born and raised in India, Jagdish Bhagwati studied at Cambridge, MIT, and Oxford before returning to India in 1961 to work at the Indian Statistical Institute and the Delhi School of Economics. In 1968 he went back to MIT, where he worked for twelve years before moving to Columbia University. Currently, he is Special Adviser to the United Nations on Globalization and External Adviser to the World Trade Organization. Jagdish Bhagwati has published numerous articles and books on virtually all subfields of international economics, notably on trade, development, and trade policy. In 1971 he founded the *Journal of International Economics*, the foremost journal in the field today. Bhagwati's influence outside the academic community is steadily increasing. Among his better-known books are *Protectionism* (1988) and *The World Trading System at Risk* (1991).

why this attention did not last very long and give a number of reasons why the strategic trade policy arguments are not important in practice. Before addressing these issues, we explain the main economic implications of imposing a tariff or quota to protect a domestic industry characterized by market power, see sections 11.2 and 11.3. The discussion in these two sections is based on Bhagwati (1965).

11.2 Market power and tariffs

The analyses and discussions in Chapters 9 and 10 have demonstrated that international trade reduces the market power of domestic firms. Conversely, therefore, we expect protection to increase domestic market power. In contrast to the perfect competition analysis of Chapter 8, however, the effects of protection depend on the form it takes. In general, as first shown by Jagdish Bhagwati (1965) and demonstrated in this section and the next, quantitative restrictions such as quotas create larger distortions and generate more domestic market power than tariffs.

Figure 11.2 illustrates the case considered by Bhagwati. There is a single producer in the domestic market facing a downward sloping demand curve, with concomitant marginal revenue curve (MR), and an upward sloping marginal cost curve (MC). In the absence of international trade, the domestic supplier is a monopolist and output would be determined by equality of marginal cost and marginal revenue at point C, such that the firm would charge the monopoly price p_{mon}. Recall that, if this were a competitive industry, output would be determined by equality of price and marginal cost, that is at point B leading to price p_{comp}. If there is free international trade, and assuming that this is a small country facing competition from price-taking foreign suppliers[1] at the price p_{world}, the

---

[1] It is not explained why the market structure at home and abroad is different.

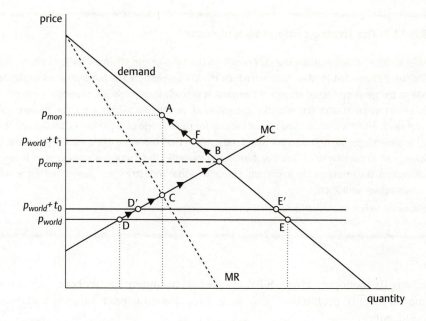

Fig. 11.2 Market power and tariff

domestic firm would produce at the point where marginal cost is equal to the world price level, that is at point D. The difference between domestic demand at point E and domestic supply at point D would be imported from abroad.

Imposing a tariff such that $p_{world} + t < p_{comp}$

If the government decides to protect the domestic firm by imposing a specific tariff t, the (welfare) consequences are initially similar to the analysis in Chapter 8. As long as the world price plus the tariff is below the competitive equilibrium price, as illustrated in Figure 11.2 for tariff t_0, the domestic firm increases output from point D to D', domestic demand falls from point E to E', and imports from abroad also decrease.

Imposing a tariff such that $p_{comp} < p_{world} + t < p_{mon}$

The analysis starts to deviate from the competitive analysis in Chapter 8 once the government imposes a 'prohibitive' tariff, such that the world price plus the tariff is above the competitive equilibrium price, as illustrated for tariff t_1 in Figure 11.2. If the domestic market were competitive, any tariff increase above the competitive price would have no further effects. The price equilibrium would remain at point B, price and quantity would be constant, and imports would be zero. If there is a single domestic firm, however, an increase of the tariff beyond the competitive price level enables the domestic firm to use its monopoly power by lowering output and increasing price and profits, up to the level $p_{world} + t_1$, that is at point F. Note that the *threat* of imports keeps the monopolist from

---

Box 11.1 **The strategic importance of sugar**

After months of negotiations the EU Council (in the form of the Ministers for Agriculture, see Chapter 13) decided in May 2001 to reduce the EU support for the production of sugar. As one of the most protected sectors in Europe it is virtually impossible for developing countries to export sugar to the EU, with the exception of ex-colonies which are given preferential treatment. The 300 million Euro annual subsidy for the storage of sugar will be abolished. The EU is currently paying 650 Euro per ton of sugar, more than twice the world market price, and is levying an import tariff of 310 per cent. Consequently, the European consumer is heavily subsidizing the strategically important European sugar industry. The guaranteed price will remain active until 2006.

Information source: NRC Handelsblad (2001*b*).

---

exercising its monopoly power fully, even when no imports actually occur, such that raising an already prohibitive tariff leads to a domestic price increase and reduces domestic output.

Imposing a tariff such that $p_{mon} < p_{world} + t$

If the government raises the prohibitive tariff even further, such that the world price plus the tariff exceeds the monopoly price, the domestic firm maximizes profits at the monopoly price and does not raise the price any further, that is the equilibrium remains at point A.

Note that, as the tariff level increases from 0 to $p_{mon} - p_{world}$, the domestic quantity and price combination first moves from point D to point B, and then from point B to point A. Any further tariff increases have no effect.

11.3 The non-equivalence of tariffs and quotas

In Chapter 8 we have briefly discussed how the imposition of a tariff and a quota leading to the same level of imports results in the same welfare effects and price level, see Box 8.1. This so-called equivalence between tariffs and quotas no longer holds if there is domestic market power. This is illustrated in Figure 11.3 for the Bhagwati framework explained in the previous section (one domestic firm and price-taking foreign suppliers). First, suppose the country imposes a tariff such that the world price plus the tariff is below the competitive price. As explained in section 11.2, and illustrated in Figure 11.3, this leads to domestic production at point A, domestic demand at point B, and imports equal to the

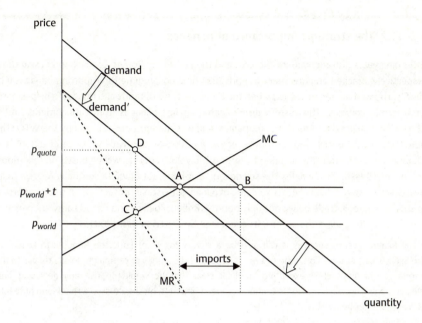

Fig. 11.3 Market power and quota

difference between points B and A. Second, suppose that *instead* of imposing a tariff, the government decides to impose a quantitative import restriction equal to the import level under the tariff (the difference between points B and A). Does this change the domestic equilibrium? Yes, it does. To understand this, we have to consider the strategic possibilities available to the domestic firm if either tariffs or the quota are imposed, as indicated by marginal revenue.

Under the tariff, the marginal revenue curve for the domestic supplier is equal to $p_{world} + t$. As a result of the quota, however, the domestic firm's demand curve essentially shifts to the left by the extent of the quota, as indicated by the arrows in Figure 11.3. Consequently, the domestic firm's marginal revenue curve is generated by this restricted demand curve. After allowing for the restricted foreign imports, the domestic firm can again exercise its monopoly power, leading to the equality of marginal revenue and marginal cost at point C and the price p_{quota}, as determined by point D.

Clearly, if domestic firms enjoy some market power, protection of the domestic industry with quota rather than tariffs leads to higher prices and lower output. Using a similar partial equilibrium welfare analysis as in Chapter 8, quotas therefore lead to larger welfare losses. The clear policy message is therefore: if you *must* protect the domestic industry, use a tariff rather than a quota.

Box 11.2 **The strategic importance of bananas**

After nine years of trade warfare the USA and the EU, led by Robert Zoellick and Pascal Lamy respectively, reached an agreement in April 2001 on a new regime for importing bananas into the EU. The warfare began in 1993 when the EU set up a mix of tariffs and quotas to help exports from former colonies. This system discriminated against bananas from Latin America, most of which are shipped by American companies, and was therefore ruled illegal by the WTO. The new system will consist of a tariff-only regime by 2006 (in line with WTO 'tariffication', see Chapter 12). In the transitional period, starting 1 July 2001, quotas will be based on the import volume of 1994–6. This benefits the struggling, near-bankrupt Chiquita company relative to its rival Dole, which has diversified its sourcing of bananas. Personal contacts seem to be important in striking strategic trade deals; not only because Robert Zoellick and Pascal Lamy are personal friends, but also behind the scenes, as suggested by *The Economist* (2001*a*):

If the banana accord survives it will also be a victory for Trent Lott, the Republican Leader of the Senate. Last year Mr Lott, who has received tens of thousands of campaign dollars thanks to the efforts of Chiquita's chief executive, made it clear that he would oppose any deal that hurt the company. This week Mr Lott is touring Europe. In Brussels, he should drop a thank-you note into Mr Lamy's letter box.

Information source: *The Economist* (2001*a*).

11.4 Strategic trade policy

One of the most controversial topics in the new trade literature is the suggestion that active government intervention, through tariffs, quotas, subsidies, or otherwise, may be able to raise domestic welfare by shifting oligopoly profits from foreign to domestic firms. The debate started in the 1980s, when there was great concern about American international competitiveness, with a series of papers by James Brander and Barbara Spencer (1983, 1985). The general idea is that government intervention can serve the 'strategic' purpose of altering the incentives of firms, thus deterring foreign competitors.

The main idea is conveyed quite easily in the Brander–Spencer analysis, which is based on the Cournot model of section 9.4, by simplifying the international trade aspects of the model. There are two firms, an Austrian firm (index A) and a Bolivian firm (index B), producing a homogeneous good. Both firms export to a *third* market and do not face any domestic demand. Since there are no other distortions in this partial equilibrium analysis than the monopoly power in the industry, the marginal cost of each firm is also the social cost of the resources it uses. As a result, national welfare for each country can be measured by the profits earned by its firm. Details on the discussion below are given in Technical Note 11.1 at the end of this chapter.

In the absence of government intervention, the Austrian firm maximizes its profits taking the output level of the Bolivian firm as given. Similarly for the Bolivian firm. As explained in section 9.4, this leads to two 'reaction curves' in (q_A, q_B)-space, giving the optimal response of each firm to the other firm's output level. The Cournot equilibrium is determined by the point of intersection of the reaction curves, where neither firm has an incentive to change its output decision, see Figure 11.4.

Does the Cournot equilibrium lead to the highest possible profits for the Austrian firm? No. As indicated in Figure 11.4, the Austrian firm's isoprofit curve is horizontal at the Cournot equilibrium, since it is the optimal response (maximizes profits) given the output level of the Bolivian firm. Taking the Bolivian firm's reaction curve as a restriction, the Austrian firm's profits are maximized at a point of tangency of the Bolivian firm's reaction curve with the Austrian firm's isoprofit curve, see the Brander–Spencer square in Figure 11.4.[2] Why does the Austrian firm not produce this level of output? Because it is lacking a credible pre-commitment. Given the output level of the Bolivian firm at the Brander–Spencer equilibrium, the Austrian firm has an incentive to produce a smaller level of output which would raise its profits even further.

The potential for beneficial active government intervention now becomes clear. If the Austrian government is somehow able to shift the Austrian firm's reaction curve to the right, such that it precisely intersects the Bolivian firm's reaction curve at the

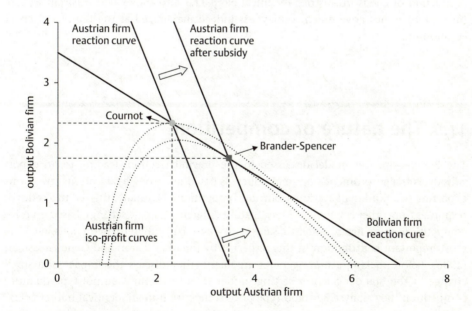

Fig. 11.4 Brander–Spencer equilibrium

[2] From your microeocomics course you may recognize this as the equilibrium which results if the Austrian firm is the Stackelberg leader.

> Box 11.3 **The strategic importance of video recorders**
>
> Imposing tariffs and quantitative restrictions are not the only means to reduce imports. A noteworthy example in this respect is the decision of France in October 1982 to change its administrative procedure for the import of video recorders, after a period in which these imports, particularly from Japan, had rapidly increased. From then on, the recorders had to enter the country through an understaffed customs office in Poitiers, a small out-of-the-way place in the midwest of France. Carefully checking to see if the instructions were written in French and taking the recorders apart to verify the stated country of origin, the French rapidly succeeded in reducing the import of video recorders from 64,000 to 10,000 per month. After complaints from Japan and other European countries and an EC-Japan agreement to 'voluntarily' restrict exports of video recorders to Europe, the French government reversed the measure.
>
> Information source: Lanjouw (1995: 11).

Brander–Spencer equilibrium, it will have made this point a credible equilibrium. In essence, the Austrian government would then give its firm a strategic advantage. Several options are available, but Technical Note 11.1 shows that one strategy which works for the Austrian government is giving an export *subsidy* of exactly the right amount to the production of goods in Austria. Technical Note 11.1 also shows that Austrian welfare (firm profit minus government outlays) is indeed maximized at the Brander–Spencer equilibrium.

11.5 **The nature of competition**

The Brander–Spencer model discussed in the previous section, leading to an export subsidy as the government's optimal policy, is based on strong assumptions (two firms exporting to a third market using Cournot competition). Naturally, this led to a series of responses from other economists investigating different strategic settings, based on price competition, more firms, domestic sales, entry and exit, differentiated goods, etc. The most important contribution in this respect is by Jonathan Eaton and Gene Grossman (1986). Before making a more general argument, they discuss the impact of a small change in the Brander–Spencer setting: rather than analysing Cournot-type quantity competition they analyse Bertrand-type price competition in an identical framework.

Consider, therefore, again an Austrian and a Bolivian firm exporting to a third market, not facing any domestic demand. Since the firms are engaged in price competition we assume that the goods are imperfect substitutes to facilitate the analysis;[3] if the Austrian

---

[3] With homogeneous goods Bertrand price competition would drive the price down to marginal costs, leaving no possibility of strategically transferring profits and effectively eliminating market power.

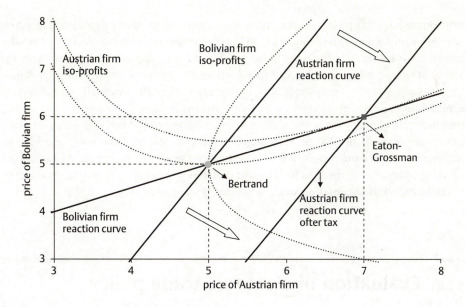

Fig. 11.5 Eaton–Grossman equilibrium

firm raises its price, this increases the demand for the Bolivian firm and vice versa. The absence of other distortions ensures that the marginal cost of each firm is also the social cost of the resources it uses, such that national welfare for each country is equal to the profits earned by its firm. Technical details on the discussion below are given in Technical Note 11.2 at the end of this chapter.

In the absence of government intervention, the Austrian firm maximizes its profits by choosing its price and taking the price level of the Bolivian firm as given. Similarly for the Bolivian firm. This leads to two 'reaction curves' in (p_A, p_B)-space, giving the optimal response of each firm to the other firm's price level. In contrast to section 11.4, these reaction curves are upward sloping: if the Bolivian firm raises its price, the demand for the Austrian firm's product increases, which allows the Austrian firm to raise its price as well. Analogous to the analysis in section 11.4, the Bertrand equilibrium is determined by the point of intersection of the reaction curves, where neither firm has an incentive to change its pricing decision, see Figure 11.5.

The Bertrand equilibrium does not lead to the highest possible profit level for the Austrian firm, which is determined by the point of tangency of the Bolivian firm's reaction curve with the Austrian firm's isoprofit curve, see the Eaton–Grossman square in Figure 11.5. This time, however, the Austrian government can ensure that the Austrian firm's reaction curve is shifted to the right to intersect at the Eaton–Grossman point by levying an export *tax* of exactly the right amount. As Krugman (1990: 251) put it:

So what Eaton and Grossman show is that replacing the Cournot with a Bertrand assumption reverses the policy recommendation. Given the shakiness of any characterization of oligopoly behavior, this is not reassuring.

Why do we have this reversal of the policy recommendation? Using terms introduced by Bulow, Geanokoplos, and Klemperer (1985), it is because with Cournot competition the choice variables are 'strategic substitutes' (higher output leads to lower marginal profitability of similar moves by the firm's rival), while with Bertrand competition the choice variables are 'strategic complements' (a higher price raises the marginal profitability of similar moves by the firm's rival). Eaton and Grossman show in a more general setting that the optimal policy recommendation depends on the choice variables being strategic substitutes (export subsidy) or strategic complements (export tax). Leaving aside the willingness of government officials who want to be re-elected to impose an export tax on an industry should the structural details demand such a policy response, it is time to evaluate the contribution of strategic trade policy.

11.6 Evaluation of strategic trade policy

For a fairly brief time period the idea of strategic trade policy, building on the framework of new trade theory, received a lot of attention, both from the international economics profession and from outside. The main reason for the outside attention is that any intellectually respectable case for intervention will quickly find support for the wrong reasons, namely as an excuse to impose arbitrary trade restrictions to protect sectors under competitive pressure from abroad. The special interest boxes in this chapter may give an idea how the Brander–Spencer idea can be misused in view of the 'strategic' importance of some protected sectors. The attention from the international economics profession is a response primarily based on this outside pressure for protection, namely to carefully scrutinize any idea that seems to support protection under some circumstances. Since the game-theoretic nature of the strategic trade policy argument makes the analyses of the scrutiny rather complex (involving the number of players, the number of time periods, the choice of strategic variables, who moves first, second, or third, the credibility of commitments, etc.) we will only briefly describe some of the main results in more general terms.

Competition for resources

The arguments in sections 11.4 and 11.5 are based on a partial equilibrium framework. By now we have become accustomed in this book to value a general equilibrium framework for investigating international trade and trade policy, as it forces us to express our ideas in a consistent way and sometimes identifies the misleading nature of partial equilibrium results. As Dixit and Grossman (1986) argue, the export subsidy in the Brander–Spencer model works because it reduces the marginal costs for the Austrian firm in the subsidized sector, which deters exports to the third market by the Bolivian firm. In a general equilibrium framework, however, the subsidized sector can only expand by bidding away resources from other sectors, thus driving up the marginal costs in those sectors. This leads to reverse-deterrence in non-targeted sectors. Constructing a tractable general equilibrium model, Dixit and Grossman show that a subsidy to a specific sector only raises national income if the deterrent effect is higher in the subsidized sector than in the sectors which are crowded out as a result of the subsidy. Optimal policy therefore requires detailed knowledge of all sectors in the entire economy.

Entry and exit

The arguments in sections 11.4 and 11.5 are based on the possibility of firms to earn supernormal profits over which firms (and countries) can compete. As argued in Chapter 10, the presence of supernormal profits will entice new firms to enter the market. This eliminates not only such profits, but also the arguments for strategic trade policy based on these profits. This line of reasoning is followed by Horstmann and Markusen (1986), who extend the Brander–Spencer framework by allowing for entry and exit of firms. The number of firms is determined by fixed costs leading to economies of scale. The authors show that a country providing a subsidy leads to a welfare loss through a reduction in scale economies or a worsening in the terms of trade.

Retaliation

There is an asymmetry in cleverness on the part of the governments in the Brander–Spencer model: the Austrian government gathers a lot of information and performs detailed calculations to determine the optimal export subsidy for its firm, while the Bolivian government does not. In an extended framework, many variants of which are analysed by Dixit and Kyle (1985), it is reasonable to assume that the Bolivian government is able to undertake similar Brander–Spencer policies. In this case the two countries end up in a prisoner-dilemma type subsidy war, leading to a welfare loss for both countries (and a welfare gain for the third country).

Informational requirements

From a practical point of view, the most important objection to the ideas underlying strategic trade policy is the enormous informational requirement to carry out such a policy, certainly if the above objections are taken into consideration. Even in the partial equilibrium framework, the Austrian government must gather information about the production structure of the home and foreign firm, about the market demand in the third country, about the type of competition in the industry (Cournot or Bertrand), and about the interaction between firms. Then it must accurately undertake detailed calculations to determine the optimal policy. If it makes a mistake, either in size or direction of the policy, national income will fall rather than rise. In a more general setting, it must gather all of this information not only for the countries directly involved in this sector, but for all countries, all sectors, and all firms in the world. It must determine the nature of competition for all these sectors and countries, it must correctly weigh and calculate the benefits of taxing or subsidizing each sector, and it must correctly predict and evaluate the response for all sectors by governments from all countries in the world. Needless to say, all of this is quite impossible. Making mistakes along the way will reduce, rather than increase national income. Moreover, it is evident that the entire process of gathering and processing so much information will put a claim on real resources which could have been used to produce goods and services.

11.7 **Application: the aircraft industry**[4]

The civil-aircraft industry is a prime example of an industry characterized by increasing returns to scale. Kenneth Arrow (1962), for example, cites the empirical regularity that after a new aeroplane design has been introduced, the time required to build the frame of the marginal aircraft is inversely proportional to the cube root of the number of aeroplanes of that model that have already been built, as illustrated in Figure 11.6. The aircraft industry is also a prime example of an industry that has been (mis)used for strategic trade policy reasons.

In view of the importance of economies of scale in the production process, attributed to learning-by-doing effects by Arrow, large companies, able to produce and sell an impressive number of similar type aircraft, enjoy a vital competitive advantage. At the

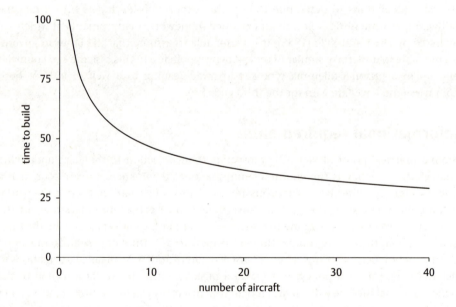

Fig. 11.6 Scale economies in the aircraft industry; index, time to build at 1 is 100

[4] The information in this section is based on *The Economist* (1997, 2000*b*, 2001*b*).

same time, the development and implementation of a newly designed type of aero-plane is extremely costly (see below), making it doubly difficult to enter the market. In the late 1960s Boeing invented the 747 jumbo jet and the European politicians were worried that the big three American firms (Boeing, McDonnell Douglas, and Lockheed), which enjoyed the benefit of a huge home market, would close down the smaller and divided European industry, so they joined forces and began to pour government money into the Airbus industry, a consortium with four parent companies (France's Aérospatiale, Germany's Daimler-Benz Aerospace, British Aerospace, and CASA of Spain).

For a long time it looked like money down the drain. Eventually, however, Airbus industry has become successful enough to present the only challenge to the Boeing dominance (Lockheed stopped producing civil aircraft in 1981 and McDonnell Douglas has merged with Boeing). Over the years, the battle between Boeing and Airbus has caused heated disputes between the American and European governments. The Americans see the struggle as a battle against subsidized competition, while the Europeans are fighting the American hegemony in a 'strategic' industry and argue that Boeing's aircraft are subsidized indirectly by the American defence budget. As *The Economist* (1997) put it: 'Any account of the civil-aircraft industry must begin with the caveat that it has never had free and fair competition. The civil-aircraft industry is the most politicised in the world—apart from the defence industry, to which it is joined at the hip.' A striking example occurred shortly after the Gulf War when the newly installed American president Bill Clinton called King Fahd of Saudi Arabia, urging him to buy $12 billion worth of Boeing and McDonnell Douglas aircraft (rather than Airbuses) made in the country that saved his hide. He did.

There have been two major attempts to force Boeing and Airbus to fight purely commercial battles. First, there was a special section written in the GATT's Tokyo round in 1979, forbidding uneconomic pricing for airliners, see Chapter 12. Second, there was a bilateral European-American deal in 1992 limiting 'launch aid' (money to help develop a new model) to 33 per cent of the total development costs, to be repaid with interest within seventeen years. This put an end to most existing arguments on subsidized aircraft, opening up new problems for the super-jumbo market instead.

For decades Airbus enviously looked at Boeing's 747 jumbo jet, representing a very lucrative share of the civil-aircraft market, where Boeing holds a monopoly. As *The Economist* (1997) put it: 'Boeing's jumbo jet has been a licence to print money: the company makes $45m on each of the $150m-jets that it produces.' Since Boeing realized that Airbus was keen to develop an alternative to its ageing 747 jumbo jet, it came up with a rather successful delaying tactic in 1992 by starting talks with the four parent companies of Airbus to jointly develop a huge super-jumbo (to carry around 800 passengers). In 1995 the cooperation fell apart and Airbus started in earnest to develop the A380, able to carry 600 passengers and supposedly 20 per cent cheaper to operate than the 747. The total development costs for the A380 are estimated to be $10.7 billion, of which, in line with the 1992 agreement, the European governments will finance 33 per cent. The A380 received a green light from Airbus officials at the end of 2000, with Singapore Airlines as launch customer, making an end to Boeing's thirty-two-year monopoly. In reaction, and after a failed attempt to sell a stretched version of the 747 which nobody wanted, Boeing is now trying to launch the 'sonic cruiser', a long-range jetliner flying just below the speed of sound, cutting an hour off transatlantic flights and three hours over the Pacific.

11.8 Conclusions

We analyse the impact of trade policy in a world characterized by imperfect competition. Tariffs and quantitative restrictions are no longer equivalent. The imposition of tariffs in general leaves the forces of foreign competition intact, be it at a lower level. This contrasts with the imposition of quantitative restrictions, which more severely restrict the strategic possibilities of foreign firms. It is therefore generally acknowledged that quotas are more restrictive than tariffs, which is one of the main reasons for the World Trade Organization to strive for 'tariffication' (the other being the clarity of the imposed trade restrictions). The so-called strategic trade policy tries to provide a competitive advantage to domestic firms by providing a credible pre-commitment. When evaluating the potential for strategic trade policy we noticed its weakness in a general equilibrium setting, the fragility of policy recommendations (type of strategic interactions, who moves first, strategic games, etc.), and most importantly from a practical perspective the enormous informational requirements for accurately performing such a policy.

Technical Notes (optional)

Technical Note 11.1 The Brander–Spencer model

The Austrian firm produces quantity q_A and the Bolivian firm produces quantity q_B. This production is exported to a third country, with price p and a linear demand curve:

(11.A1) $$p = a - b(q_A + q_B)$$

Both firms have marginal production costs c, but the Austrian government may give a production subsidy s per unit to the Austrian firm. The profit functions are therefore:

(11.A2) $$\pi_A = pq_A - (c - s)q_A; \quad \pi_B = pq_B - cq_B$$

Both firms maximize profits taking the output level of the other firm as given, which leads to the following reaction curves (see Chapter 9):

(11.A3) $$firm\ A: \ q_B = \frac{(a - c + s)}{b} - 2q_A; \quad firm\ B: \ q_B = \frac{(a - c)}{2b} - \frac{q_A}{2}$$

The intersection of the two reaction curves determines the equilibrium:

(11.A4)
$$q_A = \frac{a - c + 2s}{3b}; \quad q_B = \frac{a - c - s}{3b}$$

Taking the Bolivian firm's reaction curve into consideration the Austrian government now has to decide how high the subsidy s should be. The government's objective is to maximize the Austrian firm's profits minus the subsidy it pays:

(11.A5)
$$\pi_A - sq_A = pq_A - cq_A$$

Note that this is equivalent to maximizing the Austrian firm's profits net of subsidies. The Austrian government should therefore ensure that the Bolivian firm's reaction curve is tangent to the Austrian firm's isoprofit curve net of subsidies, as illustrated in Figure 11.4. Note that for the profit level $\bar{\pi}_A$ the Austrian firm's isoprofit curve net of subsidies is given by all combinations q_A and q_B such that

(11.A6)
$$(p - c)q_A = (a - c - bq_B)q_A - bq_A^2 = \bar{\pi}_A$$
$$\text{so } q_B = \frac{a - c}{b} - q_A - \frac{\bar{\pi}_A}{bq_A}$$

The slope of an isoprofit curve is therefore $-1 + \bar{\pi}_A / bq_A^2$. Setting this equal to $-1/2$, the slope of the Bolivian firm's reaction curve, gives: $\bar{\pi}_A = bq_A^2 / 2$. Substitute this in the equation equalizing the Austrian firm's iso-profits and the Bolivian firm's reaction curve:

(11.A7)
$$\frac{a - c}{2b} - \frac{q_A}{2} = \frac{a - c}{b} - q_A - \frac{\bar{\pi}_A}{bq_A} = \frac{a - c}{b} - q_A - \frac{bq_A^2 / 2}{bq_A}$$

Solving this equation in q_A and substituting for the other variables in the other equations determines the Brander–Spencer optimum:

(11.A8)
$$q_A = \frac{a - c}{2b}; \quad q_B = \frac{a - c}{4b}; \quad s = \frac{a - c}{4}; \quad \bar{\pi}_A = \frac{(a - c)^2}{8b}$$

Technical Note 11.2 The Eaton–Grossman model

We discuss a simple version of this model, in which an Austrian and a Bolivian firm export to a third market and compete in prices, rather than quantities. The goods produced by the two firms are imperfect substitutes for one another, in which the demand for the good rises if the other firm raises its price. Naturally, the own price effect is negative. Taking linear demand curves and constant marginal costs c, we get:

(11.A9)
$$q_A = a - p_A + p_B; \quad q_B = a - p_B + p_A$$

(11.A10)
$$\pi_A = (p_A - c)q_A; \quad \pi_B = (p_B - c)q_B$$

The remainder of this Note follows the procedure of Technical Note 11.1. Maximizing profits, taking the competitor's price as given, leads to a firm's reaction curve in (p_A, p_B)-space. The intersection of the reaction curves gives the Bertrand equilibrium:

(11.A11)
$$p_A = p_B = a + c$$

The Austrian government, strategically maximizing domestic welfare, will decide to *tax* the production of the Austrian firm, leading to the Eaton–Grossman equilibrium:

(11.A12)
$$p_A = \frac{3a}{2} + c; \quad p_B = \frac{5a}{4} + c; \quad \bar{\pi}_A = \frac{9a^2}{8}; \quad tax = \frac{3a}{4}$$

Chapter 12

International Trade Organizations

Objectives/key terms

Beggar-thy-neighbour
General Agreement on Tariffs and
    Trade (GATT)
UN Conference on Trade and
    Development (UNCTAD)
Organization of Economic Cooperation
    and Development (OECD)

Central and Eastern European
    Economic Transition Process
World Trade Organization (WTO)
United Nations (UN)

We discuss the history and functioning of the main international trade organizations.

12.1 Introduction

The basis of the present international economic order was laid during and immediately after the Second World War. The primary concern in the consultations was not to repeat the disastrous experience of the international economic relations of the interwar period. During the Great Depression in the 1930s, the 'beggar-thy-neighbour' policies, in which each country tried to transfer its economic problems to other countries by depreciating its own currency and imposing high tariffs (see for example the Hawley–Smoot Act of the USA in 1930), led to an almost complete collapse of the international trade system, further exacerbating and prolonging the economic crisis. The impact of the beggar-thy-neighbour policies on international trade is aptly illustrated by the 'spiderweb spiral', measuring the size of world imports in each month by the distance to the origin, see Figure 12.1. In a period of only four years world trade flows dropped to one-third of their

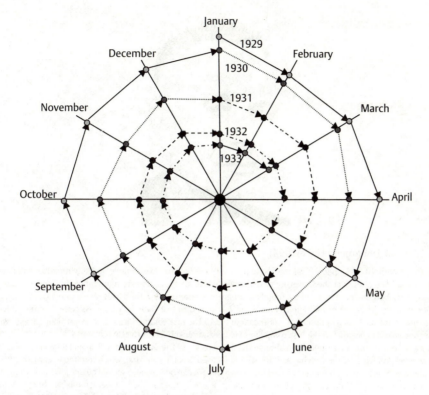

Fig. 12.1 Spiderweb spiral: world imports in million US gold $
Source: League of Nations (1933). Values in January (1929–1933): 2998, 2739, 1839, 1206, 992.

previous level (from January 1929 to January 1933, world imports fell from 2,998 to 992 million US gold $ per month).

The signing of the Charter in 1945 in San Francisco laid the foundations of the United Nations (UN) as an international organization. The system of international bodies developed afterwards is known as the United Nations family. Although consultations took place within the UN, arguably the most important international organizations—the International Monetary Fund (IMF) and the World Bank (WB) on financial issues and the General Agreement on Tariffs and Trade (GATT), later to become the World Trade Organization (WTO), on international trade issues—were eventually located outside the UN. The post-war international economic order is therefore sometimes called the GATT/WTO—IMF/WB order. Since this book focuses on international trade issues, the remainder of this chapter briefly focuses attention on international organizations dealing with international trade and trade policies, which means that the IMF and the WB will not be further discussed. Lanjouw (1995) provides a more complete overview of the international trade institutions, while Bakker (1996) provides an overview of international financial organizations.

Fig. 12.2 Jan Tinbergen (1903–1994)

The Dutch economist Jan Tinbergen was the first to receive the Nobel prize in economics in 1969 (together with Ragnar Frisch). He studied physics at the University of Leiden and wrote his thesis on extremum problems in physics and economics. Tinbergen became one of the founding fathers of econometrics in the 1930s. While working at the League of Nations, the predecessor of the United Nations, he was invited to test Haberler's business cycle theories, which resulted in *Statistical Testing of Business Cycle Theories* (1939). The first volume focused on investment activity, while the second volume constructed the first complete macroeconomic model for the United States.[1]

After the Second World War Tinbergen became the first director of the Dutch Central Planning Bureau (a think tank on economic problems for the Dutch government) and focused on policy making, which resulted in *Economic Policy: Principles and Design* (1956). Tinbergen argued that a government can only achieve several quantitative policy targets if it has an equal number of quantitative policy instruments available, the so-called 'Tinbergen rule'. Tinbergen held a part-time position at the Netherlands School of Economics (now Erasmus University Rotterdam) from 1933, but became a full-time professor of Development Planning in 1955, henceforth focusing on development problems. He gave advice to many countries and UN agencies, and lectured all over the world, which led *inter alia* to *Reshaping the International Order* (1976), a report to the Club of Rome coordinated by Tinbergen.

12.2 The World Trade Organization (WTO/GATT)

The original intention in the post-war period was to set up the International Trade Organization (ITO) for dealing with international trade issues (Havana Charter, 1948). In the end, the ITO was not set up, primarily because it was not ratified by the American Congress. As a result, the General Agreement on Tariffs and Trade (GATT), which was signed in 1947 in Geneva in anticipation of the formation of the ITO, evolved in a de facto international organization with a secretariat in Geneva. Much later, on 1 January 1995, the GATT was converted to the World Trade Organization (WTO), thus becoming an official international organization.

---

[1] Tinbergen earlier made a smaller model for the Netherlands. John Maynard Keynes did not like this work, as is evident from his book review in the *Economic Journal*. Tinbergen politely replied that Keynes had totally misunderstood his econometric methods.

The international GATT agreement is based on three principles:

1. *Non-discrimination*; as expressed in two sub-principles:

(i) *Most Favoured Nation* (MFN) treatment; if a GATT country grants a trade concession to another GATT country, this concession automatically applies to all other GATT countries as well.

(ii) *National treatment* of foreign products; apart from trade policy measures, imported goods must be treated the same as home-produced goods.

There are two main exceptions to the non-discrimination principle:

(i) *Free trade areas* and *customs unions*. If two or more countries decide to form a free trade area or a customs union, such as the countries of the European Union, discriminatory treatment is allowed, essentially because it is viewed as a move in the right direction of free trade. This is discussed in the next chapter.

(ii) *Developing countries*. Preferential treatment for imports is allowed to assist developing countries since part IV, 'trade and development', was added to the GATT in 1965. This enables the Generalized System of Preferences, see UNCTAD below.

2. *Reciprocity*. If one GATT country makes a trade concession, other GATT countries should make equivalent concessions to balance the advantages and disadvantages of trade liberalization. As explained throughout this book, taking all static and dynamic gains of trade liberalization into consideration, it is probably optimal to allow free trade regardless of whether other countries do the same. In practice, however, countries regard trade liberalization as a concession which should be reciprocated by other countries. The most important exception to this principle is for developing countries, which are not required to reciprocate.

3. *Prohibition on trade restrictions other than tariffs*. In principle, trade restrictions other than tariffs, such as quotas, are prohibited. The main reason is that, although the imposition of a tariff influences the market, its operation does not affect the market mechanism. Moreover, it is easier to negotiate on tariff reductions than on the removal of other trade measures which are more difficult to quantify. The most important exception to this principle applies in the case of balance-of-payments problems.

After the establishment of the GATT as an agreement, a series of trade liberalization rounds followed. Their successfulness in terms of the large reductions of imposed tariff rates was already illustrated in Figure 8.2. Initially, the trade liberalization rounds rapidly succeeded each other, took a limited amount of time, and involved a limited number of countries, as illustrated in Figure 12.3. As time passed, more countries became members of the GATT, such that the negotiations became more complicated and took several years to complete.

The Kennedy Round (1964–7) is often taken as the dividing line, as it involved a change in negotiating technique. In the first five rounds, negotiations took place according to the principal-supplier rule, that is there were bilateral negotiations for each product involving the principal suppliers to one another's markets. Under the MFN clause the results of the bilateral negotiations also apply to the GATT partners. This connection

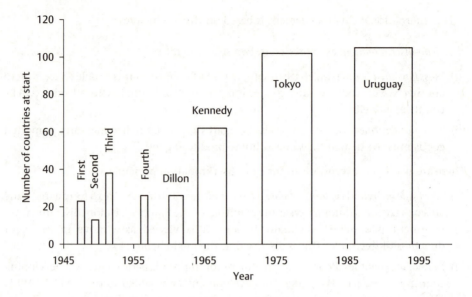

Fig. 12.3 Duration of GATT rounds and the number of countries involved

between the bilateral negotiations made it difficult to get an overall picture of the granted and received concessions, which should be balanced under the principle of reciprocity. The Kennedy Round therefore started with the aim to achieve linear tariff reductions, making it necessary to negotiate only on the exceptions. In the end, the average tariff reduction was about 35 per cent, somewhat below the target of 50 per cent, primarily because countries with already low tariffs in absolute terms were not willing to apply the same percentage reduction as countries with high tariffs in absolute terms.

To avoid the difficulties of linear tariff reductions that became apparent in the Kennedy Round, the Tokyo Round (1973–9) used the so-called 'Swiss formula' for tariff reduction, based on the parameter A (14 in the original Swiss proposal), see Figure 12.4:

$$(12.1) \qquad \text{new tariff} = \frac{A \cdot \text{old tariff}}{A + \text{old tariff}}$$

As is clear from Figure 12.4, applying this formula leads to much higher tariff reductions for initially high tariffs, thus leading to a more rapid tariff harmonization. In addition, the Tokyo Round (which was called the Nixon Round until Nixon was forced to resign as president of the USA) involved negotiations on tropical products (concessions for some products, but not for sugar), non-tariff measures (agreement on codes of conduct), agriculture (restraint on export subsidies), specific sectors (total trade liberalization for civil aircraft), and safeguards (no agreement).

Attention in the negotiations clearly shifted towards the importance of non-tariff barriers. Initially, it was thought to be a result of the successfulness of the achieved tariff reductions. As Lanjouw (1995: 12) puts it:

The metaphor applied here was of trade liberalisation representing the draining of a swamp. The reduction in tariffs symbolised letting the water level fall, uncovering what was below the surface in

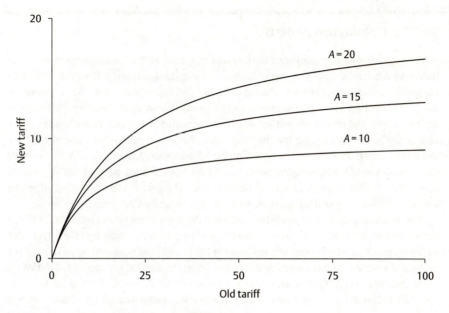

Fig. 12.4 The 'Swiss formula' for tariff reduction

the form of non-tariff barriers. However, it gradually became clear that protection by non-tariff measures was steadily increasing, so the expression 'new protectionism' became commonplace.

A clear example of the new protectionism is a 'Voluntary' Export Restraint (VER), where a country limits the number of goods exported to another country, usually as a result of the pressure exerted by the government of the importing country. VERs are against GATT rules, but do not lead to complaints to the GATT as they are imposed by the exporting country. Perhaps the most noteworthy example of a VER is the decision of the Japanese car manufacturers in the 1980s, under severe pressure from the Japanese government, which in turn was pressured by the American government, to limit the number of cars exported to the USA. Lanjouw attributes the rise of the new protectionism to a combination of factors, such as structural shifts in the international division of labour (the rise of the newly industrialized countries: Hong Kong, South Korea, Singapore, and Taiwan), cyclical movements in economic activity (the economic slowdown in the beginning of the 1980s), a diminished willingness for structural adjustment, and a mis-interpretation of the term reciprocity and the concept of trade balance surpluses and deficits (in particular in the USA, where some influential players seem to strive for bilateral trade balance with each other country, sometimes even for each good; thus trade is only 'fair' if the export of Japanese cars to the USA is of equal value as the export of American cars to Japan, leading to 100 per cent intra-industry trade).

The complications arising from the desire to stop the rise of the new protectionism and the increased number of countries involved in the GATT negotiations were responsible for the fact that the last GATT round, known as the Uruguay Round, lasted for seven years, from 1986 to 1993. In the end, substantial agreements were reached in several areas. First, the negotiations on liberalization of trade in services, an increasingly

Box 12.1 **Globalization protests**

Nowadays, international (trade) organizations tend to receive a lot of media attention whenever they hold a large meeting. The media have, of course, always covered the most important discussions and decisions of such meetings in a nice and sophisticated way. Today, however, these meetings have become main events and are headline news on the television, the radio, in the newspaper, and on the internet for weeks. Unfortunately, the media circus focuses attention on the issues surrounding the meeting rather than the meeting itself. Sometimes, the television cameras zoom in on the rioters of the 'globalization protesters', who are breaking windows, throwing bricks, spraying paint, turning over cars, setting buildings on fire, etc. At other times, they highlight the actions of the riot police, charging a building, beating up people who are lying on the ground, and, in an extreme case, shooting a protester.

Who are these globalization protesters and when did the massive violent protests start? The second part of the question is easy to answer. The first part is not. Although there had been earlier occasions at which protesters marched in the streets, the scale and aggression of the protests reached an unprecedented peak which shocked the world at the meeting of the World Trade Organization (WTO) in Seattle (USA) in December 1999. People chanted for example: 'hey, hey, ho, ho. WTO has got to go', but they were also running through the streets, wearing masks and smashing shop windows, such that Seattle was put under a curfew, the mayor declared a civil emergency, and the governor sent in the National Guard.

Explaining who the protesters are is virtually impossible, as there are so many different groups, with different, usually conflicting, ideas (if any). There were trade unionists attending a protest rally. There were colourful environmentalists in sea-turtle outfits. There were human-rights activists indicting Union Carbide for crimes against humanity. There was a French farm leader protesting against McDonald's with Roquefort cheese. As *The Economist* (1999) put it, there were 'students carrying Japanese cameras and drinking foreign coffee [who] railed that trade should be local, not global'.

Over time the protests have become even more aggressive, as for example recently at the European Union meeting in Gothenburg (Sweden) in June 2001 and at the G8 meeting (7 rich countries plus Russia) in Genoa (Italy) in July 2001, where the protester alluded to above was shot to death. Why the protests are getting so much out of hand is not clear. Some say that the internet makes it easier for the protesters to organize themselves. Others argue that the excessive media exposure generates interest from rioters around the world for the next meeting. Others still argue that the international organizations are bringing the protests upon themselves as they do not communicate the benefits of their actions to the public clearly, see for example *The Economist* (2001*d*):

Hans Eichel, the German finance minister, is the latest European grandee to come out in favour of a directly imposed EU tax as a way of making the workings of the European Union more open and less mysterious. But if ordinary people notice a deduction on their payslips marked EU, is that really going to make the Union more popular? You need to have been locked up in a convention centre for a very long time to believe that.

Information source: *The Economist* (1999, 2001*c*, 2001*d*, 2001*e*).

important part of world trade flows, led to the General Agreement on Trade in Services (GATS), a framework of principles and rules, such as MFN treatment of foreign suppliers, and for some sectors national treatment of foreign suppliers. Some subsectors were excluded (e.g. audio-visual, telecommunications, and maritime transport), for example because France feared impairing its 'cultural identity' if it had to liberalize its television programming. Second, the negotiations for the agricultural sectors eventually resulted in (i) conversion of non-tariff barriers to equivalent tariffs, (ii) tariffs to be reduced on average by 36 per cent in the next six years, (iii) a minimum foreign market share of 5 per cent after the implementation period, and (iv) reduction of export subsidies for seventeen agricultural products by 36 per cent. Third, an agreement on the protection of intellectual property rights (patents for twenty years and copyright for fifty years). Fourth, and finally, the conversion of the GATT to a full-fledged international organization, the WTO.

An important practical consequence of the establishment of the WTO is the improved dispute settlement procedure after a complaint has been made to the WTO. Not only because there are strict time limits for each stage in the procedure, but also because the system will be virtually automatic, that is the panel report written by independent experts for the dispute is automatically accepted within a specified period, unless there is a consensus in favour of rejection. This contrasts sharply with the GATT procedure in which, rather remarkably, the accused party had veto power.

At the end of 2000, the WTO had 140 member countries. The WTO organization is located on rue de Lausanne 154, CH-1211 Geneva 21, Switzerland. The WTO website (http://www.wto.org) gives details of the history of the organization, provides many (trade) statistics, gives an overview of, and background information to, the current trade topics being discussed at the WTO, and contains the list of member countries.

12.3 The United Nations (UN) and UNCTAD

The signing of the Charter in 1945 in San Francisco laid the foundations of the United Nations (UN) as an international organization, becoming operative in October of the same year after ratification by sufficiently many countries. Under the guidance of the Secretary General (at the time of writing Kofi Annan) and the Secretariat located in New York City, the large UN system deals with many different aspects of human life and organization, such as human rights, international justice, security, military and peace-keeping operations, and economic, social, cultural, and development issues. In the economic sphere, the most important body is ECOSOC, the Economic and Social Council, which coordinates the work in the economic and social fields. In this respect, and to give an idea of the size of the UN family of organizations, ECOSOC's main involvement can be subdivided as follows:

- *Programs and Funds*; such as the UN Conference on Trade and Development (UNCTAD), the UN Development Programme (UNDP), the Office of the UN High Commissioner for Refugees (UNHCR), the UN Children's Fund (UNICEF), etc.

- *Functional Commissions*; such as the Commission for Social Development, the Commission on Human Rights, the Commission on Sustainable Development, the Commission on the Status of Women, etc.
- *Regional Commissions*; such as the Economic Commission for Africa (ECA), the Economic Commission for Europe (ECE), the Economic Commission for Latin America and the Caribbean (ECLAC), the Economic and Social Commission for Asia and the Pacific (ESCAP), and the Economic and Social Commission for Western Asia (ESCWA).
- *Specialized (independent) Agencies*; such as the International Labour Organization (ILO), the Food and Agriculture Organization of the UN (FAO), the UN Educational, Scientific and Cultural Organization (UNESCO), the World Health Organization (WHO), the World Bank group, and the International Monetary Fund (IMF).

For various reasons, the developing countries became increasingly dissatisfied with their role in the world economy during the 1950s and 1960s. One reason, forwarded by the development economists Raul Prebisch and Hans Singer, was the argument that over longer periods of time the terms of trade is turning against the developing

---

Box 12.2 **The terms of trade: are high export prices good or bad?**

The ratio of export prices to import prices of a country is called the terms of trade. Now ask yourself if it is good or bad to have high export prices. If you have the interests of a firm in mind, you may be inclined to go along with the popular reasoning of businessmen in the newspaper: the dollar is overvalued, which implies that our export prices are too high such that we cannot compete effectively anymore with foreign firms (followed by threats on factories which will be closed down and jobs which will be lost). The suggestion is that high export prices are bad. In Chapter 1, however, we argued that an important characteristic of international economics is the general equilibrium approach. We have to look at the complete picture, in which 'high' export prices reflect the interplay of economic forces on the supply side *and* the demand side, perhaps caused by the fact that we produce high-quality goods in popular demand. In this interpretation high export prices are good, as they lead to higher welfare levels. This is illustrated in Figure 12.5 in a neoclassical equilibrium framework in which the country, which exports manufactures, initially reaches welfare level U_0. If the price of manufactures, the export good, rises the economy is able to reach the higher welfare level U_1. A simple analogy is to think of yourself as a country: you want the price of your export goods (labour services) which earns you an income to be as high as possible, and the price of your import goods (all goods and services you consume) to be as low as possible.

As discussed in the main text, the Prebisch–Singer hypothesis suggests that the terms of trade is deteriorating for developing countries. According to Krugman and Obstfeld (2000: 103), however, for the group of *advanced* countries as a whole the terms of trade deteriorated in the periods 1973–74 (first oil crisis) and 1979–80 (second oil crisis). Over a longer time period the net effects are minimal: in three decades (1970–97), the average terms of trade for the advanced countries deteriorated by only 6 per cent.

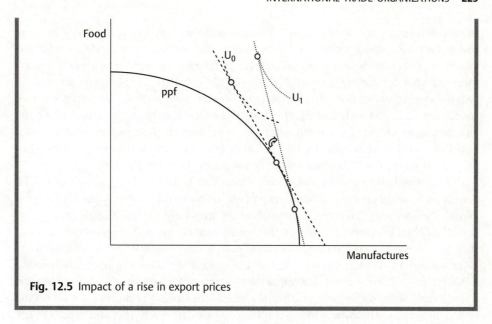

Fig. 12.5 Impact of a rise in export prices

countries, as these countries tend to be dependent for their export earnings on a limited number of primary products with falling relative prices. According to this argument, developing countries are forced to produce and export ever increasing quantities of their primary products to finance the imports of manufactured goods from developed countries. There have been many empirical studies trying to test the Prebisch–Singer hypothesis of deteriorating terms of trade for developing countries. All in all, it is fair to say that the hypothesis is far from proven, see Box 12.2. A second reason for the dissatisfaction of developing countries with their role in the world economy was the phenomenon of 'tariff escalation', referring to the fact that developed countries tend to levy low tariffs for the imports of primary products necessary in the early stages of the production process, and high tariffs for the imports of processed goods, leading to high effective rates of protection for the later stages of the production process, see Chapter 8, Table 8.1. A third reason for dissatisfaction was the GATT principle of non-discrimination, as the developing countries argued that they needed preferential treatment because they *are* less developed, a variant of the infant-industry argument. The developing countries, united in the Group of 77 (now containing more countries) wanted to set up an organization concentrating on their interests. This aim was realized at the first UNCTAD session in Geneva in 1964, establishing UNCTAD as a permanent international organization, with a secretariat and a Secretary General (a post first held by Raul Prebisch). Plenary UNCTAD sessions take place every three or four years.

As an organization, UNCTAD does not have executive power. Instead, UNCTAD conference resolutions are recommendations for the UN General Assembly. After the confrontational approach at the first UNCTAD conference, which did not lead to any substantial results, the second UNCTAD conference at New Delhi in 1968 was more consensus based, which led to the Generalized System of Preferences (GSP). Under this system, OECD countries apply non-reciprocal preferential tariffs to imports of (primary) products from developing countries to raise export earnings and stimulate growth. To provide a legal basis for GSP, an addition (part IV) was made to the GATT system in 1965, see section 12.2. UNCTAD and the GATT/WTO are therefore both concerned with trade and development issues, the main difference being that the GSP system of UNCTAD is based on a unilateral decision by OECD countries (which can also be unilaterally withdrawn), while the GATT agreements are binding contractual obligations.

Multinational, or Transnational, corporations, which have active branches in several countries, have become increasingly important in the world economy after the Second World War, see also Chapter 15. To analyse the impact of multinationals on international trade and investment flows and their general influence on the economic and social structure of (developing) nations, ECOSOC set up the Commission on Transnational Corporations in 1974, followed by the UN Centre on Transnational Corporation (UNCTC) in 1975 to support the work of the Commission. Over the years, there has been a remarkable shift in the general attitude towards the impact of multinationals on the economic system, particularly by developing countries, from a hostile and negative view in the 1960s and 1970s to a much more positive view in the 1980s and 1990s. The earlier negative picture was partly due to the political meddling of multinationals in the host countries, for example the active involvement of the American International Telephone and Telegraph Company (ITT) in attempts to bring down Salvador Allende, the Marxist President of Chile, because of fears of nationalization of ITT assets by the Allende government. The more recent positive picture on the impact of multinationals arises from the realization that the large investments by these companies, and the local knowledge and productivity spillovers created as a result of these activities, can be of vital importance for a successful development process, as explained in more detail in Chapters 14–16. Since 1991, the UN research in this area is summarized annually in UNCTAD's *World Investment Report*, at present arguably UNCTAD's most important publication.

Virtually all people in the world now live in a country that is a member of the UN. At the time of writing this chapter (summer 2001), the UN had 189 member countries. The address of the Spokesman for the Secretary General is United Nations, S-378 New York, NY 10017, USA. The UN website (http://www.un.org) gives extensive information on the structure of the organization, its history, the current issues being discussed, and the list of member countries. The history and work of UNCTAD is available at the UNCTAD website (http://www.unctad.org). Since both UNCTAD and the WTO are active in the fields of international trade and development these organizations work together, for which they established the International Trade Centre (ITC), 54–6 rue de Montbrillant, Geneva, Switzerland. The ITC website (http://www.intracen.org) contains trade documentation, detailed trade statistics per country, and the ITC magazine.

12.4 **Organization for Economic Cooperation and Development (OECD)**

The final international body to be briefly discussed in this chapter is the Organization for Economic Cooperation and Development (OECD), which was established in 1961 as the successor to the Organization for European Economic Cooperation (OEEC). The latter organization, comprising West European countries and Turkey, was established in 1948 to implement the Marshall Aid programme, by which the USA was assisting post-war recovery in Europe. At the end of the 1950s the OEEC had attained its objectives. Its transition to the OECD, in part to coordinate aid to developing countries, allowed Canada and the USA to become full members. In the 1970s membership was extended to Japan, Finland, Australia, and New Zealand. At the end of the twentieth century, and partially as a result of the breakdown of the Iron Curtain, Mexico, South Korea, Poland, the Czech Republic, Slovakia, and Hungary joined the OECD, see Figure 12.6.

The OEEC played an important role in the 1950s in reducing quantitative trade barriers (quotas) in Europe, leaving the reduction of tariffs to the GATT. Plans to form a free trade area were not successful, as there was a division between the countries which later formed the European Economic Community (EEC) and the countries which later formed the European Free Trade Area (EFTA). Eventually, many EFTA countries joined the EEC and formed the European Union (EU), see the next chapter. The OECD plays an important role as a consultation forum on trade policy issues for the developed nations, without the necessity to come to any direct agreements, which is a matter for the GATT/WTO. The OECD serves a mediating role in this respect, for example when (i) arguing in favour of

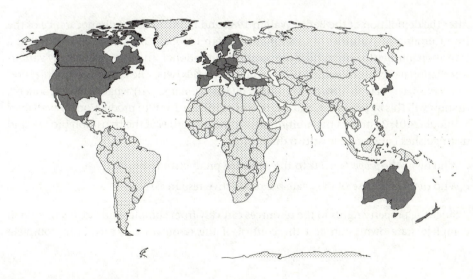

Fig. 12.6 OECD member countries

positive adjustment policies in the OECD countries in the 1970s for those sectors of the economy which could no longer compete successfully with the newly industrializing countries, or (ii) when examining the agricultural question in the 1980s and producing a report in 1987 (later approved by the OECD council) with a method of reducing the effects of different national measures to a common denominator, making them comparable and negotiable, or (iii) when the OECD council adopted guidelines for multinationals (e.g. on transfer prices) and decided to apply the principle of national treatment to multinationals.

The OECD's Development Assistance Committee (DAC) plays an important role in coordinating national aid programmes to developing countries. The DAC strives for a reduction of tied aid, in which the recipient country is obliged to spend the development assistance in the donor country or in a group of countries linked to the donor country. In general, the effectiveness of development assistance diminishes if aid is tied rather than untied, see Brakman and van Marrewijk (1998) for a general overview of (unilateral) international transfers and tied aid.

At the time of writing this chapter (summer 2001), the OECD had thirty member countries. The OECD secretariat is located on rue André Pascal 2, F-75775 Paris Cedex 16, France. The OECD website (http://www.oecd.org) gives details of the organization, provides many excellent statistics and reports, and contains the list of member countries with useful links to online data sources for each country.

12.5 Case study: economic transition in Central and Eastern Europe[2]

After the demolition of the Berlin Wall in 1989 and the subsequent disappearance of the Iron Curtain, the countries of Central and Eastern Europe (CEE) started to embark on a transition journey to reform their economic organizational structures, assisted by various international organizations and professional policy advisers. The economic organization of every society has to answer three basic questions, namely (i) what will be produced, (ii) how will this be produced, and (iii) to whom will the fruits of production be available? Schmidt (2001: 2) stresses the multi-dimensional properties of the transition process and distinguishes between at least two dimensions:

- Who owns the *property rights* to the available productive resources?
- Who *controls* the use of the available productive resources?

Since the property rights to the resources can vary from complete private ownership to complete state ownership and the control of the resources can vary from complete

---

[2] The discussion in this section is based on Schmidt (2001).

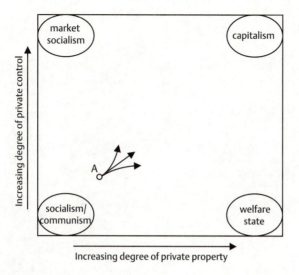

Fig. 12.7 Economic systems

private control to complete government control, as illustrated in Figure 12.7, we can distinguish four benchmark extremes of different economic systems, none of which is to be found in the real world. At one extreme we have socialism/communism with state property and state control. At the opposite extreme we have capitalism ('laissez faire') with private property and private control. On the other diagonal of the matrix in Figure 12.7 we have hypothetical extremes with state property and free markets, dubbed market socialism (see the China case study in Chapter 17), and private property with state regulation, dubbed welfare state. The transition process in the CEE countries is multi-dimensional, if only because countries can choose a different mix of the more or less one-dimensional *privatization* (moving from state ownership to private ownership) and *deregulation* (moving from state control to private control) policies, even starting from the same initial conditions, as illustrated by point A and the (curved) arrows in Figure 12.7. Thus 'transition', which must be accompanied by institutional change, can mean different things to different countries at the same time or to the same country at different times.

The transition process also involves a change in the mix of output. This is illustrated in Figure 12.8, where we have drawn a production possibility frontier (ppf) of food and manufactures for a CEE country. Suppose that the government, which is initially in control of the productive resources, ensures that the economy is producing and consuming at point A on the ppf.[3] As a result of privatization and deregulation, the ultimate objective is for the economy to produce and consume at point B, which produces more food and less manufactures and better represents the people's preferences. During the

---

[3] Many experts argue that the CEE economies were not actually producing *on* the ppf, but somewhere *inside* the ppf as a result of various inefficiencies.

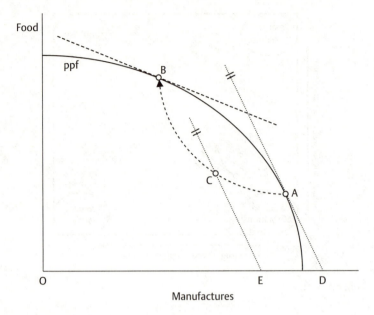

Fig. 12.8 Economic transition

transition phase from point A to point B, however, society has to reorganize itself. Capital has to be moved from one sector to another or completely discarded. People have to relocate, be educated for a new job, get used to the new organization of society and its institutional changes, etc. All of this implies that during the transition phase the economy will not be efficiently organized, such that it is producing *inside* the production possibility frontier. We therefore assume that, after a number of years, the CEE economy is producing at point C, rather than at point A. When measured at the initial equilibrium relative prices of point A, a standard procedure followed by statisticians, this implies a measured loss in real output from OD to OE. At the early stages of the transition process we can therefore expect a decline rather than a rise in measured output.[4] Moreover, depending on the speed and efficiency of the transition process, and the willingness and readiness for people to get used to the new environment, these early stages can last a long time. As Schmidt (2001: 7) remarks:

When meeting and working with colleagues in CEE one cannot escape being struck by the extra-ordinary difficulties which the communist regime must have imposed on everyday life there (with an almost universal lack of personal freedom as its most poignant feature), and by the deep traces it has left in human attitudes even today. By their very nature privatization and deregulation are legal acts, the formalities of which can in principle be arranged on fairly short notice. But then? Then everybody has to get going in the new environment, but the adaptation (human and otherwise) required for that to happen in any effective way is a very complex process and takes much more time than was originally perceived, certainly in the West.

---

[4] It is important to note that this measured decline will exaggerate the actual welfare loss if the economy was initially producing the wrong output mix, which does not reflect people's preferences.

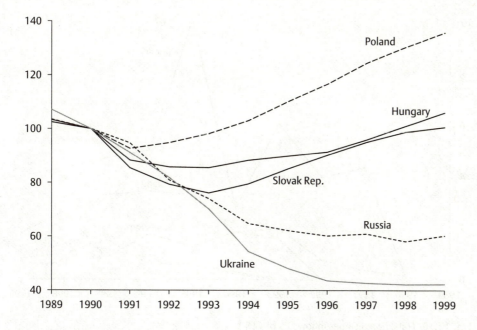

Fig. 12.9 Transition: GDP per capita, 1995 constant $, index (1990 = 100)

The extent of the decline in output and the length of time of the initial stage is illustrated for a selection of countries in Figure 12.9, using an index (1990 = 100) of per capita GDP measured in constant 1995 $. Poland, which followed a 'big bang' strategy of rapid reform, is the most successful CEE transition country. Per capita GDP dropped until 1991 (to 93 per cent) and started to rise thereafter (to 136 per cent in 1999). Hungarian GDP dropped until 1993 (to 86 per cent) before it started to rise (to 106 per cent in 1999). Similarly for the Slovak Republic, which just recovered to its 1990 level in 1999. The other two countries, Russia and the Ukraine, show just how dramatic the measured decline in output can be (to 58 per cent and 42 per cent, respectively), and how long the fall in output can last (up to 1998 for Russia, 1999 for the Ukraine).

Figure 12.10, finally, illustrates the positive influence of foreign knowledge and capital in a successful transition process. Prior to 1990, there were virtually no foreign direct investments (see also Chapters 1 and 15) into the CEE countries, measured as net inflows relative to GDP in Figure 12.10. Hungary and Poland, both rather successful transition economies, are also the most successful countries in attracting foreign direct investments, reaching levels above 4 per cent in 1998 and 1999 (for Hungary after an impressive, and clearly unsustainable, peak of 10 per cent in 1995). The other countries, in particular Russia and the Ukraine, were not nearly as successful in attracting foreign investors, who were not convinced of the commitment to the processes of privatization and deregulation.

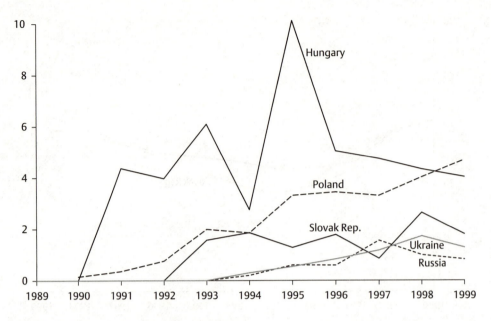

Fig. 12.10 Transition: FDI net inflows (% of GDP)

12.6 **Conclusions**

We briefly discuss the history and functioning of the main international trade organizations. The GATT deals most directly with international trade problems and has been successful in reducing trade barriers in a series of complicated negotiation rounds. It was replaced by the WTO, which has a more effective dispute settlement mechanism. Of the many UN organizations we reviewed the functioning of UNCTAD in particular, focusing on the problems of developing nations. The OECD, in contrast, is a club of advanced nations, also coordinating their interactions with developing countries. The process of CEE economic transitions illustrates the enormous and time-consuming problems of adjusting a country's economic organization and institutional framework.

Chapter 13
Economic Integration

Objectives/key terms

Preferential trade agreement   Free trade area/customs union

Trade-creation/trade-diversion   Regionalism/multilateralism

European Union (EU)   EU enlargement

We review some of the many preferential trade agreements in the world, with special attention to Europe and EU enlargement. The rising popularity of economic integration, known as 'regionalism', is analysed in a neoclassical and new trade framework.

13.1 Introduction

Since a regional economic integration agreement gives preferential treatment to the members of the agreement, but not equal treatment to non-members as would be in line with the Most Favoured Nation (MFN) clause of the GATT/WTO, any such agreement violates the non-discrimination principle of the GATT/WTO. As explained in Chapter 12, however, regional economic integration agreements can be exempted from the non-discrimination principle, either because a move towards uninhibited trade flows among a group of countries is seen as a step in the right direction of free trade, or because a preferential trade agreement provides an impulse to the growth and development process of less developed countries.

At the beginning of 2001, the European Union, under the guidance of Pascal Lamy, the European trade commissioner, decided to push through huge tariff reductions for forty-eight of the world's poorest countries. All goods, except arms, will be imported into Europe free of tariffs. Some goods, such as bananas, sugar, and rice, will be phased out later. Michael Finger, an economist at the World Bank, estimates that the forty-eight poorest countries' exports will grow by 15–20 per cent, or about $1.4 billion, per year. He also notes that the upsurge in exports will come at the expense of other developing countries, producing similar goods, which are not in the group of forty-eight, such as Swaziland.[1] These two effects, the increase of trade for the countries receiving a

---

[1] *The Economist*, 3 March 2001, p. 77.

Fig. 13.1 Jacob Viner (1892–1970)

Born in Montreal, Canada, of Romanian immigrant parents, Jacob Viner was, according to Mark Blaug (1985: 256), 'a leading interwar price and trade theorist and quite simply the greatest historian of economic thought that ever lived'. He received his Ph.D. in 1915 at Harvard University, written under the supervision of Frank Taussig, and worked at the University of Chicago, where he became editor of the *Journal of Political Economy*, before moving to Princeton in 1946. Viner's *Studies in the Theory of International Trade* (1937) provides the basis for much of our current views and knowledge on the history of international economics, particularly on the pre-scientific fallacies of the mercantilists in the seventeenth and eighteenth centuries. In 1950 Viner wrote *The Customs Union Issue*, identifying the trade-creation and trade-diversion effects, which became the basis for all subsequent work on customs unions and free trade areas.

preferential treatment and the reduction of trade for countries who do not, were described for the first time by Jacob Viner (1950), referring to it as trade-creation and trade-diversion, respectively. This chapter discusses the welfare consequences of preferential trade policies in general and gives an overview of the most important regional trade agreements in the world. An overview of the empirical issues that play a role in estimating the impact of regional trade agreements will be given in Chapter 17.

Section 13.2 gives a description of different types of regional economic integration agreements. Section 13.3 analyses the main economic consequences of economic integration based on the neoclassical framework explained in Part II of this book. Section 13.4 gives a brief overview of some of the main regional economic integration agreements that are active today, from which it will be clear that there is an increasing tendency for the countries of the world economy to organize themselves in a decreasing number of large trading blocks. Section 13.5 analyses the consequences of this empirically observed tendency in a general equilibrium framework based on the imperfect competition and intra-industry trade models of Chapters 9 and 10 of Part III of this book. Section 13.6 describes the economic integration process after the Second World War of the countries currently forming the European Union, arguably the world's most successful economic integration agreement. Section 13.7 discusses the process of EU enlargement to accommodate the Central and Eastern European countries that wish to join the EU after the fall of the Berlin Wall in 1989. Section 13.8 concludes.

13.2 Types of regional economic integration

Regional economic integration, in which a group of countries eliminates (artificial) barriers to international trade and competition on a regional rather than a global scale, has become increasingly popular since the Second World War. For the integration of final goods markets and factors of production, we can distinguish between the following types of economic integration agreements, possibly on a sectoral level only, or possibly excluding some sectors (the examples below are further discussed in the sequel of this chapter):

- *Preferential trade agreement (PTA)*. In such an agreement, tariffs or other trade restrictions are reduced among the members of the agreement for some goods or services, sometimes unilaterally. There is no general reduction of internal tariffs, nor a common external tariff. An example is provided by the preferential treatment given by the countries of the European Community to their former colonies in Africa, the Caribbean, and the Pacific (known as the ACP countries) under the Lomé Convention.

- *Free trade area (FTA)*. The members of a free trade area eliminate internal tariffs and other measures which restrict trade between its members, without any common trade policy relative to other countries. The lack of an external trade policy requires the use of certificates of origin for goods crossing the borders and other measures to prevent 'deflection' of trade, that is taking advantage of arbitrage opportunities by importing goods from outside the free trade area via the country with the lowest barriers to imports. Examples are the European Free Trade Area (EFTA) and the North American Free Trade Area (NAFTA).

- *Customs union*. Like a free trade area, a customs union abolishes internal tariffs and other trade restriction among the members of the union. In addition, the customs union develops a common trade policy, such as common external tariffs, relative to other countries. An example is provided by the European Economic Community (EEC).

- *Common market*. In this case, the member countries allow not only for the free movement of goods and services, but also for the free movement of factors of production, such as capital and labour. A common market gradually moves to an integrated (or internal) market if the member countries also eliminate other, more concealed barriers to trade arising from differences in national policy, for example regarding product standards or taxation. An example is provided by the European Union (EU).

- *Economic union*. An extension of the common/internal market is an economic union, in which case there is also harmonization of the institutional framework, regarding competition policy, procurement, etc., and a fair degree of policy coordination. The economic union therefore provides the counterpart in the real sphere of a monetary union, in which case there is sufficient policy coordination to allow for one currency. A combined example is provided by the EU's Economic and Monetary Union (EMU).

13.3 Neoclassical theory of economic integration

Jacob Viner (1950) provided the first rigorous analysis of the ways in which a customs union can affect trade flows and resource allocations. He identified trade-creation and trade-diversion, see below, and argued that if trade-creation is dominant, the customs union raises welfare for the members of the customs union and world welfare. The

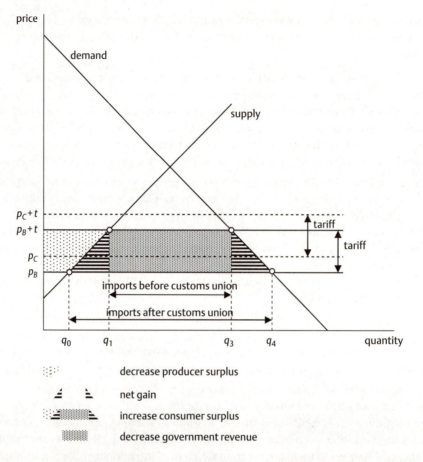

Fig. 13.2 Customs union and welfare I: trade-creation

main consequences of economic integration in a partial equilibrium framework are illustrated in Figures 13.2 and 13.3, depicting the demand and supply schedule for a specific good for Austria. We assume that Austria is a small country relative to two other countries, called Bolivia and Congo. The price for the good in Bolivia is equal to p_B, in Congo it is equal to p_C. We also assume that Austria initially imposes a specific tariff t on imports of the good from both Bolivia and Congo. We analyse the impact of economic integration if Austria decides to form a *customs union* with Bolivia, in which case the specific tariff t for imports from Bolivia is eliminated. Relative to Congo, for which the tariff is still in place, Bolivia therefore gets preferential treatment within the customs union with Austria.

I Customs union with the most efficient producer: trade-creation

Figure 13.2 depicts what happens if Bolivia is a more efficient producer than Congo, in which case p_B is lower than p_C. Before the formation of the customs union, Austria

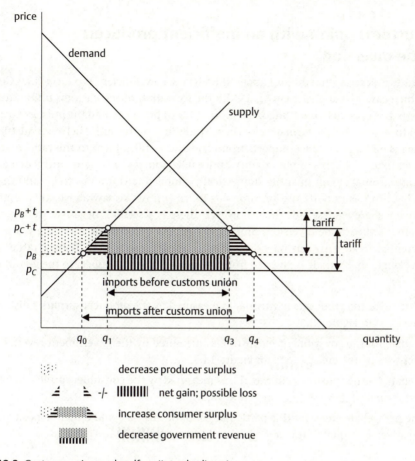

Fig. 13.3 Customs union and welfare II: trade-diversion

imports $q_3 - q_1$ goods from Bolivia, and the price in Austria is equal to $p_B + t$. After the formation of the customs union, the tariff t between Austria and Bolivia is eliminated, such that the price in Austria falls to p_B, quantity demanded increases from q_3 to q_4, quantity domestically supplied falls from q_2 to q_1, and imports from Bolivia rise from $q_3 - q_2$ to $q_4 - q_1$, hence the term trade-creation.

- Welfare for the producers in Austria, as measured by the producer surplus, falls by the area ⬚ in Figure 13.2.
- Welfare for the government in Austria, as measured by the government revenue, decreases by the area ▦ in Figure 13.2.
- Welfare for the consumers in Austria, as measured by the consumer surplus, increases by the area ▦ in Figure 13.2.
- The net welfare effect for this particular good is therefore a *gain* for Austria equal to the area ◿ in Figure 13.2.

II Customs union with an inefficient producer: trade-diversion

Figure 13.3 depicts what might happen if Bolivia is a less efficient producer than Congo, in which case p_B is higher than p_C. Before the formation of the customs union, Austria imports $q_3 - q_1$ goods from Congo, the more efficient producer, and the price in Austria is equal to $p_C + t$. After the formation of the customs union, the tariff t between Austria and Bolivia is eliminated. Since imports from Congo are still subject to the tariff t, and p_B is lower than $p_C + t$, this implies that the price falls from $p_C + t$ to p_B, quantity demanded increases from q_3 to q_4, quantity domestically supplied falls from q_2 to q_1, and there is trade-creation as imports rise from $q_3 - q_2$ to $q_4 - q_1$. As we saw above, this results in positive welfare effects. This time, however, there is a second, negative, welfare effect operative, called trade-diversion. Since the customs union with Austria gives Bolivia preferential treatment, Austria now starts to import goods from Bolivia rather than from Congo, that is trade is diverted from the more efficient producer to the less efficient producer.

- Welfare for the producers in Austria, as measured by the producer surplus, falls by the area ⠿ in Figure 13.3.
- Welfare for the government in Austria, as measured by the government revenue, decreases by the area ▦ in Figure 13.3.
- Welfare for the consumers in Austria, as measured by the consumer surplus, increases by the area ⬛ in Figure 13.3.
- The net welfare effect for this particular good for Austria could either be positive or negative; it is equal to the area ⬜ minus ‖‖‖‖‖‖ in Figure 13.3.

III The welfare effects of a customs union: general equilibrium

In the above partial equilibrium analysis, the positive welfare effects arise from the Harberger triangles measuring the efficiency gains from trade-creation. The negative welfare effects arise from the reallocation of resources from the more efficient to the less efficient producer as a result of trade-diversion. As mentioned above, Jacob Viner therefore argued that the net welfare effect of creating a customs union is positive if the trade-creation effects dominate the trade-diversion effects. This topic was analysed in the literature that followed, see Lipsey (1960) and Lloyd (1982) for an overview. The potential positive welfare benefits of the formation of a customs union, which after all eliminates artificial barriers to trade, was convincingly demonstrated by Murray Kemp and Henry Wan Jr. (1976).

Kemp-Wan proposition

Consider any competitive world trading equilibrium with a neoclassical production structure, with any number of countries and commodities, with no restrictions whatever on the tariffs and other commodity taxes of individual countries, and with cost of transport fully recognized. Now let any subset of the countries form a customs union. Then there exists a common tariff vector and a system of lump-sum compensatory payments involving only members of the union, such that each individual, whether a member of the union or not, is not worse off than before the formation of the union.

The formal proof of the proposition is based on a fundamental theorem of neoclassical general equilibrium theory and beyond the scope of this book, see Debreu (1959).[2] This theory is able to derive very general results with respect to the number of goods and countries involved because it is based on two strong assumptions: perfect competition and a neoclassical production structure. This means that imperfect competition, economies of scale, knowledge spillovers, etc. are ruled out. Note that the partial equilibrium analysis above suggests that there may be negative welfare effects if trade-diversion dominates trade-creation, which requires a decline of international trade flows of the countries forming the customs union relative to the rest of the world. To rule out this possibility Kemp and Wan argue that it is possible for the countries forming the customs union to impose a common tariff vector which leaves world prices, and therefore the trade and welfare of non-members, at their pre-union prices. The elimination of trade barriers within the union then leads to efficiency gains, which in principle enables welfare gains for each union member through a system of lump-sum transfers.

13.4 Regional trade agreements

All members of the GATT/WTO are bound to notify the regional trade agreements (RTAs) in which they participate. Almost all members participate in at least one such agreement. The GATT has received 124 notifications of RTAs (relating to trade in goods). Since the creation of the WTO in 1995, 90 additional arrangements covering trade in goods or services have been notified. Since new agreements sometimes replace old agreements, the WTO estimates that of the 214 notifications 134 are currently in force. In this section we briefly discuss the main RTAs in the world, with the exception of Europe, which is dealt with separately in section 13.6.

---

[2] In this literature the weak phrase in the proposition that an individual 'is not worse off' after the formation of the customs union actually means that in general there is room for welfare improvement.

Africa

At present, the most important regional trade agreement in Africa is the Common Market for Eastern and Southern Africa (COMESA), which was established in December 1994 and replaced a former preferential trade area, operative since 1981. COMESA currently consists of twenty member states, with a population of over 385 million people. Its task is to promote peace and security in the region and enhance economic prosperity through economic integration. It is therefore implementing a free trade area, and is scheduled to introduce a common external tariff schedule for third parties by 2004. The COMESA Centre is located on Ben Bella Road, PO Box 30051, Lusaka, Zambia.

Fig. 13.4 COMESA countries. COMESA members not listed on the map: Comoros, Mauritius, Rwanda, and Seychells

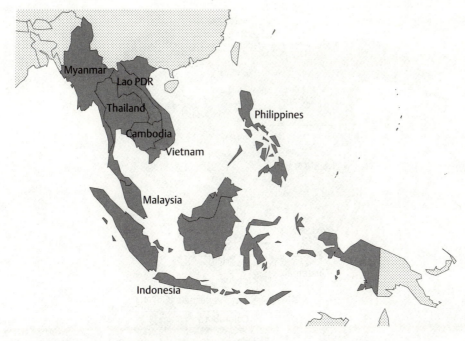

Fig. 13.5 ASEAN countries. ASEAN members not listed on the map: Brunei Darussalam and Singapore

The COMESA website (http://www.comesa.int) provides background information to the organization, statistical data, and information by state.

Asia

The most important regional trade agreement in Asia is the Association of South-East Asian Nations (ASEAN), established by five countries in 1967, but currently consisting of ten countries, with almost 500 million inhabitants. The ASEAN countries work together in several areas (political, economic, cultural, and social), and decided to form the ASEAN Free Trade Area (AFTA) in 1992, to be established by 2004. A commitment towards further economic integration was announced as ASEAN Vision 2020 at the 1997 Kuala Lumpur meeting, although many outside observers remain sceptical of the actual progress which will be made in the future. The ASEAN secretariat is located at 70A Jalan Sisingamangaraja, Jakarta 12110, Indonesia. The website (http://www.asean.or.id) provides up-to-date news of the organization, an overview of the various areas of co-operation (political and security, economic, and functional), information on the ASEAN summits, and statistical information.

America

The American continents have been very active in the formation of regional trade agreements, starting with Latin America in the 1950s. In the drive towards industrialization

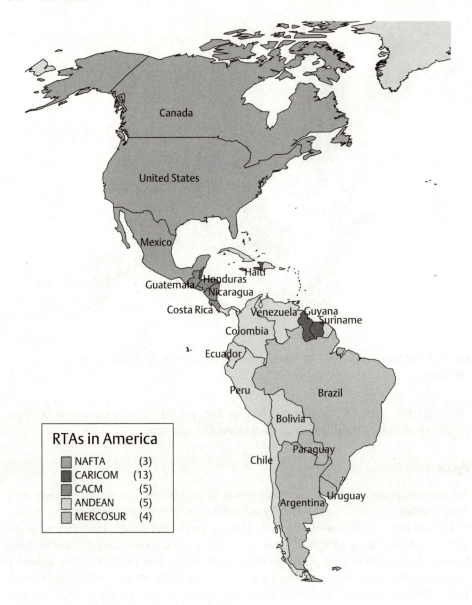

Fig. 13.6 Regional trade agreements in America

by import substitution, and realizing that for many countries in the region the domestic market was too small to allow for efficient production, regional free trade agreements were set up to increase the size of the local market. This resulted in, for example, the Central American Common Market (CACM), the Caribbean Community (CARICOM), the Andean Pact (ANDEAN), and the Mercado Commun del Sur (MERCOSUR), although some of these agreements were not energetically implemented.

Table 13.1 FTAA intra- and inter-regional trade flows, bn US $, 1999 (% of total)

	NAFTA	MERCOSUR	ANDEAN	CACM	CARICOM
NAFTA	703 (73%)	43 (4%)	43 (2%)	16 (2%)	9 (1%)
MERCOSUR		18 (2%)	6 (1%)	0 (0%)	0 (0%)
ANDEAN			5 (1%)	1 (0%)	1 (0%)
CACM				3 (0%)	0 (0%)
CARICOM					1 (0%)

Source: Inter-American Development Bank.

In North America, the agreements started in 1965 with the USA–Canada Auto Pact, involving tariff-free trade in motor vehicles and parts. A few years later on the other side of the US border the *maquiladores* in Mexico, processing or assembling parts imported from the USA and subsequently exported to the USA, started to expand and develop, in part because import duties were only charged on the value added and not on the total value. After some years of negotiations these three countries, Canada, Mexico, and the USA, launched the North American Free Trade Agreement (NAFTA). The American fears of a rapid move of companies and loss of jobs to Mexico, called the 'giant sucking sound' by Ross Perot in the presidential election campaign (which he lost), were unsubstantiated in the years of rapid economic growth following the establishment of NAFTA.

Since the Summit of the Americas in Miami, December 1994, talks are now under way to unite the economies of the western hemisphere in a single free trade agreement, the Free Trade Area of the Americas (FTAA). There are nine negotiating groups, on market access, investment, competition policy, etc. with the objective to establish the FTAA by 2005, see also the FTAA website (http://www.ftaa-alca.org). As is clear from Table 13.1, which gives the intra-regional and inter-regional trade flows between the various trading blocs, by far the largest trade flows in the FTAA area are the NAFTA intra-regional trade flows (73 per cent of the total), that is trade between Canada, Mexico, and the USA. For those countries, the establishment of the FTAA appears to be of relatively minor importance. For all other trading blocs, however, the largest trade flows derive from the inter-regional trade with the NAFTA countries, such that for all other countries establishment of the FTAA is a more important step towards free trade.

13.5 Regionalism and the new trade theory

In the course of the twentieth century, after the Second World War, the process of trade liberalization through multilateral negotiations within the GATT framework became increasingly difficult and time-consuming as more countries joined the GATT, see Chapter 12. At the same time, regional trade agreements, such as in Western Europe and North America, became increasingly popular and more powerful as many countries were organizing themselves in such agreements, which became known as 'regionalism'. On the basis of the Kemp–Wan proposition discussed in section 13.3, one might think that this process, the apparent shift away from multi-lateralism towards regionalism, might be seen as a step in the right direction by trade policy experts, although worldwide liberalization would be better still. Instead, at the end of the 1980s and the beginning of the 1990s many trade policy experts and trade economists were worried about the shift from multilateralism towards regionalism. First, because of fears that countries that join a regional trade agreement might be more protectionist towards countries outside the trading bloc than they were before. Second, because the Kemp–Wan proposition in which no individual country is made worse off after the formation of a customs union is based on (i) the imposition of external tariffs that keep world prices and trade with non-members fixed, and (ii) a complicated internal transfer scheme among the members of the customs union, both of which are not observed in reality. Third, because the Kemp–Wan proposition is based on perfect competition and neoclassical production, such that it does not allow for imperfect competition, increasing returns to scale, and external effects.

Paul Krugman (1991) developed a simple, tractable, general equilibrium model based on the intra-industry trade framework of Chapter 10 to substantiate the fears of the trade policy experts regarding the shift from multilateralism to regionalism. As usual, his work illustrated the main issues involved, such that it received consider-able attention and became the starting point of subsequent analysis and discussion, see for example De Melo and Panagariya (1993). In his first contribution Krugman assumes that a group of countries forming a trading bloc uses its monopoly power with respect to the rest of the world by imposing the 'optimal' tariff, as derived in Chapter 8. As a result, the tariff rate increases as the number of trading blocs falls. Since we do not observe increasing tariff rates in reality after the formation of a new trade bloc, which might start a process of retaliation, we discuss Krugman's model in this section for a *given* tariff rate, which is eliminated for those countries forming a trade bloc. This is not only closer to what we observe in reality, it also does not affect the main results and insights of the analysis and is easier to derive analytically, see also Krugman (1993).

Suppose the world consists of a large number N of 'provinces', each producing one unit of a unique good or variety (for this assumption, see also Chapter 17).[3] Whether or not production takes place under increasing returns to scale or imperfect competition is unimportant. A collection of provinces may form a country, such that a large country may contain more provinces, each producing a unique good, than a small country, but the country level is basically irrelevant in the sequel. The price charged domestically is 1. If c_i is the consumption level for a good produced in

---

[3] One 'unit' could, of course, refer to 1 billion, or 4 billion, or whatever the number of goods produced.

province i, the identical utility function for all economic agents is given by (see also equation 10.2):

$$(13.1) \qquad U = \left[\sum_{i=1}^{N} c_i^{\rho} \right]^{1/\rho} ; \qquad 0 < \rho < 1, \quad \varepsilon \equiv 1/(1-\rho) > 1$$

As explained in Chapter 10, this specification implies that consumers have a love-of-variety and that goods produced in different provinces are imperfect substitutes for one another, with the parameter ε as the elasticity of substitution. The world is divided into b symmetric trading blocs. There is free trade for all provinces within each trading bloc, such that the price charged for a good produced within the trading bloc is 1. Each trading bloc imposes a uniform *ad valorem* tariff t on all imports from outside the trading bloc, such that the price charged for such goods is $1+t$. We are interested in the welfare effects in this simple set-up of the formation of a smaller number of larger trading blocs, that is we are interested in the welfare effects of a fall in b.

Suppose, for example, that the world is initially divided into ten trading blocs of equal size. The inhabitants of any trading bloc then have access to 10 per cent of the world's varieties produced inside the trading bloc and freely traded at the price 1, and 90 per cent of the world's varieties imported from outside the trading bloc, subject to the tariff t, at the price $1+t$. The income available to the inhabitants of a trading bloc derives from the income generated by the production of varieties inside the trading bloc and the tariff revenue levied on imports from outside the trading bloc.

A reduction of the number of trading blocs in the world to, say, eight implies that the inhabitants of any trading bloc have access to 12.5 per cent of the world's varieties produced inside the trading bloc and freely traded at the price 1, and 87.5 per cent of the world's varieties imported from outside the trading bloc at the price $1+t$. At first sight this might seem beneficial as a larger fraction of goods is available at a lower price. However, we have seen in section 13.3 that the total welfare effect depends on the balance between the trade-creation and the trade-diversion effect. Note that the term trade-diversion is not entirely appropriate in this set-up, since all goods are imperfect substitutes for one another. Instead, it should be interpreted in this framework as a diversion away from consumption of goods produced outside the trading bloc towards goods produced inside the trading bloc, that is the increase from 10 to 12.5 per cent of the share of goods produced inside the trading bloc can be viewed as an increase in the fraction of goods whose *relative* price is distorted compared to the rest of the world. The latter interpretation makes the main effects derived in this model readily understandable. It can be shown, see Technical Note 13.1, that total world welfare (normalized to 1 for total free trade, that is if there is only one trading bloc) as a function of the tariff t, the elasticity of substitution between varieties ε, and the number of trading blocs b is equal to:

$$(13.2) \qquad \text{total welfare} = \frac{[b^{-1} + (1-b^{-1})(1+t)^{1-\varepsilon}]^{\varepsilon/(\varepsilon-1)}}{b^{-1} + (1-b^{-1})(1+t)^{-\varepsilon}}$$

Figure 13.7 illustrates the total welfare level given in equation (13.2) as a function of the number of trading blocs b, in panel a for different values of the tariff rate t, and in panel b for different values of the elasticity of substitution ε. The main conclusions are:

1. Total welfare falls as the number of trading blocs b decreases for a large range of parameter settings. Only if the number of trading blocs is already fairly small, in Figure 13.7 ranging from three to six, is a further reduction in the number of trading blocs welfare improving.[4]

2. Total welfare is, of course, maximized if there is free trade (only one trading bloc). This welfare level is also approached in this set-up if the number of trading blocs becomes very large because then the relative price distortion disappears (the share of goods produced within the trading bloc then approaches zero).

3. An increase in the tariff rate t imposed on imports from outside the trading bloc leads to (i) a reduction in the welfare level and (ii) an increase in the number of trading blocs where the minimum welfare level is reached, see Figure 13.7a. To some extent the connection between high tariffs and regionalism is ambivalent, where part (i) is the bad news and part (ii) is the good news (as a fall in b implies that the minimum is reached sooner if tariffs are high).

4. An increase in the elasticity of substitution ε leads to (i) a reduction in the welfare level and (ii) an increase in the number of trading blocs where the minimum welfare level is reached, see Figure 13.7b. These results can be understood by realizing that if it is easier to substitute one variety for another the distortive effect of the tariff is stronger. The connection between the elasticity of substitution and regionalism is therefore, like the connection between tariffs and regionalism, also ambivalent.

The advantage of the model in this section is that it highlights in a simple framework the main issues involved in the move towards regionalism and the fact that it provides a clear warning signal that this move could be detrimental to world welfare. Moreover, it shows how these issues depend on the elasticity of substitution between different goods and the tariff level imposed in the world economy. It should be noted, however, that the picture of the move toward regionalism emerging from the analysis in this section is somewhat too gloomy, as it does not take into consideration the costs of transporting goods and services. As repeatedly pointed out by Krugman (1991, 1993), in reality large trading blocs are formed between neighbouring countries, be it in Europe, America, Africa, or Asia, which account for a large share of a country's trade flows as the cost of transportation is low for neighbouring countries. Eliminating trade barriers within such 'natural' trading blocs, as Krugman calls them, therefore removes distorted relative prices to a larger extent than estimated on the basis of the share of income in the world economy of the countries in the trading bloc, therefore more rapidly leading to an increase in world welfare than suggested by the analysis in this section.

---

[4] In Krugman (1991), which is based on the 'optimal' tariff approach, the minimum was reached at three trading blocs for a large range of elasticities of substitution.

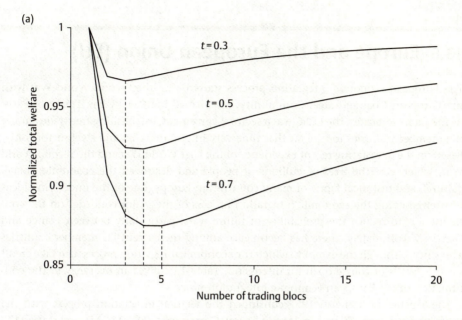

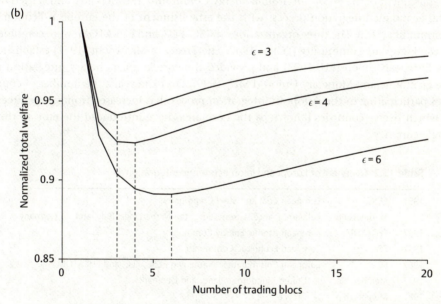

Fig. 13.7 Regional trade agreements and total welfare. Dashed lines indicate where the minimum level is reached. ad (a) $\varepsilon = 4$, ad (b) $t = 0.5$

13.6 **Europe and the European Union (EU)**

The European economic integration process started after the Second World War with the European Coal and Steel Community, established in 1951 by the Treaty of Paris. As the name indicates, the ECSC was a sectoral agreement, establishing free trade among the member countries for the (at that time very important) coal and steel sectors only. Based on the devastating recent experience of the First World War and the Second World War, which cost the lives of millions of people and destroyed the economic, social, cultural, and historical fabric of many countries in Europe, one of the underlying ideas of strengthening the economic integration process of the major countries on the continent was to reduce the probability of future wars, particularly between France and Germany. Fortunately, there has been peace among the current EU member countries ever since, although the extent to which the economic integration process can take credit for this fact is of course open for discussion. Table 13.2 gives an overview of the continuation of the European economic integration process.

The Treaties of Rome in 1957 continued the sectoral integration process with the establishment of the European Atomic Energy Community (EURATOM), and started the total economic integration process with the establishment of the European Economic Community (EEC). The three organizations (ECSC, EEC, and EURATOM) were combined in the European Community (EC) in 1967. The Treaty of Maastricht (1991) established the European Union (EU, 1993) and provided the criteria for monetary integration in the Economic and Monetary Union (EMU, 1999). Over the years, the number of countries participating in the European integration process has increased from six to fifteen, of which twelve countries (known as the Euro area) have introduced the Euro as their single currency.[5]

Table 13.2 Overview of European Union economic integration

1951	ECSC	European Coal and Steel Community
	Membership	Belgium, France, Luxembourg, the Netherlands, Italy, and W. Germany
1957	EURATOM	European Atomic Energy Community
1957	EEC	European Economic Community
1967	EC	European Communities; combining ECSC, EEC, and EURATOM
1973	Membership	+ United Kingdom, Ireland, and Denmark
1981	Membership	+ Greece
1986	Membership	+ Spain and Portugal
1990	Membership	+ East Germany (reunification of West and East Germany)
1993	EU	European Union
1995	Membership	+ Finland, Austria, and Sweden
1999	EMU	Economic and Monetary Union

[5] Current exceptions are the United Kingdom, Denmark, and Sweden.

The objective of the EEC Treaty was the establishment of a common market, which also allows for the 'four freedoms':

1. *Free movement of goods*. The common market requires not only the removal of tariffs and quantitative restrictions, but also the dismantling of other obstacles to free movement of goods. Most important in this respect was the Cassis de Dijon case in 1979. According to German regulations Cassis de Dijon, a French fruit liqueur, did not contain enough alcohol (17 per cent rather than the minimum 32 per cent), and was therefore forbidden. The European Court of Justice ruled that a product legally brought to the market in one country of the EU also has to be accepted in another country. This principle ensures that different national regulations are mutually recognized, except for hazardous products, or in the case of health, safety, or environmental reasons.

2. *Free movement of persons*. Workers have a right to work anywhere else in the EU (right of free movement) and individuals have the right to establish businesses anywhere else in the EU (right of establishment).

3. *Free movement of services*. The Cassis de Dijon verdict also holds for services, such that services offered in one EU country can also be offered in another EU country. The free movement of persons and that of services are related, as the export of services frequently requires physical presence in the customer country.

4. *Free movement of capital*. Although capital controls were still operative in some countries until the late 1980s, restrictions on capital flows between EU countries have now been eliminated.

The main institutions of the European Union are:

- *The Council of the European Union*; also known as the Council of Ministers, this central decision-making body meets in many different forms (as heads of states, or as Ministers for Foreign Affairs, Agriculture, Transport, etc.).

- *The European Commission*; administers and initiates policy in the EU. The Commission mediates between the member states and represents the EU in international negotiations.

- *The European Parliament*; this body, involved in decision and law making, is democratically chosen by the people of the EU member countries every four years, but has (too) limited power.

- *The European Court of Justice*; provides judicial safeguards and is concerned with the interpretation of EU law, including actions brought before the court between member states and between the Commission and a member state.

- *The European Central Bank (ECB)*; a largely independent institution responsible for the monetary policy of the Euro area, with price stability as the primary objective.

Two other European economic integration agreements outside the EU, as illustrated in Figure 13.8, should be mentioned in this section. First, the Stockholm Convention established the European Free Trade Association (EFTA) in 1960. In the course of the twentieth century, many EFTA countries joined the EU, such that EFTA currently consists only of Iceland, Norway, Liechtenstein, and Switzerland. Second, the Central

European Free Trade Area (CEFTA) was established in 1993 to reduce tariffs and other trade barriers and increase intra-regional trade. All CEFTA countries want to join the EU and have applied for EU membership, which brings us to the next section on future EU enlargement.

13.7 Future enlargement of the European Union

Soon after the fall of the Berlin Wall in 1989, the EC established diplomatic relations with the countries of Central Europe, removed import quotas on a number of products, extended the Generalized System of Preferences (GSP, see Chapter 12), and concluded trade and cooperation agreements with many central European countries. In 1993 at the Copenhagen European Council, the member states agreed that 'the associated countries in central and eastern Europe that so desire shall become members of the European Union'. All of this provided the candidate country meets the Copenhagen Criteria, that is:

● has achieved stability of institutions guaranteeing democracy, the rule of law, human rights, and respect for and protection of minorities;

● has achieved the existence of a functioning market economy as well as the capacity to cope with competitive pressure and market forces within the Union;

● has achieved the ability to take on the obligations of membership, including adherence to the aims of political, economic, and monetary Union;

● has created the conditions for its integration through the adjustment of its administrative structures, so that European Community legislation transposed into national legislation is implemented effectively through appropriate administrative and judicial structures.

As summarized in Table 13.3 and shown in Figure 13.8, there are no less than thirteen candidate countries which have applied for membership of the EU. As recommended by the European Commission, accession negotiations were opened by the European Council in 1998 with six of these countries, the accession countries for short.[6] For brevity, EU-15 refers to the fifteen current EU member countries, 'EU-21' also includes the six accession countries, and 'EU-28' includes all candidate countries. To assist in the decision-making process, the European Commission collects data not only on the current EU member countries, but also on the candidate countries. The discussion below is based on these data, some of which are illustrated in Figure 13.9, as summarized in Table 13.4, also providing information on the USA and Japan for comparison purposes.

---

[6] With the exception of Turkey, the same now holds for the other candidate countries. Since it is likely that the first group of accession countries listed in Table 13.3 will also be the first to join the EU, I maintain the distinction accession countries–candidate countries as listed in Table 13.3 also in the text.

Table 13.3 Different groups of European countries

Group	Member countries
EU-15	Belgium, France, Luxembourg, the Netherlands, Italy, Germany, United Kingdom, Ireland, Denmark, Greece, Spain, Portugal, Finland, Austria, and Sweden
Accession	Cyprus, Czech Rep., Estonia, Hungary, Poland, and Slovenia
'EU-21'	EU-15 + accession countries
Candidate countries	Accession countries + Bulgaria, Latvia, Lithuania, Malta, Romania, Slovakia, and Turkey
'EU-28'	EU-15 + candidate countries

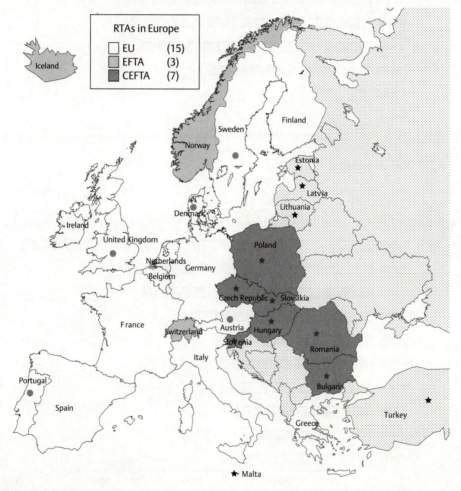

Fig 13.8 Regional trade agreements in Europe. The circles indicate former EFTA members that joined the EU; the stars indicate potential EU entrants; EU members not listed on the map: Luxembourg; EFTA members not listed on the map: Liechtenstein

As suggested by the Copenhagen Criteria, there are substantial differences between the EU-15 countries and the candidate countries, which also differ substantially among themselves. The candidate countries, most of which were formerly centrally planned economies, are transforming into a more market oriented economy, revising their laws and institutions, protecting human rights, and guaranteeing democracy.

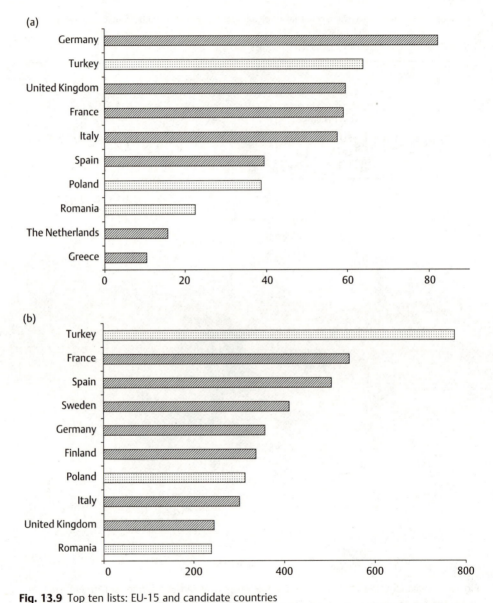

Fig. 13.9 Top ten lists: EU-15 and candidate countries

Data source: See Table 13.4. Candidate countries have a lighter shading. (a) Population (million), (b) size (1000 km²), (c) GDP (billion PPS), (d) GNP/cap (PPS).

(continued)

(c)

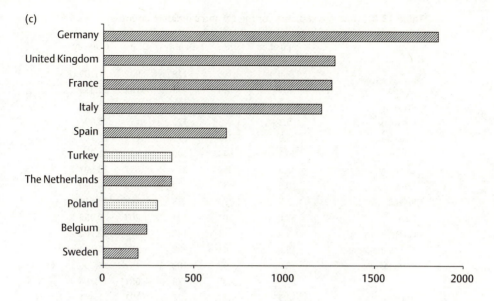

(d)

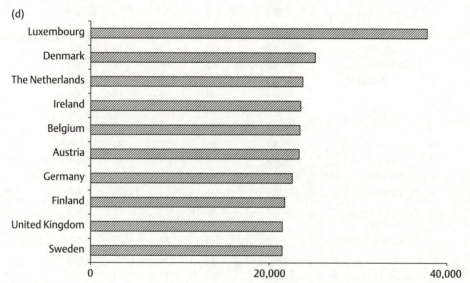

Fig 13.9 (continued)

This does not mean that meeting the EU requirements will result in a straitjacket which makes all countries look alike; we certainly want to preserve the rich cultural, historical, and social diversity which makes Europe such a fascinating continent.

Figure 13.9 illustrates 'top ten' lists for the EU if we include the candidate countries. In terms of population, the current 'big 4' EU-15 countries (Germany, UK, France, and Italy) would be joined by Turkey, ranked second with 64 million inhabitants.

Table 13.4 Economic statistics for the EU and candidate countries

Country	Population	Size	Density	GDP	GDP/cap
EU-15	376.0	3,195	118	7,937	21,109
Austria	8.1	84	96	189	23,333
Belgium	10.2	31	329	239	23,431
Denmark	5.3	43	123	133	25,094
Finland	5.2	337	15	113	21,731
France	59.1	544	109	1,263	21,371
Germany	82.2	357	230	1,857	22,591
Greece	10.5	132	80	149	14,190
Ireland	3.7	70	53	87	23,514
Italy	57.6	301	191	1,207	20,955
Luxembourg	0.4	3	145	16	37,700
The Netherlands	15.8	41	385	375	23,734
Portugal	10.0	92	109	157	15,700
Spain	39.4	505	78	681	17,284
Sweden	8.9	411	22	191	21,461
United Kingdom	59.6	244	244	1,280	21,477
Candidate countries	170.0	1,862	91	1,225	7,220
Bulgaria	8.2	111	74	39	4,700
Cyprus	0.8	9	89	14	17,100
Czech Republic	10.3	79	130	129	12,500
Estonia	1.4	45	31	11	7,700
Hungary	10.0	93	108	107	10,700
Latvia	2.4	65	37	14	5,800
Lithuania	3.7	65	57	23	6,200
Malta	0.4	0.3	1,333	4	8,800
Poland	38.7	313	124	298	7,700
Romania	22.5	238	95	128	5,700
Slovakia	5.4	49	110	53	9,800
Slovenia	2.0	20	100	30	15,000
Turkey	63.9	775	82	377	5,900
EU-15	376.0	3,195	118	7,937	21,109
Accession countries	63.0	559	113	588	9,307
'EU-21'	439.0	3,754	117	8,525	19,411
Candidate countries	170.0	1,862	91	1,225	7,220
'EU-28'	546.0	5,057	108	9,162	16,790
USA	272.0	9,373	29	8,146	29,993
Japan	127.0	378	335	2,979	23,549
USA; index, EU-15 = 100	72.0	293	25	103	124
Japan; index, EU-15 = 100	34.0	12	284	38	112

Source: European Commission (2000). Data are for 1999; population in millions; size in 1,000 km²; density in people per km²; GDP in billion purchasing power standard (pps); GDP/cap in pps; for groups of countries: see Table 13.3.

Poland and Romania, ranked seventh and eighth, would also make it to the top ten. In terms of size, with 775,000 km^2 Turkey would be the EU's largest country, substantially exceeding France, Spain, and Sweden, ranked 2–4. Again, Poland (ranked seventh) and Romania (ranked tenth) would join the top ten. In terms of economic power, the impact of the candidate countries is less substantial, with Turkey ranked sixth (barely ahead of the Netherlands and only 20 per cent of Germany's GDP) and Poland ranked eighth. In terms of GDP per capita, none of the candidate countries makes it to the top ten, where small countries (Luxembourg, Denmark, and the Netherlands) are in the lead.

As a whole, the EU-15 already represents a formidable economic power, second only to the USA. Although, with 376 million inhabitants, the EU-15 has more people than the USA (which has 272 million inhabitants), the American GDP level is slightly higher (+3 per cent) as a result of the about 42 per cent higher GDP level *per capita* (corrected for purchasing power) in the USA. On average, there are 118 people per km^2 in the EU-15, four times as high as the USA, which has an area almost three times as large. When compared to Japan, the EU-15 has about three times as many people, with a living space per capita about three times as large, earning a total income of about 2.5 times Japan's income level.

If all thirteen potential EU entrants were actually to join the EU, resulting in an 'EU-28', the EU's population would rise by about 45 per cent (to 546 million) and the EU's area would increase by 58 per cent, leading to an 8 per cent drop in population density. Moreover, since the average income level per capita for the candidate countries is only one-third of the EU-15's level, the EU's income per capita level would drop by 20 per cent, and the EU's total income level would rise by a modest 15 per cent. In view of the sizeable problems of EU-enlargement with all candidate countries, for example the tensions associated with accommodating Cyprus and Turkey in connection with the membership of Greece or the long road ahead in structural adjustment for Bulgaria and Romania, this is not likely to occur in the next decade. In the foreseeable future, enlargement by the joining of the accession countries, resulting in an 'EU-21', is more likely. This would increase the EU's population and size by about 17 per cent, and income level by about 7 per cent, resulting in a drop of income per capita by 8 per cent.

After long and painful negotiations which nearly failed and of which, according to *The Economist* (2000a), Germany's chancellor Gerhard Schröder complained that it 'makes me sick', a major step forward in the EU enlargement process was taken in December 2000 in Nice, France. The Nice Treaty agreed on:

- *Majority voting*; more decisions can be taken with qualified majority, such as for trade negotiations in services. Other areas, such as tax and social-security policy, remain subject to national vetoes.

- *Rebalancing votes*; adjustment of the votes for the European Council, European Parliament, and the Committees for the EU-15 and for twelve candidate countries (with the exception of Turkey), see Table 13.5.

- *European Commission*; the big countries give up the second commissioner from 2005. The maximum size of the commission may be put at twenty after 2007.

Table 13.5 Division of EU power after the Treaty of Nice

	European Council	European Parliament	Committees[a]
Germany	29	99	24
France	29	72	24
Italy	29	72	24
United Kingdom	29	72	24
Spain	27	50	21
The Netherlands	13	25	12
Belgium	12	22	12
Greece	12	22	12
Portugal	12	22	12
Sweden	10	18	12
Austria	10	17	12
Denmark	7	13	9
Finland	7	13	9
Ireland	7	12	9
Luxembourg	4	6	6
EU-15 total	237	535	222
Poland	27	50	21
Romania	14	33	15
Czech Rep.	12	20	12
Hungary	12	20	12
Bulgaria	10	17	12
Slovakia	7	13	9
Lithuania	7	12	9
Latvia	4	8	7
Slovenia	4	7	7
Estonia	4	6	7
Cyprus	4	6	6
Malta	3	5	5
Total	345	732	344

[a] This holds for (i) the Economic and Social Committee, and (ii) the Committee of the Regions.

• *Flexibility*; groups of eight countries or more may pursue greater integration in certain areas (for example, the Euro countries may decide on closer coordination of their financial and tax policies).

The rebalancing of the votes has given more power to the big EU countries, afraid of losing their power in an expanded EU with more countries. Most important in this respect is, of course, the number of votes in the Council, where many (= more than 80 per cent) of the EU's decisions are now made by majority voting. After the enlargement, a qualified majority requires not only about 74 per cent of the Council votes, but also the backing of at least 62 per cent of the population. The population rule ensures that

Germany, as the most populous nation, becomes the EU's most powerful member, despite the fact that the big 4 countries all get 29 votes in the Council. Nonetheless the small countries, that is all countries except the big 4, have a disproportionately large influence in the Council as it requires a smaller population for them to get 1 vote in the Council than the EU average. The democratic principle 'one man one vote' does not hold here; in this respect 1 person from Luxembourg is about as important as 5 Irishmen, 12 Dutchmen, 20 Frenchmen (or Englishmen or Italians), or 28 Germans.

13.8 Conclusions

There are many regional trade agreements in the world, in which countries are economically integrating by, for example, granting free access to their markets for the member countries (free trade area), in addition to pursuing a common external trade policy (customs union). We discuss some examples in Africa (COMESA), Asia (ASEAN), America (NAFTA, CACM, ANDEAN, CARICOM, MERCOSUR), and Europe (EU, EFTA, CEFTA). The rising popularity of economic integration is known as regionalism, to be contrasted with the multilateral WTO framework of removing trade barriers. Although a regional trade agreement in general increases welfare through increased trade flows (trade-creation), the discriminatory nature of the agreement which benefits insiders may reduce welfare through a shift toward less efficient producers (trade-diversion). A small new-trade general equilibrium model shows that the latter effect may be stronger for a fairly large range of trading blocks and elasticities of substitution, thus in general warning for a move away from multilateralism to regionalism. This argument seems to lose much of its force if the local nature of the regional agreements (and thus the high trade shares) are taken into consideration. The European Union presents the most powerful and successful economic integration scheme to date. Many Central and East European countries want to join the EU, which requires large structural and political changes, both for the applicants and for the (rather undemocratic) political decision process of the EU.

Technical Notes (optional)

Technical Note 13.1 Regionalism model

Using the exact price index P defined in equation (10.A4), in the Regionalism model we get

$$
P \equiv \left[\sum_{i=1}^{N} p_i^{1-\varepsilon} \right]^{1/(1-\varepsilon)}
$$

$$
(13.A1) \qquad = \left[\sum_{i=1}^{N/b} 1 + \sum_{(N/b)+1}^{N} (1+t)^{1-\varepsilon} \right]^{1/(1-\varepsilon)} = \{N[b^{-1} + (1-b^{-1})(1+t)^{1-\varepsilon}]\}^{1/(1-\varepsilon)}
$$

Thus, once we know the income level I in a trading bloc, equation (10.A4) gives us the demand for a particular variety, namely:

(13.A2) $\quad c_j = p_j^{-\varepsilon} P^{\varepsilon-1} I = \begin{cases} \dfrac{I}{N(b^{-1} + (1-b^{-1})(1+t)^{1-\varepsilon})}, & \text{for } j \in \text{ trading bloc} \\[3mm] \dfrac{(1+t)^{-\varepsilon} I}{N(b^{-1} + (1-b^{-1})(1+t)^{1-\varepsilon})}, & \text{for } j \notin \text{ trading bloc} \end{cases}$

The income level I of a trading bloc is the sum of the production value N/b and the tariff revenue t levied per unit on the c_j goods sold of the $N(1-b^{-1})$ varieties imported from outside the trading bloc. Using the equation above, this implies:

(13.A3) $\qquad\qquad I = \dfrac{N}{b} + \dfrac{N(1-b^{-1})t(1+t)^{-\varepsilon} I}{N(b^{-1} + (1-b^{-1})(1+t)^{1-\varepsilon})}$

Solving this equation for the income level I gives

(13.A4)
$$\left[1 - \frac{(1-b^{-1})t(1+t)^{-\varepsilon}}{(b^{-1} + (1-b^{-1})(1+t)^{1-\varepsilon})} \right] I = \frac{N}{b}$$

$$\left[\frac{(b^{-1} + (1-b^{-1})(1+t)^{1-\varepsilon}) - (1-b^{-1})t(1+t)^{-\varepsilon}}{(b^{-1} + (1-b^{-1})(1+t)^{1-\varepsilon})} \right] I = \left[\frac{b^{-1} + (1-b^{-1})(1+t)^{-\varepsilon}}{(b^{-1} + (1-b^{-1})(1+t)^{1-\varepsilon})} \right] I = \frac{N}{b}$$

$$I = \frac{N}{b} \left[\frac{(b^{-1} + (1-b^{-1})(1+t)^{1-\varepsilon})}{b^{-1} + (1-b^{-1})(1+t)^{-\varepsilon}} \right]$$

As shown in Chapter 10 the welfare of a trading bloc is equal to I/P. Since there are b trading blocs in the world, and using the above, total world welfare is equal to

(13.A5)
$$b \frac{I}{P} = b \frac{N}{b} \left[\frac{(b^{-1} + (1-b^{-1})(1+t)^{1-\varepsilon})}{b^{-1} + (1-b^{-1})(1+t)^{-\varepsilon}} \right] \frac{1}{N^{1/(1-\varepsilon)}(b^{-1} + (1-b^{-1})(1+t)^{1-\varepsilon})^{1/(1-\varepsilon)}}$$

$$= N^{\varepsilon/(\varepsilon-1)} \frac{[b^{-1} + (1-b^{-1})(1+t)^{1-\varepsilon}]^{\varepsilon/(\varepsilon-1)}}{b^{-1} + (1-b^{-1})(1+t)^{-\varepsilon}}$$

The figures in the text depict this total welfare level, normalized to unity if there is one trading bloc (global free trade).

Part Four

New Interactions

Part IV (New Interactions) brings the reader up to date with recent developments in international economics which have occurred in the last decade or so. These are based on new interactions between international economics and other fields of economics; with economic geography leading to a better explanation of location, with international business leading to a better explanation of multinational firms, and with economic growth theory leading to a better understanding of international differences in growth and development. Chapter 17 discusses the general implications of the insights that we have learned throughout this book for practical trade policy modelling.

Chapter 14

Geographical Economics

Objectives/key terms

Zipf's Law	Gravity equation
Cumulative causation	Agglomeration
Multiple equilibria	Stability/optimality
Simulations	Location

Blending some of the insights of the neoclassical trade model and the new trade model, in conjuction with factor mobility, allows us to provide a simple theory of location and agglomeration which is able to explain some empirical observations (such as Zipf's Law and the gravity equation).

14.1 Introduction

One of the most remarkable aspects of the global economic system is the unequal distribution of population and economic activity across the earth, see also Chapter 1. Millions of people are living close together in New York, Moscow, and Beijing. At the same time, there are large, virtually empty spaces available in the United States, Russia, and China. As we will illustrate in section 14.2, the distribution of people and economic activity across space is not only remarkably unequal, it is also remarkably regular, both in terms of a pattern across space (Zipf's Law) and in terms of the interaction between economic centres (the gravity equation). The question arises, obviously, why economic activity is so unequally distributed, and why these regularities occur.

It has long been evident that these aspects cannot be adequately explained using a neoclassical framework. In particular, economies of scale and imperfect competition, interacting with some form of local advantages, are essential. This implies that it is rather complicated to *endogenously* determine the size of economic activity in different locations in a general equilibrium framework. It is therefore, in retrospect, not surprising that such an endogenous, general equilibrium determination of economic size was only fairly recently developed, in particular as it was awaiting the development of the appropriate tools for this endeavour in other fields of economics. The path-breaking contribution of

Fig. 14.1 Paul Krugman (1953–)

Krugman was born in a suburb of New York City and received his BA from Yale (1974) and his Ph.D. from MIT (1977). He worked at Yale, MIT, Stanford, and MIT (again), before moving to Princeton. He is probably, and deservedly, the most influential international economist around today, well known both in the academic world and, thanks to his lucid prose, outside. As was to be expected, he described his style best himself. 'There are several different ways of doing good economics … But what has always appealed to me, ever since I saw Nordhaus practice it on energy, is the MIT style: small models applied to real problems, blending real-world observation and a little mathematics to cut through to the core of an issue.' He has used the MIT style splendidly to start off three new fields of study so far: new trade theory, target zone models, and geographical economics. For the source of the quote, see the Collier laudatio on the internet when Paul Krugman received his honorary doctorate in Berlin: http://www.wiwiss.fu-berlin.de/w3/w3collie/krugman/laudatio.html

the American economist Paul Krugman appeared in 1991. Since then many prominent researchers have published work on refinements, generalizations, and applications in this rapidly developing research area, which has become known as 'geographical economics' and combines elements from international economics, industrial organization, economic geography, spatial economics, urban economics, and endogenous growth.[1]

14.2 Zipf's Law and the gravity equation

This section discusses two regularities in the unequal distribution of people and economic activity across space, namely (i) regarding the distribution pattern of centres of activity and (ii) regarding the interactions between these centres of activity.

Distribution pattern (Zipf's Law)

The regularity in the distribution pattern, known as Zipf's Law, is most easily illustrated using a concrete example. Take the largest urban agglomeration in India. In 1991, the most recent year for which we have reliable data available, this was Bombay with more than 12.5 million inhabitants. Give this city rank number 1. Then take the second largest urban agglomeration (Calcutta, with more than 11 million inhabitants) and give this rank number 2. The third largest city (Delhi, with 8.4 million inhabitants) is given rank number 3, etc. Once you have arranged all 165 urban Indian agglomerations for which data are available in this way, you take the natural logarithm of the city size and the city rank. When the latter are plotted in a scatter diagram, the outcome is an almost perfect straight line, see Figure 14.2.

---

[1] For a while the term 'new economic geography' was popular. It was replaced by the term 'geographical economics', partly in order not to offend the older and respected economic geography literature.

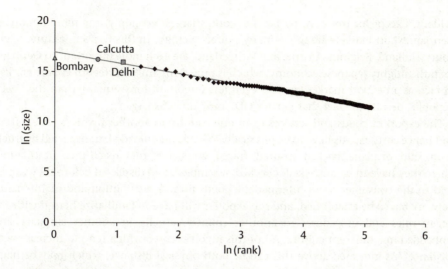

Fig. 14.2 Zipf's Law for India
Source: Brakman, Garretsen, and van Marrewijk (2001). Data are for urban agglomerations, 1991.

Obviously, there is a negative relationship between size and rank by construction. The puzzling feature is why this is an almost perfect log-linear straight line. A simple linear regression of the data plotted in Figure 14.2 gives (*t*-values in parentheses):

$$(14.1) \qquad \ln(population_i) = \underset{(528.4)}{16.94} - \underset{(-138.4)}{1.048} \ln(rank_i); \quad R^2 = 0.992$$

This regression explains 99.2 per cent of the variance in city size. Based on this estimate, we would predict the size of the population of urban agglomeration number 100, for example, to be 182,000 people. This is very close to the actual size of number 100 (Tumkur), which consists of 180,000 people. This regularity in the distribution of city sizes holds not only for India, but also for the United States, Brazil, France, China, Russia, etc.[2] Apparently, hitherto poorly understood economic forces play an important role in determining the size distribution of cities, regardless of the economic structure, organization, wealth, and history of a nation. Ever since George Kingsley Zipf (1949) presented evidence on this regularity, scientists have been searching, rather unsuccessfully, for an adequate explanation.

Interaction (gravity equation)

There is also a pattern in the interaction between centres of economic activity. It is known as the 'gravity equation', and is related to Zipf's Law. The gravity equation, too, is most easily illustrated using a concrete example, for which we focus on the export flows of Germany, the dominant European economy. In 1998 France was the largest export market for Germany, with a value of $60.3 billion. The second largest German export market was the USA ($51.1 billion), followed by the UK, Italy, the Netherlands, Belgium, Austria, and Switzerland. The 'local' flavour of this top-export market list is immediately

---

[2] The website for this book presents evidence for many countries in the world.

evident. Except for the USA, by far the world's largest economy, the most important German export markets are in Germany's direct vicinity. In this respect, its tiny neighbours, Holland, Belgium, Austria, and Switzerland, are each more important to Germany than the mighty Japanese economy, which is only Germany's thirteenth export market. In fact, as an export market Japan is even less important for Germany than the Czech Republic, despite the fact that Japan's GDP is 67 times as large.[3]

The export of goods and services from one country to another involves time, effort, and hence costs. Goods have to be physically loaded and unloaded, transported by truck, train, ship, or plane, packed, insured, traced, etc. before they reach their destination. There they have to be unpacked, checked, assembled, and displayed before they can be sold to the consumer or an intermediate goods firm. A distribution and maintenance network has to be established, and the exporter will have to familiarize herself with the (legal) rules and procedures in another country, usually in another language and embedded in a different culture. All of this involves costs, which tend to increase with 'distance'. As indicated above this can be both physical distance, which may be hampered or alleviated by geographical phenomena such as mountain ranges or easy access to good waterways, or political, cultural, or social distance, which also require time and effort before one can successfully engage in international business.

We use the term 'transport costs' as a shorthand notation for both types of distance described above. As these costs increase it will become more difficult to trade goods and services between nations. As a proxy for transport costs we calculated the 'distance to Germany' for all German export markets, taking the coordinates of the geographic centre of each nation as the hypothetical centre of economic activity. Also taking into consideration the size of the potential export market as measured by a country's GDP, a simple regression yields the following result (*t*-value in parentheses):

$$(14.2) \qquad \ln(export_i) = \underset{(-0.40)}{0.281} + \underset{(34.86)}{1.033 \ln(GDP_i)} - \underset{(-12.77)}{0.869 \ln(distance_i)}; \quad R^2 = 0.926$$

This simple relationship, which explains 92.6 per cent of the variance in German export size, is illustrated with respect to the distance to the German market in Figure 14.3, that is after correcting the size of the export flow for the size of the destination market using the estimated coefficient of equation (14.2). The five small German neighbours mentioned above are in the top left corner and are all more important export markets than Japan, certainly after the GDP correction, which is in the bottom right corner. Since the actual German exports to Japan are below the regression line in Figure 14.3, the export flows from Germany to Japan are low even after correcting for the large distance. The empirical relationship known as the 'gravity equation', first applied to international trade between nations by Jan Tinbergen (1962), holds quite generally for all countries, irrespective of, but influenced by, wealth, development level, cultural, political, and sociological organization, and history. Since one of the main objectives of geographical economics is to provide a better understanding of the unequal distribution of economic activity across space and its regularities in terms of distribution pattern and interaction, it is time to have a closer look at the basic structure of this model.

---

[3] In 1998 Japan's GDP was $3,783 billion, the Czech Republic's GDP was $56 billion (The World Bank).

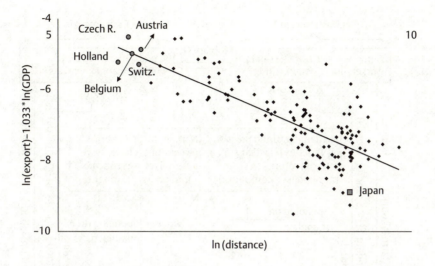

Fig. 14.3 German exports and distance
Sources: World Bank (GDP), OECD (exports), and Britannica Atlas (distance).

14.3 **The structure of the model**

This section gives a non-technical overview of the general structure of the geographical economics model, as illustrated in Figure 14.4 (with so-called 'callouts' *a–g*). Our presentation will only identify two regions, labelled 1 and 2. There are two sectors in the economy, as usual manufactures and food. Consumers in region 1 consist of farmworkers and manufacturing workers. Similarly for region 2. The farmworkers earn their income by working for the farmers in their region. If they own the farm it is as if they hire themselves. They then play a dual role, both as farmers and as farmworkers. The income stream of the farmworkers is part of a bilateral transfer: they receive an income from the farmer (the farm wage rate) and in return they have to supply labour services to the farmer. All such bilateral transfers are indicated with double-pointed arrows in Figure 14.4. The closed-pointed arrow refers to the direction of money flows, that is of income and spending. What the flow represents exactly is indicated along the line connecting the arrow points. The open-pointed arrow refers to the direction of goods flows. These are indicated in parentheses and italics along the line connecting the arrow points. The farmers in region 1 use the labour services of the farmworkers from region 1 to produce food under constant returns to scale and perfect competition. They sell this food to the consumers, either in region 1 or in region 2. There are no transport costs for food.

The manufacturing sector consists of N_1 firms in region 1 and N_2 firms in region 2. Each manufacturing firm produces a differentiated good, that is it produces a unique variety of manufactures, using only labour under internal economies of scale. This implies that the firms have monopolistic power, which they use in determining the price of their product. There are transport costs involved in selling a manufactured good in another region.

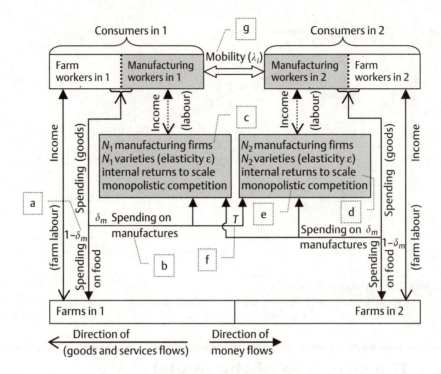

Fig. 14.4 Structure of the geographical economics model

These costs do not arise if the manufactured good is sold in the region in which it is produced. As a result of the transport costs involved in exporting manufactured goods to another region, firms will charge a higher price in the other region than at home. The manufacturing workers earn their income (the manufacturing wage rate) by supplying labour to the firms in the manufacturing sector of their region.

Demand

The consumers spend their income on food and manufactures. Since food is a homogeneous good they do not care if it is produced in region 1 or in region 2. As there are no transport costs for food, it fetches the same price in both regions (implying that farmers earn the same wage in both regions). The optimal spending of income I is determined in two stages. At the first stage the consumers decide how much to spend on food and manufactures in general. Using the Cobb–Douglas utility function of Chapter 7 (section 7.3), we already know the outcome: a constant share δ_m of income is spent on manufactures and $1 - \delta_m$ on food (callout a). At the second stage the consumers decide how much of their income to spend on a particular variety of manufactures. Using the Dixit–Stiglitz approach of Chapter 10 (section 10.3) gives demand as in equation (10.4), with $\delta_m I$ as the income term since income $(1 - \delta_m)I$ is spent on food (callout b). As discussed in Chapter 10, this results in a constant price elasticity of demand ε (callout c).

Supply

Food production is characterized by constant returns to scale and is produced under conditions of perfect competition. Workers in the food industry, which is used as numéraire, are assumed to be immobile. Given the total labour force, which we will normalize to 1, a fraction $1 - \delta_m$ works in the food sector.[4] Production in the food sector equals, by choice of units, food employment: $F = (1 - \delta_m)$. Since farmworkers are paid the value of marginal product, their wage is 1. Production in the manufacturing sector is characterized by the internal economies of scale of Chapter 10: $l_i = f + mx_i$, where l_i is the amount of labour necessary to produce x_i units of variety i. The coefficients f and m are, respectively, the fixed and marginal labour input requirements (callout d). The market structure for manufactures is one of monopolistic competition (see Chapter 10), leading to a constant mark-up of price over marginal costs. Entry and exit into the manufacturing sector until (excess) profits are zero gives the constant optimal scale of production for each variety, see Technical Note 10.2. This production size per variety determines the number of varieties produced in a region (callout e).

Transport costs

Transport costs are modelled using *iceberg* transport costs, as discussed in Chapter 9. The parameter $T \geq 1$ denotes the number of goods that need to be shipped to ensure that 1 unit of a variety of manufactures arrives per unit of distance ($=$ the distance between regions 1 and 2). We assume that the distance of a location to itself is 0 (callout f).

Box 14.1 The relevance of transport costs

Adam Smith noted the importance of locations near the coast with lower costs of transport, 'so, it is upon the sea-coast, and along the banks of navigable rivers, that industry of every kind naturally begins to sub-divide and improve itself, and it is frequently not till a long time after that those improvements extend themselves to the inland part of the country.'

Many measures, such as travel time, have been constructed to estimate transport cost. The most straightforward measure in international trade is the difference between the so-called CIF (Cost, Insurance, Freight) and FOB (Free On Board) quotations of trade. CIF measures the value of imports from the point of entry, while FOB measures the value from a carrier in the exporting 'port'. The difference between these two values is a measure of the cost of getting an item from the exporting country to the importing country. The ratio $[(\text{CIF}/\text{FOB}) - 1] \times 100\%$, reported in Table 14.1, thus provides an estimate of the transport costs, although it clearly underestimates the actual transport costs of international trade (note that products with very high transport costs are not traded at all). Different goods have, of course, different transport costs. Goods with a high value added have a relatively low CIF/FOB ratio, while perishable goods have a higher

---

[4] We imposed that the fraction of the workers in the manufacturing sector is equal to the fraction of income spent on manufactures and normalized the work force to 1. This eases notation without substantially affecting the (dynamic) equilibrium, as discussed in Brakman, Garretsen, and van Marrewijk (2001).

ratio. For the USA, for example, the *ad valorem* freight rate is 7.6 per cent for food and live animals, but only 2.25 per cent for machinery and transport equipment.

The shipping costs are higher for countries located far away from major markets (New Zealand) and for landlocked countries (Nepal). For example, the landlocked developing countries (not shown in the table) have on average 50 per cent higher transport costs than coastal developing economies. Since a doubling of trading cost appears to reduce economic growth by 0.5 per cent for developing countries and a large part of Africa is landlocked, this partially explains Africa's poor growth performance.

As a final indication of the importance of transport costs, we can compare freight costs with other trade costs, like tariffs. For the USA, industry level transport costs as a percentage of imports ranges from 1.9 to 8.5 per cent, with a mean of 4.8 per cent. Industry level tariffs range from 0.5 to 14.4 per cent, with a mean of 4.1 per cent. Transport costs as such, therefore, seem to be at least as important as policy induced trade barriers. Note, however, that the mnemonic transport costs T used in the main text are inclusive of such policy induced trade barriers (as are cultural, sociological, etc. barriers). Although data are always subject to measurement error, the impression remains that trade costs are substantial, and cannot be ignored.

Information source: Radelet and Sachs (1998), Davis (1998), and Hummels (1999*a*,1999*b*).

Table 14.1 Estimated transport costs, based on CIF/FOB ratio, 1965–1990

Country	Transport costs (%)
Australia	10.3
Austria	4.1
Canada	2.7
Denmark	4.5
France	4.2
W. Germany	3.0
Greece	13.0
Ireland	5.0
Italy	7.1
Japan	9.0
The Netherlands	5.6
New Zealand	11.5
Norway	2.7
Philippines	7.6
Portugal	10.3
Singapore	6.1
Spain	6.4
Sweden	3.5
Switzerland	1.8
Thailand	11.0
United Kingdom	6.0
United States	4.9

Source: Radelet and Sachs (1998).

14.4 **Multiple locations and equilibrium**

Now that we have introduced two regions and transport costs it becomes important to know where the economic agents are located. We therefore have to (i) specify a notation to show how labour is distributed over the two regions, and (ii) investigate what the consequences are for some of the demand and supply equations discussed in section 14.3. To start with point (i), we have already introduced the parameter δ_m to denote the fraction of the labour force in the manufacturing sector, such that $1 - \delta_m$ is the fraction of labour in the food sector. We now assume that of the labourers in the food sector a fraction ϕ_i is located in region i, and of the labourers in the manufacturing sector a fraction λ_i is located in region i. Figure 14.5 illustrates the division of labour. The boxes for the manufacturing sector are shaded, as in Figure 14.4, to indicate that their size can increase or decrease as a result of the mobility of the manufacturing workforce.

Point (ii) involves more work. We will concentrate on region 1. Similar remarks hold for region 2. It is easiest to start with the producers. Since there are $\phi_1(1 - \delta_m)$ farmworkers in region 1 and production is proportional to the labour input, food production in region 1 equals $\phi_1(1 - \delta_m)$, which is equal to the income generated by the food sector in region 1 and the wage income paid to farmworkers there. As a result of transport costs, the wage rate paid to manufacturing workers in region 1 will in general differ from the wage rate paid to manufacturing workers in region 2. We will identify these with a sub-index, so W_1 is the manufacturing wage in region 1. From now on, whenever we speak of 'the wage rate' we refer to the manufacturing wage rate. If we know the wage rate W_1 in region 1, we know from the mark-up pricing rule that the price charged in region 1 by a firm located in region 1 is equal to mW_1/ρ. The price this firm will charge in region 2 is T times higher than in region 1 as a result of the transport costs. Note that this holds for all N_1 firms located in region 1. Finally, since there are $\lambda_1\delta_m$ manufacturing workers in region 1, the number of firms N_1 located in region 1 is $N_1 = \lambda_1\delta_m/f\varepsilon$, which is proportional to the number of manufacturing workers in region 1 (see Chapter 10).

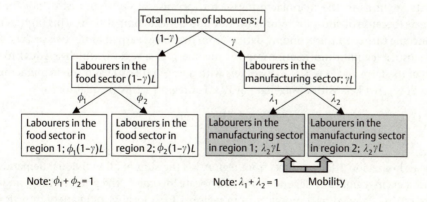

Fig. 14.5 Division of labour over the regions

The price a firm charges to a consumer for a unit of a variety depends both on the location of the firm (which determines the wage rate the firm will have to pay to its workers) and on the location of the consumer (which determines whether or not the consumer will have to pay for the transport costs of the good). As a result, the price index of manufactures will differ between the two regions. Again, we identify these with a sub-index, so P_1 is the price *index* in region 1. We can, however, be more specific since we just derived the price a firm will charge in each region, and how many firms there are in each region. Substituting this in the demand function gives (see Technical Note 14.1):

$$(14.3) \qquad P_1 = \left[\underbrace{\lambda_1 W_1^{1-\varepsilon}}_{\substack{locally \\ produced}} + \underbrace{\lambda_2 T^{1-\varepsilon} W_2^{1-\varepsilon}}_{imported} \right]^{1/(1-\varepsilon)}$$

Thus, the price index in region 1 is essentially a weighted average of the price of locally produced goods and imported goods from region 2. The impact of location on the consumption decisions of consumers requires us to know their income level, which brings us to the determination of equilibrium below.

We now have to establish the equilibrium relationships to tie up any loose ends. Together with the shaded boxes in Figure 14.4, referring to the mobility of firms and manufacturing workers, this determines the spatial distribution of economic activity. We proceed in three steps. First, we explain the *short-run* equilibrium relationships, that is for a *given* distribution of the manufacturing labour force. Second, we discuss the dynamics, that is how we move through a sequence of short-run equilibria (without factor mobility) over time to a *long-run equilibrium* (with factor mobility). Third, the *analysis* of both short-run and long-run equilibria is rather complex, so it is dealt with in section 14.5.

Short-run equilibrium

In the short run, the distribution of the manufacturing workforce over the regions is given and cannot be changed instantaneously. We therefore want to establish the equilibrium relationships for an arbitrary distribution of the labour force. There are no profits for firms in the manufacturing sector (because of entry and exit), nor for the farmers (because of constant returns to scale and perfect competition). This implies that all income earned in the economy derives from the wages earned in the two sectors. This gives us the equilibrium relationship for income I_i in a region, which is equal to the sum of the farm wages ($\phi_i(1 - \delta_m)$ workers with a wage rate of 1) and the manufacturing wages ($\lambda_i \delta_m$ workers with a wage rate of W_i). For region 1 this is equal to:

$$(14.4) \qquad I_1 = \underbrace{\lambda_1 \delta_m W_1}_{\substack{manufacturing \\ income}} + \underbrace{\phi_1(1 - \delta_m)}_{\substack{food \\ income}}$$

Demand in region 1 for products from region 1 is the sum of all individual demands by consumers in region 1. It depends on the aggregate income I_1, the price index P_1, and the price mW_1/ρ charged by a producer from region 1 for a locally sold variety in region 1. Similarly, demand in region 2 for products from region 1 depend on aggregate income I_2, price index P_2, and the price TmW_1/ρ charged by a producer from region 1 for a good sold in region 2. Total demand for a producer in region 1 is the sum of the demand from region 1 and the demand from region 2, which depends on income in *both* regions, transport costs, and the price charged relative to the price index. Equating total demand to the supply determines equilibrium in the manufacturing sector (see Technical Note 14.2):

$$(14.5) \qquad W_1 = [I_1 P_1^{\varepsilon-1} + I_2 T^{1-\varepsilon} P_2^{\varepsilon-1}]^{1/\varepsilon}$$

Intuitively, the equation makes perfect sense; wages in region 1 can be higher if this region is located close to large markets. The attractiveness of a region is related to the purchasing power of all regions and relative to the distance from the market. The advantage of using a general equilibrium approach is that the price indices and income levels, which play a crucial role, are determined endogenously.

Given the distribution of the manufacturing work force λ_i, we have now derived the short-run equilibrium equations for region 1. They are equations (14.3), determining price index P_1, (14.4), determining income level I_1, and (14.5), determining the wage rate W_1. Similar equations hold for region 2, giving a total of six non-linear short-run equilibrium equations, discussed below and analysed in section 14.5.

Discussion of symmetric example

We briefly discuss three possible short-run equilibria in a two-region version of the model. The two regions are identical in all respects, except possibly regarding the distribution of the manufacturing labour force. In particular, we also assume that the farmworkers are equally divided over the two regions, that is $\phi_1 = \phi_2 = \frac{1}{2}$. For clarity, we reiterate the short-run equilibrium equations for both regions.

$$(14.3') \qquad P_1 = [\lambda_1 W_1^{1-\varepsilon} + \lambda_2 T^{1-\varepsilon} W_2^{1-\varepsilon}]^{1/(1-\varepsilon)}; \qquad P_2 = [\lambda_1 T^{1-\varepsilon} W_1^{1-\varepsilon} + \lambda_2 W_2^{1-\varepsilon}]^{1/(1-\varepsilon)}$$

$$(14.4') \qquad I_1 = \lambda_1 \delta_m W_1 + (1 - \delta_m)/2; \qquad I_2 = \lambda_2 \delta_m W_2 + (1 - \delta_m)/2$$

$$(14.5') \qquad W_1 = [I_1 P_1^{\varepsilon-1} + I_2 T^{1-\varepsilon} P_2^{\varepsilon-1}]^{1/\varepsilon}; \qquad W_2 = [I_1 T^{1-\varepsilon} P_1^{\varepsilon-1} + I_2 P_2^{\varepsilon-1}]^{1/\varepsilon}$$

Although we have stripped the short-run equilibrium of the geographical economics model now down to its bare essentials in its simplest version (two regions, identical in all respects except for the manufacturing labour force), it only yields to analysis in three special cases for the distribution of the manufacturing labour force, discussed below.

• *Spreading*; panel *a* of Figure 14.6.

Suppose the two regions are identical in *all* respects, that is the manufacturing workforce is also evenly distributed $\lambda_1 = \lambda_2 = \frac{1}{2}$. Naturally, we then expect the wage rates of the short-run equilibrium to be the same for the two regions. Can we explicitly calculate this wage rate? Yes, if you're clever enough. One way to proceed is to guess an equilibrium wage rate, and then verify if you guessed right. This turns out to work if you guess that the equilibrium

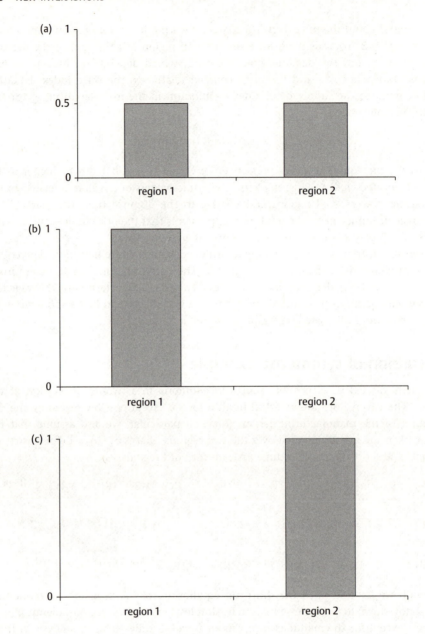

Fig. 14.6 Distribution of the manufacturing labour force; three examples. (a) Spreading, (b) agglomerate in region 1, (c) agglomerate in region 2

wage rates are $W_1 = W_2 = 1$ (use these values to calculate the price index in equation (14.3′) and the income level in equation (14.4′), then substitute the result in equation (14.5′) to verify that $W_1 = W_2 = 1$). Note that in the spreading equilibrium all variables are the same for the two regions, therefore the real wages are the same as well.

• *Agglomeration in region* 1; panel *b* of Figure 14.6.

Suppose now that all manufacturing activity is agglomerated in region 1 ($\lambda_1 = 1$), such that there are no manufacturing labourers in region 2 ($\lambda_2 = 0$). Can we determine the equilibrium? Yes. Using the same procedure as above shows that $W_1 = 1$ is a solution.

• *Agglomeration in region* 2; panel *c* of Figure 14.6.

This is the mirror image of the second situation described above.

We were able to derive the short-run equilibrium analytically for three separate cases: $\lambda_1 = 0$ (agglomeration in region 2), $\lambda_1 = \frac{1}{2}$ (spreading), and $\lambda_1 = 1$ (agglomeration in region 1). Unfortunately, these are the only three cases. In all other circumstances, and recall that λ_1 can vary all the way from 0 to 1 so there are infinitely many other cases, one cannot derive the short-run equilibrium analytically. So we have to find another way to determine these equilibria, and explain what they mean in economic terms. We will do that numerically rather than analytically, see section 14.5.

Dynamics and long-run equilibrium

The introduction of factor mobility implies that the shaded boxes in Figures 14.4 and 14.5, illustrating the structure of the model, can change in size over time, which in turn implies that the short-run equilibrium changes. Recall that labour is the only factor of production. We assume that the mobile workers react to differences in the *real* wage *w*, which adequately measures the utility level achieved. For different regions, the real wage is $w_r = W_r P_r^{-\delta}$, see the Technical Notes. The adjustment of the short-run equilibrium over time is very simple. If the real wage for manufacturing workers is higher in region 1 than in region 2 we expect that manufacturing workers will leave region 2 and settle in region 1. If the real wage is higher in region 2 than in region 1, we expect the reverse to hold. We let the parameter η denote the speed with which manufacturing workers react to differences in the real wage, and use the simple dynamic system:

$$(14.6) \qquad \underbrace{\frac{d\lambda_1}{\lambda_1}}_{\substack{change \\ labour\ in\ 1}} = \underbrace{\eta}_{\substack{adj. \\ speed}}\ \underbrace{(w_1 - \bar{w})}_{\substack{wage \\ difference}};\ \text{where } \bar{w} = \underbrace{\lambda_1 w_1 + \lambda_2 w_2}_{average\ real\ wage}$$

Note that $\bar{w}$ denotes the average real wage in the economy. A similar equation holds for region 2. Although this is essentially an ad hoc dynamic specification, it can be grounded in evolutionary game theory, see Weibull (1995), or otherwise justified, see Brakman, Garretsen, and van Marrewijk (2001). Now that we have specified how the manufacturing workforce reacts to differences in the real wage between regions, we can also note when a long-run equilibrium is reached. This occurs when one of three possibilities arises, as summarized in Table 14.2, namely (i) if the distribution of the manufacturing workforce between regions 1 and 2 is such that the real wage is equal in the two regions, not necessarily the symmetric equilibrium, (ii) if all manufacturing workers are located in region 1, or (iii) if all manufacturing workers are located in region 2.

Table 14.2 When is a long-run equilibrium reached?

Possibility 1	Possibility 2	Possibility 3
If the real wage for manufacturing workers in region 1 is the same as the real wage for manufacturing workers in region 2	All manufacturing workers are located in region 1 (agglomeration in region 1)	All manufacturing workers are located in region 2 (agglomeration in region 2)

Chapter 14 tool: Computer simulations

In section 14.4 we argued that the short-run equilibrium (for a given distribution of the man-ufacturing workforce) can be solved analytically in only three special cases. For all other situations, however, we can provide numerical solutions based on computer simulations to get a better grip on the economic forces active in the model. Simulations are becoming an increasingly popular tool in economics (see also Chapter 15) now that easy-to-use software has become widely available and personal computers are powerful and affordable enough to solve problems beyond the reach of mainframe computers only two decades ago. We first explain how computer simulations are performed.

Equations (14.3'–14.5') determine income I_r, price index P_r, and wage rate W_r in region r, respectively, given (i) the distribution λ_r of the manufacturing workforce, and (ii) the para-meters of the model, that is the share of income δ_m spent on manufactures, the transport costs T, and the elasticity of substitution ε. If we have found a solution for these three equations for each region, we have found a short-run equilibrium in which world demand for food and each variety of manufactures is equal to world supply and no producer is earning excess profits. Five requirements must be met to perform simulations.

1. We must be clear what it is we are solving for. The short-run equilibrium determines the *endogenous* variables: income I_r, price index P_r, and wage rate W_r for each region r (and in doing so also gives us the real wages, see below). So we must determine numeric values of I_r, P_r, and W_r for which equations (14.3'–14.5') hold.

2. It must be realized that the solutions for the endogenous variables depend on the values of λ_r (the distribution of the mobile labour force, fixed in the short run) and the values of all the *parameters* (δ_m, ρ, ε, and T). This implies that we cannot start to find solutions for the endogenous variables before specifying values for the exogenous variables and parameters. Table 14.3 lists these for the 'base-scenario', in which the share of income spent on manufactures δ_m is fairly low at 0.4, the substitution parameter ρ is 0.8, and the transport costs T are 1.7. The parameter σ will be discussed below.[5]

3. We must find a *solution method*, that is a well-specified procedure that will lead us to solv-ing equations (14.3'–14.5') for numeric values of the endogenous variables, given the chosen

---

[5] Note that ε can be determined from $\varepsilon = 1/(1 - \rho)$. Why did we choose this set of base-scenario parameters? To some degree, the choice is arbitrary. The share of income spent on manufactures δ_m and the elasticity of substitution $\varepsilon = 1/(1 - \rho)$ between varieties have been chosen based on reasonable empirical estimates. Given the choice of δ_m and ρ, the value of the transport costs T is chosen to demonstrate an important aspect of the geographical economics model as illustrated in Figure 14.7 and discussed below.

levels of the exogenous variables and parameters. Several options are available at this point, but in this case the order of equations readily suggests a solution method, labelled sequential iterations. It works as follows:

(i) Guess an initial solution for the wage rate in the two regions, say $(W_{1,0}, W_{2,0})$, where 0 indicates the number of the iteration (we will use $W_{1,0} = W_{2,0} = 1$).

(ii) Using $(W_{1,0}, W_{2,0})$ calculate the price indices $(P_{1,0}, P_{2,0})$ and the income levels $(I_{1,0}, I_{2,0})$ as implied by equations (14.3′) and (14.4′).

(iii) Using $(I_{1,0}, I_{2,0})$ and $(P_{1,0}, P_{2,0})$ as calculated in step (ii) determine a new possible solution for the wage rate $(W_{1,1}, W_{2,1})$ as implied by equation (14.5′).

(iv) Repeat steps (ii) and (iii) until a solution is found.

4. We must specify a *stopping criterion*. The above description of the solution method casually mentioned in step (iv) to 'repeat steps (ii) and (iii) until a solution is found', but when is a solution found? How close should we get to be satisfied that the numeric values we found are indeed a solution to equations (14.3′–14.5′)? We used as a stopping criterion the condition that the absolute value of the relative change in the wage rate should not exceed some small value σ from one iteration to the next for all regions r:

(14.7)
$$\left| \frac{W_{r,iteration} - W_{r,iteration-1}}{W_{r,iteration-1}} \right| < \sigma, \text{for all } r.$$

5. Finally, we must choose a *programming language* and write a small program to actually perform the above calculations. Again, several options are available, but we used Gauss[®], a widely used mathematical programming language, for our simulations.[6]

Table 14.3 Base-scenario parameter configuration

$\delta_m = 0.4$	$\rho = 0.8$	$T = 1.7$	$\sigma = 0.0001$

14.5 **Computer simulations: getting started**

Table 14.3 did not specify the distribution of manufacturing workers, which is necessary for performing simulations. However, we do not only want to use simulations to find a solution for a parameter setting of the model, but also want to learn something about the structure of the model. In this case, by investigating how the short-run equilibrium changes if the distribution of the manufacturing workers changes. Varying λ_1 between 0 and 1 gives a complete description of all possible distributions of the mobile workforce.

---

[6] The simulation exercises in the Study Guide are based on a more user-friendly Excel program.

We focus attention on the real wage in region 1 relative to the real wage in region 2, as it gives us an indication of the dynamic forces operating in the model, see equation (14.6). Once we find a short-run equilibrium for a distribution of the mobile labour force, it is easy to calculate the relative real wage w_1/w_2.

Figure 14.7 illustrates how the relative real wage in region 1 (w_1/w_2) varies as the share of the mobile workforce in region 1 (λ_1) varies. It is the result of 59 separate simulations in which the value of λ_1 is gradually increased from 0 to 1. Each time, the short-run equilibrium is calculated using the procedure described above. Then the relative real wage is calculated, giving 1 observation in the Figure. What can we learn from it?

First, we argued that the mobile workforce has an incentive to move to regions with a higher real wage, such that a short-run equilibrium is also a long-run equilibrium if the real wage for the mobile workforce is the same in all regions. A long-run equilibrium therefore requires that the relative real wage is 1, as long as there are mobile labourers in both regions. It is only when a long-run equilibrium implies complete agglomeration (one region ends up with all mobile labourers, either $\lambda_1 = 0$ or $\lambda_1 = 1$) that the relative real wage is not equal to one (see points A and E).[7] In Figure 14.7 the long-run equilibria B, C, and D are reached for $w_1/w_2 = 1$. There are two types of long-run equilibria: (i) spreading of manufacturing production over the two regions (point C), and (ii) complete agglomeration of manufacturing production in either region (points A and E). The Figure illustrates that there is a third type of long-run equilibrium in which manufacturing production is *partially* agglomerated in one of the two regions (points B and D), leading to a total of five long-run equilibria. It would have been very hard to find equilibria B and D analytically.

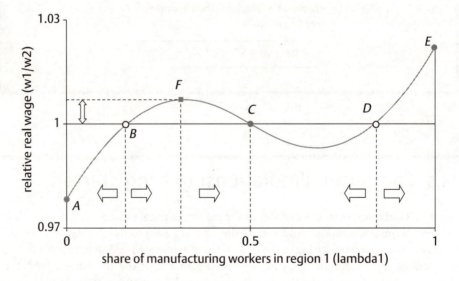

Fig. 14.7 The relative real wage in region 1, base scenario

---

[7] If there is complete agglomeration the relative real wage cannot actually be calculated since there are no manufacturing workers in one of the regions. Points A and E in Figure 14.7 are therefore limit values.

Second, the Figure gives us a clear feel for the dynamics of the system, allowing us to distinguish between stable and unstable equilibria. Suppose, for example, that $\lambda_1 = F$ in Figure 14.7. Note that the mobile workforce is smaller in region 1 than in region 2. As illustrated, the associated short-run equilibrium implies $w_1/w_2 > 1$, as indicated by the double-pointed arrow. The higher real wage in region 1 gives the mobile labourers an incentive to move from region 2 to region 1. This migration process into region 1 represents an increase of λ_1 in Figure 14.7. Migration will continue until the spreading equilibrium at point C is reached, where the real wages are equalized. Similar reasoning, leading to the spreading equilibrium at point C, would hold for any arbitrary initial distribution of the mobile labour force strictly in between points B and D, which could therefore be called the 'basin of attraction' for the spreading equilibrium. The spreading equilibrium is a stable equilibrium, in the sense that any deviation of the mobile labour force from point C within its basin of attraction will activate economic forces to bring us back to it. Similar reasoning holds for the two complete agglomeration equilibria, points A and E, each with its own basin of attraction (from point A to point B, and from point D to point E, respectively). These stable equilibria are illustrated with closed circles in Figure 14.7. In contrast, the partial agglomeration long-run equilibria, points B and D, are *un*stable, illustrated with open circles. If, for whatever reason, we are initially at point B or D, a long-run equilibrium is reached in the sense that the real wages are equal for regions 1 and 2. However, any small perturbation of this equilibrium will set in motion a process of adjustment leading to a different (stable) long-run equilibrium. For example, a small negative disturbance of λ_1 at point B leads to complete agglomeration of manufacturing activity in region 2, while a positive disturbance leads to spreading.

Computer simulations: stability

The main identifying characteristic of regions in the geographical economics model is the transport costs, assumed to be zero within a region, but positive between two different regions. The term 'transport costs' is a shorthand notation for many different types of obstacles to trade between locations, such as tariffs, language and culture barriers, and indeed the costs of actually getting goods or services at another location (see also Box 14.1). An important question is thus what the impact is of a change in the transport costs. To answer this question we repeat the simulation procedure giving rise to Figure 14.7 for both higher ($T = 2.1$) and lower ($T = 1.3$) transport costs. The results are summarized in Figure 14.8, which suggests the following conclusions:

1. If transport costs are large, the spreading equilibrium is the only stable equilibrium. It makes intuitive sense that if manufactures are difficult to transport from one region to another the dynamics of the model lead to spreading of manufacturing activity; distant provision of manufactures is too costly, such that they need to be provided locally.

2. If transport costs are small, the spreading equilibrium is unstable while the two agglomerating equilibria are stable. An initial share of the mobile workforce λ_1 in between 0 and 0.5 serves as the basin of attraction for complete agglomeration in region

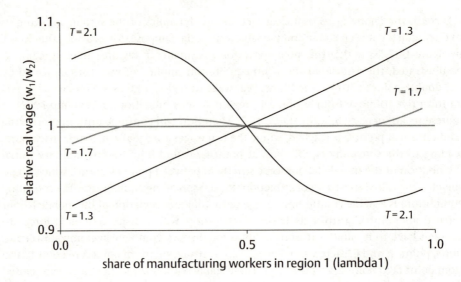

Fig. 14.8 The impact of transport costs

2, while an initial λ_1 in between 0.5 and 1 serves as the basin of attraction for complete agglomeration in region 1. Again this makes sense intuitively. With very low transport costs, the immobile market can be provided effectively from a distance, which therefore does not pose a strong enough force to counter the advantages of agglomeration.

3. For a range of intermediate values of transport costs (here for example if $T = 1.7$) there are five long-run equilibria. Three of those five, namely spreading and the two agglomeration equilibria, are stable. The other two equilibria are unstable. In this situation, the transport costs are high enough to allow for the local provision of manufactures (spreading). Simultaneously, the transport costs are low enough to allow for the provision of the immobile market from a distance (agglomeration).

The suggestions of the impact of a change in the transport costs on the stability of agglomeration and spreading in the geographical economics model, as discussed above on the basis of Figure 14.8, hold in fact quite generally. Fujita, Krugman, and Venables (1999) and Neary (2001) show that:

- For all transport costs *below* a critical level, labelled the *sustain point*, complete agglomeration of manufacturing activity in one region is a stable long-run equilibrium. If the transport costs exceed the critical sustain point level, agglomeration is not 'sustainable', that is agglomeration is an unstable equilibrium.

- For all transport costs *above* another critical level, labelled the *break point*, spreading of manufacturing activity over the two regions is a stable equilibrium. If the transport costs are lower than the critical break point level, the spreading equilibrium 'breaks', that is spreading is an unstable equilibrium.

- The sustain point occurs at a higher level of transport costs than the break point. There is thus *always* an intermediate level of transport costs at which agglomeration of manufacturing activity is sustainable while simultaneously spreading of manufacturing activity is a stable equilibrium. Note that the transport cost level chosen in Table 14.3 ($T = 1.7$) lies in between the break point and the sustain point, such that (i) the spreading equilibrium is stable, and (ii) the agglomeration equilibria are sustainable, as illustrated in Figure 14.8.

The analysis is summarized in Figure 14.9 in (T, λ_1)-space, where the arrows indicate the direction in which the mobile manufacturing workforce will migrate as a result of differences in the relative real wage between the two regions. For each of the three stable equilibria the 'basin of attraction' is indicated, that is the area of initial parameter settings (T, λ_1) which will converge to this equilibrium, see the bottom of Figure 14.9.

It is important to point out the *hysteresis* or path-dependency aspect of the model, that is history matters. Suppose that transport costs are initially high, say $T = 2.5$ in Figure 14.8. Then spreading of manufacturing activity is the only stable long-run equilibrium. Now suppose that transport costs start to fall given that the spreading equilibrium is established, say to $T = 1.7$. This will have no impact on the equilibrium allocation of manufacturing production since spreading remains a stable equilibrium. Only after the transport costs have fallen even further, below the breakpoint B in Figure 14.9, will the spreading equilibrium become unstable. Any small disturbance will then result in complete agglomeration of manufacturing production in one region. It is not possible to predict beforehand which region this will be, but suppose that agglomeration takes place in region 1. Given that region 1 contains all manufacturing activity assume now that the transport costs start to rise again, perhaps because of the imposition of trade

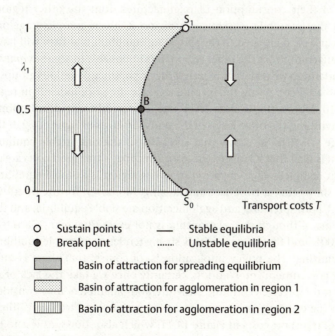

Fig. 14.9 Stability: sustain points and break point

barriers, say back to $T = 1.7$. What will happen? The answer is: nothing! Agglomeration of manufacturing activity remains a stable equilibrium. So for the same level of transport costs ($T = 1.7$) the equilibrium that becomes established depends on the way this level of transport costs is reached, on history. Obviously, predictions of what will happen if parameters change are considerably harder in models characterized by path-dependency.

14.6 **Welfare**

Brakman, Garretsen, and van Marrewijk (2001) are the first to analyse in detail the welfare aspects of the geographical economics model. Here I only illustrate one of their findings, namely the link between stability and welfare maximization. As we have seen above, depending on the parameter configuration of the model, the active economic forces may drive the manufacturing workers towards agglomeration or spreading of economic activity. The obvious question arises whether the equilibrium thus established is 'good', in the sense that it is welfare maximizing.

Obviously, different allocations of manufacturing activity will have different welfare implications for different sets of people. Given transport costs T it is, for example, clear that the mobile workforce will generate a higher welfare level in the complete agglomeration equilibrium than in the spreading equilibrium, since in the latter they have to import part of their consumption of manufactures from the other region. It is also obvious that the immobile workforce in region 2, given complete agglomeration in region 1, is worse off compared to the spreading equilibrium as they will have to import all their manufactures from the other region. It is impossible to argue *ex ante* which effect is more important, so we will have to weigh the importance of various groups, using their size as weight, after correcting the income level for the price index P_i in region i.

Figure 14.10 depicts the welfare level reached for different distributions of manufacturing activity and the three levels of the transport costs of Figure 14.9. If the transport costs are large ($T = 2.1$), we know that spreading is the only stable equilibrium. From Figure 14.10 it is clear that it is also welfare maximizing. If transport costs are low ($T = 1.3$) we know that complete agglomeration in either region is a stable equilibrium. Again, Figure 14.10 shows that it is welfare maximizing. Moreover, for the intermediate transport cost level, both spreading and agglomeration are stable equilibria, and they are local welfare maxima. Although the relationship is not exact, Brakman, Garretsen, and van Marrewijk (2001) find that there is a fairly strong tendency for stable equilibria also to be welfare maximizing. The policy implication is, of course, that there is only a limited incentive for government intervention, certainly once we take the lack of government knowledge on the precise economic structure and parameters into consideration. The link between the distribution of manufacturing activity and welfare is illustrated for a larger range of transport costs in Figure 14.11, which also shows, as was to be expected, that the maximum attainable welfare falls if transport costs increase.

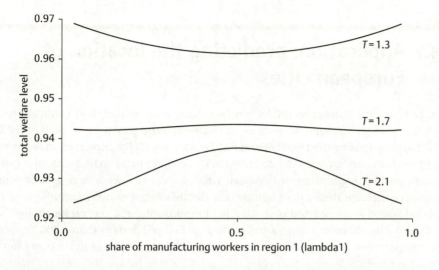

Fig. 14.10 Distribution of manufacturing and welfare

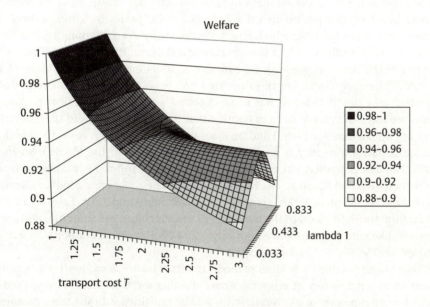

Fig. 14.11 Allocation of manufacturing production and total welfare

14.7 Application: predicting the location of European cities

The geographical economics model has been succesfully modified in various ways to explain empirical phenomena, such as Zipf's Law and the gravity equation. One of the nicest applications by the Dutch economist Dirk Stelder (2000), however, makes only a slight modification of the model described in this chapter to see to what extent it can be used to predict the location of European cities. Stelder defines a large grid of square locations on a truncated map of Europe. The distance between two locations is in principle calculated as the shortest path (that is 1 for horizontal and vertical neighbours, $\sqrt{2}$ for diagonal neighbours). Stelder's grid of Western Europe has more than 2,800 locations. Sea transportation is made possible at a few places, which are part of the network but do not act as potential locations for cities. The model allows for specific costs for transportation across land, across sea, and in hubs where (un)shipping can take place. The grid is also extended with a third dimension (height) to take the extra transportation costs into account when goods have to cross mountains.

The Stelder model starts with a flat initial distribution in which all locations on the grid are of equal size. The model simulations then calculate the redistribution of economic activity based on differences in real wages, given the parameter configuration. The location and size of the cities which emerge in the long-run equilibrium depend on the chosen parameter values and on the geographical shape of the economy. Figure 14.12 shows a model run that produces an equilibrium of 94 cities with $\delta_m = 0.5$, $\varepsilon = 5$ and $T = 1.57$.[8] The open circles are the simulated outcomes and the closed circles the 94 largest actual cities in 1996. As was to be expected with a flat initial distribution, the model produces an optimal city distribution that is more evenly spread than in reality. Large agglomerations like Paris, London, Madrid, and Rome are not correctly simulated, because population density is for historical reasons higher in the North than in the South. The model predicts too many large cities in Spain and too few cities in the UK, the Netherlands, and Belgium. The results are nevertheless relatively good for Germany. The Ruhrgebiet, Bremen, Berlin, Frankfurt, Stuttgart, and Munich (and also Vienna) are not far from the right place. In the periphery of various countries some cities also appear correctly, like Lille, Rouen, Nantes, Bordeaux, and Nice in France, Lisbon and Porto in Portugal, and Seville and Malaga in Spain.

Stelder points out that these kinds of model results of course *should be* wrong. A good fit would mean 'total victory of economics over all other social sciences because then the whole historical process of city formation would be explained with the three parameters δ_m, ε and T'. One of his objectives of the model is to clarify to what extent pure economic factors have contributed to the city formation process, concluding that even the basic model can produce city hierarchies if applied in spaces closer to geographic reality.

---

[8] The apparently peculiar choice of T results from a different parameterization used by Stelder, which we have respecified here using our parameterization.

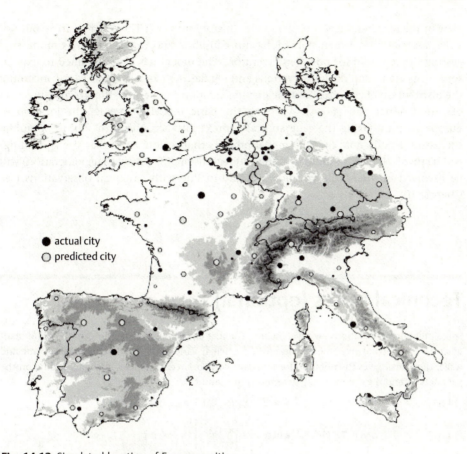

Fig. 14.12 Simulated location of European cities

14.8 Conclusions

Blending some of the insights of the neoclassical trade model (perfect competition and constant returns to scale) and the new trade model (monopolistic competition, increasing returns to scale, and varieties of manufactures) combined with factor mobility (migration to regions with high real wages), allows us to provide a simple theory of location and agglomeration. The dynamic migration process implies that we distinguish between short-run equilibria (in which the distribution of manufacturing activity is given), and an adjustment path leading to a long-run equilibrium (either spreading of manufacturing activity, or complete agglomeration). Using computer simulations to gain further insights into the model, we showed that for high transport costs spreading of manufacturing activity is a stable outcome, while for low transport costs agglomeration is a stable outcome. In an intermediate range, both agglomeration and spreading are stable outcomes, which points to some problems of predicting the effect of policy changes in view of the hysteresis aspect of the model (history matters). There is a positive, but not strict, association between stable long-run equilibria and the welfare maximum, suggesting limited need for policy intervention. The model has been modified to explain some important empirical observations and regularities (such as Zipf's Law, concerning the distribution of city sizes, and the gravity equation, concerning the size and direction of international trade flows). Applying the basic model to predict the location of European cities, taking the geographical context into account, turns out to be mildly successful. Finally note that the model predicts that regions of similar size (spreading) will be involved in intra-industry trade and regions of different size (agglomeration) will be involved in inter-industry trade, roughly in line with empirical observations (see Chapter 10).

Technical Notes (optional)

Some preliminary equations are given below. The first equation gives spending on food and manufactures, the second gives the demand for a particular variety, the third defines real income and wage, the fourth gives the notation for transport costs between regions r and s, depending on the parameter T and the distance D_{rs} between regions r and s.

$$(14.A1) \qquad F = (1 - \delta_m)I; \quad PM = \delta_m I$$

$$(14.A2) \qquad c_j = p_j^{-\varepsilon}[P^{\varepsilon-1}\delta_m I], \quad \text{where } P \equiv \left[\sum_{i=1}^{N} p_i^{1-\varepsilon}\right]^{1/(1-\varepsilon)} \qquad \text{for } j = 1, \ldots, N$$

$$(14.A3) \qquad \text{real income}: y = IP^{-\delta}; \quad \text{real wage}: w = WP^{-\delta}$$

$$(14.A4) \qquad T_{rs} = T^{D_{rs}}, \quad \text{note}: T_{rs} = T_{sr}, \quad \text{and} \quad T_{rr} = T^0 = 1$$

Technical Note 14.1 Derivation of the price index

The number of firms in region s equals: $\lambda_s \delta_m / f\varepsilon$
The price of a firm located in region s charges in region r equals: $mW_s T_{rs}/\rho$

Substituting these two results in the price index for manufactures, see equation (14.A2), and assuming that there are $R \geq 2$ regions, gives the price index for region r:

$$(14.A5) \qquad P_r = \left[\sum_{s=1}^{R} \left(\frac{\lambda_s \delta_m}{f\varepsilon}\right)\left(\frac{mW_s T_{rs}}{\rho}\right)^{1-\varepsilon}\right]^{1/(1-\varepsilon)} = \left[\left(\frac{m}{\rho}\right)\left(\frac{\delta_m}{f\varepsilon}\right)^{1/(1-\varepsilon)}\right]\left(\sum_{s=1}^{R} \lambda_s W_s^{1-\varepsilon} T_{rs}^{1-\varepsilon}\right)^{1/(1-\varepsilon)}$$

It can be shown, see Brakman, Garretsen, and van Marrewijk (2001, ch. 4), that the parameter normalization $m = \rho$ and $f = \delta/\varepsilon$ does not essentially affect the dynamic behaviour of the model, although it does affect the welfare level. Applying this normalization considerably simplifies notation as it reduces the awkward constant in square brackets on the right-hand side of equation (14.A5) to 1. Using that normalization implies that equation (14.3) is a special case for $R = 2$ and $r = 1$.

Technical Note 14.2 Derivation of manufacturing equilibrium

Equation (14.A2) gives the demand for an individual consumer in a region. Replacing the income level I with the income level I_s of region s, the price index P with the price index P_s of region s, and the price p_j of the manufactured good with the price mW_rT_{sr}/ρ which a producer from region r will charge in region s, we get the demand in region s for a product from region r:

$$(14.A6) \qquad \delta_m I_s (mW_r T_{sr}/\rho)^{-\varepsilon} P_s^{\varepsilon-1} = \delta_m (m/\rho)^{-\varepsilon} I_s W_r^{-\varepsilon} T_{sr}^{-\varepsilon} P_s^{\varepsilon-1}$$

To fulfil this consumption demand in region s note that T_{sr} units have to be shipped and produced. To derive the total demand in all $R \geq 2$ regions for a manufactured good produced in region r, we must sum production demand over all regions (that is, sum over the index s in the above equation and multiply each entry by T_{sr}):

$$(14.A7) \qquad \delta_m (m/\rho)^{-\varepsilon} \sum_{s=1}^{R} I_s W_r^{-\varepsilon} T_{sr}^{1-\varepsilon} P_s^{\varepsilon-1} = \delta_m (m/\rho)^{-\varepsilon} W_r^{-\varepsilon} \sum_{s=1}^{R} I_s T_{sr}^{1-\varepsilon} P_s^{\varepsilon-1}$$

In equilibrium this total demand for a manufactured good from region r must be equal to its supply $(\varepsilon - 1)f/m$, see Chapter 10. Equalizing these two gives

$$(14.A8) \qquad (\varepsilon - 1)f/m = \delta_m (m/\rho)^{-\varepsilon} W_r^{-\varepsilon} \sum_{s=1}^{R} I_s T_{sr}^{1-\varepsilon} P_s^{\varepsilon-1}$$

which can easily be solved for the wage rate W_s in region r:

$$(14.A9) \qquad W_r = \left[\rho m^{-\rho} \left(\frac{\delta_m}{(\varepsilon - 1)f} \right)^{1/\varepsilon} \right] \left(\sum_{s=1}^{R} I_s T_{sr}^{1-\varepsilon} P_s^{\varepsilon-1} \right)^{1/\varepsilon}$$

As in Technical Note 14.1, the awkward constant in square brackets on the right-hand side disappears if we impose the normalization $m = \rho$ and $f = \delta/\varepsilon$. Doing that implies that equation (14.5) is a special case for $R = 2$ and $r = 1$.

Chapter 15
Multinationals

Objectives/key terms

Multinationals	Transnationality index
Foreign direct investment	Mergers and acquisitions
Horizontal/vertical mergers	Transfer pricing
OLI framework	Hard disk drives

Multinational firms, with increasing shares in world production, investment, and trade flows, represent the most visible part of the 'globalization' phenomenon. We evaluate some empirical evidence and analyse the economic forces behind multinational firms.

15.1 Introduction

When I start to get hungry from shopping in the centre of the world's largest harbour, Rotterdam, I order a Big Mac at McDonald's, washing it down with Coca-Cola before driving back in my Toyota. If I fly eight hours to the west to visit my friend in Washington DC, I rent a Toyota, after eating a Big Mac and drinking Coca-Cola at the airport. If I fly eighteen hours to the east to visit my in-laws in the Philippines, the Toyota taxi stops at McDonald's so that I can eat a Big Mac and drink Coca-Cola. In Holland, the USA, and the Philippines, and virtually everywhere else in the world, I can therefore consume the products of McDonald's, Coca-Cola, and Toyota. The fact that the same company is producing and selling products in more than one country—such a company is called a 'multinational corporation' (henceforth multinational, for short)—and sometimes is producing and selling its products virtually all over the world, is probably the most visible aspect of the worldwide international economic links summarized under the label globalization. Since multinational production, investment, and trade is becoming ever more important, see sections 15.2 and 15.3, and none of the preceding chapters has devoted explicit attention to these phenomena, it is time to fill that gap in this chapter.

Fig. 15.1 Joseph Schumpeter (1883–1950)

Born in Austria, where he was briefly Minister of Finance after the First World War, Schumpeter emigrated to the USA in 1932, where he worked at Harvard University. At the early age of 28 he wrote *Theory of Economic Development* (1912), which gave a pivoting role to the dynamic, innovating entrepreneur for achieving technical progress and a positive rate of profit on capital. As Blaug (1986: 215) puts it, Schumpeter 'stressed the fact that scientific and technical inventions amount to nothing unless they are adopted, which calls for as much daring and imagination as the original act of discovery by the scientist or engineer'. Moreover, he emphasized that economic progress consists not only of new machines and products, but also of new sources of supply, new forms of organization, and new methods of production. Schumpeter distinguished sharply between the entrepreneur, doing things in a new way and earning 'profit', and the capitalist, providing the capital required to finance a new venture and earning 'interest'. In 1942 he wrote *Capitalism, Socialism, and Democracy*, a book predicting the arrival of socialism. Another Schumpeter must-have in any economist's cupboard is *History of Economic Analysis* (1954), which appeared four years after his death, on the history of economic thought with many important remarks scattered about in hundreds of footnotes.

Table 15.1 lists the twenty largest multinational firms in 1997, ranked by foreign assets. Toyota is listed as number 6, but McDonald's and Coca-Cola, mentioned in the introduction above, do not make it to the top twenty (they are in the top 100). The top twenty list contains six American, five German, and three Swiss firms. There is also a sectoral concentration, with seven automotive, four petrol, and three electronics firms. The ranking based on foreign assets as a measure of multinationality is, of course, arbitrary. The largest firm in this respect, the American firm General Electric, has foreign assets valued at $97 billion, out of total assets of $304 billion. Its foreign sales are $25 billion, out of total sales of $95 billion, and it employs 111,000 persons abroad, out of a total of 276,000 employees. The UNCTAD/Erasmus University database in the World Investment Report therefore also calculates the relative average of these three indicators of multi-nationality, labelled the Transnationality index. For General Electric this calculation results in (see Table 15.1):

$$(15.1) \qquad \frac{1}{3}\left(\frac{97}{304} + \frac{25}{91} + \frac{111}{276}\right) \times 100\% = 33\%$$

The Transnationality index is much lower than for the Swiss electronics firm Asea Brown Boveri (96 per cent) or the Swiss food firm Nestlé (93 per cent). The highest Trans-nationality index, however, is achieved by the Canadian beverages and media company

Table 15.1 Top twenty multinational corporations, ranked by foreign assets, 1997

Corporation	Country	Industry	Assets		Sales		Employment		TN Index
			Foreign	Total	Foreign	Total	Foreign	Total	
1 General Electric	USA	Electronics	97	304	25	91	111	276	33
2 Ford Motor	USA	Automotive	73	275	48	154	174	364	35
3 Shell Group	NL/UK	Petroleum	70	115	69	128	65	105	59
4 General Motors	USA	Automotive	0	229	51	178	—	608	29
5 Exxon	USA	Petroleum	55	96	105	120	—	80	66
6 Toyota	Japan	Automotive	42	105	50	89	—	159	40
7 IBM	USA	Computers	40	82	49	79	135	269	54
8 Volkswagen	Ger.	Automotive	—	57	43	65	134	280	57
9 Nestlé	Switz.	Food	32	38	48	48	220	226	93
10 Daimler	Ger.	Automotive	31	76	46	69	75	300	44
11 Mobil	USA	Petroleum	30	44	37	64	22	43	60
12 FIAT	Italy	Automotive	30	69	20	51	95	242	41
13 Hoechst	Ger.	Chemicals	29	34	24	30	—	137	77
14 Asea BB	Switz.	El. equip	—	30	30	31	201	213	96
15 Bayer	Ger.	Chemicals	—	30	—	32	—	145	83
16 Elf	France	Petroleum	27	42	26	42	41	84	58
17 Nissan	Japan	Automotive	27	58	28	50	—	137	51
18 Unilever	NL/UK	Food	26	31	45	46	263	269	92
19 Siemens	Ger.	Electronics	26	67	40	61	201	386	52
20 Roche	Switz.	Pharmac.	—	38	13	13	42	52	82

Source: UNCTAD/Erasmus Universtiy database, *World Investment Report* (1999). Sales and assets in billion US $; employment in thousands; TN index = Transnationality index (%), the average of three ratios: foreign assets to total assets, foreign sales to total sales, and foreign employment to total employment.

Seagram, not listed in Table 15.1. In general, therefore, the most international oriented companies in this respect are to be found in the smaller developed countries.

15.2 The size and structure of multinationals

Multinationals are rapidly becoming more important in the global economic system. Sales of foreign affiliates of multinational firms have risen from 23 per cent of world GDP in 1982 to 45 per cent of world GDP in 1999, see Figure 15.2a. This is, of course, not an entirely correct comparison since, unlike GDP, sales are not a value added measure. As Figure 15.2b shows, however, the gross product of foreign affiliates relative to world GDP is also estimated to have increased substantially in this period, from 5 per cent in 1982 to 10 per cent in 1999. Since both sales and gross product of foreign affiliates has roughly doubled relative to world GDP in this period, we are not surprised to see in Figure 15.2c

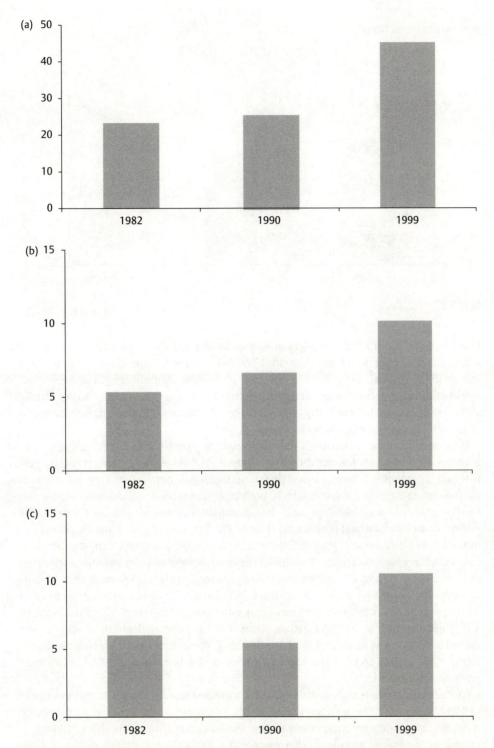

Fig. 15.2 Growing importance of multinationals. (a) Sales of foreign affiliates (% world GDP), (b) gross product of foreign affiliates (% world GDP), (c) exports of foreign affiliates (% world GDP), (d) exports of foreign affiliates (% of world exports)

Source: UNCTAD, World Investment Report (2000).

(continued overleaf)

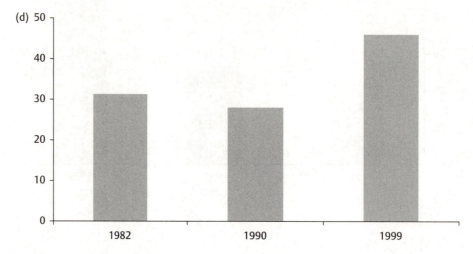

Fig 15.2 (continued)

that the same holds for the exports of foreign affiliates, increasing from 6 per cent of world GDP in 1982 to 11 per cent in 1999. International trade flows become more important in general, such that the rise in exports of foreign affiliates relative to total world exports has increased less dramatically, from 31 per cent in 1982 to 46 per cent in 1999. We conclude that currently almost half of all international trade flows are exports of foreign affiliates of multinational firms.

How does a company become a multinational? By operating and controlling foreign affiliates. This requires foreign direct investment (FDI) in either of two ways, namely through (i) greenfield investments, that is setting up a new production location, or (ii) through mergers and acquisitions. In both cases, host country assets are placed under the governance of multinational firms, but greenfield investments also contribute to the growth of an international production system. The majority of FDI, some 78 per cent, is in the form of mergers and acquisitions, which, as the name suggests, can be subdivided into a small number of mergers (less than 3 per cent), with headquarters in both countries or in one country, and a larger number of acquisitions, with headquarters in the home country and the affiliate in the host country. Acquisitions, in turn, can be minority (with 10–49 per cent of a firm's voting shares), majority (foreign interest of 50–99 per cent), or full (foreign interest of 100 per cent). In terms of the number of deals, most acquisitions are full (65 per cent of all mergers and acquisitions). These distinctions are summarized in Figure 15.3. Acquisitions of less than 10 per cent of a firm's voting shares constitute portfolio investment.

Cross-border mergers and acquisitions have increased rapidly, from $75 billion in 1987 to $720 billion in 1999, see Figure 15.4. Partly as a result of the continuing process of economic and monetary integration within the European Union, the share of Western Europe as purchasers in cross-border merger and acquisition activities has risen from 44 per cent in 1987 to 72 per cent in 1999. Simultaneously, and despite the increase in absolute terms, the share of North America dropped from 43 to 18 per cent, see Figure 15.4.

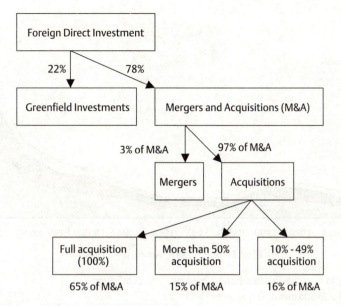

Fig. 15.3 Structure of foreign direct investment flows

Source: UNCTAD, World Investment Report (2000). Data are for 1999, the estimate 78%–22% is in value terms, relative to the average of inflow and outflow FDI (Table I.1), the other percentages are on number of deals (Table IV.1).

We can distinguish between three types of mergers and acquisitions.[1]

- *Horizontal* mergers and acquisitions between competing firms in the same industry. By consolidating their resources the merging firms aim to achieve synergies and often greater market power. Typical industries are pharmaceuticals, automobiles, petroleum, and several services industries.

- *Vertical* mergers and acquisitions between firms in client–supplier or buyer–seller relationships. The firms seek to reduce uncertainty and transaction costs as regards forward and backward linkages in the production process. Typical industries are electronics and automobiles.

- *Conglomerate* mergers and acquisitions between companies in unrelated activities. The firms seek to diversify risk and deepen economies of scope.

Horizontal mergers and acquisitions constitute the largest component of cross-border mergers and acquisitions. They have also become relatively more important over time, increasing from 55 per cent in 1987 to 72 per cent in 1999, see Figure 15.5. In contrast, conglomerate mergers and acquisitions have become relatively less important over time, falling from a high of 42 per cent in 1991 to 27 per cent in 1999, as firms tend to increasingly focus on their core business. The share of vertical mergers and acquisitions is limited, and tends to fluctuate wildly from year to year.

[1] See UNCTAD (2000: 101).

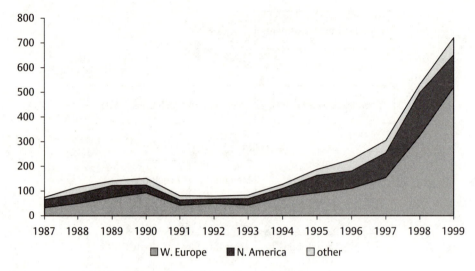

Fig. 15.4 Rapid increase in cross-border mergers and acquisitions
Source: UNCTAD, World Investment Report (2000).

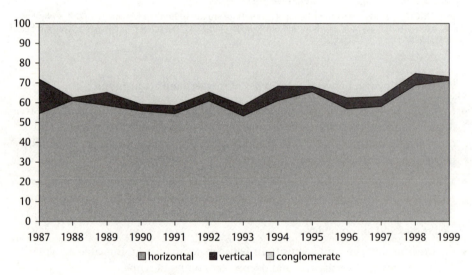

Fig. 15.5 Mostly horizontal cross-border mergers and acquisitions
Source: UNCTAD, World Investment Report (2000).

15.3 Foreign direct investment

A firm can become a multinational, that is control by means of ownership productive assets in more than one country, through foreign direct investment (greenfield investments and mergers and acquisitions). Data on foreign direct investment have been systematically gathered on a global scale for a surprisingly short period of time: the UNCTAD just celebrated the tenth anniversary of the *World Investment Report* in 2000. This work has clearly demonstrated the growing importance of foreign direct investment and multinational production and trade (UNCTAD's preferred term is transnational, rather than multinational).

In the period 1970–97 worldwide real GDP, measured in constant 1995 US $, rose from $13.5 trillion to $30.6 trillion. This is an increase of 127 per cent, or roughly 3 per cent per year, see Figure 15.6a. Measured similarly, worldwide international trade flows rose from $3.8 trillion in 1970 to $13 trillion in 1997, an increase of 243 per cent for the period, or almost 5 per cent per year. The steady growing importance of international trade flows, which as a share of world GDP increased from 28 per cent in 1970 to 43 per cent in 1997, is illustrated in Figures 15.6a and 15.6b. Finally, also measured in constant 1995 US $, worldwide foreign direct investments rose from $66 billion to $436 billion, an increase of 562 per cent, or more than 7 per cent per year. As illustrated in Figure 15.6a, therefore, foreign direct investments rose even more rapidly than international trade flows. It is also clear from the Figure that foreign direct investments are much more volatile, with large peaks and troughs, than either trade flows or production levels. This is also evident from Figure 15.6c, showing the volatile increase of foreign direct investments as a share of world GDP from 0.49 per cent in 1970 to 1.42 per cent in 1997.

The three panels of Figure 15.7 give a breakdown of the geographic distribution of foreign direct investments, that is inflows, outflows, and net flows, for eight global regions: Western Europe, Central and Eastern Europe, Africa, North America, Latin America and the Caribbean, Japan, the Asian newly industrialized countries (NICs),[2] and Other Asia. Although all data are in billions of current US $, please note the differences in scale on the vertical axes of the three panels of Figure 15.7.

As is evident from Figure 15.7a, the major destinations of foreign direct investment flows are to be found in the developed nations of Western Europe and North America, together accounting for approximately 70 per cent of the world inflows of foreign direct investment, roughly equally divided between them. Other sizeable inflows occur in Latin America, the Asian NICs (with a dip in 1998 following the Asian currency crisis), and Other Asia (mostly China). Japan, Africa, and Central and Eastern Europe receive rather limited inflows of foreign direct investment.

As illustrated in Figure 15.7b, the dominant sources of foreign direct investment are the developed countries in Western Europe, rising to 63 per cent of the world total in 1998, with North America, at 25 per cent in 1998, as second main source at a respectable distance. Together, the developed countries of Western Europe and North America are therefore the source of more than 80 per cent of the world foreign direct investment flows, as well as the destination of more than 70 per cent of those flows. Japan and the Asian NICs are also a sizeable source of foreign direct investment, at 15–20 per cent of the world total (again with a dip in 1998), but the other regions are not.

Finally, by combining the above information, Figure 15.7c shows that the dominant source of *net* foreign direct investment flows are the countries in Western Europe

---

[2] In Figure 15.7 these are: Hong Kong, Indonesia, Korea, Malaysia, Singapore, Taiwan, and Thailand.

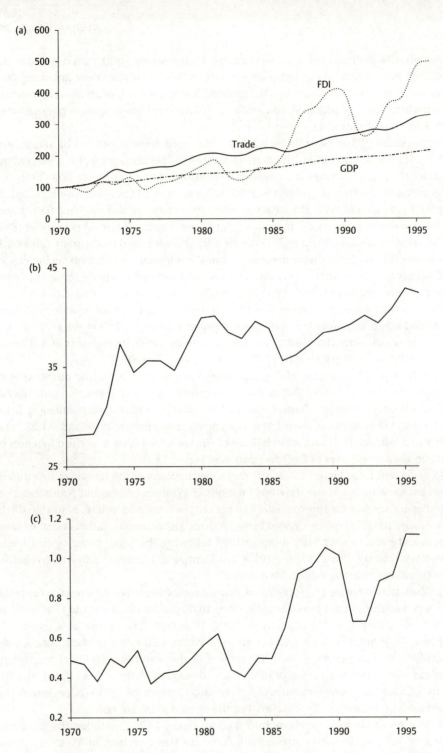

Fig. 15.6 Development of world GDP, FDI, and trade. (a) GDP, trade, and FDI (1970 = 100), (b) trade (% of GDP), (c) FDI, net inflows (% of GDP)

Source: World Bank Development Indicator CD-ROM, 1999. GDP index based on constant 1995 $.

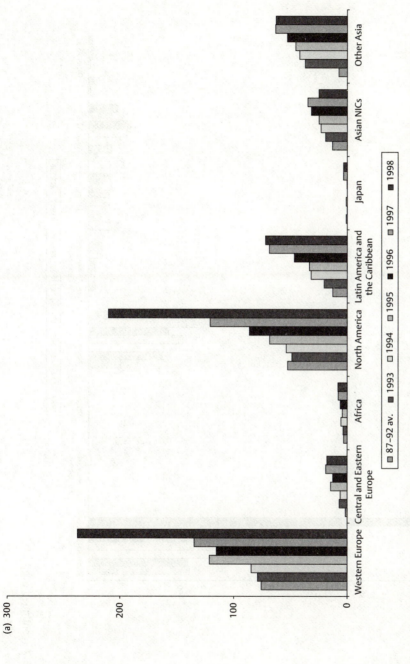

(a) 300

200

100

0

Western Europe   Central and Eastern   Africa   North America   Latin America and   Japan   Asian NICs   Other Asia
                 Europe   the Caribbean

■ 87–92 av.   ■ 1993   □ 1994   □ 1995   ■ 1996   □ 1997   ■ 1998

Fig. 15.7 Foreign direct investment flows. (a) FDI inflows (billions of $), (b) FDI outflows (billions of $), (c) net FDI flows (billions of $).
Source: UNCTAD, World Investment Report (1999).

(continued overleaf)

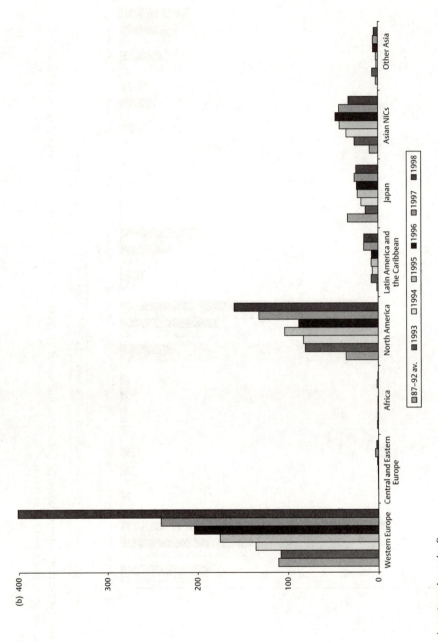

(b)

400						
300						
200						
100						
0						

Western Europe   Central and Eastern Europe   Africa   North America   Latin America and the Caribbean   Japan   Asian NICs   Other Asia

■87–92 av. ■1993 □1994 □1995 ■1996 □1997 ■1998

Fig. 15.7 (continued overleaf)

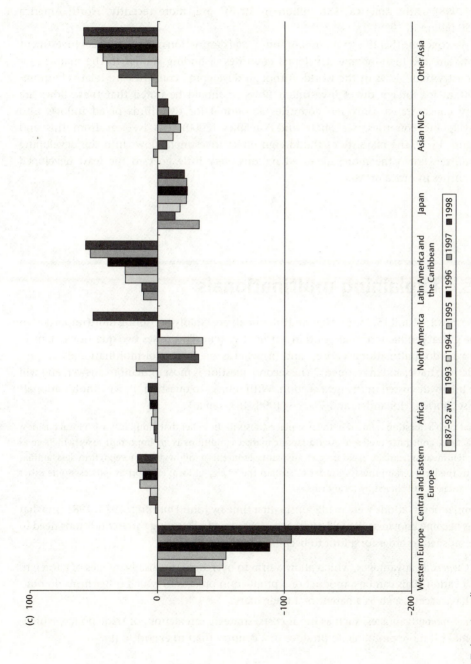

Fig. 15.7 (continued)

($169 billion in 1998). Japan ($21 billion in 1998) and the Asian NICs ($8 billion in 1998), are also small sources of net foreign direct investment flows. The main net destinations of foreign direct investment flows are Other Asia (mostly China, $58 billion in 1998), Latin America ($56 billion in 1998), and, more recently, North America ($50 billion in 1998).

We conclude that the predominant source *and* destination of foreign direct investment flows are the high-income developed countries, a finding similar to the main intra-industry trade flows in the world. Although developing countries are relatively unimportant for foreign direct investment flows, it should be noted that these flows are very concentrated: only ten countries accounted for two-thirds of all inflows into developing countries, see Shatz and Venables (2000).[3] As is clear from this and Figure 15.7*a*, the majority of the foreign direct investment flows into the developing countries go to the more advanced nations, very little goes to the least developed countries in Africa or Asia.

15.4 Explaining multinationals

Sections 15.2 and 15.3 show that multinationals are rapidly becoming more important in the global production, trade, and investment system. This poses two questions, namely (i) why do multinationals arise?, and (ii) what is the impact of multinationals on production, trade, and investment? The second question is most difficult to answer, and will be briefly discussed in the next section. With respect to question (i), why multinationals arise, Bowen, Hollander, and Viaene (1998: 463) remark:

That such a question is raised in the first place attests to the belief that familiarity with local business practices, consumer preferences and labour market conditions is an important asset which gives local firms an advantage over foreign transplants. From this it follows that a foreign firm, less familiar with the local terrain must, in order to sustain the rivalry of local enterprises, possess some other advantages, not shared by local firms.

Similar observations were made for the first time by John Dunning (1977, 1981) in what has become known as the OLI approach. According to Dunning three conditions need to be satisfied in order for a firm to become a multinational:

- *Ownership* advantages, which allow a firm to overcome the disadvantages of a foreign location. This can be a product or a production process to which other firms do not have access, such as a patent or a trade mark.
- *Location* advantages, such as input costs, strategic interaction, or trade policy, which make it more profitable to produce in a country than to export to it.

---

[3] Argentina, Brazil, Chile, China, Hungary, Indonesia, Malaysia, Mexico, Poland, Singapore. Of these flows China received 30.6 per cent.

- *Internalization* advantages, which make it more profitable for a firm to undertake foreign production itself, rather than dealing with a foreign partner more familiar with the local environment.

The extensive empirical literature on firm characteristics associated with multinational firms, representing the sources of the ownership, location, and internalization advantages of Dunning, has recently been reviewed by Markusen (1995, 1998).[4] The latter study produces the following list of main firm and industry characteristics for multinationals.

1. Multinationals are associated with high ratios of R&D relative to sales.

2. Multinationals employ large numbers of scientific, technical, and other 'white-collar' workers as a percentage of their workforce.

3. Multinationals tend to have a high value of 'intangible' assets (market value minus the value of tangible assets, such as plant and equipment).

4. Multinationals are associated with new and/or technically complex products.

5. Evidence suggests that multinationality is negatively associated with plant-level scale economies.

6. Multinationals are associated with product-differentiation variables, such as advertising to sales ratios.

7. A minimum or 'threshold' level of firm size seems to be important for a firm to be a multinational, but above that level firm size is of minimal importance.

8. Multinationals tend to be older, more established firms.

In the international economics literature, the above firm and industry characteristics clearly lead us into the realm of imperfect competition, product differentiation, and increasing returns to scale, see Chapters 9 and 10. The discussion below can therefore build upon the main insights already derived in these chapters. Points 5 and 7 above, distinguishing between plant level and firm level economies of scale, have been crucial in understanding why and when multinationals arise in a general equilibrium framework.[5] Rather than elaborating on the individual contributions in this area, the next section will explain in some detail the general structure and main results of a recent representative model of multinational activity by James Markusen and Anthony Venables.

Box 15.1 **Transfer pricing**

When firms are operative in more countries, each having different tariffs and different corporate income taxes, this raises the possibility of 'transfer pricing', that is the setting of prices on intrafirm transactions to minimize tax and tariff payments and maximize corporate profits, see Horst (1971). Although, according to international principles, the dutiable value of these

---

[4] See Markusen (1995) and Caves (1996) for further references.
[5] Important early contributions are: Helpman (1984, 1985), Markusen (1984), and Ethier (1986).

transactions should be the arm's-length price, that is the price which would be charged to an outside buyer, exporters have some manoeuvring space when declaring a value for duty. Declaring a high import value increases the tariff payments to be made and at the same time shifts profits from the importing country to the exporting country. The latter will be beneficial if the importing country has a higher corporate tax rate than the exporting country. The overall payments of the firm therefore depend on the tariff duty relative to the difference in taxation rates.

In a small partial equilibrium model Bowen, Hollander, and Viaene (1998: 474–9) show that transfer pricing may also influence the firm's location decision. Assuming that the marginal production costs are the same in Home and Foreign, that the transfer prices may vary in a range with a minimum and a maximum, and allowing for the possibility to set up a production plant either in Home only or in both Home and Foreign, they show that a Home plant alone is optimal if the taxation of profits is low compared to the taxation of profits in Foreign. Otherwise, as the taxation rates become more equal, it is optimal to establish two production plants. Empirical studies, for example by Grubert and Mutti (1991) who study US multinational activity in thirty-three countries, found ample evidence of income shifting into countries with low tax rates. Moreover, host country corporate taxes have a negative impact on export sales of local subsidiaries, but not on local sales.

15.5 **Multinationals in general equilibrium**

As argued in Chapter 1, international economists are not truly satisfied with an explanation of empirical observations until they can construct a general equilibrium model producing similar results. The last decade of the previous century has seen large improvements in this respect in trying to explain multinational firms and their impact on the international trading system in a general equilibrium framework. As pointed out above, we restrict attention to the Markusen and Venables (1998) model, which focuses on horizontal multinationals. As shown in section 15.2, this comprises the majority of foreign direct investments. As in previous chapters, we analyse two countries, Austria and Bolivia, and two types of industries, manufactures and food. The food sector produces a homogeneous good under constant returns to scale, using capital K and labour L as inputs, in a perfectly competitive market. There are no transport costs for food, which will be used as numéraire. The production function for food is (compare equation (4.1)):[6]

$$(15.2) \qquad F_A = K_A^{\alpha_f} L_{Af}^{1-\alpha_f} \qquad F_B = K_B^{\alpha_f} L_{Bf}^{1-\alpha_f}; \quad 0 < \alpha_f < 1$$

---

[6] The complete specification of the model is a bit too involved for this book, even in the Technical Notes section, so we refer the reader for details to Markusen and Venables (1998).

Recall that α_f measures the capital intensity of the production process. Also note that the capital used in the production process of food in equation (15.2) does not have a sub-index f, in contrast to the labour used. This will be explained below. If we know the amount of capital and labour used in the food sector, we can derive the wage rate and the rental rate by equating them to the marginal product of labour and capital, respectively.[7]

Multinationals may arise in the production of the manufactures, a homogeneous good, in a framework of imperfect competition using the Cournot model explained in Chapter 9. To model point 2 of section 15.4, arguing that multinational production is (high-skilled) labour intensive, we assume that the production process of manufactures uses no capital.[8] The entire capital stock in both countries is therefore employed in the production of food, such that there is no need for a sub-index f in equation (15.2). In accordance with points 5 and 7 of section 15.4, arguing that multinationals are characterized by firm level and plant level fixed costs, there are increasing returns to scale in the production process of manufactures. This will be modelled as a somewhat more complex version of the production process of Chapter 10.

The production of manufactures, which uses only labour, is characterized by the following parameters (identical in both countries).

- c — the (constant) marginal production costs in terms of labour. Together with the wage rate in the country of production this determines the marginal costs of production.

- t — the amount of labour needed to transport one unit of manufactures from Austria to Bolivia, or vice versa. As argued by Dunning, it is necessary to have a location advantage for explaining multinationals, that is an incentive to produce in a country rather than to export to it, which is provided in this framework by the transport costs t.

- F — the firm level fixed costs in terms of labour. Since each firm has to incur these costs only once, it provides the ownership advantage in Dunning's framework. Presumably, the firm level fixed costs represent investments in research and development, employing white-collar workers for the technically more complex manufactures products, in accordance with points 1–4 of section 15.4.

- G — the plant level fixed costs in terms of labour. The firm can decide, at a cost, to set up more than one production plant, which enables the firm to avoid the transport costs t. Naturally, the firm only sets up multi-plant production if it is profitable to do so.

We can now distinguish between four different types of firms in the manufactures sector, as summarized in the decision process of Figure 15.8. First, the firm can decide in which country, Austria or Bolivia, it will establish its headquarters. In conjunction with the wage rate, this determines the level of the firm-specific and plant-specific fixed cost in the country of establishment. Second, the firm can decide whether or not to establish a production plant in the other country.[9] The advantage is, of course, the fact that this

---

[7] Which is equal to the value marginal product of labour and capital because food is the numéraire.

[8] To emphasize the distinction between high-skilled versus low-skilled labour, the reader may reinterpret the capital stock K in this chapter as low-skilled labour and the labour stock L as high-skilled labour. The production of manufactures is then high-skilled labour intensive and the production of food low-skilled labour intensive.

[9] The logical possibility of incurring firm-specific fixed costs in one country and one plant specific cost in the other country (vertical multinational) is not taken into consideration, see Markusen et al. (1996).

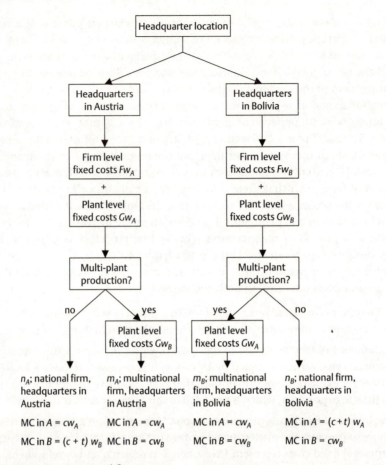

Fig. 15.8 Decision process and firm types

allows the firm to avoid the transport costs of exporting goods to the other country. The disadvantage is that the firm has to incur extra fixed plant costs in the other country. If the firm does *not* establish a production plant in the other country we will call it a *national* firm, n_A if it is established in Austria and n_B if it is established in Bolivia. If the firm does establish a production plant in the other country we will call it a *multinational* firm, m_A if the headquarters are established in Austria and m_B if the headquarters are in Bolivia. If M_{AA}^n are the sales of manufactures in Austria of a national firm established in Austria, M_{AB}^n are the sales of manufactures in Bolivia of a national firm established in Austria, and similarly for M_{AA}^m and M_{AB}^m for multinational firms, the cost functions for firms with headquarters in Austria are therefore:

$$
\text{(15.3)} \quad
\begin{aligned}
&\text{national firm}: \quad (F+G)w_A + cw_A \overbrace{M_{AA}^n}^{\substack{domestic\\sales}} + (c+t)w_A \overbrace{M_{AB}^n}^{\substack{foreign\\sales}} \\
&\text{multinational firm}: \quad (F+G)w_A + Gw_B + cw_A \underbrace{M_{AA}^m}_{\substack{domestic\\sales}} + cw_B \underbrace{M_{AB}^m}_{\substack{foreign\\sales}}
\end{aligned}
$$

Box 15.2 **Top business locations**

Firms take many different factors into consideration before deciding where to locate their new business. The quality of the labour force is important, as is political and social stability, the quality of infrastructure (roads, telecommunications, railroads, air connections), the links to suppliers and demanders, unemployment, inflation, etc. Each year the Economist Intelligence Unit evaluates many of these aspects and produces an updated list of the locations for the best business climate worldwide. In 2001, the Netherlands topped the list, in part because of its many tax treaties with other nations. The USA dropped from first to second place, just ahead of the UK and Canada.

The best location depends, of course, on the type of business the firm wants to establish. Suppose, focusing on Europe only, that a firm wants to establish an efficient distribution centre with good links to other parts of Europe. Then, according to Buck Consultants International, the Netherlands is again the best location, followed by Belgium and France. However, if a firm wants to establish a European headquarters the UK is ranked first, followed by the Netherlands and (tied) Belgium and Germany. If a firm wants to establish a high-tech European production site, the UK is ranked first, followed by Ireland and France. Although these lists, as summarized in Table 15.2, tend to draw a lot of media attention and may be flattering for high-ranked countries, we should not overemphasize their importance. Investment location decisions by firms may involve millions or billions of dollars and are therefore not taken lightly. Firms decide where to put up shop after carefully scrutinizing many possible locations for their advantages and disadvantages taking the particular firm situation into consideration, not on the basis of a list published by a magazine or a consulting firm.

Information source: NRC Handelsblad (2001*e*)

Table 15.2 Top business locations, 2001

Best business climate worldwide[a]	Best location European headquarters[b]	Best location European distribution centre[b]	Best location European high-tech production[b]
1 The Netherlands	UK	The Netherlands	UK
2 USA	The Netherlands	Belgium	Ireland
3 UK	Belgium (3/4)	France	France
4 Canada	Germany (3/4)	UK	Germany
5 Switzerland	France	Germany	The Netherlands
6 Ireland	Ireland	Ireland	Belgium

[a] According to the Economist Intelligence Unit.
[b] According to Buck Consultants International.

The remainder of the model is familiar from the previous chapters. The utility function in both countries is as specified in Chapter 7 (Cobb–Douglas), with δ_m as the share of income spent on manufactures. This implies that the price elasticity of demand is equal to 1, such that the optimal pricing rule for a firm is equal to its market share, see Technical Note 9.2 for details. Firms will enter the market for manufactures in both countries until (excess) profits are equal to zero. Finally, general equilibrium obviously requires full employment of labour and capital, as well as market clearing for food and manufactures in both countries.

15.6 Characterization of equilibrium

The main strong point of the current multinational models is the ability to *endogenously* determine the market structure. Firms may or may not decide to establish headquarters in a country. Similarly, they may or may not decide to establish another production plant in the other country. Whether or not they make these decisions is determined within the model, thus determining the nature of market competition endogenously. The market equilibrium outcome depends, of course, on the parameters and the size and distribution of the capital and labour stock.

Unfortunately, the main strong point of the current multinational models also constitutes its main weakness, as illustrated in Figure 15.9. The flexibility of the model, which enables a firm in manufactures to be a national firm in either country, or a multinational firm with headquarters in either country, opens up four logical possibilities: n_A, n_B, m_A, and m_B. This implies, in turn, that there are $2^4 = 16$ possible equilibrium market structures, of which we can delete only one (there has to be at least one firm), see Figure 15.9. The reader will of course realize that it is tiresome, if not virtually impossible, to analyse fifteen different regimes for a large range of parameter values or endowment distributions. Imagine the possibility of distinguishing between national firms, horizontal multinationals, *and* vertical multinationals, as some models do, in a world of five countries; it would increase the range of possible firms to $3 \cdot 5 = 15$, and the range of possible regimes to $2^{15} - 1 = 32,767$. It is clear that such a number of possibilities cannot be analysed without a powerful tool to assist the researcher.

To present the main results of the multinational model more clearly, we will group the fifteen regimes of Figure 15.9 into three aggregate types; (i) the shaded regimes in Figure 15.9 with *only national* firms, (ii) the three regimes on the right of Figure 15.9 with *only multinational* firms, and (iii) the other regimes with a *mixed* composition of firms (nationals and multinationals).

Figure 15.10 recalls the impact of different distributions of the world endowment of capital and labour between the two countries in the Edgeworth Box, see Chapter 6. At point C, in the centre of the Edgeworth Box, the capital–labour ratio is the same in the two countries, and they are exactly equal in size. Going from point C to the north-east

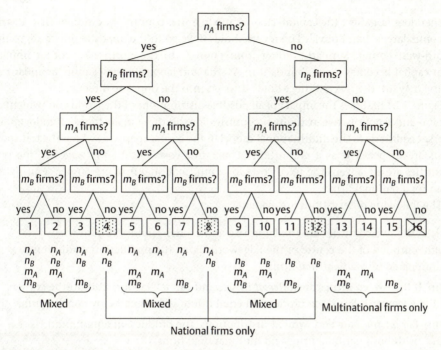

Fig. 15.9 Possible national/multinational regimes

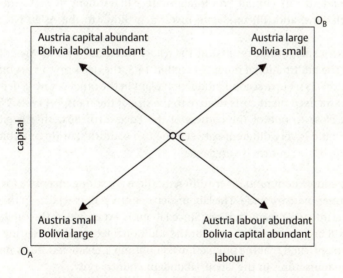

Fig. 15.10 Endowment distributions in the Edgeworth Box

corner does not affect the capital–labour ratio in either country, but implies that Austria becomes larger than Bolivia. The reverse holds if we go in the opposite direction, to the south-west corner. Similarly, going from point C to the north-west corner implies that capital becomes more abundant in Austria and labour becomes more abundant in Bolivia. Again, the reverse effect holds if we go into the opposite direction.

Figure 15.11a shows the impact of all possible distributions of the world endowment of capital and labour between the two countries for the three main types of endogenous market equilibria of the multinational model in the base scenario, in which the transport costs are 15 per cent as a proportion of marginal costs and (if the wages in the two countries are equalized) the fixed costs for a multinational firm are 60 per cent higher than for a national firm.

The following observations are evident.

(i) If the two countries are *similar* in size and capital–labour ratio (in the neighbourhood of the centre of the Edgeworth Box), the production equilibrium is dominated by *multinational* firms.

(ii) If the two countries are *different* in size and capital–labour ratio (in the corners of the Edgeworth Box), the production equilibrium is dominated by *national* firms.

(iii) For *intermediate* endowment distributions, the production equilibrium is *mixed*, with both national firms and multinational firms.

All three observations are in striking correspondence with the empirical facts discussed in sections 15.2 and 15.3, namely (i) large foreign direct investment flows between similar developed nations, (ii) virtually no foreign direct investment flows to the small least developed nations, and (iii) moderate investment flows to the Asian NICs and Latin America.

How can we explain these results? As the reader will recall from the description of the structure of the multinational model in section 15.5, the decision to start multinational production, that is set up a second production plant in the other country, depends on the size of the extra fixed plant costs relative to the size of the transport costs. Now suppose that we are close to one of the corners of the Edgeworth Box, that is either (*a*) the endowment ratio is very different between the two countries, or (*b*) one country is very small and the other country is very large:

(a) If the endowment ratio is very different, there is a strong incentive for Heckscher–Ohlin type inter-industry trade. The labour-rich country will specialize in the production of the labour intensive manufactures. Since labour is expensive in the capital abundant country it will be too expensive to incur the additional fixed costs of setting up an extra production plant, such that the production equilibrium is characterized by national firms producing manufactures in the labour-abundant country only.

(b) If one of the countries is very small, it is important to realize that there are economies of scale associated with the production of manufactures. This makes the small country unattractive as a home base for production (as it will be impossible to recuperate the fixed costs domestically) and as the basis for a foreign affiliate (the small market implies that the transport costs are fairly low if this market is serviced from abroad). The

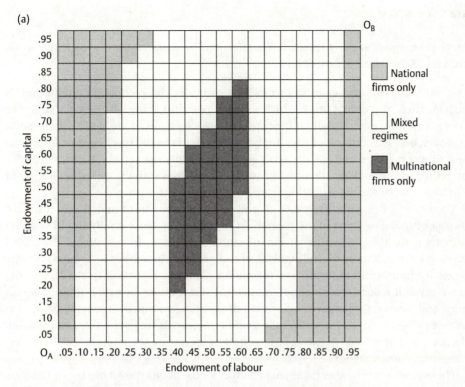

(a)

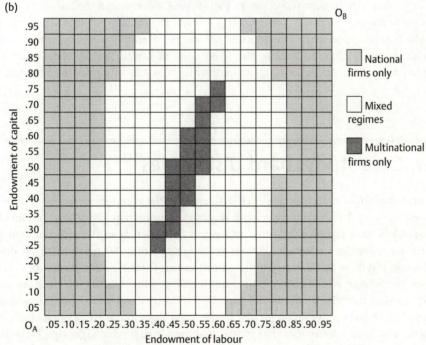

(b)

Fig. 15.11 Characterization of main regimes

Reprinted from Journal of International Economics, 46, Markusen and Venables, *Multinational firms and the new trade theory*, 194–5, copyright (1998), with permission from Elsevier Science.

production equilibrium is therefore characterized by national firms producing manufactures in the large country only.

In both case (*a*) and case (*b*) of different countries the production equilibrium is characterized by national firms, which explains point (ii) above. At the same time, the above reasoning explains why multinationals arise if countries are similar, as in point (i) above, because similar countries imply similar wage rates (no specialization incentive) and similar market size (large transport costs to the other market which can be avoided by setting up a subsidiary abroad). The intermediate cases with the mixed results, point (iii) above, represent the transition from one extreme to the other.

The economic reasoning in cases (*a*) and (*b*) also enables us to understand the main impact of changing some of the parameters in the model. Since economies of scale are important for the production of manufactures, a decrease in the size of the global economy makes it more difficult to recuperate fixed costs investments. As fixed costs are larger for multinational firms than for national firms, a reduction in the size of the economy will reduce the range of endowment distributions in which multinationals arise, and increase the range of endowment distributions in which national firms arise, as shown in Figure 15.11*b*. Growth in the world economy, as we have witnessed for many decades, therefore leads to the opposite effect of increasing the importance and occurrence of multinationals.

The outcome of two other parameter changes for the main types of market equilibria is similar to the situation depicted in Figure 15.11*b*. First, a decrease in the transport costs of 10 per cent makes it relatively less attractive to incur the extra fixed costs of setting up a subsidiary abroad and therefore reduces the range of endowments in which multinationals arise. Second, increasing the fixed costs of multinational firms relative to national firms also reduces the range of endowments in which multinationals arise.

15.7 Case study: hard disk drives[10]

The manufacture of hard disk drives (HDD), an essential component for the computer business, is a very dynamic industry, with revenues of more than $30 billion, product life cycles of less than eighteen months, and prices falling at more than 40 per cent per annum for more than a decade. Fifteen years ago not only 80 per cent of all drives production was done by US firms but the same was true for the assembly activities. As we will see, the pressure of globalization has rapidly changed the structure of doing business, as measured by the value chain, in this high-tech industry dominated by multinationals.

Figure 15.12 gives a simplified picture of the main steps in the HDD value chain, the sequence and range of activities that go into making a final product. Ignoring R&D there are four major steps in the value chain: (i) electronics—this includes semiconductors,

---

[10] This section is based on Brakman, Garretsen, and van Marrewijk (2001).

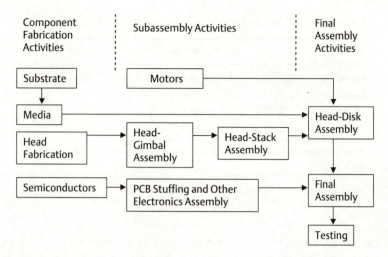

Fig. 15.12 The Hard Disk Drive value chain
Simplified version of Gourevitch *et al.* (2000).

printed circuit boards (PCBs) and their assembly; (ii) heads—devices that read and write the data, which are manufactured in stages with labour-intensive subassembly activities, such as head-gimbal assembly (HGA) and head-stack assembly (HSA); (iii) media—the material on which the information is stored,[11] and (iv) motors—which spin the media with extreme precision.[12] Producers locate the production of the many discrete steps in the value chain around the world for various reasons. The final assembly of the disk, which gives it the 'Made in Singapore' or 'Made in Taiwan' label, is only one, and not necessarily the most important, aspect in this process. As Gourevitch, Bohn, and McKendrick (2000), discussing the structure of Seagate, the world's largest manufacturer of HDDs, put it:

Although Seagate has kept control over almost all production, it has globally dispersed its operations to an extraordinary degree. A single component may be worked on in five countries and cross two oceans while Seagate is building it up through its value chain. Seagate develops new products (and processes) at seven locations in the United States and Singapore. It assembles disk drives in Singapore, Malaysia, Thailand, and China. In heads, the company fabricates its wafers in the United States and Northern Ireland, and cuts them into bars and assembles them into HGAs in Thailand, Malaysia, and the Philippines. It makes media in Singapore and motors in Thailand. It manufactures printed circuit cables in Thailand and assembles the electronics onto printed circuit boards in Indonesia, Malaysia, and Singapore. It is the largest nongovernment employer in Thailand and Singapore.

Table 15.3 gives four different indicators of nationality of production for the HDD industry. The large majority (88.4 per cent per unit of output) of HDDs is made by US

---

[11] According to Gourevitch, Bohn, and McKendrick (2000: 304): 'Typically, aluminum blank substrates are nickel-plated and polished before the platters are sputtered and finished. As with heads, media are a very high-technology aspect of HDD production.'

[12] The Japanese Nippon Densan company has about a 75 per cent worldwide market share in motors.

Table 15.3 Hard Disk Drives; indicators of nationality of production

Measure[a]	USA	Japan	SE Asia	Other Asia	Europe	Other
Nationality of firm	88.4	9.4	0.0	2.2	0.0	0.0
Final assembly	4.6	15.5	64.2	5.7	10.0	0.0
Employment	19.3	8.3	44.0	17.1	4.7	6.5
Wages paid	39.5	29.7	12.9	3.3	8.5	6.1

Source: Gourevitch et al. (2000, table 2) (data for 1995). All numbers as percentage of world total.
[a]Nationality of firm (% of unit output); location of final assembly; employment in value chain; and wages paid in value chain, respectively.

firms. But in sharp contrast to fifteen years ago, only 4.6 per cent of the final assembly of HDDs is done in the USA. Most final assembly of disks now takes place in SE Asia (64.2 per cent), which means the bulk of employment is in SE Asia (44 per cent), rather than in the USA (19.3 per cent), although the value of wages paid is much higher in the USA (39.5 per cent) than in SE Asia (12.9 per cent). Essentially, the HDD industry currently has two concentration clusters. The first is Silicon Valley in the USA, with a substantial share of research, design, development, marketing, and management (with a smaller counterpart in Japan). The second is in South-East Asia, which dominates final assembly, most labour-intensive subassemblies, and low-tech components, such as baseplates.

15.8 Conclusions

Multinational firms, with increasing shares in world production, investment, and trade flows, represent the most visible part of the 'globalization' phenomenon. The largest multinational firms are established in the OECD countries, with a concentration in certain sectors (electronics, petroleum, automotive, and chemical). Most foreign direct investment (FDI) arises from (majority) acquisitions, rather than from greenfield investments or mergers. Most FDI is horizontal, that is within the same industry, rather than vertical or conglomerate. Moreover, most FDI is from OECD countries to OECD countries, with Western Europe and Japan as the largest net sources and Latin America and Other Asia (non-NICs) as the largest net destinations (notably China). The OLI framework argues that a firm must have ownership, location, and internalization advantages before deciding to become a multinational. Empirical research finds that multinationals are R&D intensive, have a high value of intangible assets, produce differentiated goods, and make new or complex products.

An important accomplishment of the modern general equilibrium models of multi-nationals is the ability to determine the market structure endogenously, that is the existence and distribution of national and multinational firms is determined by the production functions and the distribution of endowments. In general, and in accordance with the stylized facts, multinational firms dominate if countries are more similar, while national firms dominate if countries differ in size or relative factor endowment abundance. The main disadvantage of the modern general equilibrium models of multinationals is the rapidly increasing number of cases to be studied, which sometimes makes it hard to keep a clear overview of the results. When discussing the Hard Disk Drive industry we saw that similar types of activity tend to cluster in certain regions (R&D in Silicon Valley and final assembly in South-East Asia), and that the 'nationality' of the final product depends very much on the used indicator.

Chapter 16

New Goods, Growth, and Development

Objectives/key terms

New goods	Variety/quality
Kaldor's stylized facts	Neoclassical growth model
Solow residual	Endogenous growth model
Discount rate	Geography experiment

The stylized facts of economic growth, with ever increasing welfare levels, cannot adequately be explained by the neoclassical growth model. Focusing instead on the importance of new goods (variety/quality), we stress the role of the profit-seeking entrepreneur for dynamic innovations. The geography approach may be useful in explaining the localization of and large swings in economic prosperity.

16.1 Introduction

After my alarm clock woke me up this morning, I made breakfast in the microwave oven. While driving to work in my car I called my wife with my mobile phone to remind her to buy Madonna's new compact disc. As soon as I arrived at work, I turned on the electric light and my computer, eager to check for new e-mails.

You probably didn't notice anything peculiar in the above three sentences, although you may have been wondering what a description of my morning activities is doing in a book on international economics. Two hundred years ago, however, the first three sentences would have been utter nonsense for everybody, even for a well-educated person. He or she would not know what an alarm clock is, or a microwave oven, nor be familiar with a car, a mobile phone, a compact disc, electric light, a computer, or e-mail. In fact, someone living one hundred years ago, rather than two hundred, would also have been unaware of the above mentioned goods and services, with the exception perhaps of cars and electric light. Indeed, come to think of it, I myself could not have imagined twenty

Fig. 16.1 Paul Romer (1955–)

After studying mathematics, physics, and economics at the University of Chicago, where he received his Ph.D. in economics, Romer worked at Rochester, Chicago, and Berkeley, before settling at Stanford University. He was the instigator and most important developer of 'endogenous growth theory', which seeks to better understand the economic forces leading to innovation and improvements in standards of living. It all started with Romer's 'Increasing Returns and Long Run Growth', published in the *Journal of Political Economy* in 1986. His research in this area culminated in 'Endogenous Technological Change', published in the same journal in 1990. We should also mention his 1994 work 'New goods, old theory, and the welfare costs of trade restrictions' on the difficulty of comprehending, appreciating, and measuring the importance of *not* introducing new goods and services in an economy, published in the *Journal of Development Economics*.

years ago that I would be writing these words on a portable computer, that I would be able to reach my family with my mobile phone while walking around virtually anywhere in Europe, or that I would work together with other economists in Holland, Cyprus, Italy, Luxembourg, Poland, England, and the United States by sending files back and forth as e-mail attachments.

Our lives have drastically changed over the past 200 years, 100 years, or even twenty years. It is much more comfortable than it has ever been in the past. We are able to do things (watch television, play laser tag games), visit places (Hawaii, the Kilimanjaro, the moon), and see things (even molecules, using a scanning tunnelling microscope) that were unheard of before. The quality of our lives has improved, in short, not only because we are now able to produce and consume *more* goods and services (larger houses, bigger cars, more hamburgers), but also, and probably more importantly, because we are now able to produce and consume entirely *new* goods and services, which better fit our preferences, or enable us to fulfil hitherto hidden needs and desires. All of this is an ongoing process. We can thus rest assured that only twenty years from now, we will have witnessed the birth of yet another large range of unknown, fascinating, useful, or otherwise interesting and worthwhile new goods and services, provided we last that long.

If new goods and services are so important for raising the standard of living and improving our well-being, the issues, problems, and policies affecting the creation and introduction of new goods and services will, of course, have been intensively and exhaustively analysed within the economic paradigm. Well . . . no, not exactly. These issues have, in fact, received only limited attention for a long time, with the noteworthy exceptions of Young (1928) and Schumpeter (1934). The main reason is probably, as pointed out by Paul Romer (1994: 9), the fact that:

Once we admit that there is room for newness—that there are vastly more conceivable possibilities than realized outcomes—we must confront the fact that there is no special logic behind the world we inhabit, no particular justification for why things are the way they are. Any number of arbitrarily small perturbations along the way could have made the world as we know it turn out very differently.

The issue is illustrated in Figure 16.2. Suppose the domestic production possibility frontier is given by the shaded area in Figure 16.2, and we have to decide whether it is better for the economy to produce at point A or at point B. The problem of

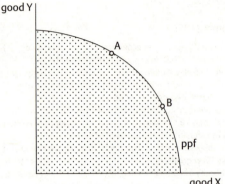

good X   **Fig. 16.2** A complete world

acknowledging the importance of new goods starts exactly at the first word of the previous sentence: 'suppose'. As soon as we do that, and as soon as we draw a production possibility frontier, as we do in Figure 16.2, we already presuppose that both good X and good Y already exist, that is they have been invented and it is possible to produce them. The large majority of economic analysis focuses on efficiency and optimality considerations within this framework. This leads, of course, to important insights and policy prescriptions. What if, instead, good Y has not yet been invented and is not actually produced? This drastically changes the questions we must try to answer. Why has good Y not been invented? At what cost could it be invented and introduced? What are the gains for an individual firm and for society as a whole of inventing, producing, and introducing good Y? The starting point of the analysis is, therefore, supposing not that something exists, but that it does not. We return to this in the next chapter.

16.2 **Modelling new goods**

What is a new good? Well, if we say it is something that was not there before, any production activity undertaken by producers results in new goods. If the baker takes the loaves out of the oven, he has produced new goods. If I were to buy a Big Mac at McDonald's, it would also be classified as a new good. Clearly, this is not what we have in mind when we are talking of new goods, although at some point in time both examples could have been classified as such; the bread I buy (called 'Waldkorn') did not exist twenty years ago, and the Big Mac was invented by Jim Delligatti in 1968. Let's say a new good is something that was not there before, which substantially deviates from any other good or service ever produced before.

Where does this leave us? Necessarily in a grey area. Mobile telephones are fairly new goods (although pre-dated by their bulkier ancestors for a longer time than you might think). In connection with an enormous antenna network, mobile phones are able to deliver services previously unavailable. You would probably also classify digital versatile disks (DVDs) and DVD players as fairly new goods. But are they? DVDs enable you to enjoy a movie on your television at home any time you want. But isn't that service already provided by VCRs, which also allow you to easily tape a movie?[1] No, a DVD fan might say, the services of DVDs were not already provided by VCRs because a VCR cannot deliver the same clear image and high-quality sound as a DVD, which makes DVDs a new good. We do not want to go too deeply into this type of discussion, but it is at least clear that there are essentially two types of new goods. First, there are new goods which deliver (consumer) services which were previously unavailable, such as the ability to fly, to talk on a mobile phone, to play a computer game, etc. We have already called such new goods 'varieties' in Chapter 10. Second, there are new goods which deliver similar (consumer) services as before, but of a better quality, such as the introduction of colour television instead of black and white, the introduction of compact discs instead of the LP record, a more comfortable house because of better insulation, etc. We will call such new goods 'quality' improvements.

The variety approach

How do we model the introduction of new goods? Based on our classification, there are two possible roads to follow, namely the modelling of the introduction of new varieties and the modelling of quality improvements. We have seen the variety approach already in Chapter 10. The essence of the variety approach is based on the Dixit–Stiglitz specification by the term N, indicating the number of varieties available on the market. In the Krugman model of Chapter 10 and the Ethier interpretation of section 10.8, the number of varieties increases if the extent of the market increases.

The Krugman and Ethier variety approach is illustrated in Figure 16.3. At time $t = 0$ the economy is in autarky and $N_{t=0}$ varieties are available to the consumers (or the final goods producers if the varieties are intermediate goods). At time $t = 1$ the economy is engaged more actively in international trade, which increases the extent of the market and therefore increases the number of available varieties to $N_{t=1}$. The variety approach is also used in a more dynamic setting of endogenous growth, in which case the number of available varieties may increase either as a result of an increase in the extent of the market, or as a result of active R&D efforts by firms to invent and introduce new varieties. In the latter case, Figure 16.3 depicts the evolution of the economy over time even in a stagnant population, see Romer (1990) and Grossman and Helpman (1991a).

The quality approach

The accumulated impact of quality improvements can be enormous. Take, for example, automobile production. Cars have been around for more than 100 years. They first became a widely available popular means of transportation in the United States in 1908 when Henry Ford started building the model T. Now millions of cars are produced and

---

[1] I know there are DVD players available that do this too, but they are still relatively expensive.

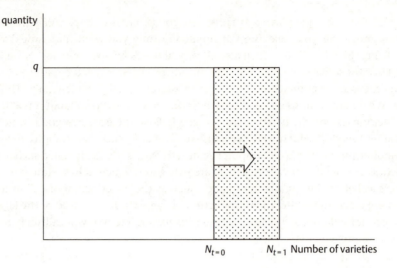

Fig. 16.3 New goods and variety

sold worldwide, the main markets being Japan, Europe, and America. To many people, cars have therefore been available for decades. One could argue that cars today deliver similar services (transportation) as cars did forty years ago. On the other hand, cars today are of so much better quality and deliver so much more power, comfort, safety, and pleasure, that they are not at all comparable to the cars of forty years ago. Most cars now have safety glass, anti-lock breaks, power steering, airbags, better fuel efficiency, more comfortable seats, and even navigational systems to help you find your way in a strange city. Indeed, it is no exaggeration to conclude that the most expensive Rolls-Royce available on the market forty years ago, which only the happy few could afford, delivers worse transportation comfort and safety than the Volkswagen Golf does today, which more than half the population of the developed nations can afford.[2] All of this as a result of gradual improvements in quality.

The modelling of quality improvements is more complicated than the modelling of increases in product variety. Pioneering work was performed by Gene Grossman and Elhanan Helpman (1991a, 1991b) and Philippe Aghion and Peter Howitt (1992). The general modelling strategy, known as the 'quality ladder' approach, is illustrated in Figure 16.4, where we distinguish between sixteen different varieties. Since we are concerned with quality improvements, the number of varieties will remain fixed. All goods can be produced at different quality levels. An increase in the quality level, as measured on the vertical axis in Figure 16.4, is able to better fulfil a consumer's preferences for the same quantity of output, or leads to higher productivity for the same quantity of output if it is an intermediate good.

---

[2] Driving a 40-year-old Rolls-Royce will give you other types of enjoyment than driving a brand new Volkswagen Golf.

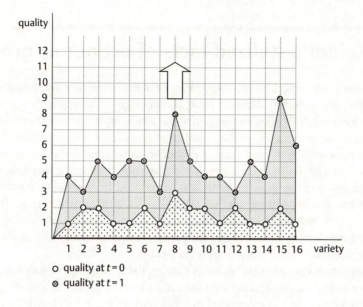

Fig. 16.4 Quality ladders

Increases in the quality level are the result of Research and Development efforts by competing firms, trying to improve upon the current state-of-the-art technology. If a firm is successful in developing a quality improvement, this leads to a discrete increase in the quality level, which is therefore measured in integers {1, 2, 3, ...} in Figure 16.4. A successful innovation allows the firm to temporarily drive its competitors out of the market and earn monopoly profits, until the firm itself is driven out of the market by the next successful innovator.

The open dots in Figure 16.4 illustrate the state-of-the-art technology at time $t=0$. Variety number 8 is produced initially at the highest quality level ($q=3$). The shaded dots in Figure 16.4 illustrate the state-of-the-art technology at time $t=1$. As drawn, all varieties have improved in quality, indicating that the R&D efforts led to successful innovations for all products. Variety number 8 has increased in quality from $q=3$ to $q=8$. Within the structure of this model, this indicates that there have been five successful innovations for variety 8 between time $t=0$ and $t=1$. Innovators in sectors number 2 and 12 have been less successful in that time period, since the quality improved only by one step in those two sectors. Most successful innovations have occurred in sector 15, where quality improved from $q=2$ to $q=9$, indicating seven successful innovations.

The R&D efforts in this approach are driven by the prospect of (temporarily) earning monopoly profits. Note that we discussed two distinct ways of modelling new goods, the variety approach and the quality approach. However, since both approaches lead to very similar economic outcomes, as clearly demonstrated by Grossman and Helpman (1991a), and the quality approach is analytically more complicated than the variety approach, we focus on the variety approach in the endogenous growth model of section 16.6. First, however, we turn to dynamics, empirics, and the neoclassical growth model.

16.3 Kaldor's stylized facts of economic growth

After the discussion above on the importance of introducing new goods and services in an economy, an inherently dynamic issue, it is appropriate to explicitly investigate the economic forces underlying the evolution of the prosperity of nations. As we will see, the analysis of economic growth and international economics is closely linked. The neo-classical economic growth model uses a production structure similar to the neoclassical trade model of Part II. To overcome some of the shortcomings of neoclassical growth theory, the endogenous growth model was introduced in the 1980s, shortly after the arrival of the first new trade models, and using a similar structure as in Part III. Throughout this chapter, we present the most important empirical facts of economic growth and development, indicating how particular economic models may be useful in explaining these facts, and where support is lacking.

In an important contribution Nicholas Kaldor (1961) suggests the following 'stylized facts' of economic change and development in capitalist societies as a starting point for the construction of theoretical models (see also Burmeister and Dobell 1970: 65).[3]

1. The continued growth in the aggregate volume of production and in the productivity of labour at a steady trend rate.

2. A continued increase in the amount of capital per worker.

3. A steady rate of profit on capital.

4. Steady capital–output ratios over long periods.

5. A steady investment coefficient, and a steady share of profits and wages.

Two of these stylized facts are illustrated in Figure 16.5 for the USA. The first, and most striking, fact is the steady trend rate increase in per capita output. Since Figure 16.5a uses a (natural) logarithmic scale, the slope of the income graph represents the growth rate of the economy, see Chapter 16 tools. Over a longer time period, the slope of the income graph for the USA is indeed surprisingly steady. Using the Maddison data of Table 16.1 below, the compounded per capita growth rate for the USA in the period 1870–1990 has been 1.75 per cent. Applying a simple rule of thumb, see again Chapter 16 tools, this implies a doubling in per capita output every $70/1.75 - 40$ years. On the remarkable stability of the American growth in output per capita Charles Jones (1995: 497) remarked:

an economist living in the year 1929 . . . 'fits a simple linear trend to the natural log of per capita GDP for the United States from 1880 to 1929 in an attempt to forecast per capita GDP today, say in 1987. How far off would the prediction be?' . . . the prediction is off by only about 5 percent.

Figure 16.5b shows part of Kaldor's stylized fact number 5 by depicting gross investment as a percentage of income. Arguing that the investment rate is steady, as Kaldor does, may

---

[3] Kaldor mentions a sixth stylized fact, see below.

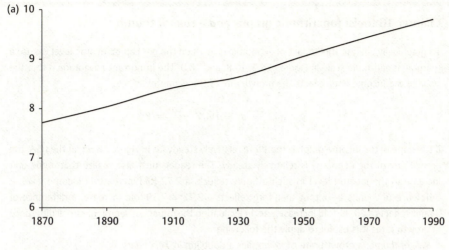

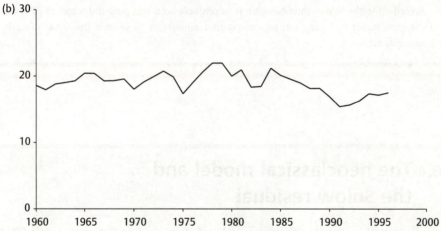

Fig. 16.5 Income and investment in the USA. (a) USA GDP per capita, 1985 US $, logarithmic scale, (b) USA, gross investment (% of GDP)
Source: Table 16.1 and World Bank Development Indicators CD-ROM, 1999.

be pushing it, but it is clear that over a longer time period there is no trend up or down in the relative investment level, but only fluctuations around the average of 19 per cent.

Kaldor's other stylized facts are clearly related. If the investment level as a percentage of income is roughly steady, which must of course be driven by a fairly steady rate of profit, we are not surprised to find a steady capital–output ratio, such that capital per worker and output per worker will be rising over time. Section 16.5 will review some more evidence.

Chapter 16 tools: logarithmic graphs and a rule of thumb

To graphically analyse the impact of economic growth on the per capita income level we use a (natural) logarithmic scale in Figures 16.5, 16.8, and 16.9. The important advantage is that the *slope* of the income line reflects the *growth rate* of the economy, since:

$$y \equiv \ln(Y) \Rightarrow dy = d\ln(Y) = \frac{dY}{Y} \equiv \tilde{Y}$$

If the slope of the income graph is therefore relatively steady, as in Figure 16.5a for the USA, the *growth rate* of the economy is relatively steady. The reader must also realize that a one-unit increase in the income level in such a figure reflects a 2.72-fold increase in income level. A difference of 2 units in output therefore reflects a $2.72^2 = 7.39$-fold increase, a difference of 3 units reflects a 20.09-fold increase, etc. In evaluating the impact of seemingly small difference in growth rates it is useful to apply the following

Rule of thumb: a growth rate of x% implies a doubling in 70/x years.

According to the rule of thumb, which is surprisingly accurate, output doubles in 70 years if the growth rate is 1 per cent, whereas output doubles in 35 years if the growth rate is 2 per cent, etc.

16.4 The neoclassical model and the Solow residual

The neoclassical model of economic growth was developed by Robert Solow (1956), for which he received the Nobel prize. It can, with some difficulty, explain Kaldor's stylized facts. The starting point of the analysis is a neoclassical aggregate production function, with constant returns to scale and the possibility to substitute between two factors of production, capital K and labour L, to produce output Y.

$$(16.1) \qquad Y_t = AK_t^\alpha L_t^{1-\alpha}$$

Increases in the output level can therefore be explained through an increase in one of the two factors of production. The capital stock increases through gross investment I, and decreases due to depreciation of capital μK, where μ is the rate of depreciation. The number of available labourers increases through the (exogenous) growth rate of the population n. If we let a sub-index t denote the time period, we therefore get:

$$(16.2) \qquad K_{t+1} - K_t = I_t - \mu K_t; \quad L_{t+1} - L_t = nL_t$$

Entrepreneurs will, of course, invest in new capital only if it is profitable to do so. Frank Ramsey (1928) provides pioneering work in this area, and is therefore co-founder of the neoclassical growth model. We can, however, significantly simplify the analysis by positing, in accordance with stylized fact number 5, that the economic agents invest a constant fraction s of income into new capital goods, that is $I_t = sY_t$. This simple framework suffices to show that the capital–labour ratio $k \equiv K/L$ evolves over time to a constant steady state rate, see Technical Note 16.1, given by

$$(16.3) \qquad\qquad sAk_t^\alpha = (\mu + n)k_t$$

The left-hand side of equation (16.3) represents the increase in the capital–labour ratio through gross investments, which depend on the savings rate s and the per capita output level AK^α. It is a concave function, as illustrated in Figure 16.6, which reflects the decreasing marginal product of capital if more capital is used for a given level of labour. The right-hand side of equation (16.3) represents the required investment level to keep the capital–labour ratio constant, $(\mu + n)k$, by compensating for the rate of depreciation μk and the increase in labour nk. It is a linear function. The capital–labour ratio will increase if the investments are larger than what is required to keep the capital–labour ratio constant. This is illustrated for $k = 4$ in Figure 16.6, where the investment level at point G is larger than what is required to compensate for depreciation and labour force growth at point F, thus leading to an increase in the capital–labour ratio. The economy will evolve over time to the steady state equilibrium point E.

Can the model sketched so far explain Kaldor's stylized facts? No, it cannot. The main difficulty is the fact that the economy evolves over time to a constant capital–labour ratio and a constant level of output per worker. To allow for an *increasing* level of output per capita, the neoclassical growth model imposes *exogenous* technological change. The easiest way to do this is by allowing the productivity constant A in equation (16.1) to increase over time, and thus be time dependent (A_t). Changing equation (16.1) accordingly and writing

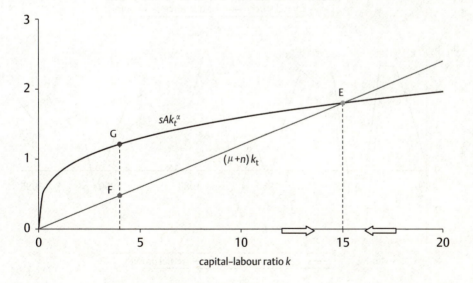

Fig. 16.6 Steady state equilibrium in the neoclassical growth model. Parameters: $A = 4$, $\alpha = 0.3$, $s = 0.2$, $\mu = 0.1$, $n = 0.02$.

the result in relative changes, see Chapter 5, gives

$$\tilde{Y}_t = \underbrace{\tilde{A}_t}_{\substack{\text{technical} \\ \text{change}}} + \underbrace{\alpha\tilde{K}_t}_{\substack{\text{capital} \\ \text{increase}}} + \underbrace{(1-\alpha)\tilde{L}_t}_{\substack{\text{labour force} \\ \text{increase}}} \Rightarrow$$

(16.4)

$$\tilde{A}_t = \underbrace{\tilde{Y}_t}_{\substack{\text{to be} \\ \text{explained}}} - \underbrace{[\alpha\tilde{K}_t + (1-\alpha)\tilde{L}_t]}_{\text{'explained'}} = \text{Solow residual}$$

The first part of equation (16.4) shows that increases in output $\tilde{Y}_t$ are the result of investments in capital $\alpha\tilde{K}_t$, changes in the labour force $(1-\alpha)\tilde{L}_t$, and improvements in technology $\tilde{A}_t$. Since improvements in technology are not explained within the model, it is called the Solow residual. It is calculated as given in the second part of equation (16.4).

Figure 16.7 shows the decomposition of economic growth into an 'explained' part from increases in the capital stock and the labour force, and the unexplained part of the Solow

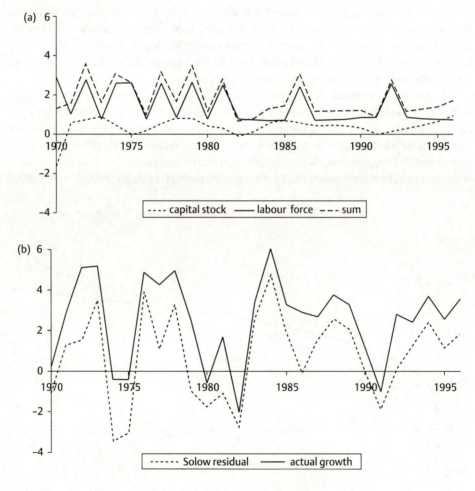

Fig. 16.7 'Explained' growth and Solow residual. (a) USA 'explained' economic growth (%), (b) USA actual growth and Solow residual
Source: World Bank, World Development Indicators CD-ROM, 1999.

residual. As is evident from Figure 16.7b, the Solow residual represents a sizeable part of the actual growth rate (usually more than one-third), which it follows closely. This fact and the fact that it is necessary to impose exogenous technological change to allow the economy to grow, represent the major drawbacks of the neoclassical growth model.

16.5 Empirical pictures

Table 16.1 presents income per capita for a selection of currently developed and currently less developed countries for a longer time period (1870–1990), as pioneered by Angus Maddison (1991). The data are in constant 1985 US $. The evolution of income per capita as given in Table 16.1 is illustrated using a logarithmic scale in Figure 16.8 for the developed countries and in Figure 16.9 for the less developed countries.

As is evident from the various panels of Figure 16.8, the fairly steady growth rate for the USA, as also depicted in Figure 16.5 and in accordance with Kaldor's first stylized fact, is the exception for the currently developed countries rather than the rule. Among the countries experiencing large swings in the speed of economic development are Australia and Austria, with a period of stagnation from 1910 to 1950, Japan and the Netherlands, with a period of stagnation in the interbellum, and Italy and Japan, with a period of very rapid increase after the Second World War. Note the impressive performance of Japan, which managed to maintain per capita real GDP growth rates above 8 per cent for decades.

Studying the panels of Figure 16.8, the reader may be inclined to conclude that there is a convergence of income per capita levels over time, since all graphs move to a narrow range in 1990. That conclusion would be false, however, since the sample of countries depicted in Figure 16.8 are currently developed countries with similar income per capita levels. If we eliminate this 'sample bias', as we should according to De Long (1988), income per capita does not converge over time. The question of convergence or divergence of income per capita over time is rather complex and has resulted in numerous empirical studies.

We get a feel for De Long's argument if we inspect Figure 16.9, which depicts an impressive variation in the development of economic prosperity over time. Argentina, for example, was considerably wealthier in 1900 than Brazil, which has now caught up. Income per capita levels were stagnant in many countries, including Korea and the Philippines from 1910 to 1950, Indonesia, China, India, Pakistan, Thailand, and Taiwan from 1900 to 1950, and, worst of all, Bangladesh which experienced stagnant or declining income per capita levels for almost the entire century. In contrast, Korea, Taiwan, and more recently China have managed to maintain per capita real growth rates above 6 per cent for decades. The impact of such differences is mind-boggling. Korea, for example, was estimated by Maddison to have real per capita GDP in 1900 of $549. Fifty years later, in 1950, there was virtually no change at an income level of $564. Only thirty-seven years later, in 1987, income had exploded to $4,143, a more than seven-fold increase in less than four decades.

Table 16.1 Income per capita levels (1985 US $)

Country	1870	1890	1910	1930	1950	1970	1990
(a) Currently developed countries							
Australia	3,143	3,949	4,615	3,963	5,970	9,747	13,514
Austria	1,442	1,892	2,547	2,776	2,869	7,547	12,976
Belgium	2,009	2,654	3,146	3,855	4,229	8,235	13,320
Canada	1,330	1,846	3,179	3,955	6,112	10,200	17,070
Denmark	1,543	1,944	2,856	4,114	5,227	9,575	14,086
Finland	933	1,130	1,560	2,181	3,481	7,838	14,012
France	1,582	1,955	2,406	3,591	4,176	9,245	14,245
Germany	1,223	1,624	2,256	2,714	3,542	9,257	14,288
Italy	1,216	1,352	1,891	2,366	2,840	7,884	13,215
Japan		842	1,084	1,539	1,620	8,168	16,144
The Netherlands			2,965	4,400	4,708	9,392	13,078
Norway	1,190	1,477	1,875	3,086	4,541	8,335	15,418
Sweden	1,401	1,757	2,509	3,315	5,673	10,707	14,804
Switzerland			2,979	4,511	6,546	12,208	15,650
UK	2,693	3,383	3,891	4,287	5,651	8,994	13,589
USA	2,244	3,101	4,538	5,642	8,605	12,815	18,258

Country	1900	1913	1950	1973	1987
(b) Currently less developed countries					
Argentina	1,284	1,770	2,324	3,713	3,302
Bangladesh	349	371	331	281	375
Brazil	436	521	1,073	2,504	3,417
Chili	956	1,255	2,350	3,309	3,393
China	401	415	338	774	1,748
Colombia	610	801	1,395	2,318	3,027
India	378	399	359	513	662
Indonesia	499	529	484	786	1,200
Korea	549	610	564	1,790	4,143
Mexico	649	822	1,169	2,349	2,667
Pakistan	413	438	390	579	885
Peru	624	819	1,349	2,357	2,380
Philippines	718	985	898	1,400	1,519
Taiwan	434	453	526	2,087	4,744
Thailand	626	652	653	1,343	2,294

Source: Maddison (1991), as reported in Barro and Sala-i-Martin (1995).

The empirical evidence presented in this section leads to two conclusions. First, economic growth rates can differ drastically between nations for long periods of time. To be fair to Kaldor, we must note that he included this as his sixth stylized fact, not mentioned in section 16.3. Second, history provides us with examples of countries with a steady development of income over time, such as the USA and Colombia, and with examples of stagnations and booms, such as Australia and Japan.

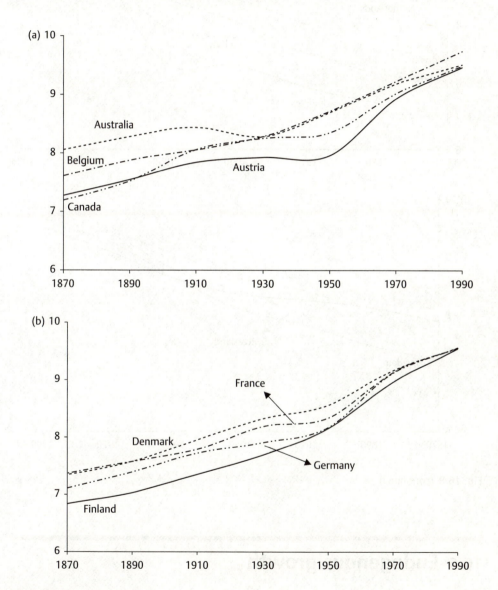

Fig 16.8 Income per capita I, 1985 US $, logarithmic scale
Source: Table 16.1.

(*continued overleaf*)

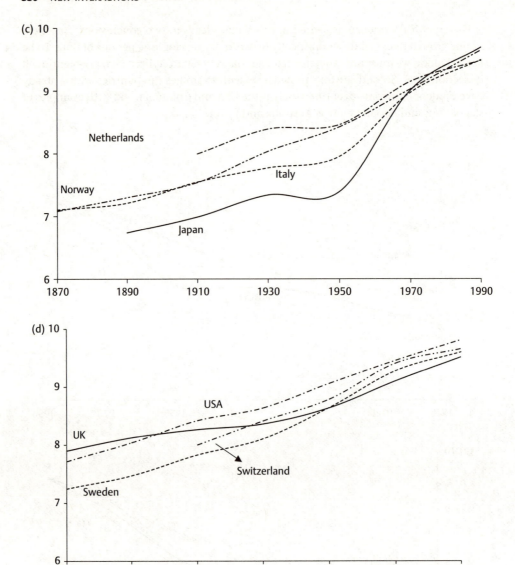

Fig. 16.8 (continued)

16.6 Endogenous growth

The large differences in economic development discussed in section 16.5, the large
Solow residual in empirically explaining economic growth rates as discussed in
section 16.4, and the fact that the neoclassical growth model depends on exogenous

technical change to allow the economy to continue growing, together resulted in the desire to provide an alternative explanation for the dynamic forces underlying the variation in economic growth rates. The search for this alternative explanation, which is now known under the label 'endogenous growth', was led by Paul Romer (1986, 1990). In his review Romer (1994*a*) mentions five basic facts, in addition to Kaldor's

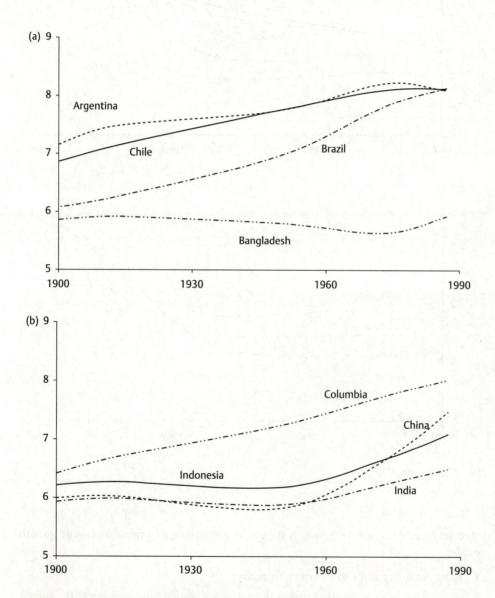

Fig 16.9 Income per capita II, 1985 US $, logarithmic scale
Source: Table 16.1.

(*continued overleaf*)

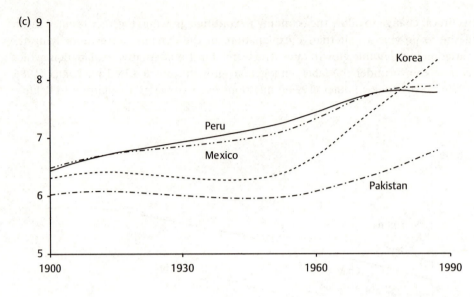

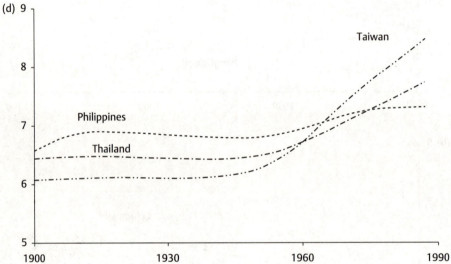

Fig. 16.9 (continued)

stylized facts of section 16.3, which should be accommodated in an economic growth model.

1. There are many firms in a market economy.
2. Discoveries differ from other inputs in that many people can use them at the same time (non-rival goods).
3. It is possible to replicate physical activities.

4. Technological advance comes from things that people do.

5. Many individuals and firms have market power and earn monopoly rents on discoveries.

A good is a rival good if only one person can use it at the same time. I can work on a computer, and so can you. But we cannot work on the same computer at the same time. A computer is therefore a rival good, as is a desk, a chair, a copy machine, etc. Knowledge is, in general, a non-rival good. I can apply the principles of addition, subtraction, or double entry bookkeeping at the same time as you can. The combination of facts 2 (non-rivalness) and 3 (replication) implies that there must be increasing returns to scale. The argument is simple. Let $Y = F(K, L; A)$ be the production function, in which K is capital, L is labour, and A represents the state of technology. If I can in principle replicate the physical production process, there must be constant returns to scale in capital K and labour L; increasing these inputs by the factor $\lambda > 1$ must increase output by the same factor λ, that is $F(\lambda K, \lambda L; A) = \lambda F(K, L; A)$. If an increase in the state of technology or knowledge A, which is a non-rival good, by the same factor λ (however measured) has any positive productive influence on output, there must be increasing returns to scale at the aggregate level: $F(\lambda K, \lambda L; \lambda A) > F(\lambda K, \lambda L; A) = \lambda F(K, L; A)$.

Increasing returns to scale in production of course give rise to imperfect competition (fact 5), though to a limited extent as there are many firms in a market economy (fact 1). Since accumulating knowledge, testing and developing new products, and achieving scientific breakthroughs is costly and takes a lot of effort from talented individuals (fact 4), a proper model of economic growth should allow these efforts to be determined and remunerated within the model. Those, in a nutshell, are the requirements for an endogenous growth model. We will use a discrete version of the canonical model by Grossman and Helpman (1991a, ch. 3), giving it the Ethier (1982) intermediate goods interpretation (see Chapter 10) to explain the basic structure of endogenous growth models. There are N different varieties x_i which are imperfect substitutes of one another, with an elasticity of substitution equal to $\varepsilon \equiv 1/(1 - \rho) > 1$. The varieties are intermediate goods in the production process of one final good Y. If we let the sub-index t denote time and use the fact that the varieties will be produced in identical quantities, we get

$$(16.5) \qquad Y_t = \left(\sum_{i=1}^{N_t} x_{it}^{\rho} \right)^{1/\rho} = N_t^{(1/\rho)-1} \underbrace{[N_t x_t]}_{L_x/m}; \quad x_{it} = x_t \quad \text{for all } i$$

The model uses only labour as a factor of production, and distinguishes between two types of activity, labourers in the production process L_X and labourers in the research and development sector $L_{R\&D}$. In the equilibrium analysed below, the distribution of labourers over these two activities is stable over time. If m is the marginal labour required to produce one unit of a variety of intermediate goods, the total production level of intermediates $N_t x_t$, the term in square brackets in equation (16.5), must be equal to L_X/m. As is clear from (16.5), output Y_t can rise over time if N_t increases. To keep the term $N_t x_t$ constant, the production level per variety x_t must fall. This is illustrated for the three periods t_0, t_1, and t_2 if the term $N_t x_t = 10$ in Figure 16.10.

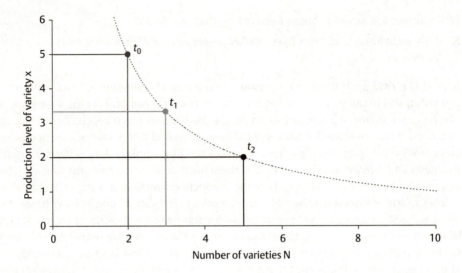

Fig. 16.10 Evolution of N_t and x_t over time

We assume that the working population is constant, that is $L_t = L$ for all t, and use the wage rate as numéraire, $W_t = 1$ for all t. This brings several simplifications. First, the income level in the economy is constant, because entry and exit in the research and development sector will ensure that (excess) profits are zero and the wage bill is constant, such that the income level is $W_t L_t = L$ for all t. Second, since the wage rate is constant the price charged for a particular variety is also constant (use the optimal pricing rule of Chapter 9 to get: $p_t = mW_t/\rho = m/\rho$ for all t). Since the entrepreneur charges a higher price than the marginal costs of production, she earns an operating profit. Technical Note 16.2 shows that this operating profit π_t in period t is inversely related to the number N_t of varieties on the market as follows.

$$(16.6) \qquad \pi_t = (1 - \rho) \frac{L}{N_t}$$

Equation (16.6) clearly demonstrates the economic forces behind an endogenous growth model. A producer who has invented and patented a new variety of intermediate goods is able to derive an operating profit from the production of those goods by asking a higher price than marginal costs. These profits present a clear incentive to engage in R&D activities for inventing and developing new varieties. The profits are eroded in two ways.

- *Future* profits are evaluated using a discount rate θ, see Box 16.1. The higher the discount rate, the lower the present value of all future discounted profits, and therefore the smaller the incentive to invest in R&D.

- An increase in the number of varieties N_t increases competition and erodes future profits, see equation (16.6). If g is the growth rate of the number of varieties, which will be constant in this model, an increase in g erodes future profits faster and therefore, just like an increase in the discount rate θ, reduces the incentive to invest in R&D.

Box 16.1 **Discounting the future**

Consumers care not only about current consumption levels, but also about future consumption levels. This is important to determine their savings decisions, that is the supply of funds which can be used by firms to finance investment decisions. To reflect the preference for current consumption by consumers, and take uncertainty about future developments into account, economic growth models assume that the agents value future consumption using the discount rate $\theta > 0$. Consumption t periods from now is then 'discounted' by the factor $[1/(1+\theta)]^t$. In most models, as here, the discount rate is equal to the interest rate. Suppose we take into consideration only three periods, in which profits are 10 in each period. Total discounted profits if the discount rate $\theta = 0.1$ are:

$$\left(\frac{1}{1.1}\right)^0 10 + \left(\frac{1}{1.1}\right)^1 10 + \left(\frac{1}{1.1}\right)^2 10 = 10 + 9.09 + 8.26 = 27.35$$

The weight given today to the profits two periods from today is therefore only 8.26, rather than 10. This effect is stronger if the discount rate rises. If $\theta = 0.2$, we get:

$$\left(\frac{1}{1.2}\right)^0 10 + \left(\frac{1}{1.2}\right)^1 10 + \left(\frac{1}{1.2}\right)^2 10 = 10 + 8.33 + 6.94 = 25.27$$

which shows that profits two periods from now are given a weight of only 6.94, rather than 10. A rise in the discount rate therefore reduces the present value of investments. To conclude, Technical Note 16.3 uses the fact that if the positive constant a is smaller than 1, the term $[1 + a + a^2 + a^3 + \cdots]$ converges to $1/(1-a)$.

The benefits of investing in R&D have to be confronted with the costs of inventing a new variety. Essentially, these investment costs are equivalent to the fixed costs in the intra-industry trade model of Chapter 10. The costs in terms of labour of inventing a new variety in period t are assumed to be F/N_t. Note that the required amount of labour for inventing a new variety falls over time as the number of varieties increases. This represents a knowledge spillover, which makes it less costly to develop new varieties as the technical capabilities and knowledge level of the economy increase. Without these knowledge spillovers, the output level of the economy would eventually stop rising (once it is no longer profitable to invest in new varieties). With the knowledge spillovers, the economy will grow steadily forever, as shown in Technical Note 16.3. The growth rate of the economy is higher if

(i) the labour force is higher (increasing returns to scale ensure that size is important)
(ii) the fixed costs of investment F are lower, and
(iii) the discount rate is lower.

It is important to realize that the brief explanation of the endogenous growth model above has turned the appreciation in the economics profession for monopoly power and imperfect competition around, although not 180 degrees. We used to hammer into our students' heads that monopolies are bad and inefficient, and that imperfect competition should be viewed as a distortion. Once we acknowledge, however, that there are increasing returns to scale at the aggregate level, as explained above, we know the economic equilibrium must be characterized by some form of imperfect competition. If we then also acknowledge that most economic progress derives from conscious and costly investment in research and development, which has to be recuperated somehow, it is only a small step to start to appreciate the fact that successful firms are able to exercise their monopoly power in a market of imperfect competition, thus generating operating profits which recuperates the costly investments in R&D. Without those monopoly profits, the economy would ultimately stop growing. It is the main contribution of Joseph Schumpeter to point out these links.

16.7 An experiment in geographical economics

One important empirical characteristic of economic growth, namely the large swings in economic prosperity (long periods of stagnation or decline, followed by periods of rapid growth), is not explained by either the neoclassical growth model or the endogenous growth model, both of which focus on steady growth of income per capita. Brakman, Garretsen, and van Marrewijk (2001, ch. 10) argue that these large swings are better explained by the geographical economics model of Chapter 14. We illustrate this by briefly discussing a simulation dynamics experiment.

We extend the geographical economics model to twelve cities located, like a clock, at equal distances on a circle. This so-called racetrack economy is discussed in the Study Guide. To allow for the simultaneous existence of economic centres of different size and avoid bang-bang[4] (corner) solutions, we introduce congestion costs, leading to higher production costs as economic activity concentrates in a certain location (for details, see Brakman, Garretsen, and van Marrewijk 2001). We focus attention on the impact of a gradual, but step-wise, fall in the transport costs T (the other parameters of the model will remain fixed), as follows:

1. We set the transport costs at a very high level, namely $T = 3$.
2. We randomly select an initial distribution of manufacturing labour across the twelve cities.
3. Since the initial distribution is not a long-run equilibrium, manufacturing workers migrate to cities with higher real wages until a long-run equilibrium is reached.
4. Given the long-run equilibrium established in step 3, we now give a shock to the system by lowering the transport costs from $T = 3$ to $T = 2.9$.

---

[4] See van Marrewijk and Verbeek (1993).

5. The distribution of manufacturing activity over the twelve cities, which was a long-run equilibrium in 3, will, in general, no longer be an equilibrium after the change in transport costs in 4. This sets in motion a new process of labour migration to cities with higher real wages until a new long-run equilibrium is reached for the new level of transport costs (similar to 3).

6. We continue to shock the system along the lines of 4 and 5 by gradually, but step-wise, lowering transport cost to $T = 2.8$, $T = 2.7$, etc.

The fact that we analyse a twelve-city setting has the advantage that it allows for a much richer structure and more surprising economic interactions than the two-city setting. The disadvantage is, however, that it is more difficult to succinctly present and interpret the results of the simulations. We will therefore concentrate on the degree of agglomeration of economic activity by reporting a widely used empirical measure of industry concentration: the Herfindahl (1950) index, see for example Martin (1994), which is simply defined as the sum of the squared shares of manufacturing in each city. Thus, for example, if there are three cities and all manufacturing is located in one city, the Herfindahl index is: $1^2 + 0^2 + 0^2 = 1$. If manufacturing activity is equally divided over two of the three cities the Herfindahl index is: $0.5^2 + 0.5^2 + 0^2 = 0.5$. If the manufacturing activity is equally divided over all three cities the Herfindahl index is: $0.33^2 + 0.33^2 + 0.33^2 = 0.33$, etc. In general, the Herfindahl index is higher if economic activity is more agglomerated.

During the simulation experiment manufacturing activity is reallocated over the twelve cities 800 times. Figure 16.11 gives an overview of the evolution of the extent of agglomeration, as measured by the Herfindahl index. At each vertical dashed line in Figure 16.11, there has been an exogenous fall in transport costs. Initially, there does not

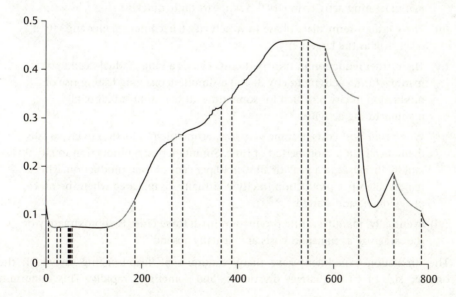

Fig. 16.11 Evolution of agglomeration, the Herfindahl index

appear to be a lot of change in economic structure, say roughly up to reallocation number 130. Further reductions in transport costs start to set in motion a long process of increasing agglomeration of economic activity, reaching a peak at about 0.46, roughly from reallocation 480 to 580. As transportation costs continue to fall, the agglomeration of economic activity starts to decrease again, with a slight revival during the transition process from reallocation 650 to 730, as further discussed below. Eventually, as transport costs are virtually absent (in the end $T = 1.01$) manufacturing activity is roughly equally spread over the twelve cities.

In the initial phase, when transport costs are very high and manufacturing activity is relatively evenly spread, reductions in transport costs have very limited effects (roughly the range from $T = 3.0$ to $T = 2.2$). This is illustrated by the low number of reallocations after a fall in transport costs needed to reach a new long-run equilibrium (sometimes only 1, 2, or 3 reallocations; in one case no reallocation is required). In this phase the Herfindahl index is about 0.075. Note that this is *lower* than what the index would be if manufacturing activity were perfectly evenly spread over the twelve cities (namely 0.083), an indication that the Herfindahl index is not a perfect measure of agglomeration.[5]

The evolution of manufacturing activity during the simulation is shown in Figure 16.12 for a selection of cities (3, 6, and 9). Again, as in Figure 16.11, a vertical dashed line indicates an exogenous change in the transport costs, which sets in motion a new adjustment process to reach a new long-run equilibrium. Figure 16.12 dramatically illustrates the large swings in economic prosperity.

  (i) There is an initial phase, in which all cities are roughly equal in size.

 (ii) Then the process of agglomeration starts. City 6 rapidly attracts a lot of manufacturing activity, while city 3 increases in size more slowly. In contrast, manufacturing activity in city 9 disappears quite quickly.

(iii) There is an intermediate phase in which city 6 becomes smaller and city 3 takes over as the largest city.

(iv) The further reduction in transport costs causes a long gradual decline of manufacturing activity in city 3, and a simultaneous long-lasting rise of production in city 6, which for some time attracts almost half of all manufacturing activity.

 (v) When transport costs become very low, economic production in city 6 falls dramatically in a short period of time. Simultaneously, production in city 9 rapidly increases to a peak of almost 30 per cent of total production. This is remarkable since production in city 9 virtually disappeared when the process of agglomeration started.

(vi) Eventually, manufacturing production in all three cities is approximately of the same size as transport costs are virtually absent.

The simulation experiment gave many examples of 'leap-frogging' in which the economic size of cities changes drastically, and sometimes rapidly. This important

---

[5] Any one-dimensional measure of agglomeration has its disadvantages.

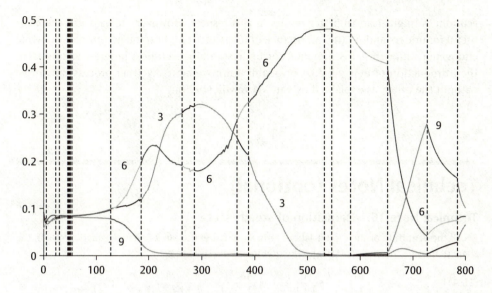

Fig. 16.12 Dynamics of city size; cities 3, 6, and 9

empirical aspect of economic growth cannot be explained using either neoclassical or endogenous growth theories, but is more readily understood in a geographical economics framework.

16.8 **Conclusions**

Most inhabitants of the OECD countries have become accustomed to ever increasing per capita income levels. Historically, however, many countries have experienced long-lasting periods of stagnation as well as periods of extremely rapid increase. These and other stylized facts of economic growth cannot adequately be explained by the neo-classical growth model, which focuses on investment in capital goods as the main engine for growth, not only because it must rely on exogenous technical change to keep the economy growing, but also because of the large Solow residuals. To circumvent these shortcomings, we turn attention to endogenous growth models, in which entrepreneurial innovation in a world characterized by increasing returns to scale and imperfect competition is the main engine for economic growth. Innovation is modelled either as the invention of new goods and services or the development of quality improvements. In both cases Joseph Schumpeter has pointed out the essential role of monopoly profits to entice the entrepreneur to undertake innovative activities. The empirically observed large swings in economic growth cannot be explained by either neoclassical or endogenous growth theories. We argue that an elaboration of the geographical economics might lead to better results in this respect. However, neoclassical theory is useful for understanding the importance of investment and capital accumulation, while endogenous growth is instrumental for understanding technical progress arising from the introduction of new varieties or quality improvements. Neither process can thrive without the other, as explained by van Marrewijk (1999).

Technical Notes (optional)

Technical Note 16.1 Derivation of steady state

Recall the definition of the capital–labour ratio $k = K/L$, use the rate of change equation (16.2), the share of income invested, and the production function (16.1) to get:

$$(16.A1) \qquad k_{t+1} = \frac{K_{t+1}}{L_{t+1}} = \frac{I_t + (1-\mu)K_t}{(1+n)L_t} = \frac{sAK_t^\alpha L_t^{1-\alpha}}{(1+n)L_t} + \frac{1-\mu}{1+n}\frac{K_t}{L_t} = \frac{s}{1+n}Ak_t^\alpha + \frac{1-\mu}{1+n}k_t$$

Now subtract k_t on both sides of the equation and simplify to derive the rate of change of the capital–labour ratio. Finally, put the resulting equation equal to zero to derive the steady-state capital–labour ratio, as given in equation (16.3) of the main text.

$$(16.A2) \qquad k_{t+1} - k_t = \frac{s}{1+n}Ak_t^\alpha - \frac{\mu+n}{1+n}k_t = 0 \quad \Leftrightarrow \quad sAk_t^\alpha = (\mu+n)k_t$$

Technical Note 16.2 Derivation of operating profit

First, note that the operating profit for a variety in period t is the difference between the price p_t charged and the marginal cost mW_t of producing one unit, times the number x_t of goods sold, that is $\pi_t = (p_t - mW_t)x_t$. Using the optimal pricing rule $mW_t = \rho p_t$, this reduces to $\pi_t = (1-\rho)p_t x_t$. The total value of production of manufactures $N_t p_t x_t$ must be equal to the income level L (see the main text), such that $p_t x_t = L/N_t$, which gives equation (16.6) in the main text.

Technical Note 16.3 Derivation of the endogenous growth rate

If the discount rate is θ, see Box 16.1, the growth rate of the number of varieties is g, such that $N_t = N_0(1+g)^t$, and we define $a^{-1} = (1+g)(1+\theta)$, then the present discounted value at time 0 of operating profits from time t using (16.6) is $(1-\rho)La^t/N_0$. The value at time 0 of developing a new variety is the sum of all future profits:

$$(1-\rho)\frac{L}{N_0}[1 + a + a^2 + a^3 + \cdots] = \frac{1-\rho}{1-a}\frac{L}{N_0}$$

As explained in the main text, the cost of inventing a new variety at time 0 is equal to F/N_0. Equilibrium in the R&D sector requires equality of cost and benefits, which gives

$$1 - a = (1-\rho)\frac{L}{F}, \quad \text{or} \quad (1+g) = \frac{F}{(1+\theta)[F - (1-\rho)L]}$$

The growth rate of the economy is therefore higher if (i) the labour force is higher (increasing returns to scale make the size of the economy important), (ii) the fixed costs of investment F are lower, and (iii) the discount rate is lower.

Chapter 17

Applied Trade Policy Modelling

Objectives/key terms

Demand bias

Linder hypothesis

Applied general equilibrium

Dynamic costs of trade restrictions

Armington assumption

Applied partial equilibrium

Dupuit triangle

Case study: China

We briefly discuss some of the problems and procedures of applied trade policy modelling, on both the demand and the supply side of the economy, and in both a partial and a general equilibrium framework. Next, we turn to the problem of measuring the hidden costs of trade restrictions, illustrated by a case study of China.

17.1 Introduction

We have almost come to the end of *International Trade and the World Economy*. In the preceding chapters we presented many theories on international economic phenomena, developed in reaction to and illustrated by empirical information on the world economy. Moreover, we reviewed various implications of these theories for international economic policies. Readers with a practical orientation may wonder at this stage if they have learned enough and are ready to start working on applied trade policy problems at ministries, research institutes, consulting firms, banks, and the like. In this respect, I am afraid we have to be modest and give a dual answer: (i) you have learned a lot, but (ii) there is a lot more to learn before you can start working on applied trade policy:

(i) All the material presented to you in the previous chapters is essential information before you can start working on applied trade policy. We have given a fairly complete, thorough, and up-to-date overview of the most important international economic theories. When working in applied trade policy *all* these elements will come back to you;

perfect competition, constant returns to scale, factor abundance, technology differences, imperfect competition, increasing returns to scale, multinationals, geographic concentration, the international economic order, new goods, development, etc. It is all used and combined in many different ways in applied trade policy.

(ii) After finishing their Ph.D.s Joseph Francois and Kenneth Reinert, the editors of *Applied Methods for Trade Policy Analysis: A Handbook*, started working at the US International Trade Commission (USITC) in Washington DC where they discovered (1997: 3): 'Within a few weeks of our arrival at the USITC, it became apparent that there was a broad set of tools required for our jobs that were rather different from those emphasized in academia.' Since they continue to argue that their 560-page handbook only represents an *introduction* to the tools needed for applied trade policy analysis, it is obvious that the remainder of this chapter cannot adequately cover and teach these tools.

The sequel of this chapter gives a brief overview of the main problems and procedures of applied trade policy modelling, first partial equilibrium and then general equilibrium, and concludes with a discussion on the hidden costs of trade restrictions which are not measured in any applied trade policy model. Before we get started, however, we list the main characteristics of applied trade policy analysis (see Francois and Reinert 1997):

1. *Detailed policy orientation.* This indicates a commitment by the applied researcher to sectoral and institutional details of a policy, and thus the willingness to learn about trade data nomenclatures, input–output relationships, industrial classification schemes, and details on imposed trade and domestic policies (quotas, tariffs, VERs, subsidies, etc.)

2. *Non-local changes in policy parameters from distorted base equilibria.* Theoretical models frequently analyse the impact of small changes starting from an initial non-distorted equilibrium. Applied trade policy models, instead, start from a base equilibrium with the relevant distortions from government policy built into it and analyse the impact of the policy changes actually under consideration.

3. *Accurate and current data.* The outcome of policy experiments in a model depend on the functional forms used to describe technology and agents' behaviour, the base data used to describe the initial equilibrium, and the behavioural elasticities of the functional forms. The analyst must choose the share and elasticity parameters accurately, and use

Fig. 17.1 Léon Walras (1834–1910)

Born in a small town in Normandy, France, Léon Walras studied in Paris and was active in various fields (journalism, clerk at a railway company, director of a bank) before he was appointed as a professor of political economy at the University of Lausanne in 1870. There he finished his work on the two-part *Elements of Pure Economics* (1844–70), which he revised several times. It was largely neglected in his own time, inaccessible as it was to contemporary readers. Using marginal utility theory and maximization, he was the first to write down and solve a multi-equation model of general equilibrium in all markets. For this he now receives wide recognition. As Schumpeter remarked (quoted in Blaug 1986: 264): 'As far as pure theory is concerned, Walras is in my opinion the greatest of all economists.'

current data for 'calibration' (a procedure to ensure that the model fits the data), which usually involves a trade-off between accuracy and currency of data.

4. *Model structure determined by the data*. Since the applied researcher is trying to answer practical questions, the model structure is to a fair extent determined by the data. In a homogeneous-goods, perfect-competition framework, for example, it is hard to explain two-way trade in similar goods. Nonetheless, this is what we observe in the data. Applied researchers therefore sought a practical way of modelling two-way trade, which they found on the demand side of the economy, to which we now turn.

17.2 Demand

In their theories international economists pay, in general, little attention to the demand side of the economy, focusing instead on supply factors, such as differences in technology, endowments, increasing returns to scale, and imperfect competition, for explaining international trade flows. Applied trade policy modellers have long recognized that the demand side plays a crucial role for better understanding empirically observed trade flows, for example to explain the phenomenon of intra-industry trade (two-way trade in identical or similar products). This section briefly discusses three aspects of the demand side: demand bias, the Linder hypothesis, and the Armington assumption.

Demand bias

To derive the Heckscher–Ohlin result in the factor abundance model discussed in Part II of this book we assumed that all consumers in all countries have identical homothetic preferences. Figure 17.2 illustrates what may happen if this assumption is not valid. Consider again the case of Austria and Bolivia, producing food and manufactures using capital and labour as factors of production. If the production of manufactures is capital intensive and Austria is relatively capital abundant, the production possibility frontier for Austria is relatively biased towards the production of manufactures, as explained in Chapter 7 and illustrated in Figure 17.2. Let p_m/p_f be the relative price of manufactures in the international trade equilibrium. Austria then produces at point Pr_A and Bolivia at point Pr_B in Figure 17.2, such that, in accordance with the Rybczynski result, Austria produces relatively more manufactures. This time, however, we assume that Austrian consumers have a demand bias towards the consumption of manufactures, that is at the price ratio p_m/p_f Austrians want to consume relatively much less food than Bolivians. As illustrated in Figure 17.2 with the two coinciding trade triangles, this demand bias can result in Austria *im*porting manufactures and exporting food, despite the fact that Austria produces relatively more manufactures than Bolivia and in contrast to the Heckscher-Ohlin result. Demand bias may therefore also explain the Leontief paradox, see Chapter 7, if American consumers have a preference for capital intensive products.

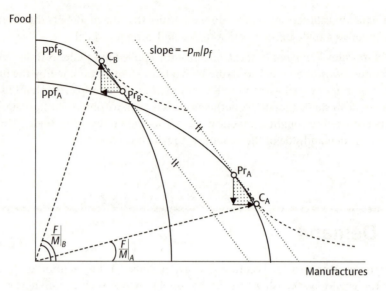

Fig 17.2 Impact of demand bias on international trade

Linder hypothesis

Linder (1961) presents a different explanation for the direction of trade in differentiated manufactures. He argues that producers in each country manufacture goods to satisfy the needs of the consumers in that country. Since not all consumers are alike and some prefer goods with different characteristics, international trade provides a means to obtain these other goods and benefit from a wider variety of goods. This part is similar to Krugman's formalization of the intra-industry trade model explained in Chapter 10. Linder continues, however, by arguing that countries with similar standards of living will consume similar types of goods. The high-income countries, with large amounts of capital per worker, will therefore have similar tastes and largely trade with other high-income countries. This is also what we observe in the data. The other side of the coin of the Linder hypothesis is, of course, that poor countries will consume similar types of goods and trade largely with other poor countries. In contrast, the data show that poor countries tend to trade with rich countries. According to Linder this can be explained by assuming that trade in raw materials and agricultural products is based on the neoclassical factor abundance theory, while Linder's theory applies to trade in differentiated manufactures.

Armington assumption

One of the problems of applied research in international economics is the phenomenon of two-way trade in the same product category, which cannot adequately be explained by perfect competition models with homogeneous goods. Part III of this book, which discusses literature developed in the 1980s and 1990s, has sought an explanation on the supply side of the economy in an imperfectly competitive environment in which each *firm* produces a unique variety of manufactures, which is an imperfect substitute for any other variety of manufactures. Earlier, however, applied research has addressed this problem in a practical way on the demand side of the economy, keeping intact the framework of perfect competition and homogeneous goods, by using the 'Armington (1969) assumption' in which each *country* (or region) produces a unique good. These country goods, say x_1 and x_2 for countries 1 and 2, are imperfect substitutes and combined to produce a composite utility good, say U_1 for country 1, for example as follows:

$$(17.1) \qquad U_1 = \left[\underbrace{a_{11}x_1^\rho}_{\substack{domestic\\good}} + \underbrace{a_{21}x_2^\rho}_{\substack{imported\\good}} \right]^{1/\rho} \quad ; \quad 0 < \rho < 1$$

The approach can easily be extended to accommodate more countries, while the parameter ρ and the constants a_{ji}, which may vary per country, are chosen to reproduce the actual trade flows between countries. Note the similarity between the (CES) Armington assumption and the Ethier interpretation of the Krugman model in Chapter 10.

17.3 **Partial equilibrium models**

The basic disadvantage of partial equilibrium models in applied trade policy modelling, the fact that such models do not take many economic factors into consideration, is simultaneously the most important advantage of these models. If the trade policy question the researcher is trying to address is limited in scope, perhaps concerning one or only a few sectors in a single country and a few policy variables, applied partial equilibrium models allow for a rapid and transparent analysis. The methodology used is quite similar to the theoretical approach explained in Chapter 8. The applied researcher, however, is not interested in the potential theoretical costs of trade restrictions, but in actually estimating the size of these costs for a specific set of policies in a specific set of markets.

To estimate these costs the applied researcher has to calculate the actual size of the Harberger triangles in a market structure for which the observed prices and quantities (produced, imported, and consumed) and the imposed trade restrictions are consistent with the empirically observed data (an example of point (ii) in the introduction to this chapter). She is therefore operative in a 'second-best' world in which the initial equilibrium is influenced by the currently imposed trade restrictions. A simple example is given in Figure 17.3, in which the researcher has to estimate the effect of increasing the imposed tariff rate from the current level t_0 to the newly suggested level t_1 for a small country which cannot influence the price p_0 of the good on the world market. We know from Chapter 8 that the net welfare loss to society of imposing the tariff rate t_0 relative to free trade is equal to the sum of the Harberger triangles C in Figure 17.3. Now note that increasing the tariff rate from t_0 to t_1 not only leads to an extra welfare loss equal to the triangles C in Figure 17.3 but also magnifies the impact of the initial distortion, leading to an additional welfare loss equal to the rectangles B in Figure 17.3. Moreover, when compared to a policy of free trade, the net welfare loss of imposing a tariff t_1 is equal to the sum of triangles A and C and rectangles B.

Before calculating the size of the Harberger triangles, which as we saw do not actually have to be triangles, the researcher has to undertake a few actions. She has to collect data on observed prices and quantities. She has to estimate the slope of the demand and supply functions, perhaps by using estimated elasticities for demand and supply based on econometric studies. She has to accommodate and quantify the type of trade policy imposed on the market, see Laird (1997) for further details. Finally, she has to decide if domestic goods and imported goods are perfect substitutes (as in Figure 17.3) or imperfect substitutes (based on the Armington assumption), see Box 17.1 for an example.

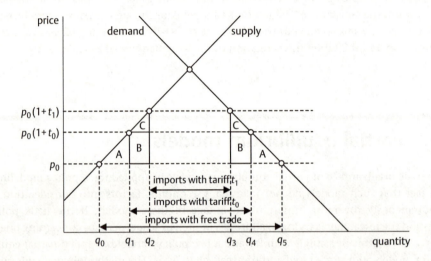

Fig 17.3 Partial equilibrium and second-best

Box 17.1 **US steel protection**

Francois and Hall (1997) use partial equilibrium methods to estimate the impact of US steel protection in 1992. After a period in which the US steel industry threatened to file hundreds of antidumping and countervailing duty complaints, negotiations began in the 1980s on Voluntary Export Restraints (VERs), which led to agreements with nineteen countries and the European Community. By the end of the 1980s, after the dollar had reduced considerably in value, the quotas had largely ceased to be binding. The US president announced in 1989 the phasing out of the VERs by 1992. Renewed search for protection by the US steel industry did not lead to new VERs, but to antidumping and countervailing duties. This episode allows Francois and Hall to compare the transition from bilateral quotas to bilateral tariffs.

The estimated costs of protection for the US steel industry are illustrated in Figure 17.4 for three types of products: cut-to-length steel plate, cold-rolled products, and corrosion resistant products. Depending on the type of trade policy and the methodology used, the sum of the estimated costs varies from $305 million to $877 million. We can draw two main conclusions. First, the costs of protection are higher if imports are imperfect substitutes for domestic products. Compare, for example, the $121 million estimated costs of tariffs for cut-to-length steel plate in the imperfect substitutes case with the $42 million in the perfect substitutes case. The size of these differences depends, of course, crucially on the elasticity of substitution between domestic and imported goods. Second, within each methodology the estimated costs of protection are higher for quotas than for tariffs. Compare, for example, the $73 million estimated costs of quotas for cold-rolled products with the $50 million of tariffs in the perfect substitutes case. These differences arise from the distribution of the tariff equivalent government revenue (see Chapter 8).

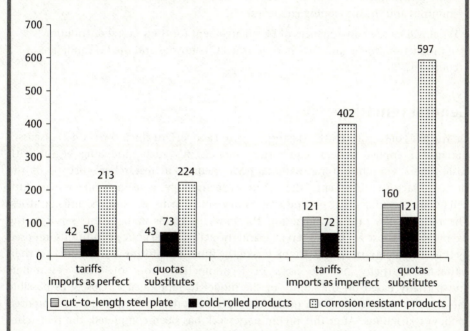

Fig. 17.4 US steel industry, estimated costs of protection
Source: Francois and Hall (1997).

17.4 **General equilibrium models**

If an applied researcher is trying to answer more ambitious questions, involving a range of trade policy measures, a range of sectors, and/or a range of different countries, she will use applied general equilibrium models (AGE; also known as computable general equilibrium models, CGE) which take into consideration the simultaneous effects of all proposed policy measures for all sectors and countries. The use of such models, which in general should give better and more detailed answers to the posed questions, has become much more popular over the last two decades as a result of improved data availability, more readily available computing power, and the development of user-friendly software to use this computing power. Some questions to be answered this way are:

- What is the impact of the formation of the North American Free Trade Area (NAFTA) for wages, employment, and production in Mexico, Canada, and the USA?

- What is the impact of the GATT's Uruguay Round on trade and welfare for the OECD countries and the developing countries?

- What will be the consequences of EU enlargement for the sectoral distribution of production, trade, and GDP both for the EU countries and the EU candidate countries?

General remarks

On the basis of the first (NAFTA) question posed above, Drusilla Brown (1992) discusses the use of applied general equilibrium models. All such modelling begins with basic general equilibrium international trade theory. The researcher must specify the stocks of factor endowments, the nature of technology, consumer preferences, firm behaviour, etc. for a range of products, endowments, firms, consumers, and countries. The model takes into consideration the flows of goods and (factor) services, the payments for those goods and services, and the actual trade policy conditions imposed by the various countries. The parameters of the functional forms in the model are then estimated, partially on the basis of (econometric) work of other researchers and partially based on the ability of the model to reproduce as closely as possible the actually observed data on production, prices, consumption, trade, and imposed (policy) restrictions. After this preliminary work has been completed, the researcher can perform counterfactual experiments by solving the model again after changing one or several policy parameters to determine the economic impact of the policy changes.

The applied models deviate from the theoretical models not only by identifying a large number of sectors and factors of production, but also in some other ways:

- Most models differentiate industry sales by destination, frequently using a constant elasticity of transformation (CET) aggregation procedure, making the production possibility frontier between the exportable variety and the domestic variety concave rather than linear. Increasing returns to scale are usually modelled as a fixed investment in capital and labour before production can begin, with variable costs proportional to output.

- Factor markets are modelled in different ways. Sometimes capital and labour can move freely between sectors within a country, but not between countries. Sometimes a Keynesian approach is used in which the real wage is fixed and employment may vary.

Sometimes the labour supply is fixed, but capital can move freely to or from the rest of the world at an exogenous world rental rate.

• In many cases an Armington-type assumption is used.

• The researcher models the economic structure of some, but not all, countries in the world. Countries that are not explicitly modelled are usually captured with ad hoc excess demand functions depending on relative prices.

The historical development of the applied general equilibrium models has largely coincided with the theoretical developments in Parts II, III, and IV of this book. Brown (1992) distinguishes three main applied general equilibrium policy approaches:

1. *Static models with perfect competition and constant returns to scale.* The first models were based on the neoclassical approach of Part II, static in nature with constant returns to scale and perfect competition, the main difference being the incorporation of the Armington assumption to allow for two-way trade. Estimating the impact of NAFTA is then largely an exercise in calculating trade-creation and trade-diversion effects, although this time taking the factor supply restraints into consideration, see Chapter 13. In evaluating five type (1) studies on the impact of NAFTA, Brown (1992: 56–7) concludes: 'the differentiated product-CRS models show small welfare gains of less than 1 percent of GNP, though the welfare effects are positive for the participating countries.'

2. *Static models with imperfect competition and increasing returns to scale.* The second set of applied general equilibrium models is based on the various approaches discussed in Part III of this book, static in nature, but incorporating imperfect competition and increasing returns to scale. They were developed in part in reaction to points of critique of the applied models in (1) above, in particular with respect to the necessity to incorporate (Armington) country-specific production differentiation to explain two-way trade. As Brown (1992: 41) puts it: 'the fact that it is a convenient assumption does not make it a good assumption for empirical analysis.' She argues that a framework of product differentiation at the firm level, based on increasing returns to scale, is more suitable in many cases, not only because firms will incorporate the elasticity of demand in their pricing decisions, but also to allow greater intersectoral specialization. As discussed in Part II, potential gains from trade then also arise from increased competition, more efficient use of scale economies, productivity increases as a result of increased specialization, and love-of-variety. In evaluating four type (2) studies on the impact of NAFTA, Brown (1992: 57) concludes: 'models that ... incorporate IRS ... show welfare gains for Mexico in the range of 2 to 4 percent.'

3. *Dynamic models.* The third generation of applied general equilibrium models is dynamic in nature and based on the work discussed in Part IV of this book, incorporating labour migration, investments, capital movements, and multinational firms. This can be done by specifying the time path for one of the exogenous variables (as in the geographical economics experiment of section 16.7), by endogenizing the growth of some of the variables of the system (as in the Solow model of section 16.4), or by explicit intertemporal optimization by firms and consumers (as in the endogenous growth

model of section 16.6). In evaluating three type (3) studies on the impact of NAFTA, Brown (1992: 57) concludes: 'The addition of international capital flows suggests... welfare gains for Mexico of 4 to 7 percent. Finally, endogenizing productivity growth produces much larger welfare effects, possibly in the range of 10 percent of Mexican GNP.'

As the above description on the use of applied general equilibrium models suggests, the theoretical developments in international economics, prompted by the search for models that are better able to explain the empirical observations, have gradually led to an increase in the estimated costs of trade restrictions. The earlier constant returns–perfect competition models used for evaluating major policy changes, such as NAFTA or the Uruguay Round (see Box 17.2), estimated the potential gains in a range below 1 per cent of GNP. The second generation of models, based on imperfect competition and increasing returns to scale, estimated the potential gains in a range up to about 4 per cent of GNP. Finally, the third generation of models, taking some dynamic issues into consideration, estimate the potential gains in a range up to 10 per cent of GNP. The estimated costs of trade restrictions has thus gradually increased over time to more substantial importance. Nonetheless, as the rest of this chapter argues, there are good reasons to believe, and there is supporting evidence in favour of this belief, that for all their sophistication these models *still* underestimate the importance of international access through trade, foreign direct investment, capital flows, etc.

Box 17.2 **Assessing the dynamic impact of the Uruguay Round**

Using a Korea-based model, Francois, McDonald, and Nordström (1997) analyse the difference between static and dynamic effects of the GATT's Uruguay Round for six groups of countries: (i) Korea, (ii) Japan, (iii) Other Asia, (iv) North America, (v) Europe, Australia, and New Zealand, and (vi) the Rest of the World. Their analysis is based on three different hypotheses. First, the regional capital stocks are assumed to be fixed. Second, capital can accumulate in each region with a fixed savings rate. Third, capital can accumulate in each region with an endogenous savings rate (in which the real return to capital is equal to the benchmark level in the long run).

In line with the discussion in section 17.4, and as illustrated in Figure 17.5, the estimated impact of the Uruguay Round for the different regions is small if the capital stock is fixed, ranging from 0.1 per cent of GDP for North America, Europe, and the Rest of the World to 2.1 per cent of GDP for Korea. In general, the Uruguay Round turns out to be 'capital friendly', that is the imposed policy changes lead to increased capital accumulation and larger welfare gains for most regions (Japan and North America are the exception). Korea's GDP, for example, is estimated to increase by 2.7 per cent rather than 2.1 per cent. Finally, if we consider a more complete dynamic model, with endogenous determination of savings using the simple closure rule given above, welfare gains are substantially larger for all regions, even for Japan (from 0.4 to 0.9 per cent) and North America (from 0.1 to 0.4 per cent). The most dramatic improvement is for Korea (an estimated increase of 9.2 per cent).

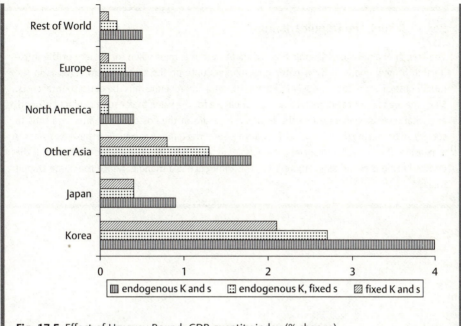

Fig. 17.5 Effect of Uruguay Round, GDP quantity index (% change)
Source: Francois, McDonald, and Nordström (1997); K = capital stock, S = savings rate, Europe includes Australia and New Zealand. Estimated effect for Korea with endogenous K and S is 9.2% (out of range for figure).

17.5 Measuring what is not there: the Dupuit triangle

As far as we know, the first analysis of the value of a new good to society, that is the first attempt to try to measure the value of something that does not yet exist, was provided by the French engineer Jules Dupuit in 1844. As head of an engineering district, he was responsible for building roads, bridges, and canals. He was therefore interested in developing practical rules for determining if a specific project should be built, for which he described a demand curve and a revenue curve, which allowed him to identify an important problem associated with the introduction of new goods.

The main issue is illustrated in Figure 17.6, depicting a downward sloping demand curve for a good, say a bridge, that has not yet been introduced. The vertical axis represents the price to be paid each time the bridge is crossed. If the price is too high (above p_{max}) nobody will use the bridge. If the price is zero, the bridge will be used most intensively at q_{max}. As we know from standard microeconomic theory, the area under the demand curve measures the value of the bridge to the consumers at any given quantity. At a price of 0, for example, the total value of the bridge to consumers is equal to the area $Op_{max}q_{max}$.

Box 17.3 **Tool: the Dupuit triangle**

The French engineer Jules Dupuit tried to measure the surplus value for society of the intro-duction of new goods. If firms enter new markets until profits are driven to zero, as in the monopolistic competition model of Chapter 10, total firm revenue must be equal to total costs. Since the area under the demand curve is a measure for the value to consumers of a new good, and total revenue generated by the firm is a measure of the costs for the firm, and thus to society, of producing this new good if profits are zero, the difference between these two areas is a measure of the surplus to society as a whole generated by introducing the new good. If the demand curve is linear, as in Figure 17.6, this difference is a triangle, hence the name Dupuit triangle.

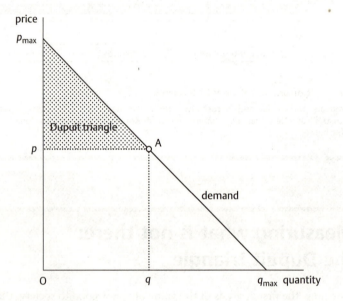

Fig. 17.6 The Dupuit triangle

Suppose, then, that a private company is interested in building this bridge, and evaluates whether or not it is worthwhile to go ahead with the project. In Figure 17.6, we assume that the firm charges price p, resulting in q crossings of the bridge and total revenue pq, equal to the area $OpAq$ in Figure 17.6. How the firm determines the price p it charges for one crossing of the bridge is immaterial for our argument. What is important, is the fact that the total area under the demand curve at q, that is the area $Op_{max}Aq$, is strictly *less* than the revenue generated by the firm from the crossings of the bridge, the area $OpAq$. The difference between the value to consumers and the revenue for the firm, that is the triangle $p_{max}Ap$, represents a welfare gain for which the firm building the bridge is not compensated in terms of revenue. If the firm decides that the total revenue generated by the bridge is not enough to compensate it for the costs of building and maintaining the bridge, for argument's sake because the revenue is exactly equal to the total costs, it will decide not to build the bridge. Paul Romer (1994), who labels $p_{max}Ap$ the Dupuit triangle, then argues that the *welfare loss* to society of *not* building the bridge is equal to the Dupuit triangle in Figure 17.6.

In general, the above reasoning makes clear that there are costs involved, in terms of a welfare loss to society as a whole, of *not* introducing a good on the market. The Dupuit triangle can be interpreted as a measure for this welfare loss.[1] Moreover, it is evident that we cannot rely on market forces to ensure that all new goods which are valuable to society will actually be introduced, because the firm introducing a new good can only appropriate part of the surplus it generates.[2]

17.6 More on the dynamic costs of trade restrictions

In Chapter 8 we analysed the impact of imposing trade restrictions, both in a partial equilibrium framework and in a general equilibrium framework. To calculate the costs of such trade restrictions, we try to estimate the size of the Harberger triangles, see also section 17.3. In general, such estimated costs of trade restrictions are in the neighbourhood of 1 per cent of GDP, or 2–4 per cent of GDP in a framework of imperfect competition and increasing returns to scale, see section 17.4. Despite the fact that this amounts to the sizeable sum of \$290–1,170 *billion* on a global scale in 1997, the costs of trade restrictions appear to be moderate in relative terms. The endogenous growth model of section 16.6 argues that increases in economic welfare arise primarily from developing new varieties and producing quality improvements of existing varieties. As argued in section 17.5, the costs of *not* introducing a new good on the market can be measured by the Dupuit triangle.

Romer (1994b) combines these insights by pointing out that one of the most important consequences of imposing trade restrictions is the fact that they might lead to new goods and services *not* being available on the market, leading to an underestimation of the actual costs of trade restrictions. This is illustrated in Figure 17.7 for a country that does not produce the good in question. Without trade restrictions, the equilibrium is at

---

[1] As a student of mine noted, the Dupuit triangle probably overestimates this loss. If the bridge is not built an alternative means of crossing the river, such as a ferry, will be viable. The ferry will have a similar Dupuit triangle which mitigates the welfare loss of not building the bridge.

[2] Price discrimination cannot solve this problem, as explained in Romer (1994).

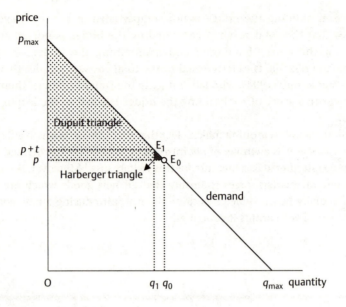

Fig. 17.7 Harberger triangle and Dupuit triangle

point E_0, leading to quantity demanded q_0 at the world price level p. If the country imposes an import tariff t, we should distinguish between two possibilities.

(i) The good is still imported from abroad. The price rises to $p + t$, which leads to a welfare loss for the economy equal to the Harberger triangle in Figure 17.7.

(ii) The good is no longer imported from abroad, perhaps because the foreign producer can no longer recuperate its fixed costs. The welfare loss for the economy is equal to the Dupuit triangle in Figure 17.7.

Romer essentially argues that when we are estimating the costs of trade restrictions we tend to focus our attention almost exclusively on the small Harberger triangles in Figure 17.7, rather than on the large and much more important Dupuit triangles. This practice is understandable, since it is easier to measure the costs of something you can observe (the Harberger triangles) than something that is not there (the Dupuit triangles of the goods and services not introduced on the market).

Using a model quite similar to the framework presented in section 16.6, Romer (1994) illustrates his argument for a small developing economy, say Developia, which does not invent its own capital goods. Instead, those intermediate capital goods and services are invented abroad. After a successful innovation, the foreign inventors face the decision whether or not to introduce the intermediate good on Developia's market, which gives them an operating profit as the price they charge will be higher than the marginal costs of production and transport. They will only introduce the new intermediate good on Developia's market if the operating profits are higher than the fixed costs of introduction, say for setting up a local consulting office. This criterion determines the number of varieties introduced on the market. Romer discusses the impact of 'expected' versus 'unexpected' tariffs for Developia's market, but I prefer to give it the 'static' versus 'dynamic' interpretation of Brakman and van Marrewijk (1996).

Suppose the government of Developia imposes an *ad valorem* tariff τ on the purchases of all foreign goods. The *static* effect of this tariff policy is an increase in price leading to inefficiency and a welfare loss calculated as the sum of all Harberger triangles as illustrated in Figure 17.7. When measured as the percentage reduction in output relative to the output level without tariffs, this leads to a welfare loss of τ^2 per cent in Romer's model.[3] The *dynamic* effect of this tariff policy also takes into consideration the fact that the reduction in operating profits for the foreign entrepreneurs will induce some of them not to introduce the intermediate good on Developia's market. Calculation of the dynamic welfare loss therefore also includes the Dupuit triangles of Figure 17.7. In Romer's model, the dynamic welfare loss is equal to a $2\tau - 2\tau^3 + \tau^4$ per cent reduction in output. Figure 17.8 illustrates the difference between static and dynamic loss. For example, $\tau = 0.2$ if the static welfare loss in output is 4 per cent (at point E_0), while the dynamic welfare loss is 39 per cent (at point E_1)! This suggests a huge underestimate of the costs of trade restrictions using Harberger triangles.

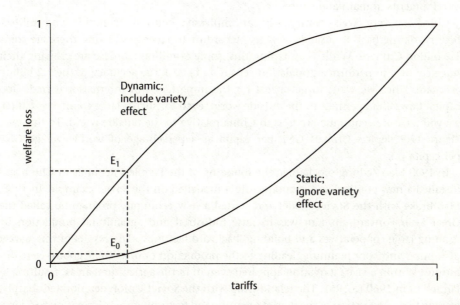

Fig. 17.8 Dynamic costs of trade restrictions

---

[3] For details on these calculations we refer the reader to Romer (1994).

17.7 **China, a case study**

The main difficulty of calculating the dynamic costs of trade restrictions as explained in section 17.6 is the fact that even if you think that the dynamic costs are much more important than the static costs, it is almost impossible to estimate their size. Again, how do you estimate the size of the welfare loss as a result of goods and services that are not introduced using a generally accepted methodology? It is virtually impossible, at least for the moment. Nonetheless, we can provide circumstantial evidence that the dynamic costs are more important than the static costs. My favourite example is the difference in economic development between North Korea and South Korea after the Korean ceasefire in 1953. North Korea isolated itself economically from virtually all outside influences, thus not benefiting from the knowledge increases and inventions of new goods and services in the rest of the world. The result was a stagnant, or slowly deteriorating, North Korean economy for more than five decades, eventually resulting in large famines. The developments in North Korea contrast sharply with those in South Korea, which aggressively focused on expansion on the world market, using knowledge and capital goods from all over the world, leading to an enormous rise in living standards, see Figure 16.9c. Unfortunately, lack of reliable data on the North Korean economy prevents me from going into further detail here.[4] Instead, we will briefly focus attention on the developments in mainland China.

China is a very large country, with an impressive cultural, economic, and military history, dating back thousands of years. According to recent estimates, there are some 1.2 billion Chinese. While I am typing this, some 6 million Chinese are crossing their huge country to perform a population census and check the accuracy of the 1.2 billion estimate. Since we want to get a feel for the importance of international trade and capital flows and openness to the outside world, even for such a large country as China, we will measure economic progress in China relative to the outside world. To this end, Figure 17.9 depicts China's GNP per capita as a percentage of world average GNP per capita.

In 1949 Mao Zedong proclaimed the founding of the People's Republic of China and installed a new political and economic order modelled on the Soviet example. In 1958, Mao broke with the Soviet model and started a new economic programme called the Great Leap Forward. Its aim was to raise industrial and agricultural production by forming large cooperatives and building 'backyard factories'. The results of the market disruption and poor planning, leading to the production of unsaleable goods, were disastrous. Within a year, starvation appeared even in fertile agricultural areas, resulting in famine from 1960 to 1961. The relationship with the Soviet Union deteriorated sharply, leading to the restriction of the flow of scientific and technological information to China, and the withdrawal of all Soviet personnel in 1960. When compared to the world average, the impact of the Great Leap Forward shows up in Figure 17.9 as a deterioration of

---

[4] Similar examples of neighbours with different openness of economic systems, and corresponding differences in economic development are: East versus West Germany, and Thailand versus Myanmar.

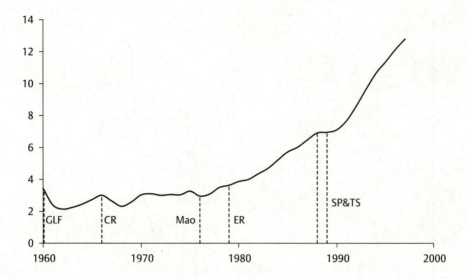

Fig. 17.9 Economic development in China

Source: World Bank, World Development Indicators CD-ROM, 1999; GLF = Great Leap Forward, CR = Cultural Revolution, Mao = Mao's death, ER = Economic Reform, SP&TS = Student Protest & Tianannan Square.

China's living standards from an already low 3.44 per cent in 1960 to an even lower 2.14 per cent in 1962 (a relative decline of 38 per cent!).

In the early 1960s Liu Shaoqi and his protégé Deng Xiaoping took over direction of the party and adopted pragmatic economic policies at odds with Mao's revolutionary vision. In 1966, when the Chinese economy had almost recuperated from the consequences of the Great Leap Forward and Chinese per capita GNP had bounced back to 3.00 per cent of the world average, Mao started the Cultural Revolution, a political attack on the pragmatists who were dragging China back toward capitalism. The Red Guards, radical youth organizations, attacked party and state organizations at all levels. Again, Mao's insightful ideas were disastrous to the Chinese standard of living, which dropped to 2.32 per cent of the world average in 1968, see Figure 17.9 (this time 'only' a relative decline in position of 23 per cent). The Chinese political situation stabilized after some years along complex factional lines, stabilizing the Chinese living standards to slightly above 3 per cent of the world average and leading to the reinstatement of Deng Xiaoping in 1975, who was stripped of all official positions only a year later by the Gang of Four (Mao's wife and three associates).

Mao's death in September 1976 set off a scramble for succession, leading to the arrest of the Gang of Four and the reinstatement of Deng Xiaoping in August of 1977. In a pivotal meeting in December 1978 the new leadership adopted Economic Reform policies to expand rural incentives, encourage enterprise autonomy, reduce central planning, open up to international trade flows with the outside world, establish foreign direct investment in China, and pass new legal codes in June of 1979.

The positive consequences of the Economic Reforms for the Chinese standard of living were enormous, dramatically illustrating the dynamic costs of trade restrictions. The

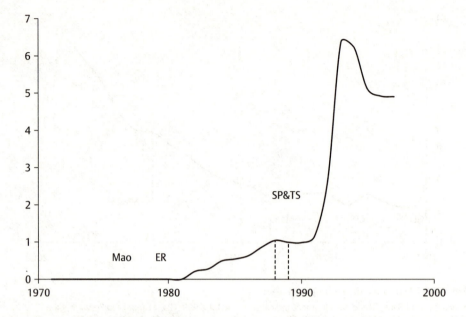

Fig. 17.10 Capital inflows into China net foreign direct investment (% of GNP)
Source: World Bank, World Development Indicators CD-ROM, 1999; GLF = Great Leap Forward, CR = Cultural Revolution, Mao = Mao's death, ER = Economic Reform, SP&TS = Student Protest & Tianannan Square.

policy of openness is illustrated in Figure 17.10 for the net foreign direct investment flows into China as a percentage of GNP. There are no data available prior to 1971, but as illustrated by Figure 17.10 there were *no* foreign direct investments into China from 1971 to 1979 (we can be sure that this also held for a long period preceding 1971). After the Economic Reforms, foreign direct investments into China rose rapidly to a stagnating level of about 1 per cent of GNP in the period 1988–91, followed by a continued rise to a peak of more than 6 per cent of GNP in 1993 and 1994, and stabilizing at around 5 per cent of GNP thereafter (remember that these are percentages of a rapidly increasing GNP level, see Figures 16.9*b* and 17.9).

The period of temporary stagnation in 1988–90 is indicated by the term *Student Protests & Tiananmen Square* in Figures 17.8 and 17.9. At the end of the 1980s party elders feared, in reaction to student demonstrators, that the reform programme was leading to social instability and called for greater centralization of economic controls. The political debate culminated in university students in Beijing camping out at Tiananmen Square to protest against those who would slow reform. Martial law was declared and military force was used against the protesters, leading to hundreds of casualties. Eventually, this only temporarily stopped the reform process as younger, reform-minded leaders began their rise to top positions and Deng Xiaoping renewed his push for a market-oriented economy, as sanctioned by the Party Congress in 1992.

The impact of the economic reform programme, interrupted temporarily by the events surrounding Tiananmen Square, is clearly visible in Figure 17.9. As a percentage of the world average, the Chinese standard of living rose from 3.6 per cent in 1979 to

6.9 per cent in 1988, where the increase was interrupted for a year, to continue rising to 12.8 per cent in 1997 (a relative increase of 250 per cent in eighteen years!). As far as economic prosperity is concerned Deng Xiaoping, who died in 1997, has been extremely important for the Chinese people.

17.8 Conclusions

As explained in the introduction to this chapter, we can only scratch the surface in describing the many issues at stake in applied trade policy modelling, which in general involves the use of accurate and current data, a model structure determined by the data, a detailed policy orientation, and the analysis of non-local changes in policy parameters from distorted base equilibria. Applied researchers have used the demand side of the economy to solve some practical problems in matching models and data, for example by incorporating demand bias, the Linder hypothesis, and the Armington assumption.

If the trade policy question the researcher is trying to address is limited in scope, perhaps concerning one or only a few sectors in a single country and a few policy variables, applied partial equilibrium models, based on estimating the size of the Harberger triangles, allow for a rapid and transparent analysis. If the researcher is trying to answer more ambitious questions, involving a range of trade policy measures, a range of sectors, and/or a range of different countries, she will use applied general equilibrium models which take into consideration the simultaneous effects of all proposed policy measures for all sectors and countries. There are roughly three types of applied general equilibrium models: (1) constant returns and perfect competition, (2) increasing returns and imperfect competition, and (3) dynamic models. In general, the estimated costs of trade restrictions increases as we move from type (1) to type (2), and from type (2) to type (3) models.

We conclude the chapter by arguing that none of the applied general equilibrium models can really measure the importance of international economic contacts through the exchange of goods, capital, foreign direct investment, knowledge, ideas, etc. The main reason is that imposing trade restrictions may result in goods and services *not* being introduced on the market. We use the Dupuit triangle to estimate the costs of goods that are not introduced, which is a tricky procedure even in a theoretical framework. Using a simple model, we show that such costs can be substantial (and much larger than the empirically estimated costs in applied general equilibrium models). A case study of China's recent history gives at least some suggestive·evidence in favour of this view.

Chapter 18

Concluding Remarks

18.1 Introduction

In the preface of this book we stated that the objective is to give a succinct, fairly complete, up-to-date, and thorough introduction to the forces underlying 'real' international economics. In this final chapter of *International Trade and the World Economy* we briefly review the most important results of international economics discussed in the previous chapters, both for international trade and trade policy.

The world economy

Chapter 1 presents basic information on the structure of the world economy, in terms of land area, population, GDP, etc. The differences between countries are large, particularly for per capita incomes. International trade flows, which are increasing faster than world production, are dominated by relatively small European and South-East Asian countries. We emphasized that a surplus on the current account translates into an outflow of capital, and vice versa. We also emphasized that international economists, in trying to explain the empirical observations, value the consistency of a general equilibrium approach, as opposed to the loose ends of a partial equilibrium approach.

18.2 International trade

The four-part organization of the book broadly coincides with four different modelling approaches to explain international trade flows. After reviewing each in turn, we discuss the gains from trade and the type of trade explained by each approach.

Classical technology differences

Chapters 2 and 3 analyse the classical driving forces behind international trade flows: technological differences between nations. If another country can produce a good more cheaply than we ourselves can make it (opportunity costs), it is better to import this good from abroad. To determine a country's strong (export) sectors as well as its terms of trade, only comparative costs are important, not absolute cost differences (which largely determines the welfare level and the wage rate). Comparative advantages are empirically measured using the Balassa index of normalized export shares.

Neoclassical factor abundance

Chapters 4 to 7 analyse the neoclassical incentive for international trade based on differences in relative factor abundance. The production structure uses capital and labour to produce labour-intensive food and capital-intensive manufactures under perfect competition and constant returns to scale. There is a one-to-one connection between the prices of final goods and the rewards to the factors of production, that is if we know the former we can derive the latter, and vice versa. If trade between nations equalizes the prices of food and manufactures, it therefore also equalizes the wage rate and the rental rate (factor price equalization). If the price of labour-intensive food rises, this raises the wage rate and reduces the rental rate. The opposite holds if the price of manufactures rises (Stolper–Samuelson). Moreover, the changes in the factor prices are larger in relative terms than the changes in the final goods prices (magnification effect). Similarly, for given prices of the final goods, an increase in the available amount of capital leads to an increase in the production of (capital intensive) manufactures and a reduction in the production of food. The opposite holds for an increase in the available amount of labour (Rybczynski effect). When combined with neutral (identical and homothetic) pre-ferences, the above implies that under free trade the capital abundant country will export (capital intensive) manufactures (Heckscher–Ohlin).

New trade; imperfect competition and increasing returns to scale

Chapters 9 and 10 discuss the new trade theories, based on imperfect competition and increasing returns to scale. Profit maximizing firms in an imperfectly competitive market charge a mark-up of price over marginal costs, the size of which depends on the price elasticity of demand and on the degree of competition. Perceived differences in elasticity of demand lead to international trade flows, and possibly beneficial 'reciprocal dumping'. Imperfect competition leads to a deviation between the marginal rate of substitution and the marginal rate of transformation, and thus to a sub-optimal outcome. The empirically observed prevalence of intra-industry trade (two-way trade in similar products), mea-sured using the Grubel–Lloyd index, may be explained with the Krugman model, in which each firm produces a unique variety with economies of scale under monopolistic competition.

New interactions; geography, business, and growth

Chapters 14–16 analyse more recently acquired insights derived from combining international economics with other fields of economics. The geographical economics approach blends the factor abundance model (perfect competition and constant returns to scale) and the new trade model (monopolistic competition, increasing returns to scale, and varieties of manufactures) with factor mobility (migration to regions with high real wages) to provide a simple theory of location and agglomeration. This approach explains some empirical observations and regularities, such as Zipf's Law (on the distribution of city sizes) and the gravity equation (on the size and direction of international trade flows). Similarly, the new theories on multinational firms, which are particularly active in the OECD countries and control rising shares in world production, investment, and trade flows, combine imperfect competition and returns to scale with production and strategy approaches from the business literature to endogenously determine the market structures operative in different countries of the world. In accordance with the stylized facts, multinational firms dominate if countries are more similar, while national firms dominate if countries differ in size or relative factor endowments. Chapter 16 combines economic growth theories with different approaches in international economics to explain economic dynamics and development. The neoclassical growth model focuses on investment in capital goods. It exhibits large Solow residuals and must rely on exogenous technical change to keep the economy growing. The endogenous growth models focus on entrepreneurial innovation in a world characterized by increasing returns to scale and imperfect competition. The empirically observed large swings in economic growth may be explained by a dynamic version of the geographical economics model.

Gains from trade

The gains from international trade depend on the structural details of the model in question. In the classical approach, trade is based on differences in technology between nations. If another country can produce a good (relatively) more cheaply than we ourselves can make it, it is better to import this good from abroad. In the neoclassical approach, trade is based on differences in (relative) factor abundance between nations. International trade then leads to efficiency gains by equalizing the marginal rate of substitution for all countries. In the new trade approach, international trade is based on imperfect competition and increasing returns to scale. Trade flows then lead to welfare improvements as a result of increased competition (pro-competitive gains from trade), a better use of scale economies, or an increase in the extent of the market, which raises the number of available varieties (Krugman) or the production level through positive externalities (Ethier).

Types of trade explained

International trade models are designed to explain different types of trade, that is they are usually the result of attempts to better understand empirical observations. Classical and neoclassical trade models were developed to explain inter-industry trade, that is the exchange of different products (for example cloth in exchange for wine). At the time of development of these models, the emphasis was on the production of homogeneous goods by firms with limited market power. Both approaches are therefore better suited to explain trade flows between *dis*similar countries than between similar countries. Empirically, however, the largest trade flows are between similar (high-income) countries, to a considerable extent based on intra-industry trade, that is the exchange of similar products (two-way trade). New trade theories, based on increasing returns to scale and imperfect competition, were developed to explain these phenomena in a time in which product differentiation by firms with considerable market power is becoming more important. More recently still, geographical economics and the theory of multinationals were developed to better understand the location decisions of firms, the rising importance of multinationals, economic agglomeration, and the market structures of countries.

18.3 Trade policy

We distinguish between three types of trade policy, namely (i) standard trade policy based on the classical and neoclassical approaches of Parts I and II, (ii) new trade policy, or strategic trade policy, based on the new trade models of Part III, and (iii) applied trade policy, based on a practical mix of many different theoretical approaches. We review each of these below, with a brief digression into regional integration, to conclude with some remarks on the hidden costs of trade restrictions.

Standard trade policy

Chapter 8 analyses the impact of trade policy on the size of trade flows and the distribution of welfare effects for the classical and neoclassical models. In general, there are both winners and losers of imposing trade restrictions, which makes the demand for protection (lobbying) understandable. Among the winners are protected domestic producers and, in terms of tariff revenue, the government. The main losers are the foreign producers, the domestic consumers, who pay for the increased profits and the tariff revenue, and the country as a whole, in terms of an efficiency loss (Harberger triangles). The main difference between tariffs and quotas rests in the question who receives the tariff-equivalent government revenue. The foreign country can try to reap this benefit by establishing a 'voluntary' export restraint. Imposing a tariff always leads to a net welfare loss for a small country, which cannot influence its terms of trade. Within a neoclassical framework, a large country, which can influence its terms of trade, might benefit from a net welfare gain by imposing an 'optimal' tariff based on its monopoly power. This argument breaks down under a system of retaliation leading to tariff wars, which clarifies the necessity of multilateral trade negotiations.

New trade policy

Chapter 11 analyses the impact of trade policy based on the new trade models with imperfect competition. Tariffs and quantitative restrictions are no longer equivalent. The imposition of tariffs in general leaves the forces of foreign competition intact, albeit at a lower level. This contrasts with the imposition of quantitative restrictions, which more severely restrict the strategic possibilities of foreign firms. Quotas are therefore more restrictive than tariffs, which is one of the main reasons for the World Trade Organization to strive for 'tariffication' (the other being the clarity of the imposed trade restrictions). The so-called strategic trade policy tries to provide a competitive advantage to domestic firms by providing a credible pre-commitment. When evaluating the potential for strategic trade policy we noticed its weaknesses in a general equilibrium setting, the fragility of policy recommendations (type of strategic interactions, who moves first, strategic games, etc.), and most importantly from a practical perspective the enormous informational requirements for accurately implementing such a policy.

Regional integration

We apply the insights from both standard trade policy and new trade policy to discuss the costs and benefits of the many regional trade agreements (for example, a free trade area or a customs union). The rising popularity of economic integration known as regionalism is to be contrasted with the multilateral WTO framework of removing trade barriers. Although a regional trade agreement in general increases welfare through increased trade flows (trade-creation), the discriminatory nature of the agreement which benefits insiders may reduce welfare through a shift toward less efficient producers (trade-diversion). The European Union presents the most powerful and successful economic integration scheme to date. Many Central and East European countries want to join the EU, which requires large structural and political changes, both for the applicants and for the (rather undemocratic) political decision process of the EU.

Applied trade policy

Chapter 17 analyses applied trade policy, involving the use of accurate and current data, a model structure determined by those data, a detailed policy orientation, and the analysis of non-local changes in policy parameters from distorted base equilibria. Applied researchers have used the demand side of the economy to solve some practical problems in matching models and data, for example by incorporating demand bias, the Linder hypothesis, and the Armington assumption. For simple trade policy questions researchers use an applied partial equilibrium model, based on estimating the size of the Harberger triangles. For more complicated questions researchers use applied general equilibrium models, which take into consideration the simultaneous effects of all pro-posed policy measures for all sectors and countries. There are roughly three types of applied general equilibrium models: (1) constant returns and perfect competition, (2) increasing returns and imperfect competition, and (3) dynamic models. In general, the estimated costs of trade restrictions increase as we move from type (1) to type (2), and from type (2) to type (3) models. Using applied trade policy models requires the mastering of many practical tools not covered in this book. However, a rudimentary version of most theoretical analysis on which the applied policy models are based *is* covered in this book.

Hidden costs of trade restrictions

We conclude our discussion on trade policy by noting that the importance of international economic contacts through the exchange of goods, capital, foreign direct investment, knowledge, ideas, etc. can hardly be overestimated. The main reason is that imposing trade restrictions may result in goods and services *not* being introduced on the market. Using the Dupuit triangle to estimate the costs of goods that are not introduced in a simple model, we show that such costs can be substantial (and much larger than the empirically estimated costs in applied general equilibrium models). Suggestive empirical evidence in favour of this interpretation is given for example by North and South Korea, East and West Germany, and the recent developments in China.

References

AGHION, P., and HOWITT, P. (1992), 'A model of growth through creative destruction', *Econometrica*, 60: 323–51.

ALLEN, W. R. (ed.) (1965), *International Trade Theory: Hume to Ohlin*, Random House, New York.

ARMINGTON, P. S. (1969), 'A theory of demand for products distinguished by place of production', *International Monetary Fund Staff Papers*, 16: 159–78.

ARROW, K. J. (1962), 'The economic implications of learning by doing', *Review of Economic Studies*, 29: 155–73.

BAIROCH, P. (1988), *Cities and Economic Development: From the Dawn of History to the Present*, paperback reprint, trans. C. Braider, University of Chicago Press, Chicago.

BALASSA, B. (1965), 'Trade liberalization and "revealed" comparative advantage', *Manchester School of Economic and Social Studies*, 33: 92–123.

—— (1966), 'Tariff reductions and trade in manufactures', *American Economic Review*, 56: 466–73.

—— (1989), '"Revealed" comparative advantage revisited', in Bela Balassa (ed.), *Comparative Advantage, Trade Policy and Economic Development*, New York University Press, New York: 63–79.

BARRELL, R., and PAIN, N. (1999), 'Domestic institutions, agglomeration and foreign direct investment in Europe', *European Economic Review*, 43: 925–34.

BARRO, R. J., and SALA-I-MARTIN, X. (1995), *Economic Growth*, McGraw-Hill, New York.

BHAGWATI, J. (1965), 'On the equivalence of tariffs and quotas', in R. E. Baldwin (ed.), *Trade, Growth, and the Balance of Payments*, North-Holland, Amsterdam.

BAKKER, A. F. P. (1996), *International Financial Institutions*, Longman, London.

BLAUG, M. (1985), *Great Economists since Keynes*, Wheatsheaf Books Ltd., Brighton.

—— (1986), *Great Economists before Keynes*, Wheatsheaf Books Ltd., Brighton.

BLOOM, L., and SACHS, J. (1998), 'Geography, demography, and economic growth in Africa', *Brookings Papers on Economic Activity*, 2: 207–95.

BOWEN, H. P., HOLLANDER, A., and VIAENE, J.-M. (1998), *Applied International Trade Analysis*, University of Michigan Press, Ann Arbor.

—— LEAMER, E. E., and SVEIKAUSKAS, L. (1987), 'Multicountry, multifactor tests of the factor abundance theory', *American Economic Review*, 77: 791–809.

BRAINARD, S. L. (1997), 'An empirical assessment of the proximity-concentration trade-off between multinationals sales and trade', *American Economic Review*, 87: 520–44.

BRAKMAN, S., and VAN MARREWIJK, C. (1996), 'Trade policy under imperfect competition', *De Economist*, 144: 223–58.

—— —— (1998), *The Theory of International Transfers*, Cambridge University Press, Cambridge.

—— GARRETSEN, H., and VAN MARREWIJK, C. (2001), *An Introduction to Geographical Economics*, Cambridge University Press, Cambridge.

BRANDER, J. A. (1981), 'Intra-industry trade in identical commodities', *Journal of International Economics*, 11: 1–14.

—— and KRUGMAN, P. R. (1983), 'A "reciprocal dumping" model of international trade', *Journal of International Economics*, 15: 313–21.

—— and SPENCER, B. J. (1983), 'International R&D rivalry and industrial strategy', *Review of Economic Studies*, 50: 707–22.

—— —— (1985), 'Export subsidies and international market share rivalry', *Journal of International Economics*, 18: 83–100.

BROWN, D. K. (1992), 'The impact of a North American Free Trade Area: applied general equilibrium models', in N. Lustig, B. P. Bosworth, and R. Z. Lawrence (eds.), *North American Free Trade: Assessing the Impact*, Brookings Institution, Washington: 26–68.

BULOW, J. I., GEANAKOPLOS, J. D., and KLEMPERER, P. D. (1985), 'Multimarket oligopoly: strategic substitutes and complements', *Journal of Political Economy*, 488–511.

BURMEISTER, E., and DOBELL, A. R. (1970), *Mathematical Theories of Economic Growth*, Macmillan, New York.

CAVES, R. E. (1996), *Multinational Enterprise and Economic Analysis*, Cambridge Surveys of Economic Literature, 2nd edn., Cambridge University Press, Cambridge.

CHAMBERLIN, E. H. (1933), *The Theory of Monopolistic Competition: A Re-orientation of the Theory of Value*, Harvard University Press, Cambridge, Mass.

CHIPMAN, J. S. (1965), 'A survey of the theory of international trade: Part 1, the Classical theory', *Econometrica*, 33: 477–519.

COLLINS, S. M. (ed.) (1998), *Imports, Exports and the American Worker*, Brookings Institutions Press, Washington.

COURNOT, A. (1838), *Recherches sur les principes mathématiques de la théorie des riches*, trans. N. Bacon (1897), Macmillan, New York.

DAVIS, D. R. (1988), 'The home market, trade and industrial structure', *American Economic Review*, 88 (Nov.): 1264–77.

DEBREU, G. (1959), *Theory of Value*, Wiley, New York.

DE LONG, J. B. (1988), 'Productivity growth, convergence, and welfare: comment', *American Economic Review*, 78: 1138–54.

DE MELO, J., and PANAGARIYA, A. (1993), *New Dimensions in Regional Integration*, Cambridge University Press, Cambridge.

DIEWERT, W. E. (1981), 'The economic theory of index numbers: a survey', in A. Deaton (ed.), *Essays in the Theory and Measurement of Consumer Behaviour*, Cambridge University Press, Cambridge: 163–208.

DIXIT, A., and GROSSMAN, G. (1986), 'Targeted export promotion with several oligopolistic industries', *Journal of International Economics*, 21: 233–50.

—— and KYLE, A. S. (1985), 'The use of protection or subsidies for entry promotion and deterrence', *American Economic Review*, 75: 139–52.

—— and NORMAN, V. (1980), *Theory of International Trade*, Cambridge University Press, Cambridge.

—— and STIGLITZ, J. (1977), 'Monopolistic competition and optimal product diversity', *American Economic Review*, 67: 297–308.

DORNBUSCH, R., FISCHER, S., and SAMUELSON, P. (1977), 'Comparative advantage, trade and payments in a Ricardian model with a continuum of goods', *American Economic Review*, 67: 823–39.

DUNNING, J. H. (1977), 'Trade, location of economic activity and MNE: a search for an eclectic approach', in B. Ohlin, P.O. Hesselborn, and P. M. Wijkman (eds.), *The International Allocation of Economic Activity*, Macmillan, London.

—— (1981), *International Production and the Multinational Enterprise*, Allen & Unwin, London.

DUPUIT, J. (1844), 'On the measurement of the utility of public works', reprinted in K. Arrow and T. Scitovsky (eds.), *Readings in Welfare Economics* (1969), Allen & Unwin, London: 35–62.

EATON, J., and GROSSMAN, G. M. (1986), 'Optimal trade and industrial policy under oligopoly', *Quarterly Journal of Economics*, 2: 383–406.

The Economist (1997), 'Peace in our time', 26 July (on *The Economist*'s website).

—— (1999), 'The new trade war', 2 Dec. (on *The Economist*'s website).

—— (2000*a*), 'So that's all agreed, then', 14 Dec. (on *The Economist*'s website).

—— (2000*b*), 'Thank you, Singapore', 30 Sept. (on *The Economist*'s website).

—— (2001*a*), 'A fruity peace', 19 Apr. (on *The Economist*'s website).

—— (2001*b*), 'A phoney war', 5 May (on *The Economist*'s website).

—— (2001*c*), 'More tomatoes, please', 21 June (on *The Economist*'s website).

—— (2001*d*), 'Visigothenburger', 21 June (on *The Economist*'s website).

—— (2001*e*), 'Picking up the pieces', 26 July (on *The Economist*'s website).

ETHIER, W. E. (1982), 'National and international returns to scale in the modern theory of international trade', *American Economic Review*, 72: 950–9.

—— (1986), 'The multinational firm', *Quarterly Journal of Economics*, 101: 805–33.

FEENSTRA, R. C., MARKUSEN, J. R., and ROSE, A. K. (2001), 'Using the gravity equation to differentiate among alternative theories of trade', *Canadian Journal of Economics*, 34: 430–47.

FRANCOIS, J. F., and HALL, H. K. (1997), 'Partial equilibrium modeling', in J. F. Francois and K. A. Reinert (eds.), *Applied Methods for Trade Policy Analysis: A Handbook*, Cambridge University Press, Cambridge: 122–55.

—— and REINERT, K. A. (1997), 'Applied methods for trade policy analysis: an overview', in J. F. Francois and K. A. Reinert (eds.), *Applied Methods for Trade Policy Analysis: A Handbook*, Cambridge University Press, Cambridge: 3–24.

—— McDONALD, B. J., and NORDSTRÖM, H. (1997), 'Capital accumulation in applied trade models', in J. F. Francois and K.A. Reinert (eds.), *Applied Methods for Trade Policy Analysis: A Handbook*, Cambridge University Press, Cambridge: 364–82.

FUJITA, M., KRUGMAN, P. R., and VENABLES, A. J. (1999), *The Spatial Economy: Cities, Regions, and International Trade*, MIT Press, Cambridge, Mass.

GANDAL, N., HANSON, G. H., and SLAUGHTER, M. J. (2000), 'Technology, trade, and adjustment to immigration in Israel', NBER working paper 7962.

GOUREVITCH, P., BOHN, R., and McKENDRICK, D. (2000), 'Globalization of production: insights from the hard disk drive industry', *World Development*, 28(2): 301–17.

GROSSMAN, G. M., and HELPMAN, E. (1991a), *Innovation and Growth in the Global Economy*, MIT Press, Cambridge, Mass.

—— —— (1991b), 'Quality ladders in the theory of growth', *Review of Economic Studies*, 58: 43–61.

GRUBEL, H. G., and LLOYD, P. J. (1975), *Intra-industry Trade: The Theory and Measurement of International Trade in Differentiated Products*, John Wiley, New York.

GRUBERT, H., and MUTTI, J. (1991), 'Taxes, tariffs, and transfer pricing in multinational corporate decision making', *Review of Economics and Statistics*, 79: 285–93.

HARBERGER, A. C. (1954), 'Monopoly and resource allocation', *American Economic Review*, 44: 77–87.

—— (1959), 'Using the resources at hand more effectively', *American Economic Review*, 49: 134–46.

HARRIS, R. (1985), 'Why voluntary export restraints are voluntary', *Canadian Journal of Economics*, 18: 799–809.

HEAD, K., RIES, J., and SWENSON, D. (1995), 'Agglomeration benefits and location choice: evidence from Japanese manufacturing investments in the United States', *Journal of International Economics*, 38: 223–47.

HELPMAN, E. (1984), 'A simple theory of international trade with multinational corporations', *Journal of Political Economy*, 92: 451–71.

—— (1985), 'Multinational corporations and trade structure', *Review of Economic Studies*, 52: 443–58.

HERFINDAHL, O. C. (1950), 'Concentration in the steel industry', unpublished Ph.D. dissertation, Columbia University.

HINLOOPEN, J., and VAN MARREWIJK, C. (2001), 'On the empirical distribution of the Balassa Index', *Weltwirtschaftliches Archiv*, 137: 1–35.

HORST, T. (1971), 'The theory of the multinational firm: optimal behavior under different tariff and tax rates', *Journal of Political Economy*, 79: 1059–72.

HORSTMAN, I. J., and MARKUSEN J. R. (1986), 'Up the average cost curve: inefficient entry and the new protectionism', *Journal of International Economics*, 20: 225–48.

HUMMELS, D. (1999a), 'Towards a geography of trade costs', Mimeo, University of Chicago.

—— (1999b), 'Have international transportation costs declined?', Mimeo, University of Chicago.

HURIOT, J.-M., and THISSE, J.-F. (eds.) (2000), *Economics of Cities: Theoretical Perspectives*, Cambridge University Press, Cambridge.

IRWIN, D. (1996), *Against the Tide: An Intellectual History of Free Trade*, Princeton University Press, Princeton.

JONES, C. (1995), 'Time series tests of endogenous growth models', *Quarterly Journal of Economics*, 495–525.

JONES, R. W. (1965), 'The structure of simple general equilibrium models', *Journal of Political Economy*, 73: 557–72.

KALDOR, N. (1961), 'Capital accumulation and economic growth', in F. A. Lutz and D. C. Hague (eds.), *The Theory of Capital*, Macmillan, London: 177–222.

KEMP, M. C., and WAN, H. Y., Jr. (1972), 'The gains from free trade', *International Economic Review*, 13 (3): 509–22.

—— —— (1976), 'An elementary proposition concerning the formation of customs unions', *Journal of International Economics*, 6 (1): 95–7.

KENEN, P. B. (2000), *The International Economy*, 4th edn., Cambridge University Press, Cambridge.

KENNEDY, P. (1995), 'The threat of modernization', *New Perspectives Quarterly*: 31–3.

KINDLEBERGER, C. P. (1973), *The World in Depression 1929–1933*, Lane, London.

KRISHNA, K. (1989), 'Trade restrictions as facilitating practices', *Journal of International Economics*, 26: 251–70.

KRUGMAN, P. (1979), 'Increasing returns, monopolistic competition and international trade', *Journal of International Economics*, 9: 469–79.

—— (1980), 'Scale economics, product differentiation, and the pattern of trade', *American Economic Review*, 70: 950–9.

—— (1990), *Rethinking International Trade*, MIT Press, Cambridge, Mass.

—— (1991), 'Is bilateralism bad?', in E. Helpman and A. Razin (eds.), *International Trade and Trade Policy*, MIT Press, Cambridge, Mass.: 85–109.

—— (1993), 'Regionalism versus multilateralism: analytical notes', in J. De Melo and A. Panagariya (eds.), *New Dimensions in Regional Integration*, Cambridge University Press, Cambridge: 58–79.

—— and OBSTFELD, M. (2000), *International Economics: Theory and Policy*, 5th edn., Addison-Wesley, New York.

LAIRD, S. (1997), 'Quantifying commercial policies', in J. F. Francois and K. A. Reinert (eds.), *Applied Methods for Trade Policy Analysis: A Handbook*, Cambridge University Press, Cambridge: 27–75.

LANCASTER, K. J. (1979), *Variety, Equity and Efficiency*, Columbia University Press, New York.

LANJOUW, G. J. (1995), *International Trade Institutions*, Longman and Open University, London.

LAWRENCE, R. Z., and SLAUGHTER, M. J. (1993), 'International Trade and American wages in the 1980s: giant sucking sound or small hiccup?', *Brookings Paper on Economic Activity 2: Microeconomics*: 161–226.

LEONTIEF, W. W. (1956), 'Factor proportions and the structure of American trade: further theoretical and empirical analysis', *Review of Economics and Statistics*, 38.

LERNER, A. P. (1952), 'Factor prices and international trade', *Economica*, NS 19.

LIESNER, H. H. (1958), 'The European common market and British industry', *Economic Journal*, 68: 302–16.

LINDER, S. (1961), *An Essay on Trade and Transformation*, Wiley, New York.

LIPSEY, R. G. (1960), 'The theory of customs unions: a general survey', *Economic Journal*, 70: 496–513.

LLOYD, P. J. (1982), '3 × 3 Theory of customs unions', *Journal of International Economics*, 12: 41–63.

MADDISON, A. (1991), *Dynamic Forces in Capitalist Development*, Oxford University Press, Oxford.

MARKUSEN, J. R. (1981), 'Trade and the gains from trade with imperfect competition', *Journal of International Economics*, 11: 531–51.

—— (1984), 'Multinationals, multi-plant economics, and the gains from trade', *Journal of International Economics*, 16: 205–26.

—— (1995), 'Incorporating the multinational enterprise into the theory of international trade', *Journal of Economic Perspectives*, 9: 169–89.

—— (1998), 'Multinational firms, location, and trade', *World Economy*, 21(6): 733–56.

—— and VENABLES, A. J. (1998), 'Multinational firms and the new trade theory', *Journal of International Economics*, 46: 183–203.

—— KONAN, D. E., and ZHANG, K. H. (1996), 'A unified treatment of horizontal direct investment, vertical direct investment, and the pattern of trade in goods and services', NBER working paper 5696, Cambridge, Mass.

MARREWIJK, C. VAN (1999), 'Capital accumulation, learning, and endogenous growth', *Oxford Economic Papers*, 51: 453–75.

—— and VERBEEK, J. (1993), 'Sector-specific capital, "bang-bang" investment and the Filippov solution', *Journal of Economics*, 57: 131–46.

MARTIN, S. (1994), *Industrial Economics: Economic Analysis and Public Policy*, Macmillan, New York.

MARTYN, H. (1701), *Considerations upon the East India Trade*, see Irwin (1996): 56–9.

MEADE, J. E. (1952), *A Geometry of International Trade*, George Allen & Unwin, London.

MIDELFART-KNARVIK, K. H., OVERMAN, H. G., REDDING, S. J., and VENABLES, A. J. (2000), 'The location of European industry', *Economic Papers*, 142, European Commission, Brussels.

NEARY, J. P. (1978), 'Short-run capital specificity and the pure theory of international trade', *Economic Journal*, 88: 477–510.

—— (2001), 'Of hypes and hyperbolas: introducing the new economic geography', *Journal of Economic Literature*, forthcoming.

NRC Handelsblad (2001*a*), 'Van nul naar record in grillige chipmarkt', 19 Jan.: 14 (in Dutch).

—— (2001*b*), 'Minder EU-hulp suiker', 23 May (in Dutch).

—— (2001*c*), 'Prijs van walvisspek stijgt explosief', 12 May: 19 (in Dutch).

—— (2001*d*), 'Japan buigt niet in ruzie schoolboek' and 'De geschiedenis blijft Japan achtervolgen', 14 July: 4 (in Dutch).

—— (2001*e*), 'Ondernemersvrouwen houden van Holland', 18 Aug.: 13 (in Dutch).

OHLIN, B. (1933), *Interregional and International Trade*, Harvard University Press, Cambridge, Mass.

OTTENS, D. (2000), 'Revealed comparative advantage: an empirical analysis', unpublished Master's thesis, Erasmus University, Rotterdam.

PORTER, M. E. (1990), *The Competitive Advantage of Nations*, Free Press, New York.

RADELET, S., and SACHS, J. (1998), 'Shipping costs, manufactured exports, and economic growth', Mimeo, Harvard.

RAMSEY, F. P. (1928), 'A mathematical theory of saving', *Economic Journal*, 38: 543–59.

RIVERA-BATIZ, L. A., and ROMER, P. M. (1991*a*), 'Economic integration and endogenous growth', *Quarterly Journal of Economics*, 106: 531–55.

—— —— (1991*b*), 'International trade with endogenous technological change', *European Economic Review*, 35: 971–1004.

ROMER, P. M. (1986), 'Increasing returns and long run growth', *Journal of Political Economy*, 94: 1002–37.

—— (1990), 'Endogenous technological change', *Journal of Political Economy*, 98: S71–S102.

—— (1994), 'New goods, old theory, and the welfare costs of trade restrictions', *Journal of Development Economics*, 43: 5–38.

RYBCZYNSKI, T. M. (1955), 'Factor endowments and relative commodity prices', *Economica*, 22: 336–41.

SAMUELSON, P. A. (1948), 'International trade and the equalisation of factor prices', *Economic Journal*, 58: 163–84.

—— (1949), 'International factor price equalisation once again', *Economic Journal*, 59: 181–96.

—— (1952), 'The transfer problem and transport costs: the terms of trade when impediments are absent', *Economic Journal*, 62: 278–304.

—— (1971), 'Ohlin was right', *Swedish Journal of Economics*, 73: 365–84.

SCHMIDT, J. A. (2001), 'Background of economic transition in Central and Eastern Europe', Lecture Notes, Erasmus University, Rotterdam.

SCHUMPETER, J. A. (1934), *The Theory of Economic Development*, Harvard University Press, Cambridge, Mass.

—— (1954), *History of Economic Analysis*, 12th printing, 1981, George Allen & Unwin, London.

SCITOVSKY, T. (1954), 'Two concepts of external economies', *Journal of Political Economy*, 62: 143–51.

SHATZ, H. J., and VENABLES, A. J. (2000), 'The geography of international investment', in G. L. Clark, M. Feldman, and M. S. Gertler (eds.), *The Oxford Handbook of Economic Geography*, Oxford University Press, Oxford.

SIEBERT, H. (1999), *The World Economy*, Routledge, London.

SMITH, A. (1776), *An Inquiry into the Nature and Causes of the Wealth of Nations*, Glasgow edition of the works and correspondence of Adam Smith, ed. R. H. Campbell and A. S. Skinner, 1981, Liberty Press, Glasgow.

SOLOW, R. M. (1956), 'A contribution to the theory of economic growth', *Quarterly Journal of Economics*, 70: 65–94.

SPENCE, A. M. (1976), 'Product selection, fixed costs and monopolistic competition', *Review of Economic Studies*, 43: 217–35.

STELDER, D. (2000), 'Geographical grids in new economic geography models', paper presented at the International Conference on the occasion of the 150th anniversary of Johann Heinrich von Thünen's death, Rostock, 21–4 Sept.

STOLPER, W., and SAMUELSON, P. (1941), 'Protection and real wages', *Review of Economic Studies*, 9: 58–73.

SUMMERS, L. H., and HESTON, A. (1991), 'The Penn world table (mark 5): an expanded set of international comparisons, 1950–1988', *Quarterly Journal of Economics*, 106: 327–68.

THWEATT, W. O. (1976), 'James Mill and the early development of comparative advantage', *History of Political Economy*, 8: 207–34.

TINBERGEN, J. (1962), *Shaping the World Economy*, Twentieth Century Fund, New York.

TIROLE, J. (1988), *The Theory of Industrial Organization*, MIT Press, Cambridge, Mass.

TREFLER, D. (1995), 'The case of the missing trade and other mysteries', *American Economic Review*, 85: 1029–46.

UNCTAD (1999), *World Investment Report 1999*, United Nations, New York.

—— (2000), *World Investment Report 2000*, United Nations, New York.

VANEK, J. (1959), 'The natural resource content of foreign trade, 1870–1955, and the relative abundance of natural resources in the United States', *Review of Economics and Statistics*, 41.

VENABLES, A. J. (1985), 'Trade and trade policy with imperfect competition: the case of identical products and free entry', *Journal of International Economics*, 19: 1–20.

VERDOORN, P. J. (1960), 'The intra-block trade of Benelux', in E. A. G. Robinson (ed.), *Economic Consequences of the Size of Nations*, Macmillan, London.

VINER, J. (1950), *The Customs Union Issue*, Carnegie Endowment for International Peace, New York.

WEIBULL, J. W. (1995), *Evolutionary Game Theory*, MIT Press, Cambridge, Mass.

WONG, K. Y. (1986), 'Are international trade and factor mobility substitutes?', *Journal of International Economics*, 20: 25–44.

WOOD, A. (1994), *North–South Trade, Employment and Inequality: Changing Fortunes in a Skill-Driven World*, Clarendon Press, Oxford.

—— (1998), 'Globalisation and the rise in labour market inequalities', *Economic Journal*, 108: 1463–82.

YOUNG, A. A. (1928), 'Increasing returns and economic progress', *Economic Journal*, 38: 527–42.

ZIPF, G. K. (1949), *Human Behavior and the Principle of Least Effort*, Addison Wesley, New York.

Index

Page numbers followed by '*t*' refer to tables; those followed by '*f*' refer to figures.